The Politics of Multiculturalism and Bilingual Education

Students and Teachers Caught in the Cross Fire

Editors

Carlos J. Ovando
Indiana University, Bloomington

Peter McLaren
University of California at Los Angeles

Boston   Burr Ridge, IL   Dubuque, IA   Madison, WI   New York
San Francisco   St. Louis   Bangkok   Bogotá   Caracas   Lisbon   London
Madrid   Mexico City   Milan   New Delhi   Seoul   Singapore   Sydney
Taipei   Toronto

McGraw-Hill Higher Education

A Division of The *McGraw-Hill* Companies

THE POLITICS OF MULTICULTURALISM AND BILINGUAL EDUCATION
STUDENTS AND TEACHERS CAUGHT IN THE CROSS FIRE

This book is printed on acid-free paper.

1 2 3 4 5 6 7 8 9 0 DOC/DOC 0 9 8 7 6 5 4 3 2 1 0

ISBN 0–07–366076–0

Editorial director: *Jane E. Vaicunas*
Sponsoring editor: *Beth Kaufman*
Developmental editor: *Cara Harvey*
Marketing manager: *Daniel M. Loch*
Project manager: *Susan J. Brusch*
Production supervisor: *Enboge Chong*
Designer: *K. Wayne Harms*
Senior photo research coordinator: *Carrie K. Burger*
Compositor: *Precision Graphics*
Typeface: *10/12 Palatino*
Printer: *R. R. Donnelley & Sons Company/Crawfordsville, IN*

Cover designer: *Mary Sailer*
Photograph by: *Nicholas Nixon*

Library of Congress Catalog Card Number: 99–63840

To:
Paulo Freire, a compañero and tireless
champion of praxis, social justice, and hope;
Students and teachers who learn from each other and
keep the joy and redemptive power of ideas alive;
Developing countries and their people suffering economic
crises, wishing that the injustices between developed and
developing countries will be resolved.
C.J.O. and P.M.

TABLE OF CONTENTS

Part I
THE MORAL AND POLITICAL CROSS FIRES
OF MULTICULTURALISM

Part II
TEACHERS AND STUDENTS CAUGHT IN THE CROSS FIRE

Acknowledgments

Peter and I thank all the chapter authors for their patience and commitment to the book project. We also thank the manuscript reviewers who provided fair and insightful suggestions to improve the organization and substance of the anthology.: Ricardo García, University of Nebraska–Lincoln; María E. Tórres-Guzmán, Teachers College, Columbia University; Martha Combs, University of Nevada; Timothy Reagan, University of Connecticut–Storrs; Maureen Gillette, College of St. Rose; Hassana Alidou-Ngame, Texas A & M University; and Elizabeth Platt, Florida State University. We also thank the entire staff of the McGraw-Hill College Division, especially Jane Vaicunas, Beth Kaufman, and Cara Harvey, for their sustained encouragement, patience, flexibility, and sense of humor. Our thanks also go to Susan Brusch for ably shepherding the editorial production phase of the book and to Dan Loch, the senior marketing manager, for making the book visible and accessible throughout the United States and internationally. Last but not least, I, Carlos Ovando, wish to thank Kristina Lindborg, Jane Lyle, and Sharon Pugh for their editorial and moral support during some of the most challenging moments of the manuscript preparation process. You are terrific!

About the Authors

MARGARITA CALDERÓN is a research scientist for the Johns Hopkins University's Center for Research on the Education of Students Placed at Risk. She is conducting longitudinal research studies in schools in the El Paso, Texas, area on effective two-way bilingual programs, academic success for language-minority students at the middle and high school levels, and building teachers' learning communities at these schools. She is also a trainer and writer for the Johns Hopkins University Success for All Foundation. She was an associate professor in the Department of Educational Leadership at the University of Texas, El Paso. For the past ten years, she has trained bilingual and English as a Second Language (ESL) teachers and teacher trainers and school administrators nationally and internationally. Her writings reflect a balance between teacher training materials, curriculum, classroom application, and scholarly research on professional development and effective schooling for language-minority students.

ARGELIA CARREÓN is affiliated with the Johns Hopkins University Success for All Foundation. She served as the director of bilingual education for El Paso Independent School District, the largest district on the U.S.-Mexico border. There, she implemented several innovative bilingual and ESL programs such as the Accelerated Two-Way Bilingual Education Program (1992). She is active in state, national, and binational conferences.

BETH CHAPPELL graduated from Gustavus Adolphus College in 1997 and teaches high school English in Minnesota.

JAMES CRAWFORD is an independent writer and lecturer based in the Washington, D.C., area. His publications include: *Best Evidence: Research Foundations of the Bilingual Education Act* (National Clearinghouse for Bilingual Education, 1997); *Bilingual Education: History, Politics, Theory, and Practice*, 3rd ed. (Bilingual Education Services, 1995); *Hold Your Tongue: Bilingualism and the Politics of English Only* (Addison-Wesley, 1992); and *Language Loyalties: A Source Book on the Official English Controversy* (University of Chicago Press, 1992). He has also served as Washington editor of *Education Week* and writer-consultant to the Stanford Working Group on Federal Programs for Limited English Proficient Students. Mr. Crawford maintains an extensive language policy web site at http://ourworld.compuserve.com/homepages/jwcrawford.

JIM CUMMINS received his Ph.D. in education psychology from the University of Alberta in 1974. He is currently a professor in the Department of Teaching, Learning, and Curriculum in the Ontario Institute for Studies in Education at the University of Toronto. His research has focused on second-language acquisition and bilingualism with particular emphasis on the social and educational barriers that limit academic success for culturally diverse students. He has served as a consultant on language planning in education to numerous international agencies. His publications include: *Bilingualism and Special Education: Issues in Assessment and Pedagogy* (Multilingual Matters, 1984); *Bilingualism in Education: Aspects of Theory, Research and Practice* (with Merrill Swain; Longman, 1986); *Minority Education: From Shame to Struggle* (with Tove Skunabb-Kangas; Multilingual Matters, 1988); *Brave New Schools: Challenging Cultural Illiteracy Through Global Learning Networks* (with Dennis Sayers; St. Martin's Press, 1995); and *Negotiating Identities: Education for Empowerment in a Diverse Society* (California Association for Bilingual Education, 1996). He is also a co-author of *Scott Foresman ESL: Accelerating English Language Learning,* a grade 1 through 8 ESL program published in 1996.

HENRY A. GIROUX received his doctorate from Carnegie-Mellon University in 1977. He taught at Boston University from 1977 to 1983. From 1983 to 1992, he taught at Miami University. He currently holds the Waterbury Chair Professorship at Pennsylvania State University. His most recent books include: *Fugitive Cultures: Race, Violence, and Youth* (Routledge, 1996); *Channel Surfing: Race Talk and the Destruction of Today's Youth* (St. Martin's Press, 1997); *Pedagogy and the Politics of Hope* (Westview/HarperCollins, 1997); and *The Mouse That Roared: How Disney Shapes Culture and Everyday Life* (Rowman and Littlefield, 1999). He is currently the director of the Waterbury Forum in Education and Cultural Studies at Penn State University. He is also on the editorial and advisory boards of numerous national and international scholarly journals. He serves as the editor or co-editor of three scholarly book series published respectively by State University of New York Press, Bergin and Garvey, and Rowman and Littlefield. Professor Giroux lectures widely on a variety of cultural, social, and educational issues in the United States and abroad.

SABRINA W.M. LAINE is a Ph.D. candidate in the Department of Educational Leadership and Policy Studies at Indiana University, Bloomington. She taught multicultural education as an adjunct faculty member at Indiana University–Purdue University–Indianapolis between 1994 and 1996. She has published articles on school choice, equity, standards, and other policy issues. She is currently a program associate and senior policy analyst at the North Central Regional Education Laboratory, Oak Brook, Illinois.

PETER MCLAREN is professor of education at the Graduate School of Education and Information Studies, University of California, Los Angeles. He received his Ph.D. in educational theory from the Ontario Institute for Studies in Education, University of Toronto. His development of a revolutionary politics of liberation has taken him throughout Europe, Latin America, and Southeast Asia, where he is considered one of the leading figures in critical pedagogy. A former elementary and middle school teacher, he is the author of *Revolutionary Multiculturalism: Pedagogies of Dissent for the New Millennium* (Westview Press, 1997); *Life in Schools: An Introduction to Critical Pedagogy in the Foundations of Education,* 3rd ed. (Longman, 1997); and *Critical Pedagogy and Predatory Culture* (Routledge, 1995).

MASAHIKO MINAMI is assistant professor of Japanese in the Department of Foreign Languages and Literatures at San Francisco State University, where he teaches courses on second-language acquisition and learning. He received his Ed.D. in human development and psychology from Harvard University. Prior to his appointment at San Francisco State, he was on the faculty of the Department of Psychology at the University of Massachusetts, Lowell. Professor Minami's research interests include psycho-sociolinguistics with a particular emphasis on cross-cultural comparisons of language development and narrative/discourse structure. He has published a number of articles and reviews and presented papers on this subject. He is co-editor of *Language Issues in Literacy and Bilingual/Multicultural Education* (Harvard Educational Review, 1991). He has also contributed chapters to books covering Asian narratives, East Asian students' experiences in the U.S. classrooms, cultural constructions of meaning, and child care quality in Japan.

JUAN S. MUÑOZ is a Ph.D. candidate in the Graduate School of Education and Information Studies, University of California, Los Angeles. He formerly served as a high school teacher and community college instructor and is extensively involved in the community, culture, and politics of East Los Angeles. He currently works in the field of alternative educational theory and practice as it relates to marginalized and disentitled students of color in urban contexts.

WARREN A. NORD is director of the Program in the Humanities and Human Values, and teaches in the Department of Philosophy at the University of North Carolina at Chapel Hill. He is the author of *Religion and American Education: Rethinking a National Dilemma* (University of North Carolina Press, 1995) and the co-author, with Charles C. Haynes, of *Taking Religion Seriously Across the Curriculum* (ASCD, 1998).

CAROLYN O'GRADY is assistant professor of education and co-director of Women's Studies at Gustavus Adolphus College in St. Peter, Minnesota. She is completing a book on the integration of service learning and multicultural education.

CARLOS J. OVANDO is professor of education and former chair of the Department of Curriculum and Instruction at Indiana University, Bloomington. He is also the current director of the Bilingual-Bicultural Education Program. He received his Ph.D. in curriculum and instruction and international comparative education from Indiana University. His research, teaching, and service focus on factors that contribute to the academic achievement of language-minority students and ethnically diverse groups. A former high school Spanish teacher, he has served as guest editor of two special issues of the *Educational Research Quarterly* and contributed to the *Handbook of Research on Multicultural Education, Peabody Journal of Education, Bilingual Research Journal, Phi Delta Kappan, Educational Leadership, Kappa Delta Pi Record,* and the *Harvard Educational Review.* He is the senior co-author (with Virginia P. Collier) of the second edition of *Bilingual and ESL Classrooms: Teaching in Multicultural Contexts* (McGraw-Hill, 1998). He is writing a book (with Colleen Larson) entitled *The Color of Bureaucracy: Institutionalizing Inequity in Multicultural School Communities* to be published by Harcourt Brace. Professor Ovando has given presentations in Canada, Costa Rica, Egypt, England, Guam, Mexico, Nicaragua, the Netherlands, the Philippines, Spain, and the United States. He has been a professor of education at Oregon State University, the University of Alaska, Anchorage, and the University of Southern California. He has also been a visiting scholar at the Instituto de Estudios Latinoamericanos, Universidad Nacional, Costa Rica, and the University of Washington, Seattle. He has worked with Mexican Americans, Athabascan Indians, Asian Americans, Pacific Islanders, African Americans, Southwestern Indians, Chamorros, Costa Ricans, and Nicaraguans. During his sabbatical leave in 1998, he interviewed six undocumented Nicaraguan high school students and their mothers who work in banana plantations in Costa Rica. A frequent speaker at state, national, and international conferences, Ovando has presented invited papers and workshops in Canada, Costa Rica, Egypt, England, Guam, Mexico, Nicaragua, the Netherlands, the Philippines, and Spain. Born in Nicaragua, Ovando emigrated to the United States at the age of 15 and has, therefore, experienced first-hand many of the academic, sociocultural, and emotional issues that confront language-minority students in the United States. In 1998, he received a Teaching Excellence Recognition Award from the School of Education at Indiana University. He is a naturalized citizen of the United States.

RICARDO PÉREZ is professor of bilingual education at the University of Texas–Pan American. There, he has coordinated the bilingual teacher education program and served as project director for several Title VII federal grants. He has also served as interim dean of the College of Education as well as chair of the Department of Curriculum and Instruction. He is past president of the Texas Association for Bilingual Education. He has also served as the south Texas university representative for the Texas Association of Chicanos in Higher Education. He is currently involved in a longitudinal study on two-way bilingual education and in the development of an instrument to assess appropriate instructional bilingual classroom strategies.

SHARON PUGH is associate professor of language education and the director of the Indiana University Student Academic Center. She is the first author of two books on metaphor, *Bridging: A Teacher's Guide to Metaphorical Thinking* (1992) and *Metaphorical Ways of Knowing* (1997), both published by the National Council of Teachers of English. She has also published articles on global multiculturalism, multicultural trade books, and issues-based education. She teaches and does research on critical reading and thinking in content instruction.

NICOLE SCHONEMANN is a Ph.D. candidate in the Department of Educational Leadership and Policy Studies at Indiana University, Bloomington. Her dissertation (in progress), "Voices of Staying and Leaving: The Interplay of Migration and Education in a Mexican Village," explores perceptions of the interplay between the phenomena of seasonal migration and education in a Mexican village with a 70 percent seasonal migration rate to the United States. She has taught social studies (grades 5 through 12) in Monterrey, Mexico, and worked for the Indiana Migrant Education Program as a summer tutor. For two years, she was the graduate assistant at the Bilingual Education Endorsement Program at Indiana University.

MARGARET SUTTON is an assistant professor of educational leadership and policy studies at Indiana University. She earned her M.A. in philosophy of education at the University of British Columbia and Ph.D. in international development education at Stanford University, where she also served for two years as an instructor and director of the master's program. Her dissertation research focused on the interactions of social science research, policy making, and ordinary understandings of cultural change in Bali, Indonesia. Prior to joining the Indiana University faculty, Sutton was the director of research, evaluation, and gender issues for the Academy for Educational Development in Washington, D.C. In this position, she contributed to the design and evaluation of programs in basic education in Asian and African nations. She has written extensively in the field of gender and education, including two recent articles in *Women in the Third World: An Encyclopedia of Contemporary Issues*. She is currently conducting research on how children in the United States learn about global society and issues. She will have an article appearing in the *International Journal of Social Education* on the history and politics of global education in the United States.

Cultural Recognition and Civil Discourse in a Democracy

Carlos J. Ovando
Indiana University, Bloomington

Peter McLaren
University of California at Los Angeles

Multicultural societies and communities that stand for the freedom and equality of all people rest upon mutual respect for reasonable intellectual, political, and cultural differences. Mutual respect requires a widespread willingness and ability to articulate our disagreements, to defend them before people with whom we disagree, to discern the difference between respectable and disrespectable disagreement, and to be open to changing our minds when faced with well-reasoned criticism. The moral premise of multiculturalism depends on the exercise of these deliberative virtues.
—Amy Gutmann, Politics of Recognition, 24

This anthology—*The Politics of Multiculturalism and Bilingual Education: Students and Teachers Caught in the Cross Fire*—examines contested political and pedagogical issues surrounding multiculturalism and bilingual education in U.S. society. The genesis of the book dates back to the 1997 annual meeting of the American Educational Research Association. With Sabrina Laine, one of the contributors, Carlos Ovando organized a symposium entitled "The Politics of Multiculturalism: Students and Teachers in the Cross fire." We hope that this book will add longer life to the ideas presented in that symposium, so that they may become a resource for reflection and debate for students, teachers, professors, and national policy makers.

Written by engaging, experienced, and thoughtful scholar/practitioners in the fields of multiculturalism and bilingual education, the anthology is organized in two interdependent parts: "The Moral and Political Cross Fires of Multiculturalism," and "Teachers and Students Caught in the Cross Fire."

The first part—"The Moral and Political Cross Fires of Multiculturalism"—establishes a conceptual framework for the book. In the first chapter, Pugh, Ovando, and Schonemann examine multicultural metaphors. Such metaphors serve as a political vehicle for evaluating our judgments of others and for imaginatively entering into their experiences. Thus, they lay the groundwork for thinking about diversity in education in subsequent chapters. In Chapter 2, McLaren and Muñoz pick up on a central theme introduced in Chapter 1, which is that language can be used to rationalize injustice or to open up understanding to challenge the status quo. Examining multiculturalism from national and global perspectives, they argue for a decentering of whiteness and a critique of the role of global capitalism. To redress inequities in society, the authors propose a revolutionary multicultural education that is driven by egalitarian principles. In Chapter 3, Giroux argues that the dismissal of cultural politics by the neo-Enlightenment left and the right does disservice to the premise of multiculturalism, which is not about self-interest and polarization of society but rather about working together for a just social order, democracy, and human freedom. In Chapter 4, Nord introduces a new dimension—the role of religion in multicultural education—with its own set of controversies. He argues, for example, for including courses in the public schools that examine the religious traditions of American society as an integral part of students' intellectual development. In Chapter 5, Laine and Sutton widen the diversity perspective by considering the politics of cultural policies in the United States, Canada, and Australia.

The second part—"Teachers and Students Caught in the Cross Fire"—sets the context for reflection and action (praxis) for students and teachers caught in the cross fire. Crawford opens up this part in Chapter 6 by examining the complex and highly politicized nature of language issues in the United States, as reflected in the paradox of bilingual education. In Chapter 7, Cummins examines the growing animosity toward the bilingual schooling of language-minority students and argues for going beyond adversarial discourse in search of common ground. In Chapter 8, Ovando and Pérez examine the limitations and promises of two-way bilingual immersion programs in Texas, drawing policy implications for multilingual and multicultural societies. In Chapter 9, Calderón and Carreón analyze sociocultural conflicts facing bilingual teachers and students along the U.S.-Mexico border, suggesting a new border pedagogy. In Chapter 10, Minami examines political issues in the schooling of Asian students, attacking the myth of Asian students as a "model" minority. In the final chapter, O'Grady and Chappell reflect on the challenges and opportunities surrounding cross-cultural service learning experiences in a Midwestern community.

Multicultural Education: Two Sides in the Battle

Multicultural education may be defined as:

> an approach to teaching and learning that is based upon democratic values and beliefs, and affirms cultural pluralism within culturally diverse societies and an interdependent world. It is based on the assumption that the primary goal of public education is to foster the intellectual, social, and personal

development of virtually *all* students to their highest potential. Multicultural education is comprised of four interactive dimensions: the movement toward equity, curriculum reform, the process of becoming interculturally competent, and the commitment to combat prejudice and discrimination, especially racism. (Bennett 1999, 11)

This broad definition touches on many of the ways in which multicultural education is currently either celebrated or denigrated. Multiculturalism may be considered a form of political compact: an agreement that affirming and promoting distinctive group identities has positive social value for both the group and society as a whole. Merelman (1994) develops the concept of the political compact as a way for historically subordinated groups to move from the margin, redefine the center, and become contenders for cultural capital. This capital consists of "credentialed intellectual ability, broad symbolic mastery, and marketable cultural talents" (1, 4). For subordinated groups to flourish, however, the political compact must be sufficiently strong and resilient to resist the blows of the dominant sectors of society.

We would like to expand this concept by noting that as long as we continue to operate within the existing capitalist social relations of the larger society, there is good reason to believe that racism and social injustice will continue to pose a serious threat to democracy and that the dream of social equality will remain largely unrealized. (See Chapter 2 by McLaren and Muñoz.) Thus, the larger implications of this book center on the issue of what type of society we want for ourselves, our students, and our own children.

Within this humanistic vision, language use also plays a pivotal function in bringing us closer together or driving us apart. So critical in fact is the power of language in shaping our attitudes toward the multicultural debate that in one form or another, all the chapters of this book reflect its importance and pervasive nature. Language is, moreover, a special domain for teachers, who work largely in the medium of words and whose relationships with students depend on their understanding of the linguistic and cultural in all human affairs.

While advocates of pluralistic education argue that broad-based multicultural education reform is exactly what schools most need to prepare students for the twenty-first century, the other side portrays multicultural education as a subversive movement with a radical anti-American and antiwhite agenda that has the potential to divide and destroy American society.

If a major goal of multicultural education is to empower *all* students, why would there be so much passionate opposition to this curricular approach? Why, for example, would such prominent authors and social critics as William Bennett, Alan Bloom, Linda Chávez, Dinesh D'Souza, Chester Finn, E.D. Hirsch, Diane Ravitch, Richard Rodríguez, Arthur Schlesinger, Jr., and Thomas Sowell write so negatively against multicultural education? D'Souza (1991), for example, argues that multiculturalism lowers academic standards by establishing preferential admission policies to colleges and universities for minority students. Finn (1984), Ravitch (1985a, 1985b), and Chávez (1991, 1995) feel that multiculturalists promote intellectual mediocrity in the curriculum. They accuse multiculturalists of substituting "feel-good" learning for academic rigor by overemphasizing self-esteem gained through reverence for one's ethnicity. Ravitch and Schlesinger have charged that multicultural education divides American society by segregating students and teaching them competing ethnocentrisms through such curricular approaches as Afrocentric education. Chávez and Ravitch also accuse multicultural educators of implementing institutional change without community consent. Bennett (1984, 1985) suggests that multicultural education undermines America's common culture by denying its Western roots and teaching the "wrong" values. He argues that an agenda that promotes diverse belief systems may even undermine Judeo-Christian traditions, thus deemphasizing traditional moral authority based on Western religious principles. Bloom (1987) and Hirsch (1987) charge that multicultural education does not prepare youth for successful participation in American society because it ignores the intellectual heritage (i.e., "Great Books") of the Western world and replaces it with ethnic content. Another charge that appears in the writings of most of the critics is that multicultural education divides American society by excluding white students from the multicultural umbrella and assuming that they do not need to enhance their self-esteem. They also claim that multicultural educators frequently treat culture and race as a single issue, thus confusing assimilation and acculturation in American society. In addition, critics accuse multicultural educators of promoting conflict by nurturing a sense of historic grievances—the blame game. Another criticism is that multicultural education infringes on the right to freedom of speech by teaching political correctness, using reverse language discrimination, and rewarding intellectual constraint (Webster 1997).[1]

How do supporters of multicultural education respond to these charges? James Banks, one of the United States' leading architects and passionate defenders of multicultural education, feels strongly that at the core of such attacks is a fear by whites that their traditional dominance over society, or hegemonic hold, is declining because of the increasing proportion of non-European Americans in the population. He rejects the neoconservative scholars' portrayal of multicultural education as antiwhite, anti-Western, and anti-American. Banks (1992, 3–24) believes that multicultural education serves as a means to put into practice the egalitarian ethos in our democracy by including content integration in the curriculum that represents multiple cultural groups. Multicultural education also examines how social, behavioral, and natural scientists construct knowledge and how their sociocultural backgrounds influence the way they create knowledge. Multicultural education works toward the eradication of prejudice, and it promotes equity pedagogy, incorporating teaching styles that complement students' varying back-

---

[1]The sum of the antimulticultural positions unveiled here were derived from Sabrina Laine's (1994) unpublished paper, "Multiculturalism: An easy target," and from Ovando and McCarty (1992), "Multiculturalism in U.S. society and education: Why an irritant and a paradox?"

grounds. Finally, multicultural education, as defined by Banks, affirms the importance of reflection and action (praxis), creating an empowering school culture for minority students by completely restructuring the organization and culture of the school. For Banks, fairly implemented multicultural education does not separate students from each other but rather has the potential to bring them together—*e pluribus unum*. His ubiquitous message is: "Multicultural education is necessary to help all of the nation's future citizens acquire the knowledge, attitudes, and skills needed to survive in the twenty-first century. Nothing less than the nation's survival is at stake" (35).

To the critics, however, multiculturalism is certainly not one of the keys to twenty-first-century survival. In their demonized version, they portray it as a social reconstructionist movement that is not aimed at engaging minority and majority students in the pursuit of knowledge in a democratic society and interdependent global community. Instead, they see it as an ideological agenda that attempts to redress perceived social, economic, cultural, and linguistic inequalities of the past (Salins 1997). Multicultural scholars such as Henry Giroux, Peter McLaren, and Donaldo Macedo often draw the neoconservatives' fire. McLaren (1998), for example, is a lightning rod for conservative criticism as he chides his fellow multicultural educators for not being radical enough in their vision of a just social class structure. In his words,

> Most educationalists who are committed to critical pedagogy and multicultural education propagate versions of it that identify with their own bourgeois class interests. One doesn't have to question the integrity or competence of these educators or dismiss their work as disingenuous—for, for the most part, it is not—to conclude that their articulations of critical pedagogy and multicultural education have been accommodated to mainstream versions of liberal humanism and progressivism. (49)

McLaren and other political radicals have particularly incited the wrath of the neoconservatives as they draw heavily from the tradition of revolutionary thought exemplified by such figures as Paulo Freire (1970), Che Guevara, and Emiliano Zapata. They find the politics of multicultural education to be interrelated with the defects of capitalism, especially in countries on the periphery of the world economy, as the gap widens between the haves and the have-nots on a global scale. (See Bissett and D.G. 1998.) According to Manning Marable (1998, 5), as of 1993, the top 1 percent of all income earners in the United States had a greater combined net wealth than the bottom 95 percent of all income earners, which means that about 2 or 3 million individuals control the vast majority of resources in this country. And it is equally difficult to turn a blind eye to the disaster the current political and economic system has wreaked on the environment.

The radical position (represented in this volume in the chapter by McLaren and Muñoz) argues that reform efforts brought about by well-intentioned multiculturalists, while affecting some advances on the long road to social justice, often merely establish the balance of competing forces (from the political left, right, and center), but only for a short time. For revolutionary multiculturalists, history has made it apparent that as long as we simply tinker with the capitalist system to increase its stability, the structural impediments to social justice remain firmly in place.

Recently, one of the editors and a student drove past the Pico-Aliso housing project in the Boyle Heights section of East Los Angeles. Pico-Aliso is the largest public housing complex west of the Mississippi River, and it has the highest concentration of gang activity in southern California and possibly the entire world. From Pico-Aliso, they drove toward the westside, past Beverly Hills to the University of California campus in Westwood. During the ride, the conversation focused on the recent activity of the Zapatista Army of National Liberation in Chiapas, Mexico. The question was posed: What is the relationship between the largely Chicano residents of Pico-Aliso, the residents who live in the huge mansions in Beverly Hills, and the Zapatistas? The relationship might strike some as rather abstract or vague, until you start thinking about the phenomenon of globalization. The housing projects are filled with undocumented immigrants who have fled Mexico, a nation caught up in a financial crisis produced by recent global economic policies spearheaded by the United States. These neoliberal economic policies are creating a small number of wealthy elite—such as the Beverly Hills executives whose corporations own the *maquiladora* factories that line the border between Mexico and the United States, and exploit cheap Mexican labor. The Zapatista Army in Chiapas is rebelling against the unimaginable poverty faced by millions of Mexicans and against the economic policies that are responsible for the sale of Indian lands that had been worked by the indigenous peoples of Mexico for centuries. In a case such as this, as in many other situations, multicultural education can provide the kind of backdrop that enables students to analyze relationally what appear to be wholly separate conditions.

The contributors to this book represent a variety of positions on the continuum of multicultural points of view. Multiculturalism must neither congeal into a dogmatic profession of faith nor simply remain at an abstract level of analysis without acting on the world. There is much room for dialogue. For example, what are the precipitating causes of racism, sexism, xenophobia, linguistic intolerance, religious bigotry, and homophobia? Are they basically personal biases, distorted ways of thinking, erroneous world views, or ideologies detached from larger economic structures? Or, conversely, are they primarily systems of classification that religion, anthropology, and science have used both wittingly and unwittingly to legitimize the social divisions under capitalism?

The departure point of multicultural education is respect for differences, without falling into a facile cultural relativism. We do not advocate an "anything goes" multiculturalism, but one that is firmly grounded in a politics of social justice, human freedom, and democracy. While we might differ as to what such a politics should look like (e.g., conservative, centrist, radical, etc.), we strongly advocate that multicultural education be guided by the acknowledgment that multiple oppressions on the basis of race, ethnicity, culture, class, gender, language, religion, and sexual orientation are inescapably interwoven into the fabric of everyday life in our society.

Proponents of multiculturalism as an ethical stance acknowledge that its appeals to tolerance and its postmodern approach to knowledge often offer teachers few tools that are useful in practice. Discussions of multiculturalism can make many teachers feel intellectually inadequate (unable to keep up with the "deconstructionists") or defensive (accused of racism and ethnocentrism). Naturally, this exclusionistic approach tends to alienate those who feel they are struggling to do the best for their students.

As one starting point, teachers can develop a deeper understanding of what is wrong with "monocultural" education and come to better recognize the extent to which they have internalized monocultural assumptions—assumptions such as a cultural deficit explanation for low achievement, a tendency to universalize the dominant culture, and lowered expectations for racial and ethnic minorities. Another important issue to understand is the extent to which minority students are disadvantaged not by their social backgrounds but by a school culture, curriculum, teaching methodology, and approach to assessment that have evolved to serve the white, European American, middle-class norm. Perhaps the single most important goal is for teachers to develop a dialogical habit of the mind and heart that prompts them to step out of their familiar class, cultural, religious, and linguistic framework and enter into the experiences of others.

We hope that this book will help teachers caught in the cross fires over multiculturalism and bilingual education to be able to come to grips with the complexity, challenges, and promises of these important theoretical and practical concerns in our diverse society and shrinking global village. We hope that the book will help prepare preservice teachers to position themselves effectively for the realities of diversity in the classrooms, institutions, and society in which they will live out their careers. This book, therefore, is intended for audiences reaching their student teaching experience, graduate students, and teachers in the field. Finally, we hope that the civility of rational discourse on these matters will increasingly take center stage in our democratic society. In Amy Gutmann's (1992) words, "The moral promise of multiculturalism depends on the exercise of these deliberative virtues" (24).

REFERENCES

Banks, J. A. 1992. Multicultural education: Nature, challenges, and opportunities. In *Multicultural education for the 21st century,* ed. C. Díaz, Washington, D.C.: National Education Association.

Bennett, C. I. 1999. *Comprehensive multicultural education: Theory and practice.* 4th ed. Boston: Allyn & Bacon.

Bennett, W. J. 1984. To reclaim a legacy: Report on the humanities in education. *Chronicle of Higher Education* 29(14): 16–21.

Bennett, W. J. 1985. Speech to the Association for a Better New York. In *Language loyalties: A source book on the Official English controversy,* ed. J. Crawford, 358–363. Chicago: University of Chicago Press.

Bissett, J., and D. G. 1998. Who owns the world? Available from http://www.worldsocialism. org/poverty.htm

Bloom, A. D. 1987. *The closing of the American mind: How higher education has failed democracy and impoverished the soul of today's students.* New York: Simon & Schuster.

Chávez, L. 1991. *Out of the barrio: Toward a new politics of Hispanic assimilation.* New York: Basic Books.

Chávez, L. 1995. Demystifying multiculturalism. In *Taking sides: Clashing views on controversial educational issues,* ed. J. Noll, 8th ed., 94–99. Guilford, Conn.: Dushking Publishing Group. Reprinted from *National Review,* 21 February 1994, 46(3): 26–30.

D'Souza, D. 1991. *Illiberal education: The politics of race and sex on campus.* New York: Free Press.

Finn, C., D. Ravitch, and R. Fancher. 1984. *Against mediocrity: The humanities in America's high schools.* New York: Holmes and Meier.

Freire, P. 1970. *Pedagogy of the oppressed.* New York: Continuum.

Gutmann, A. 1992. Introduction to *Multiculturalism and the "politics of recognition,"* by C. Taylor, 3–21. Princeton, N.J.: Princeton University Press.

Hirsch, Jr., E.D. 1987. *Cultural literacy: What every American needs to know.* Boston: Houghton Mifflin.

Laine, S. 1994. Multiculturalism: An easy target. Unpublished paper. Indiana University.

Marable, M. 1998. The left. *Social Policy* 28(3): 4–9.

McLaren, P. 1998. Che: The pedagogy of Che Guevara: Critical pedagogy and globalization thirty years after Che. *Cultural Circles* 3 (summer).

Merelman, R. M. 1994. Racial conflict and cultural politics in the United States. *Journal of Politics* 56(1): 1–20.

Ovando, C. J., and L. P. McCarty. 1992. Multiculturalism in U.S. society and education: Why an irritant and a paradox? Paper presented at the Seventh Triennial Conference of the World Council for Curriculum and Instruction, Cairo, Egypt.

Ravitch, D. 1985a. Politics and the schools: The case of bilingual education. In *Taking sides: Clashing views on controversial educational issues,* ed. J. Noll, 8th ed., 240–248, 1995. Guilford, Conn.: Dushkin Publishing Group. Reprinted from *Proceedings from the American Philosophical Society* 129(2).

Ravitch, D. 1985b. *The schools we deserve: Reflections on the educational crisis of our time.* New York: Basic Books.

Salins, P. D. 1997. *Assimilation American style: An impassioned defense of immigration and assimilation as the foundation of American greatness and the American Dream.* New York: Basic Books.

Webster, Y. O. 1997. *Against the multicultural agenda: A critical thinking alternative.* Westport, Conn.: Praeger.

PART ONE

The Moral and Political Cross Fires of Multiculturalism

Sharon Pugh   Carlos J. Ovando   Nicole Schonemann

*D*rawing on the argument that metaphor is inherent in human language and thought, this essay explores the metaphors in a broad spectrum of writings on issues of difference, multiculturalism, and multilingualism in education. Taking the position that these are always issues of both morality and imagination as well as of politics, the authors examine metaphors in three broad categories grounded in direct experience: sensory-based metaphors, especially those of sight, hearing, and taste; metaphors of struggle and conflict; and metaphors of geography, the last including movement and direction as well as water, terrain, and boundaries. Through this analysis, the authors demonstrate how metaphorical language reveals assumptions, arguments, and judgments, and how metaphorical thinking can be used to either solidify set positions or cultivate new understandings. Finally, it is argued that "strong sense" metaphorical thinking is deliberately dialectical in striving to expand perspectives on complex issues and foster imagination and empathy as essential to human morality.

CHAPTER 1

The Political Life of Language

Metaphors in Writings About Diversity in Education

Sharon Pugh,
Indiana University, Bloomington

Carlos J. Ovando,
Indiana University, Bloomington

Nicole Schonemann,
Indiana University, Bloomington

People and their cultures perish in isolation, but they are born or reborn in contact with other men and women, with men and women of another culture, another creed, another race. If we do not recognize our humanity in others, we shall not recognize it in ourselves.
Carlos Fuentes, The Buried Mirror

The Power of Metaphorical Thinking

In this chapter, we take a strong position on the importance and pervasiveness of metaphor in thought and expression. Often without our realizing it, the metaphors we use reveal our positions and attitudes. In arguments, metaphors may be used skillfully to enhance messages of acceptance or rejection along with other connotative meanings that powerfully influence how students think about themselves, others, issues, and events. Metaphors can also be used in ways that foster mutual understanding and appreciation. Therefore, teachers need to be acutely sensitive to the effects of metaphors in virtually all conversations and texts.

Our discussion first focuses on the concept of "moral imagination," referring to the capacity to reason from multiple perspectives and experience empathy. This concept is represented metaphorically in parables by science fiction author Ursula LeGuin and legal scholar Derrick Bell. We then explore different ways that metaphors have been used in writings about multicultural and bilingual education to represent particular stances in a highly politicized dialectic on the purposes and outcomes of schooling in our society. Our intent for this

3

chapter is to raise readers' awareness of how language operates in any politicized arena and use that understanding as informed teachers and responsible citizens.

The Fundamental Issue of Difference   The issue of difference is a moral one, involving questions of privilege and power. Because these questions often evoke discomfort, especially in groups whose members differ in their personal access to privilege and power, they may be avoided in classrooms. At best, they are replaced with more positive reflections of diversity. Too often, they are replaced with no questions at all. Without denying the value and importance of representing human differences in a positive light and fostering tolerance and appreciation for the similarities in the human experience, in this chapter we will emphasize the equal importance of addressing the difficult and contentious issues as well. We will do so by unpacking the complex ways in which metaphorical language can stimulate the development of our moral imagination in seeking the highest ideals of democratic pluralism.

In her parable "The Ones Who Walk Away from Omelas," Ursula LeGuin (1978) presents the heart of this moral issue by positing a city whose prosperity depends on the abominable suffering of one child. Residents of the city know about and may even witness the child's misery, but most rationally weigh the sacrifice of one individual against the well-being of all others and choose to accept the sacrifice. Only a few walk away from the city and the devil's bargain their society has struck, going into an unimaginable and perhaps nonexistent world beyond. "But they seem to know where they are going," writes LeGuin at the end, "the ones who walk away from Omelas."

Education, etymologically, means "leading out." Therefore, education, if anything, should be about coming to understand where one is going and by extension where one's society is going. Parables such as LeGuin's provide narrative metaphors that guide such understanding. Derrick Bell (1992), in his exploration of American racism, *Faces at the Bottom of the Well*, refers to LeGuin's description of Omelas as "an apt metaphor for the knowing but unspoken alliance whereby all whites are bonded . . . by racism." In his book, he offers his own bitter parable, "Space Traders," in which leaders of a superior civilization from another galaxy offer the United States a permanent supply of wealth, pollution control, and energy in exchange for all of its African American citizens. Although some debate ensues, the popular decision is to strike the bargain, which is implemented on the nation's last Martin Luther King, Jr., day:

> Crowded on the beaches were the inductees, some twenty million silent black men, women, and children, including babes in arms. As the sun rose, the Space Traders directed them, first, to strip off all but a single undergarment; then, to line up; and finally, to enter those holds which yawned in the morning light like Milton's "darkness visible." The inductees looked fearfully behind them. But, on the dunes above the beaches, guns at the ready, stood the U.S. guards. There was no escape, no alternative. Heads bowed, arms now linked by slender chains, black people left the New World as their forebears had arrived. (194)

Like the comfortable citizens of Omelas, those who stand by observing this scene have rationalized the exchange, arguing that there is no reason to believe that African Americans will suffer more where they are going than they have here or that they should be honored to sacrifice themselves for their country. These observers neither draw on the lessons of the past nor use their imaginations to put themselves in the place of others. In addition to being an issue of morality, therefore, otherness is also an issue of imagination. It concerns whether and how we use our imaginations to expand our awareness of human experience and to act on that knowledge. In his book, *Priviliged Ones: The Well-Off and the Rich in America* (1977), Robert Coles reveals how children's moral imagination is arrested by their parents' view of justice and fairness in society. As he puts it, early in their moral development, children of rich parents demonstrate empathy for poor children and want to know why the less fortunate are not as well off as they are—why they live in old houses in poor neighborhoods, wear non-brand name clothes, ride in old cars, and do not have nice toys. In response to their childrens' sense of fairness and justice, the rich parents tell them that it is basically a moral and motivational issue—that in this country, all can prosper if they believe and practice the work ethic and take advantage of the many opportunities available to them. In sum, rich parents inculcate their children to view the parents of poor children as lacking the moral fiber, right attitude, and work ethic to prosper. Eventually, rich children accept these views of the poor, and the oppressive cycle in society is reenacted in another generation.

Teachers who support the development of moral imagination in their students help take education well beyond the limits of the presumably neutral knowledge brokering that conservative critics claim is education's sole purpose. In so doing, they will inevitably encounter a third dimension of human diversity, the political, which is concerned with active participation in issues of how power, resources, and opportunities are negotiated. According to the claims of democracy, in such negotiations highest value is placed upon fairness and justice, but in their pursuit of self-interest, humans tend to fall short of this ideal, usually by excluding from participation those who can be marginalized because of differences in appearance, language, culture, nationality, or class. The politics of inclusion and exclusion work in many ways, through customs, through laws, through agencies and institutions, but most ubiquitously through language. Recently, for example, the access of language-minority students in California to meaningful education was seriously compromised with the passage of Proposition 227, a harsh antibilingual measure euphemistically called "English for the Children" (1997). (See Chapter 6 by James Crawford in this book for a more extended discussion of this legislation.)

Language is our primary human system for conceptualizing, expressing, and comprehending complex and relative meanings. As the International Reading Association and the National Council of Teachers of English (1994) insightfully put it, "Language is very much like a living organism. It cannot be put together from parts like a machine, and it is constantly changing. . . . Language does not contain meaning; rather, meaning lies in the social relationships within which language occurs. Individuals in communities make sense of language within their social relationships, their personal histories, and their collective memory" (7–9). Although it is approximate, value-laden, and changing, language is often regarded as definite, neutral, and permanent. "Look it up in the dictionary" is often the suggestion made for settling, not just beginning to pursue, the meaning of a word. But language is truly a dynamic system by which meanings can be constructed and reconstructed rather than packaged and transmitted. Language provides maps to meanings, and maps are positioned representations of reality.

For example, we are used to seeing the world represented by the Mercator map, which, in order to maintain shapes and spatial relationships on the globe, positions the Northern Hemisphere as "up" and flattens the curved surfaces so that areas near the poles are enlarged. The effect of this flattening is to distort the relative sizes of some land masses, such as Alaska in relation to Mexico. Addressing the political implications of this configuration, German historian Arno Peters (1990) created his "New World Map," which maintains land masses in proper proportion to each other but distorts continental shapes. Given the inevitability of distortion on any map, the two versions work best together, illustrating the dialectical nature of knowledge.

As a map or model of meaning, language is also by nature metaphorical. That is, metaphor is the growing tip of a living language, so that from its most basic roots it is composed of comparisons and extensions of meaning that conform to human experience over time. Therefore, to explore the political nature of language, we must study it as a phenomenon of metaphorical thinking. In their definitive analysis of metaphor, Lakoff and Johnson (1980) reach the conclusion that metaphorical thinking is a sixth, cultural sense, ". . . like seeing or touching or hearing, with metaphors providing the only ways to perceive and experience much of the world." They further emphasize the importance of realizing that "the way we have been brought up to perceive the world is not the only way and . . . it is possible to see beyond the 'truths' of our culture" (239).

Lakoff and Johnson (1980) offer not just an analysis but also an argument against what they consider a false dichotomy between the "objectivist myth" and the "subjectivist myth" of Western culture. They use the term *myth* not to disparage these perspectives as false but to emphasize that all systems of knowing are culturally constructed and reflect selected values while suppressing others. Lakoff and Johnson propose a third, more powerful myth to guide contemporary understanding, the "experiential myth," which validates both objectivity and subjectivity dialectically enjoined and allows a much broader array of values to be brought to light:

The myth of objectivism reflects the human need to understand the *external* world in order to be able to function successfully in it. The myth of subjectivism is focused on *internal* aspects of understanding—what the individual finds meaningful and what makes life worth living. The experientialist myth suggests that these are not opposing concerns. It offers a perspective from which both concerns can be met at once. (229)

What the "experientialist myth" emphasizes is that knowledge is a dynamic creation constantly unfolding throughout life and across domains as the individual interacts and negotiates with others. This account of human understanding, Lakoff and Johnson (1980) believe, provides a richer perspective on the areas most important to humanity, including interpersonal communication, mutual understanding, and self-understanding.

The richness in such "interactionally based and creative understanding" depends on diversity of experience and world views, patience and tolerance in the process of sharing understanding, and what Lakoff and Johnson (1980) call "the crucial skill of metaphorical imagination," which entails "the ability to bend your world view and adjust the way you categorize your experiences" (231). At the same time, however, it suggests the importance of critical examination of metaphors as expressions of particular perspectives that, by necessity, are partial and preferential.

Metaphorical Thought and Language in Discussions of Diversity

If we accept that metaphorical thinking is an integral part of knowledge construction and that issues of diversity involve morality, imagination, and politics, the question of how metaphors are used in discussions that relate to diversity is critical. When they represent particular perspectives on complex issues, metaphors illuminate some aspects of these issues while concealing other aspects, as exemplified in the discussion of maps above. As positioned arguments, metaphors are powerful political tools and have provided the most enduring political images: administrations characterized by their policy package (e.g., Franklin Roosevelt's New Deal or Lyndon Johnson's Great Society), political conceptualizations of otherness (e.g., the former Soviet Union as "the evil empire"), heroic characterizations of war (e.g., Operation Desert Storm) and mistakes not to be repeated (e.g., "another Vietnam"). These have shaped the way policy is understood and sometimes the formation of policy itself.

Whether such charged metaphors are regarded as patriotic slogans or objects of critical scrutiny depends largely on the hearer's willingness to suspend judgment, analyze the metaphor for its implications and exclusions, and evaluate its usefulness in terms of a framework that admits alternative positions. Instilling such a disposition to commit oneself to the effort of critical thinking is an important responsibility of formal education, according to Paul (1985), who argues that it is "human nature" to reason in terms of immediate self-interest and that learners must be helped to build larger frameworks of social justice or even their own longer-term interests. While metaphors must be grounded in some accepted understanding of reality to be considered valid (Lakoff and Johnson 1980), it is important to recognize that because they emphasize only one aspect of reality they are inherently manipulative, focusing attention on the view that the writer or speaker has chosen to emphasize. That is, metaphors are tools of conscious persuasion; they do not merely describe a situation but also serve as a heuristic that constructs understanding through shaping an influential image. A metaphor, in this sense, can create a false sense of understanding and offer relief from the responsibility to obtain a greater understanding of an issue. If accepted as a package of accomplished understanding, the metaphor has curtailed thinking. To avoid such programming, the reader or listener must assume responsibility for looking beyond the metaphor. While the metaphor may be a bridge toward understanding (Pugh et al. 1992), the reader or listener should be alert to uncovering hidden pathways as well. As extensions of the positions of their creators, metaphors vary in their impact according to their source. Simply put, the metaphors of those in power can obscure other metaphors, and they reinforce and perpetuate the power holders' version of reality and play a crucial role in the construction of social and political realities (Lakoff and Johnson 1980).

Metaphors of "Otherness" and Policy Implications   Metaphors of "otherness" are often used to restrict or deny rights and services to specific populations. For example, metaphors that describe phenomena of migration may emphasize or deemphasize the "otherness" of migrants in order to influence policies. Migration metaphors have varied over time to support or deny the entrance of specific immigrant populations and the rights to which these populations may be entitled, reflecting current attitudes toward other nationalities. A strong example of such a metaphorical argument is Charlotte Perkins Gilman's 1923 essay "Is America Too Hospitable?" (cited in Ceplair 1991), in which she compares immigrants primarily from southern and eastern Europe to invading insects:

> Our swarming immigrants do not wish for a wilderness, nor for enemies. They like an established nation, with free education, free hospitals, free nursing, and more remunerative employment than they can find at home. . . . The amazing thing is the cheerful willingness with which the Americans are giving up their country to other people, so rapidly that they are already reduced to a scant one half of the population. (289)

Gilman's "Americans," facing the loss of political and cultural power, were separated from those she considered immigrants by another metaphor, the preferred "blend."

> All Americans come from somewhere else. But all persons who come from somewhere else are not therefore American. The American blend is from a few closely connected races." (Ceplair 1991, 290)

Gilman's conceptualization of the "other" is a use of imagery to restrict understanding of commonality, deny connection, and limit political power of the populations she demeans. Similar sentiments are echoed in the contemporary package of Proposition 187, a California state initiative to deny basic social services to undocumented residents. Proposition 187's colloquial name, the "Save Our State Initiative," is itself a metaphor that implies criminal threat from immigrants (in this case, primarily from Latin America) to the well-being of California. It reads in part as follows:

> [That the People of California] have suffered and are suffering economic hardship caused by the presence of illegal aliens in this state. That they have suffered and are suffering personal injury and damage caused by the criminal conduct of illegal aliens in this state. That they have a right to the protection of their government from any person or persons entering this country unlawfully. Therefore, the people of California declare their intention to provide for cooperation between their agencies of state and local government with the

federal government, and to establish a system of required notification by and between such agencies to prevent illegal aliens in the United States from receiving benefits or public services in the State of California." (Suárez-Orozco 1995, 17)

Here, the attribution of illegality, a construction of lawmakers like those who wrote Proposition 187, has been metonymically converted into the people themselves so that they, and not just their status as defined by California law, are "illegal aliens," an identity that is further intensified by the allegation that they cause crime at the same time that they constitute it. And not only are they both crime and criminals, but they are parasites, too, a dehumanizing image that hides the nebulous nature of cost-benefit analysis when applied to migration and ignores evidence from numerous studies indicating that undocumented immigrants often contribute more to the welfare of their adopted society than they take out, in part due to fear of repercussions associated with their illegal status (Flores and Hammer 1997). In other words, the metaphors of criminality and parasitism condemn the immigrants when it is more likely that society is deriving benefit from them while according them treatment that would be considered a crime if applied to "legal" populations. Even more disturbing perhaps is that these metaphors hide the reality that the primary targets of this initiative are children. Who else would be most affected by the denial of educational services? If the metaphors had offered the images of "children as parasites" or "children as criminals," would the proposition have garnered as much political support as enabled it to pass? Through strategically managed language, proponents of this measure succeeded in focusing attention on the version of reality that served their purposes.

Teaching and Metaphor   To teach students to identify values that are both highlighted and hidden in metaphors, teachers themselves must be sensitive to the ways they portray perspectives on diversity. In discussions of multiculturalism and multilingualism in education, metaphors with their implied arguments abound, often highly charged with strong attitudes. Because of the volume of writing that has been produced, an exhaustive review of metaphorical language in discussions of diversity in education is beyond the scope of this chapter. Instead, we have sampled a broad spectrum of writings representing negative and positive perspectives toward the concept of teaching diversity. In this discussion, we have organized our analysis around three groupings of metaphors: (1) metaphors of the senses, particularly seeing, hearing, and tasting; (2) metaphors of conflict, struggle, violence, and pathology; and (3) metaphors of topography, including water, terrain, boundaries, and directionality.

These groupings do not constitute formal categories. They overlap among themselves as well as with other possible groupings, but our purpose is not to construct a taxonomy but rather to achieve a useful focus on a very complex and changing subject. This focus, we hope, will help guide educators in their own further analyses and critiques of metaphorical thinking and language.

Metaphors of the Senses

Metaphors of the senses are present in much writing about education, often in ways that encourage an appreciative view of diversity, such as the various food images—salads, soups, and casseroles—that evoke the spirit of *e pluribus unum*, unity with diversity. Food images are also used negatively, however, notably in epithets like "Oreo," banana," "apple," and "coconut," referring to people of color who have been co-opted by the dominant white culture. Visual images are also prominent, often implying equality, as in "color-blindness" or "rainbow coalition," or appreciation, as in colorful creations such as mosaics and tapestries. An example of how such metaphors lend themselves to elaboration is Esquivel's (1991) discussion of bilingual education as a "tapestry of languages":

> A tapestry is a work of creativity, but it is often put to very practical uses as carpet or curtain or wall covering. The weave of a tapestry is intricate and complex, and the visual image it presents is often made simple by its unity. A tapestry is woven by thousands of threads, but still it is one single art object. If you look at a tapestry from the underside, you see what looks like a disorderly tangle of stitches and knots and disconnected figures; if you stand in front of it, you perceive the finished surface, whose patterns are clear, whose segments are related to one another in beautiful designs. (171)

Bilingual education, Esquivel goes on to write, is a tapestry not only of languages but also of cultures, and it "brings into one process the multiple treasures of multiple peoples and their long and honorable histories" (175).

In contrast with metaphors that highlight color as aesthetically positive are those centered around notions of visibility, signifying power, or invisibility, signifying its absence. The title of Ralph Ellison's (1952) novel, *Invisible Man*, expresses the African American male's nonstatus in Ellison's time. The notion of "color-blindness," often evoked in arguments against affirmative action, continues to equate invisibility with insignificance but with the twist that it is now the issue of race itself that is hidden in the rhetoric. Stephen Steinberg (1997), in his indictment of the liberal retreat from the civil rights platform, argues that this concealment is a return to pre-civil rights complacency. "The truth is," he writes, "that it is the refusal to see race—the willful color-blindness of the liberal camp—that acquiesces to the racial status quo, and does so by consigning blacks to a twilight zone where they are politically invisible" (42).

In contrast, the image of invisibility may be used to signify power when it connotes normativeness or the privileged perspective from which others are visually defined, usually by color. For example, in apartheid-era South Africa, multiple calibrations of color measured deviation from the central unspecified norm of whiteness, the only identity that did not have to be documented. In her analysis of white preservice teachers' attempts to explore their own concepts of whiteness, McIntyre (1997) found that her participants had to struggle to recognize that their cultural lenses normalized a social hierarchy in which white dominated other races. "What was problematic in this talk," McIntyre writes, "was their failure to explore and/or question how whites continue to dominate people of color and keep this racial hierarchy in place" (83). A telling image that emerged from students' conversations about race and education was that of the "white knights" who, "dressed in teachers' clothing . . . enter their classrooms complete with a history of white dominance, privilege, and advantage" (123). This stance manifested itself in expressions of compassion and pity for poor and colored students and a wish to "save" them, but it did not peak into anger about the hierarchical system that sustains the economic inequalities. As teachers with high self-expectations, the "white knight" teachers wanted to vanquish these inequities with the swords of their own good intentions. McIntyre concludes that to break the obscuring "white bubble" in which they still focus on their own feelings and experiences, whites "need to take responsibility to educate ourselves about 'the Other' which means reading about people of color—their histories, their lived experiences in their own words. It means not relying on people of color to teach us about themselves, or about ourselves, or about racisms and the impact of racism on their/our lives. That's our responsibility . . ." (139).

Though in the researcher's own judgment incomplete, the struggle of these preservice teachers to confront the meaning of their own whiteness was still a rather remarkable undertaking in teacher education. As such, it marks some dissolution of the solid opaqueness of the "white bubble" while increasingly the benign invisibility of whiteness is threatened. Citing the multicultural demographics of Los Angeles as an example of the changing nature of cultural politics, Giroux (1994) argues that as various ethnic, racial, and cultural groups have redefined their visibility in positive terms,

> . . . dominant society no longer resorts to extermination or silencing Others; nor can it simply erase them. Cultural difference has descended on America like a fog. Dominant groups are now driving very carefully through a cultural terrain in which whiteness can no longer remain invisible as a racial, political, and historical construction. The privilege and practices of domination that underscore being white in America can no longer remain invisible through either appeal to a universal norm or a refusal to explore how whiteness works to produce forms of "friendly" colonialism. (40)

Closely related to images of invisibility are images of silence. In her analysis of the campaign to demolish Lani Guinier's candidacy for director of the Civil Rights Division of the Justice Department, Williams (1995) shows how vested assumptions and rumor displaced Lanier's own voice, either through her own writings (which even her nominator President Bill Clinton claimed not to have read) or through public statements, which she was effectively barred from making. Although Guinier's statements had been accessible in leading law journals for years,

> . . . they were utterly ignored as authoritative in the debate about who she was and what she meant. While perhaps it's just politics that everyone in Washington gets picked apart for what they say, Lani Guinier was condemned for things she never said and consistently denied. . . . Over and over I saw her picture on television, her lips moving, but the sound being given to a voice-over

that described all the awful crackpot things she meant when her lips moved like that." (144)

The combination of Guinier's silence with an authoritative voice-over speaking for her, Williams (1995) writes, "ultimately served to depersonalize her. It made her a visual aid reinforcing a stereotype" (144). In this metaphorical analysis, the subject's visual image is present but confiscated, while her silence is masked by the presence of a disembodied voice.

Metaphors of Conflict and Pathology

The experience of confusion and disorientation inherent in Giroux's image of a fog is consistent with "culture wars" and other fighting metaphors that have become familiar in discussions of multiculturalism. Conflict is not always to be viewed negatively, as Graff (1993) argues in *Beyond Culture Wars*, which has the subtitle, *How Teaching the Conflicts Can Revitalize American Education*. Graff argues that the American tradition of dissenting voices can be the basis of education through dialectical reasoning while exposing hidden agendas and silent debates. Such an approach could certainly begin with an examination of metaphorical arguments. For example, Ravitch's (1985a) characterization of advocacy campaigns as "crusades" marked by "intolerance of criticism and unyielding dogmatism" (240) is a device she uses to forge a historical chain of instances chosen to construct her analogy. Bilingual education, she argues, is yet another series of twentieth-century campaigns that include curriculum purges during the two world wars, McCarthyism, and the Vietnam War. Ravitch (1985b) alleges that "advocates press its adoption regardless of its educational effectiveness. . . . The aim is to use the public schools to promote the maintenance of distinct ethnic communities, each with its own cultural heritage and language." (247) This kind of deceptive argumentation by analogy, augmented in this instance by the writer's authority as a historian, illustrates the importance of critically examining the connotations of metaphors and determining the limits of the comparisons they present.

Metaphors of conflict and violence range from the relatively innocuous images of sports, such as level and unlevel playing fields and the hijinks of political football, to the ominous images of war, such as cultural battle lines or linguistic genocide. In this category, we also include metaphors of capitalism, often construed as benign when in fact they imply cultural battle lines drawn between the rich and the poor, the culturally empowered and disempowered. Such images include cultural capital or deprivation and the vocabulary of investment banking such as *currency*, *enterprise*, and *economic determinism*. Our best known assimilationist image, that of the melting pot, belongs in the category of violence in that it implies dissolving individuals into a boiling mixture, whether in the foundry or the kitchen, to be poured into molds of mass production. This aspect is emphasized in the following observation from the introduction to the *Before Columbus Fiction Anthology* (Strads, Trueblood, and Wong 1992):

The only accurate aspect of the melting-pot metaphor is heat—the heat of anger caused by ignorance and abuse. We can no more be melted into one alloy than we can expect the world to learn and speak Esperanto. The metaphor persists, however, and the Eurocentric point of view continues to be disseminated because it embodies a come unto me monopolistic attitude that obviates the effort to understand cultural difference—not merely racial difference. (xii)

War images are used on both sides of the multicultural/bilingual debate. Another conservative critic, Chávez (1995), argues that "multiculturalists," by whom she means vocal advocates of multicultural education, are a liberal elite group who try to hold power by using schools and government resources to maintain a rebel guard of assimilation-resisters, young people who "must be trained to think of themselves as members of oppressed minority groups" (97). Banks (1993) uses similar imagery to argue in support of multicultural education, describing ". . . well financed attacks by western traditionalists who fear . . . their own disempowerment," and asserts that this "well orchestrated attack on multiculturalism reflect[s] an identity crisis in American society" (92).

Metaphors of Deviance and Disease   An important group of metaphors associated with images of conflict and violence are those that actually criminalize or pathologize difference and opposition. According to Apple (1988), for example, the "normative gaze of mainstream educational discourse" views minority and low-income youth as "deviant entities in educational and social arrangements," a view reflected in D'Souza's (1991) reference to "cultural pathologies" in the African American community. D'Souza is actually echoing the central argument of the Moynihan Report during the Johnson administration, which has become the definitive text for placing blame for aberrance, poverty, and dependence on the inherently weak black family structure rather than viewing all these phenomena as outcomes of systemic discrimination (Steinberg 1997, 26). Geneticists (or eugenicists) have offered their evidence validating race-based social and economic inequalities as acts of nature.

On the other hand, the term "caste-like minorities" (Ogbu 1988) is a metaphor contending that inequalities are more socially than biologically constructed, although one must keep in mind that in traditional Indian society, which is the source of the metaphor, caste was considered an inborn, biological attribute. Also arguing metaphorically for the social construction of inequality, Spener (1996) describes the role of schools in socializing children into low self-expectations, a process he calls "inferiorating education," which results in part from ". . . use of clinical definition of caste-minority children's academic problems that place blame on the minority family for producing 'inferior children' . . ." (62). Using more vivid imagery, McLaren (1994) describes a media-propagated view of the African American underclass as "a population spawning mutant Willie Horton-type youths who, in the throes of bloodlust, roam the perimeter of the urban landscape high on angel dust, randomly hunting whites with steel pipes" (194).

Another pathologically based metaphor, which brings up images of a medical threat, is that of the "at-risk" student. In a continuation of the tradition of labeling marginalized student populations, the 1990s has seen the creation of this category. It is even a funding category in state and federal educational agencies (Banks 1995). Researchers, practitioners, and policy makers often use this term, and it is sufficiently broad and ambiguous to serve as an umbrella metaphor for any student who does not fit the mainstream norm and who therefore may be in need of special preventive measures or treatments to be recategorized as a "healthy" student.

Images of wounding and medical assault may express the pain of exclusion, such as Singaporean educator Su Chin Lim's (1997) term "cultural lobotomy" for the effects suffered when the Chinese government attempted to eliminate all dialects but Mandarin, suddenly cutting off millions of people's access to radio, theater, and other spoken forms of cultural expression. Williams (1997) describes the casual perpetuation of social divisions, often embodied in humor, as virulent. She tells the story of eavesdropping on a conversation among members of an affluent, well-educated family, who, after covering topics of investments, travel, and hobbies, fell to telling redneck jokes, capturing the interest of a small girl among them. "They were so pleasant and happy," Williams (1997) writes, ". . . and yet they were transporting a virus." She speculates that "that little girl will have to leave the warmth of the embracing, completely relaxed circle of those happy people before she can ever appreciate the humanity of someone who drives a pickup, who can't afford a dentist" (263)—in other words, before she has hope of getting rid of the virus.

Metaphors of Topography

The third grouping, metaphors of topography, is in many ways the most generative of the three. Because these metaphors include ideas of space, contiguity, movement, and the elements of air, water, and earth, they offer great opportunities to the imagination. They accommodate movement and so provide for a language of progress and change while raising issues of both separation and contact. They may also penetrate most deeply into the substrata of our knowledge and beliefs. In his essay, "Landscape and Narrative," Native American writer Barry Lopez (1989) describes what he calls the 'interior landscape," by which he means "the speculations, intuitions, and formal ideas we refer to as 'mind' . . . some [of which] are obvious, many impenetrably subtle." He asserts his own belief that the interior landscape is profoundly affected by where one has been in the exterior world. He writes that "thoughts are arranged . . . according to the thread of one's moral, intellectual, and spiritual development. The . . . shape of the individual mind is affected by land as it is by genes" (65).

Land Metaphors   Land metaphors play with images of divisions and separation, as well as those of comfort and familiarity. Frontiers and borders, for example, emphasize separation and difference. What is a political border other than a positioning of otherness? Anzaldúa (1987) writes that ". . . borders are set up to define the places that are safe and unsafe, to distinguish us from them. A border is a dividing line, a narrow strip along a steep edge" (3).

The image of crossing borders has been used in many ways. Borders may represent a power imbalance, where movement from one side to another is restricted by a powerful neighbor. Crossing forbidden borders can symbolize loss of self and even life, as in the film *El Norte*, or it can open the way to a new vision or understanding. In describing an experience that took him beyond that which he had previously known only through imagination, Richard Rodríguez explained, "I have trespassed the boundary; I have gone to a foreign country" (McCarthy 1994). Here, the ability to cross borders is an empowering experience. At the same time, one's own side of the border may represent a variety of meanings—familiarity, safety, and self-definition. Borders may be drawn internally, as suggested in Rodríguez's distinction between the public and private self. This is especially significant for those who have crossed a physical border and are outsiders to the dominant culture. For Rodríguez, the essential border separated the world of school, which helps create the public individual, from the world of home and community, which nurtures the private self. While acknowledging that the parent and the teacher must help the child cross the public sphere, he believes that "the border needs to be maintained. I think these are separate worlds" (McCarthy 1994).

Just as borders imply separation, center/periphery, and center/margin dichotomies, they also offer a strong imagery of power/powerlessness. Marginality implies displacement or exclusion. The image of center and marginality is a two-dimensional one, with finite edges and limited room that necessitates unequal access to the inner circle. Transposed to a sphere, edges disappear and the margin becomes ambiguous, with the potential to become a center itself. bell hooks (1984) distinguishes between being placed or left in the margins from reclaiming the margins as an authentic site of resistance, change, and power. She speaks ". . . not of a marginality one wishes to lose—to give up . . . or surrender as part of moving into the center—but rather of a site one stays in, clings to even, because it nourishes one's capacity to resist. It offers to one the possibility of radical perspective from which to see and create, to imagine alternatives, new worlds" (149–150).

Another positive image of borders, which regretfully has not been applied very frequently in culturally diverse educational settings, is that of biological diversity at the borders of varying ecosystems. For example, in an estuary, where salt and fresh waters mix, there is a remarkable wealth of plant and animal diversity. The border areas between ecosystems are generally the richest biological systems, and likewise human borderlands have the potential to be seen as rich cross-cultural, linguistic, and pedagogical settings.

Water Metaphors   Metaphors of water rely on an understanding of water as a powerful force, the location of a struggle in which nature often wins over humans. Water metaphors emphasize direction, speed, and force of movement, and especially danger. Perhaps in an effort to stress the powerful impact that it can have on a community, the phenomenon of migration is often described through water metaphors. These images range from forceful (wave or flood) to moderate (flow) to negligible (trickle), according to the degree of perceived threat. Water metaphors commonly used to describe educational methods in the teaching of language-minority populations focus on the power of water and the need for human struggle against this force. Before the Bilingual Education Act of 1968 made such methods illegal, language-minority students were frequently placed in English-only classrooms. These situations were aptly labeled "sink or swim," "immersion," or "submersion," implying an ordeal by water in which one either learned the language of instruction or did not survive. Martha Jiménez (1992) of the San Francisco Board of Supervisors explained that "[l]anguage-minority children were left to 'sink or swim' in English-only classrooms, to succeed or drown in a sea of indifference" (243).

Metaphors of water are also used in positioning otherness. Consider the pejorative terms *wetback* or *mojado*, which refer to undocumented workers from Mexico. These metaphors merge images of the journey across the Rio Grande/Bravo River with images of sweat from long hours of backbreaking agricultural labor. "Steamer class" or immersion classes for immigrants (Glazer 1997), a metonymically employed image of steamer ships bringing immigrants across the Atlantic, uses water to represent separation, distance, and difference, the crossing of a wide boundary in the course of which the non-English-speaking immigrant becomes the one coming in, the other.

Water metaphors also provide for unidirectional imagery, which again emphasizes the power of water. For example, the frequently used term *mainstream* implies a strong flow that takes one inexorably in a single direction. When we speak of migrant agricultural workers as traveling in migrant streams, we also imply surging movement in one direction, which denies the cyclical nature of seasonal migration and separates the northward movement of the workers from their southward exodus, fragmenting the rationality of their experience.

Setting Boundaries on the World

From the earth to the otherworldly, "alien" is a particularly powerful metaphor that conjures images of unknowable beings outside humanity, beyond our control and therefore threatening. This metaphor focuses not only on difference but on its ominous nature, thereby justifying renunciation and self-defense. This emphasis on difference and unacceptability is evident when we contrast "alien" with "foreigner," "visitor," or "guest worker." Different epithets are applied to different groups. A British or French national may be considered a foreigner with or without negative connotations but never an "alien."

"Alien," moreover, is often coupled with "illegal." This descriptor suggests that it is not just the act of crossing forbidden boundaries but the perpetrators themselves who are illegal, a stroke of metonymy that makes the person the crime and justifies eradication. This focus on the issue of legality seems restricted to migration; people who commit what would universally be considered more heinous illegal acts, such as murder or rape, are not confounded with their crimes in this way. Criminalizing the individual amplifies the egregiousness of an act that is not, in itself, as self-evidently villainous as assault and homicide. Making the person the crime dispenses with significant ethical questions of where entering a country without official documentation falls on a scale of offensiveness or, more important, whether current immigration policy is just. Putting an ironic twist on the metaphor of illegality, Richard Rodríguez (1996) suggests that it is the homeland and not the new country that suffers when the immigrant breaks away from family and community:

> People in California talk about the "illegals." But there was always an illegality to immigration. It was a rude act, the leaving of home. It was a violation of custom, an insult to the village. A youthful act of defiance. I know a man from El Salvador who has not talked to his father since the day he left his father's village. (It is a sin against family to leave home.) Immigrants must always be illegal. Immigrants are always criminals. They trespass borders and horrify their grandmothers. But they are also our civilization's prophets. (224)

There is a saying in Latin America, "*La necesidad tiene cara de perro.*" (Necessity has a dog's face.) The fact that people are willing to take such risks speaks much of their need to migrate. Throughout history, humans have left loved ones, familiar cultures, languages, and institutions to cross national borders in search of better opportunities for themselves and their children. There are an estimated 100 million immigrants worldwide. As national boundaries become increasingly permeable because of pull and push forces associated with free market economies, we may need to reconsider what kind of immigration policies will best promote liberty and justice for all.

CONCLUSION

One classic definition of otherness is in the ancient Chinese text, the *I Ching*, in which the fifty-sixth hexagram depicts the Wanderer, symbolized by a transient fire on a mountain top. Because "strange lands and separation are his lot," the Wanderer must remain cautious and may expect success only in small things (Wilhelm 1967, 217). In a nation founded on the principle that all are equal, no groups, whether cultural or racial, should be relegated to the status of the Wanderer, one who does not belong here and should go elsewhere, one whose freedom must be checked, one whose aspirations must be kept low.

The opposite of such distancing is empathy, the willingness to enter unsentimentally into the perspectives and experiences of others, especially those who seem very different from oneself. Metaphorical thinking works as powerfully in cultivating such dialogic awareness and the cultivation of new understandings as it does in narrowing the focus to a selected position. Borrowing from Richard Paul's (1985) distinction between "strong" and "weak" critical thinking, the former being dialogical, the latter merely technical, we propose a distinction between weak and strong metaphorical thinking. Weak metaphorical thinking, we contend, is the use of comparisons to manipulate arguments and rationalize set positions. Strong metaphorical thinking is deliberately dialectical in striving to expand perspectives on complex issues and foster imagination and empathy as the basis of human morality. With this distinction in mind, how should we proceed to illuminate the debate over language and cultural rights in democratic educational settings? What positions and steps should teachers take to guide students toward strong critical thinking and strong use of metaphors? What role can strong metaphors play in imagining a moral dimension to linguistic and cultural rights?

In her essay entitled "The Moral Necessity of Metaphor," Cynthia Ozick (1986) argues that through finding analogies between our own experiences and those of others, we develop a concept of shared humanity that renders social injustice and other forms of violence unacceptable. Metaphorical thinking imbued with morality and imagination enables the emotional understanding of others' lives. Without a fully felt sense of shared humanity with other groups, it becomes possible to abjure, exploit, enslave, and even annihilate them. Ozick concludes her essay with these words:

> Through metaphor, the past has the capacity to imagine us, and we it. Through metaphorical concentration, doctors can imagine what it is to be their patients. Those at the center can imagine what it is to be outside. The strong can imagine what it is to be weak. Illuminated lives can imagine the dark. Poets in their twilight can imagine the borders of stellar fire. We strangers can imagine the familiar hearts of strangers. (68)

And we can also imagine what Carlos Fuentes (1992) means when he reminds us that "Cultures only flourish in contact with others; they perish in isolation" (346).

STUDY QUESTIONS

1. What images or connotations does the concept of "otherness" evoke for you? What is the opposite of "otherness"? What experiences have you had with either status?
2. Why do the authors claim that imagination plays a key role in expanding and limiting understanding of others? Offer some examples of how imagination has been used to create metaphors that have either expanded or limited understanding of others.
3. What observations can you make about your own use of language in talking about others you consider different from yourself? In talking about multiculturalism in education? What observations have you made about the way people use language on these topics in general, particularly focusing on the media? Can you think of examples of commonly used metaphors and their possible effects on attitudes people hold toward each other?
4. How do people use metaphors to argue for particular positions? How can metaphors be read critically? Discuss examples from your own experience

of ways that people have used metaphors to advance their arguments or points of view.

5. At the end of the chapter, the authors propose concepts of "strong sense" and "weak sense" metaphorical thinking. What are these concepts, and what examples can you think of to illustrate them? What use can you make of this distinction?

6. What political issues concerning multicultural and bilingual education are brought out in this chapter? What moral or ethical issues? What are your political and moral stands?

KEY CONCEPTS

Metaphor

Metaphorical argument

Moral imagination

Otherness

Multiple perspectives

Political life of language

REFERENCES

Anzaldúa, G. 1987. *Borderlands: La frontera*. San Francisco: Spinsters/Aunt Lute.

Apple, M. 1988. Overview. In *Class, race, and gender in American education*, ed. L. Weis, i-vii. Albany: State University of New York Press.

Banks, J. 1993. Multicultural education: Development, dimensions, and challenges. *Phi Delta Kappan* 75(1): 21–28.

Banks, J. 1995. Multicultural education: Historical development, dimensions, and practice. In *Handbook of research on multicultural education*, ed. J. A. Banks and C. A. M. Banks, 3–24. New York: Macmillan.

Bell, D. 1992. *Faces at the bottom of the well: The permanence of racism*. New York: Basic Books.

Chávez, L. 1995. Demystifying multiculturalism. In *Taking sides: Clashing views on controversial educational issues*, ed. J. Noll, 8th ed., pp. 94–99). Guilford, Conn.: Dushkin Publishing Group. Reprinted from *National Review*, February 24 1994.

Ceplair, L., (ed.) 1991. *Charlotte Perkins Gilman: A nonfiction reader*. New York: Columbia University Press.

Coles, R. 1977. *Privileged ones: The well-off and the rich in America*. Boston: Little, Brown.

D'Souza, D. 1991. *Illiberal education: The politics of race and sex on campus*. New York: Free Press.

Ellison, R. 1952. *Invisible man*. New York: Random House.

English for the Children. 1997. English language education for children in public schools. California initiative statute (certified as Proposition 227 for the 2 June 1998 primary election).

Esquivel, R. 1991. Bilingual education helps minority children. In *Education in America: Opposing viewpoints*, ed. C. Cozic, 170–176. San Diego, Calif: Greenhaven Press.

Flores, J. L., and P. Hammer. 1997. Introduction to *Children of la frontera*, ed. J. L. Flores, 3–18. Charleston, W. V.: Clearinghouse on Rural Education and Small Schools.

Fuentes, C. 1992. *The buried mirror: Reflections on Spain and the New World*. New York: Houghton Mifflin.

Gilman, C. P. 1991. Is America too hospitable? In *Charlotte Perkins Gilman: A nonfiction reader*, ed. L. Ceplair, 288–312. New York: Columbia University Press. (Original work published 1923).

Giroux, H. 1994. Living dangerously: Identity politics and the new cultural racism. In *Between borders: Pedagogy and the politics of cultural studies*, ed. H. Giroux and P. McLaren, 29–54. New York: Routledge.

Glazer, N. 1997. *We are all multiculturalists now*. Cambridge: Harvard University Press.

Graff, G. 1993. *Beyond the culture wars*. New York: W. W. Norton.

hooks, b. 1984. *Feminist theory from margin to center*. Boston: South End Press.

International Reading Association and National Council of Teachers of English. 1994. *Standards for the assessment of reading and writing*. Newark, Del.: Authors.

Jiménez, M. 1992. The educational rights of language minority children. In *Language loyalties: A sourcebook on the official English controversy*, ed. J. Crawford, 243–251. Illinois: University of Chicago Press.

Lakoff, G., and M. Johnson. 1980. *Metaphors we live by*. Chicago: University of Chicago Press.

Le Guin, U. 1978. The ones who walk away from Omelas. In *The Norton anthology of short fiction*, ed. R. V. Cassill, 364–369. New York: W. W. Norton.

Lim, S. 1997. Talk at Indiana University, November.

Lopez, B. 1989. Landscape and narrative. In *Crossing open ground*, ed. B. Lopez, 61–72. New York: Vintage Books.

McCarthy, B. 1994. *Victim of two cultures: Richard Rodríguez*. Princeton, N.J.: Films for the Humanities.

McIntyre, A. 1997. *Making meaning of whiteness: Exploring racial identity with white teachers*. Albany: State University of New York Press.

McLaren, P. 1994. Multiculturalism and the postmodern critique: Toward a pedagogy of resistance and transformation. In *Between borders: Pedagogy and the politics of cultural studies*, ed. H. Giroux and P. McLaren, 192–224. New York: Routledge.

Ogbu, J. 1988. Class stratification, racial stratification, and schooling. In *Class, race and gender in American education*, ed. L. Weis, 163–182. Albany: State University of New York Press.

Ozick, C. 1986. The moral necessity of metaphor. *Harper's*, 62–68. May.

Paul, R. 1985. Dialectical reasoning. In *Developing minds: A resource book for teaching thinking*, ed. A. Costa, 152–160. Arlington, Va.: Association for Supervision and Curriculum Development.

Peters, A. 1990. Peters atlas of the world. New York: Harper and Row.

Pugh, S., J. Hicks, M. Davis, and T. Venstra. 1992. *Bridging: A teachers's guide to metaphorical thinking*. Urbana, Ill.: National Council of Teachers of English.

Ravitch, D. 1985a. Politics and the schools: The case of bilingual education. In *Taking sides: Clashing views on controversial educational issues*, ed. J. Noll, 8th ed., 240–248. Gilford, Conn.: Dushkin Publishing Group, 1995. Reprinted from proceedings from *The American Philosophical Society*, (129)2.

Rodríguez, R. 1996. Pocho pioneer. In *The late Mexican border*, ed. B. Byrd and S. M. Byrd, 211–224. El Paso, Texas: Cinco Puntos Press.

Suárez-Orozco, M. 1995. The need for strangers: Proposition 187 and the immigration malaise. *Multicultural Review* 4(2): 17–23, 56–58.

Spener, D. 1996. Transitional bilingual education and the socialization of immigrants. In *Breaking free: The transformative power of critical pedagogy*, ed. P. Leistyna, A. Woodrum, and S. Sherblom, 59–82. Cambridge: Harvard Educational Review.

Steinberg, S. 1997. The liberal retreat from race during the post-civil rights era. In *The house that race built*, ed. W. Lubiano, 13–47. New York: Vintage Books.

Strads, G., K. Trueblood, and S. Wong. 1992. Introduction: Redefining the mainstream. In *The before Columbus fiction anthology: Selections from the American book awards 1980–1990*, ed. I. Reed, K. Trueblood, and S. Wong, xi–xx. New York: W. W. Norton.

Wilhelm, R. C. 1967. *The I Ching or book of changes*, trans. C. Bayner, 3rd ed. Princeton, N.J.: Princeton University Press.

Williams, P. 1995. *The rooster's egg*. Cambridge: Harvard University Press.

Williams, P. 1997. The ethnic scarring of American whiteness. In *The house that race built*, ed. W. Lubiano, 253–263. New York: Vintage Books.

Peter McLaren   Juan Muñoz

*I*n this chapter, we examine the various forms of multiculturalism. We locate the
capacity for liberal and neoliberal multiculturalism to contest the disturbing effects
of global capitalism within a broader analysis linking capitalism and racism. Moreover,
we examine the interrelated dynamics between capitalism and racism in schooling contexts. Cases indicating the rise of white supremacist activities, the selective presentation of historical events, and the relentless assault on marginalized communities are
used to reinforce the importance of appropriating a reconceptualized multicultural
framework. The concepts of whiteness and color-blindness are outlined and challenged
as critical alternatives to conservative forms of multicultural critique. Finally, we
examine the twin dangers of the globalization of capital and the social positioning of
white privilege from the vantage point of critical/revolutionary multiculturalism.

CHAPTER 2

Contesting Whiteness

Critical Perspectives on the Struggle for Social Justice*

Peter McLaren and Juan S. Muñoz
University of California at Los Angeles

Any great artist is wrestling with evil, because that's what life is about. You can't talk about life without talking about evil. In talking about white supremacy, you really are talking about precisely those old historic virtues: What are you alive for? What are your callings in life? Are you willing to fight? What moral character do you have? What kind of integrity do you have? How much courage do you have? Are you brave? Are you willing to take a risk? These are basic questions.
"I'm Ofay, You're Ofay," Cornel West, 1998, p. 198

Origins of Multicultural Education

Multicultural education originated in the 1960s as an offspring of the civil rights movement and its fundamental concern with freedom, political power, and economic equality (Sleeter and McLaren 1995). It was as much a political and ethical response to conflagrations of power as it was an educational reaction to the growing concerns of teachers and parents who aligned themselves with the social, political, cultural, and economic struggles of besieged and embattled ethnic groups during the tumultuous struggles over integration. While much of the direction of multicultural education can be traced to African American activism and community involvement in struggles over the curriculum, multicultural education today has multiplied its vision, and its constituencies now include broad participation and leadership from Asian American, Latino/a, and other communities. Discussing the origins of the term *multicultural education*, Sleeter and McLaren (1995) write:

*Sections of this text appear in Peter McLaren, *Revolutionary Multiculturalism*. (Boulder, Colo.: Westview Press, 1997). We want to thank Carlos Ovando for his excellent editorial suggestions and for his support and encouragement.

> The prefix "multi" was adopted as an umbrella to join diverse groups of color. . . . The term "multiethnic education" was used to bridge racial and ethnic groups; "multicultural education" broadened the umbrella to include gender and other forms of diversity. The term "culture" rather than "racism" was adopted mainly so that audiences of white educators would listen. (12)

Mainstream liberal multiculturalism with its signature stress on diversity and its "normative grammar" of inclusion has given way in the 1990s to more heterogeneous strands on the periphery of the educational establishment that call for stronger links with workers' and women's movements, bilingual education associations, indigenous rights groups, and gay and lesbian organizations (see McLaren 1997a; 1977b). And while the increasing politicization of multicultural education has resulted in what has sometimes been seen as the "culture wars" surrounding political correctness and ethnic separatism, multicultural education in the main has remained quarantined within a fairly domesticated political project that has focused on a vociferous yet relatively nonthreatening call for ethnic diversity and inclusion. While by no means has this mainstream project congealed into a fully articulated, all-encompassing theory, it has been given a greater command than the more critical 'multiculturalisms' (i.e., Grant 1998; Kincheloe and Steinberg 1997; May 1999; McLaren 1997, Sleeter and McLaren 1995) in the public arena of programs and policy.

While our emphasis in this chapter is mainly on issues of class exploitation in the present global economy and its relationship to racism, whiteness, color-blindness, and multicultural education, we acknowledge a fundamental inter-relationship among struggles involving race, class, gender, and sexual orientation. We would like to underscore at the outset that we are not attempting to place the importance of class above race, or race above issues of gender or sexuality, but rather we are resituating the project of multicultural education *in general* from a point of view that takes seriously the current restructuring of capitalism on a global basis and is willing to consider what this might mean for challenging the hegemony of white privilege. In doing so we assume the explanatory primacy—not exclusivity—of economic determinations as our major premise.

Capitalist Social Relations and Multicultural Education

Multicultural education has received more attention over recent years since demographic studies now indicate that people of color will constitute the majority of the United States population during the twenty-first century (McLaren 1995; Sleeter and McLaren 1995). Multicultural educators recognize that the relationship between marginalized and disenfranchised groups of U.S. citizens and public education has been dramatically affected by the social, political, and economic influences texturing the communities in which they live and the schools they attend (La Belle and Ward 1994).

Mainstream multiculturalism's quest for the elusive holy grail of cultural diversity has at times offered tantalizing promises, but in our view, can unwittingly prove functional for the reproduction of capitalist relations of power and privilege and the international imperialist order and an ultimate barrier to the task of erecting a broader social movement that also includes struggles over class, gender, and sexual orientation. In fact, from the bourgeois standpoint, mainstream multicultural education has served as an educational diversion from the theoretical and programmatic contributions of leftist critiques of capitalist social relations and exhibits a generic tendency to evade the political implications of the anticapitalist struggle in general. We believe that multicultural education has in the main ignored relations of class exploitation. We are especially troubled by this structured silence because we now inhabit a historical conjuncture of globalized capitalism in which neoliberal economics and social policy are greatly exacerbating as well as racializing the social division of labor. We believe that it is time to go beyond current positions on multiculturalism and their mutual anathemas and move toward a supersession of past divisions. What multicultural education above all needs today is an advance beyond the threshold of the division between race and class, toward the point where the transformation of capitalist relations of exploitation becomes the practical terminus.

The multicultural left in the United States is caught in the powerful pincers of current economic history. The top jaw is the deregulation of the global economy, and the bottom jaw is the neoliberal philosophy that emphasizes an acceleration of cuts in social spending, including deep reductions in education spending. Abetted by their centrist adaptations to the reformist forces of progressive educators and policy makers, and under camouflage of cheap, carnival barking for liberal democratic values, much of the multicultural left is busy feathering a nest with mainstream liberals and conservatives whose work remains devoid of any substantial critique of capitalism. Having imbibed the comforting aroma of capitalism's inevitability, even some erstwhile members of the radical left are dancing on the grave of the former Soviet Union, overtly disavowing their once highly esteemed socialist ideals. The rightward lunge of the pseudo-multicultural left and its unquestionable thirst for capitulation to the disintegrative character of bourgeois liberal reforms are disheartening. The educational swamp of liberal reformism into which most educational progressives now sink is infested with the world-historical arrogance of a neoliberalism that sees the untrammeled free market as the answer to all social programs, including education, even as neoliberal reforms call for a frontal assault against public education, support a voucher system, and encourage the privatization of schooling. Liberal reformism conduces to a partial counterconstrual to its own democratic premises: By incanting "diversity" as a solution to inequality, it fails to target the underlying matrix of power relations upon which such diversity will rest, namely, the social relations of white supremacist capitalist patriarchy.

More specifically, multicultural education has been impoverished by proponents who fail to link racism to capitalist social relations but instead perceive it to be primarily a problem confined to the realm of psychological disposition, pathological attitude formation, or epistemological claims. Such proponents have gutted multicultural education of its most profound political implications such as the anticapitalist struggle and the struggle against white supremacy. In our view, multicultural education can be transformed in a satisfactory way only if it adopts a fundamental stance against capitalist relations of exploitation and addresses the process of imperialism, the social relations of production, and the construction of white privilege. Here we take the position that systematic racism is an ideology and set of social and cultural practices that grew out of slavery in which the act of discrimination created categories and criteriologies of difference and hierarchical systems of classification that served to universalize and naturalize imperialist aggression and dominant social relations of exploitation.

The ideological charter of public schooling that grounds contemporary educational practice throughout the United States is the same today as it was during the early nineteenth century: to socialize students and to assimilate them into the labor market and international division of labor. We live in a world in which the material production under capitalism is subordinate to the production of surplus value (or profit) and those who monopolize the ownership of the means of production are able to appropriate this surplus value. Rather than educate people to question their social location within the market economy, education was designed by the employer class to inculcate specific industrial skills necessary for individuals to perform within a heavily dominated manufacturing labor market so that their surplus value could be extracted by the capitalist class. And while today's global marketplace has seen sweeping new adjustments, along with vast and accelerated changes with respect to the skills necessary to succeed within it, the exploitation of the many by the few has remained a disturbing constant. We argue that critical educators need to acknowledge the process of disorganized and uneven capitalist development and commit themselves to anti-imperialist struggle against global hierarchies of power and privilege whose chief western guardian is the United States.

Capitalism's worldwide structural crisis is linked to the internal logic of the capitalist system itself and is manifested in overaccumulation and failure to utilize fully its productive capacity. The reorganization of the labor process has significantly altered the relation between capital and labor. Capital is eliminating multiple layers of management, administration, and production to lower costs. Deindustrialization, capital flight, the ascendancy of financial and speculative capital, the expansion of transnational circuits of migrant workers, and the deproletarianized surplus labor force have created radically new social conditions throughout most of the globe. We are witnessing in unprecedented scope the globalization of capital; the domination of the economy by monopolies, oligopolies, and cartels as capital investment hurriedly moves to cheaper markets offering a higher rate of exploitation; the decline of corporate taxes; tax increases on the working class in the form of state-run gambling and lotteries; and reduced social expenditures in health, education, and social services. We are also witnessing the development of "free" economic zones; a powerful business counterattack in response to sporadic minor victories by labor; the relieving of the state of any barriers that might restrict private accumulation; the state's growing indebtedness to corporate bondholders; the constitutional enshrinement of the rights of private property; the discouragement of social redistribution policies; the privatization of municipal services; a massive assault on trade unionism; draconian attacks on social assistance; a conviction that capital is self-regulating; and the drastic reduction of state interventions in the economy and social life that have grown with the development of capital (Teeple 1995). The move toward deregulation has been described as one that is tantamount to progress. For example, the *New York Times* reported that Russian free-market advocates "faced the mammoth task of civilizing their country" (Parenti 1998, 178). Of course, in reality, the globalization of the economy has brought nothing but massive unemployment and misery to Russia and the former Eastern bloc countries as well as to countries within Latin America (McLaren 1999; 1998). In the case of Latin America and Asia, the International Monetary Fund has put together multibillion-dollar bailouts in return for austerity measures that mandate major spending cuts and accelerate liberalization and deregulation in economies that are still characterized by strong state interventions.

Unfettered capitalism—what some have called "casino capitalism," "fast capitalism," or "tycoon capitalism"—is not only objectionable on ethical grounds. It does not work even within the terms of its own logic. Brenner (1998) notes, "If, after more than two decades of wage-cutting, tax-cutting, reductions in the growth of social expenditure, deregulation and 'sound finance,' the ever less fettered 'free market' economy is unable to perform half as well as in the 1960s, there might be some reason to question the dogma that the freer market, the better the economic performance" (238).

The United Nations reported that in 1996, the assets held by the world's 358 billionaires exceeded the combined incomes of countries with 45 percent of the world's people, exacerbating the rich-poor divide in the most grotesque form imaginable (Gates 1998). Manning Marable (1998) notes that between 1973 and 1989, the overall average annual income of all wage earners living in U.S. cities dropped by 16 percent. For instance, in 1990, the median annual incomes of the poorest fifth and the wealthiest fifth in Los Angeles were, $6,821 and $123,098, respectively. In Chicago, the gap was $4,743 versus $86,632. In Detroit, it was $3,109 versus $63,625. Forty million U.S. citizens today lack any form of medical insurance (5-6).

Critical multicultural education and critical pedagogy historically have set out to contest vigorously the persistence of race, class, and gender inequalities, whether they are based on the ownership of property, the possession of credentials, or the persistence of patriarchy and homophobia. Education was often criticized by multicultural educators as a way of adjusting young people to the inevitability of these inequalities rather than motivating them to claim their own historical agency by struggling against them. As a means of contesting the fact that schooling in the United States is functionally advantageous to the reproduction of class and cultural assimilation, critical educators introduced "political literacy" to students through Paulo Freire's well-known practice of "conscientization." "Conscientization" involves learning to perceive, resist, and transform the social, political, and economic contradictions within the learner's everyday world as well as within the macrostructure of social life in general (Freire 1970). And while the agenda of "conscientization" still prevails among many multicultural educators, it is undeniably the case that critical education in general has become politically domesticated. That is, it has been toned down so that it poses no significant threat to the status quo (McLaren in press a; in press b). The continued assault on public education as well as the ascendancy of neoliberal educational policy and practices have undercut the foundation for transforming multicultural educational into a larger political project that could transform structures of oppression on a wide scale. Another reason for the domestication of critical pedagogy and multicultural education has been its alignment with conservative forms of postmodern educational critique (McLaren 1995; McLaren in press a). This follows from a recession of Marxist critique in the former heartlands of educational theory—the sociology of education and curriculum studies—which have now been overtaken by the voguish apostasy of post-structuralist and postmodernist critiques with their emphasis on "power/knowledge relations" and their disabling abstention from social relations of production.

While critical pedagogy and critical multicultural education advocates do not always agree with one another on the extent to which critical education should be linked to wider social movements, they are in general agreement that the educational system should reflect the concerns of diverse groups and that individuals must learn to collaborate and organize to bring about social change even at the expense of a radical alteration of current social arrangements. More specifically, critical pedagogy and critical multicultural education offer insight into the possible dismantling of white privilege and hegemony and a counter-hegemonic position to mainstream educational positions on educational "success." According to Christine Sleeter and Carl Grant (1994), conventional educational approaches assume that all students will be guaranteed social and economic opportunities commensurate with their level of education regardless of race, class, gender, and ethnicity. As individuals increase their "human capital" through an accumulation of educational experiences, they will appreciably affect their quality of life and social standing through a "bootstrap effect." Or so the story goes. The notion that the market will reward the degree to which individuals are presumed to obtain higher levels of human capital displays the temper, if not the letter, of the mainstream position. Schools are targeted as critical junctures where human capital (knowledge and skills), is transmitted or withheld. While critical pedagogy and critical multicultural education challenges these mainstream assumptions, what rarely accompanies such critiques is a sustained critique of capitalism. Of greater significance than this lapse is its facilitating condition: the supposed separation of educational "success" from the perpetuation of those conditions disabling to the elimination of race and class privilege.

The Relationship Between Capitalism, Racism, and Multicultural Education

Antiracism is, of course, one of the key components of virtually any multicultural curriculum. However, in our view, racism is inextricably linked to capitalism. So for multicultural educators to address racism, they must also address the reality of capitalism. Ultimately, to abolish racism, we need to abolish global capitalism.

Racism occurs when the characteristics that justify discrimination are held to be inherent in the oppressed group. This form of oppression is peculiar to capitalist societies; it arises in the circumstances surrounding industrial capitalism and the attempt to acquire a large labor force. Callinicos (1993) notes the way in which Marx grasped how racial divisions between "native" and immigrant workers could weaken the working class and make it easily susceptible to exploitation. U.S. politicians take advantage of this division, which the capitalist class understands and manipulates only too well. George Bush, Jesse Helms, Pat Buchanan, Phil Gramm, David Duke, and Pete Wilson have effectively used racism to divide the working class.

Today the globalization of capital has put so much pressure on the working and middle classes in general that the dominant Anglo-European population is trying to hold on to its advantage by abolishing all initiatives that assist minority populations. Symptomatic of such contemporary racism in the capitalist economy, multicultural education today is coming under a powerful assault by anti-immigration organizations, conservative Christian fundamentalist groups, and conservative politicians who are interested in promoting a neo-liberal economic and cultural agenda. In California, the backlash from the right has led to the abolition of affirmative action for minority groups and women. It has also led to public initiatives that have abolished bilingual education, limited medical provisions and schooling for undocumented immigrants, and restricted immigration. It has also led to a growth of white supremacist organizations and citizen militia movements that support and practice racist agendas.

What is so pernicious and feral about the dominant class position is that proponents replicate one of the generic vices of mainstream education in arguing that affirmative action should be abolished on the grounds that race should not be a factor in one's ability to secure a job. They argue instead that jobs should be acquired on the basis of one's "merit" or "qualifications" alone. But what the Anglo-Europeans do not recognize when they enjoin U.S. citizens to be "color-blind" is that European Americans securely hold the structural advantage in all levels of society. They do not recognize that racism and class exploitation is still widespread in U.S. society. And what is even worse is that some conservative African Americans and Latinos/as have joined forces with the European American power elite in calling for an end to affirmative action programs. What the power elite fails to acknowledge publicly is that there has always been affirmative action for European Americans—an advantage that was secured (and is still secured today) through colonization, imperialism, and racism. Consequently, without affirmative action for people of color, the dominant European American population will function virtually uncontested. The myth of color-blindness suggests that the cultural sphere in the United States has been fully integrated and that social and economic equality have been realized. This is patently false, of course, but serves as a convenient lie, and it is in the interest of the dominant power elite to keep it alive.

Racism, which is alive and well in the United States, has had a long and deeply ingrained history. For example, more than two hundred years ago, Benjamin Franklin wrote:

> Why increase the Sons of *Africa*, by planting them in *America*, where we have so fair an Opportunity, by excluding all Blacks and Tawneys, of increasing the lovely White and Red? (cited in Perea 1995, 973)

Woodrow Wilson, considered by many to be one of the most unblemished presidents of the twentieth century, was an unrepentant white supremacist who believed that black people were inferior to white people. In fact, Wilson ordered that black and white workers in federal government jobs be segregated. Among other things, he vetoed a clause on racial equality in the Covenant of the League of Nations, and his wife told "darky" stories in cabinet meetings (Loewen 1995). The next president, Warren G. Harding, was inducted into the Ku Klux Klan in a ceremony at the White House (Loewen 1995). How many students can boast knowledge of these facts? How can U.S. history books cover up these events and hundreds of others, including the 1921 race riot in Tulsa, Oklahoma, in which whites dropped dynamite from an airplane onto a black community, destroying eleven hundred homes and killing seventy-five people (Loewen 1995)?

The experience of Latinos/as in the United States provides another example of deeply rooted racist attitudes. In his eighteenth-century study of Mexico, the historian William Robertson (1777) offered a distorted presentation that tainted the colonists' perceptions of Mexicans for generations to follow. The assessment that Robertson offered of Mexicans was fundamentally informed by his repugnantly low estimation of the character of Spaniards as well as of Mexican aboriginals, whose racial fusion gave rise to the modern biological Mexican archetype. For Robertson,

> the Mexican stood as the fiercest and most detestable of the New World peoples, inferior culturally to the Incas and in qualities of character to the North American native. By also arguing that the Spaniards who were attracted to America were the most undesirable elements of their society, Robertson offered to his readers a Mexico populated by two extraordinary breeds of scoundrels already mixing their blood. (Paredes 1978, 156).

Negative stereotypes of the Mexican continued into the twentieth century. Even as Chicanos were fighting with distinction in World War II throughout Europe, the Pacific, and North Africa, another war was raging in the United States. On the home front Chicanos/as were continuously denied the civil rights accorded to other members of American society. The Sleepy Lagoon case acutely captured this subjective application of the law. It involved the discovery of a young Anglo man's murdered body on the morning of August 2, 1942. Twenty-two Chicanos, members of the 38th Street Boys gang, were arrested and charged with the murder. The defendants were portrayed as incorrigible criminals and convicted in the court of public opinion long before they reached a court of law. Chicano historian Rodolfo Acuña (1972) offers the following summary of a report issued during the case by the Los Angeles Sheriff's Department:

> Chicanos were inherently criminal and violent . . . . Chicanos were Indians . . . Indians were Orientals and . . . . Orientals had an utter disregard for life. Therefore, because Chicanos had this inborn characteristic, they too were violent. [The report further alleged] that Chicanos were cruel for they descended from the Aztecs who supposedly sacrificed 30,000 victims a day! Chicanos . . . . could not change their spots . . . . and had an innate desire to use a knife and let blood, and this inborn cruelty was aggravated by liquor and jealousy (255).

Today the image of the undocumented worker as an illegal alien, as a "migrant" living in squalor, spreading disease, raping white women, extorting lunch money from white school children, creating squatter communities, hanging out in shopping centers, forcing Anglo schools to adopt bilingual education programs to accommodate the offspring of criminals and to appease the foreigner living on U.S. soil has served to identify Mexicans with dirt, filth, and unnatural acts, while symbolically constructing European American citizens as pure, law-abiding, and living in harmony with God's natural law (Gutiérrez 1996). These images are unambiguous extensions of racist and nativist nineteenth- and early twentieth-century Anglo-American representations of Mexicans and continue to influence Anglo perceptions about Mexicans. This is despite the substantial contribution of Mexicans to the economy as laborers and consumers, their disproportionately low use of social welfare programs, and their increasing presence among the middle-class voting public (not to mention their rich contribution to literature, the arts, and education).

Looking more recently, the Los Angeles uprisings of 1992 can be traced to extreme poverty in African American and Latino communities brought on by the effects of globalization and neoliberal economic policies and practices. The structural changes associated with the emergence of the postindustrial economy had reconfigured the city's social relations. As Los Angeles County's largest population, Latinos cannot strictly be categorized as a "race," a nationality, or an ethnic grouping since they constitute a cross section of Latin American immigrants, most of whom are "racially" mixed Mexicans and Central Americans. As a mixed or *mestizo* people, Latino ethnicities are woven from indigenous, African, Iberian, and European, as well as Asian strands. Culture, language, gender, and history, in addition to class, must be integrated when attempting to grasp multiple, overlapping racialized identities. During the uprising, however, the media's reliance on a racialized language of blacks vs. Asians vs. Latinos precluded the use of alternative explanatory categories (Valle and Torres 1995). The media lacks a semantic category—as well as a general "problematic" with which to identify and conceptualize Latino racial ambiguity as well as an analysis of class exploitation.

In the United States, neither the media nor its audiences have created a language with which to adequately reveal the nation's heterodox ensemble of racialized ethnicities and cultures. Rather, the suppression of this cultural dialogue has been conveniently institutionalized. The Census Bureau, for example, has had a very difficult time trying to figure out how to classify Latinos/as by color. In the 1940 census, Latinos/as were classified as "black" or a "racial" nonwhite group. In the 1950 and 1960 censuses, the term "white person of Spanish surname" was used. In 1970, the classification was changed to "White person of Spanish surname and Spanish mother tongue." Then in 1980, Mexican Americans, Puerto Ricans, and other Central and Latin Americans of diverse national origin were reclassified as "nonwhite Hispanic." Latinos were back to square one. Because the census used a "white/black" paradigm to classify its citizens, it has shuttled Latinos back and forth between these two extremes. In each case, the organizing principle behind the labels is the perceived presence or absence of color (Valle and Torres 1995).

The Concept of Whiteness

Much of the discussion about identity formation in the multicultural literature has focused on those groups whom the dominant culture has characterized as "ethnic." Such populations are almost invariably described as visible "minorities" and most often appear under the term "people of color." This has perpetuated the idea that phenotype, skin color, and temperament are permanently fixed and "natural" attributes of different ethnic groups. Although we recognize biological markers of race such as phenotype, skin color, and hair texture as "floating signifiers" that acquire different meanings according to shifting sociocultural, historical, and political contexts, it remains the case that race matters. Race creates significant negative effects in the lives of people of color.

Our attention has been drawn to the fact that the term *ethnic* is rarely applied to populations commonly described as "white." If you are white, you occupy a space that seemingly transcends ethnicity. Whiteness miraculously becomes the "oneness" without which otherness could not exist—the primogenitor of identity, the marker against which otherness defines itself. Whiteness functions as a frozen state—a dead zone where "traits" associated with skin color, phenotype, race, class, and gender characteristics historically associated with Anglo-Europeans are held to be perpetually raceless. Whiteness has been positioned as the backdrop against which alternative or unconventional social practices and cultural formations are judged, thus ascribing an unprecedented degree of authority and power to its membership and its ethnocentric cultural, social, and ideological expressions, while at the same time repositioning the "other" as deviant. Whiteness has become the laboratory where ethnicities are given defining characteristics, assembled, and categorized. Schools are the clinics that "treat" these ethnic groups, police their behavior, and assimilate them.

We argue, after Theodore W. Allen (1994; 1997) and Scott (1998) that whiteness is, first and foremost, a 'sociogenic' (having to do with social forces and relations) rather than a 'phylogenic' (having to do with phenotype or skin color) phenomenon. Historically, whiteness was an invention of the seventeenth century Anglo-American and United States ruling class—largely the oligarchy of owners of large colonial plantations—who endowed indentured Europeans (who were *de facto* slaves) with civil and social privileges that greatly exceeded those of their fellow African bondsmen. This was a political and economic maneuver designed to secure control of the plantocracy. The invention of the white race was primarily a means of preventing Anglo-Americans who existed in a state of chattel bond-servitude from joining forces with african bondsmen and overthrowing the plantocracy. That is, whiteness was an historical process of homogenizing the social statuses of Anglo-European tenants, merchants and planters into membership in the white race.

Within New England's system of equitably distributed small land holdings, freedom for or bond-laborers (six thousand Europeans and two thousand African Americans) would have effectively terminated the plantocracy's super-exploitation of the African and European bond laborers since the eight thousand bond-laborers would then have become part of a diversified smallholder economy. The chattelization of labor became a necessity for strengthening Virginia's tobacco monoculture. In colonial Virginia, roughly between 1676 and 1705, there was no initial status distinction between 'black' and 'white' bond-laborers. However, the small landholders of colonial Virginia had begun to oppose changes in Virginia land policy that allocated the best land to wealthy capitalist investors, and laws that forbade them from trading with the Indians. More and more landless laborers began to fight against their chattel bond-servitude. Africans and Europeans fought side by side against the plantation bourgeoisie who would routinely punish runaway laborers by adding years to their servitude, and who ordered severe restrictions on corn planting and a ban on hunting for food in the forests so that the rebelling chattel bond-laborers would starve to death.

The aim of the Anglo-American continental plantation bourgeoisie was to prepare the ground for a system of lifetime hereditary bond-servitude. But the African American and European bond-laborers began to 'confederate' and together they were too strong for the tiny colony elite to defeat. Indentured Anglo-Americans were consequently recruited into the middle classes through anomalous white-skin privileges. White skin privilege was an acknowledgment of their loyalty to the colonial land and property-owning class. There were simply too many laboring-class Europeans who had no social mobility and were thus a constant threat to the plantocracy. The white race had to be invented in order to diffuse this potential threat to ruling class hegemony. Racial oppression was systematically put into place and European Americans were brought into the white 'middle class.' This saved the ruling class the money that it would have cost them to put down constant rebellions.

As Allen (1994, 1997) notes, the social function of whiteness in this respect was social control, a practice which has colonial origins that can be traced back to the assault upon the tribal affinities, customs, laws and institutions of Africans, Native Americans, and Irish by English/British and Anglo-American colonialism. Practices of social control reduce all members of oppressed groups to one undifferentiated social status beneath that of any member of the colonizing population. With the rise of the abolitionist movement, racial typologies, classification systems, and criteriologies favoring whiteness and demonizing blackness became widespread in order to justify and legitimize the slavery of Africans and ensure the continuation of lifetime chattel bond-servitude. Today "whiteness" has become naturalized as part of our 'commonsense' reality.

As an identity formation, whiteness is rarely assailed as a racialized practice of power and privilege, exactly because of its ubiquitous and invisible presence. That is, whiteness as a racialized practice within social conventions has been expressed and interpreted as the perpetual and uncontested anchor of normality. Michael Parenti (1998) raises a series of questions about the media that progressive educators need to take seriously: How often do television newscasters or newspapers talk about "white-on-white" violence? Why have the media lavished attention on the Ku Klux Klan, magnifying its visibility, yet consistently failed to report the Klan's alignment with racism, fascism, anticommunism, and anti-Semitism? Why do the media fail to report the role played by the FBI in organizing and financing chapters of the Klan, on the pretext of infiltrating their ranks? Why do the media not give as much exposure to leftist organizations such as the National Alliance Against Racism and Political Repression headed by Angela Davis and Charlene Mitchell as they do to conservative groups? Why did the media give more national attention to Nazi-Ku Klux Klan member David Duke in his unsuccessful bid for a seat in the Louisiana state legislature than to socialist Bernard Sanders who ran for the U.S. Congress in Vermont and won? Why do the U.S. media often attribute political instability in Latin America to the nature and the culture of the Latin Americans themselves? Why do the media report a typical "Arab style" of thinking or describe the Russian people as having an "urge for order"? Can you imagine the media talking about a typical "white" way of thinking? (Parenti 1998).

Even among critical educators, little attention is given to the formation of whiteness. Whiteness is universalized as an identity that both supersedes and transcends ethnicity. Rarely in public discussions of race are we provided opportunities to recognize the many implications of racialized social practices in our everyday experiences as racialized subjects. This dilemma is symptomatic of an understanding of identity that largely forecloses consideration of its broader political dimensions. Rarely are discourses and practices that we attribute to "ethnicity" questioned beyond their expression as individual or group "attitudes" and seen instead for the economic interests that they serve and the social arrangements that they privilege.

Our policies of multiculturalism and invocations of diversity are, for the most part, grounded in an integrationist universalism that links truth to the transcendence of racial categories and status. Within such a liberal tradition, white people, as mentioned previously, are encouraged to become "color-blind," not to recognize the specificity of their own white ethnicity because to do so would reveal whiteness as an invisible marker for conceptualizing normative arrangements of social practices. Current legal definitions of race embrace the norm of color-blindness and thus disconnect race from social identity and race-consciousness. Within the discourse of color-blindness, blackness and whiteness are seen as neutral and apolitical descriptions reflecting skin color. They are seen as being unrelated to social conditions of domination and subordination and to social attributes such as class, culture, language, and education. According to Harris (1993):

> To define race reductively as simply color, and therefore meaningless . . . is as subordinating as defining race to be scientifically determinative of inherent deficiency. The old definition creates a false linkage between race and inferiority, the new definition denies the real linkage between race and oppression under systematic white supremacy. Distorting and denying reality, both definitions support race subordination. As Neil Gotanda has argued, color blindness is a form of race subordination in that it denies the historical context of white domination and Black subordination. (1768).

Canada ?

We need to recognize that most attempts at practicing a form of multiculturalism actually reconfirm existing relations of power and privilege. This is because social practices of whiteness are rarely, if ever, named, let alone interrogated in the clarion call for increasing cultural diversity. There remains a limited amount of critical discussion of the history, construction, and representation of whiteness, particularly with respect to its ability to remain the presumed default setting for so much of mainstream American culture, social relations, and intellectual activity. This has been the case from the advent of compulsory education in the United States, which was designed to provide socializing programs to train individuals both to accept and to further reify whiteness as an immutable reference point constituting normality. Within the current call for diversity in our schools and wider society, there exists little acknowledgment of, let alone complex engagement with, the processes by which racialized difference is grounded in dominant social relations of production and consumption and the existing social division of labor.

It is possible that a half century from now whites might be a minority in the United States. As they continue to feel that their civil society is being despoiled and to blame immigrants for their increasing downward mobility and the disappearance of "traditional" American values, whites fall prey to the appeal of a reactionary and fascist politics of authoritarian repression. The kindling of fascism lies in the furnace of U.S. democracy waiting for a spark to ignite a firestorm of state repression. Previous firestorms have occurred in the Watts rebellion of August 1965, the civil rights movement, and the antiwar movement of the 1960s. More recently, we have witnessed the Los Angeles uprising of April 29, 1992, and the East Los Angeles high school walkouts of 1994 over Proposition 187. The same heat has found expression in several other initiatives in California aimed directly at constituencies of color, in particular Latinos. These initiatives include Proposition 209 (the abolition of affirmative action programs) and Proposition 227 (the repeal of bilingual education). Likewise, Propositions 187, 209, and 227 constitute a "three strikes and you're out" assault on Latinos/as, who presently constitute the fastest growing community in California.

In the United States, we are living at a time of undeclared war. Each day we negotiate our way through mine-sown terrains of confrontation and uncertainty surrounding the meaning and purpose of identity. American democracy faces Janus-like in two directions simultaneously: toward a horizon of hope and coexistence and toward the burning eyes of Klansmen in sheets soiled with blood. While this current historical juncture is witnessing an unprecedented growth of white supremacist organizations living on the fringes of social life, establishment conservatives are stridently asserting nativistic and populist sentiments that barely distinguish them ideologically from their counterparts in racialist far-right groups and citizen militias. The Ku Klux Klan, Posse Comitatus, The Order, White Aryan Resistance, Christian Identity, National Alliance, Aryan Nations, American Front, Gun Owners of America, United Citizens of Justice, and militia groups have organizations in most, if not all, of the fifty states.

Social policies, drafted without the conscious contribution by disenfranchised peoples, have created the conditions for white communities to feel as if they are under siege. As social welfare spending increased from 11.2 percent to 18.7 percent of the U.S. gross national product from 1965 to 1980 (Jencks 1992), conservative writers began to assail social welfare programs as counterproductive and wasteful. If economically disenfranchised people of color are to be helped, they vociferously argued, then it should be done by private individuals or organizations and not the government. But wealthy private organizations have benefited from the hegemony of white privilege in the government and the marketplace for centuries. Unbridled capitalism in our present service economy is ruthlessly uncharitable to the poverty-stricken. Transferring the challenge of economic justice from the government into the hands of philanthropists who feel "pity" for the poor is certainly not the solution.

As attitudes toward social welfare changed, a new rhetorical strategy developed to bind the spirit and restrict access to social welfare programs. The debate over social supports became a competition between the deserving poor (elderly and the disabled), and the undeserving poor (single mothers). Benefits would be allocated according to a subjective standard of merit and deservedness. Categories of "deserving" and "undeserving" poor, designed to feed the anger of whites demanding accountability from those receiving financial assistance, were presented for public consumption.

Not surprisingly, the "deserving" sector of Americans were often the offspring of an aging white baby-boom middle class concerned with retirement and health benefits. Those members of the American "family" who were deemed undeserving were the racialized "welfare mothers or parasitic immigrants." Thus, the historical past that middle-class whites clamor for and the present that confronts them and quickens their pulse are informed by a racialized logic. This position remains steadfast regardless of significant data indicating that, historically, social welfare programs have benefited white Americans to a greater extent than any other ethnic group. The notion of who constitutes the deserving and undeserving poor marked an important shift in how people of color were perceived. The social condition of poverty has become inseparable from individual volition. According to Jencks (1992), "The popularity of the term thus signals a political shift: instead of blaming poverty on society, as we did in the late 60's, we are now inclined to blame poverty on the poor" (120).

Multicultural Education and the Challenge to Whiteness

As we survey the contemporary landscape of global capitalism, racism, and poverty, we can conclude that the challenge to multicultural educators is to choose against whiteness. We believe that an emphasis on the social and historical construction of whiteness will put a different and important focus on the problem surrounding identity formation at this particular juncture in U.S. history. When North Americans talk about race, they inevitably refer to African Americans, Asians, Latinos/as, and Native Americans, to the consistent exclusion of European Americans. We want to challenge the prevailing assumption that to defeat racism, we need to put our initiatives behind the inclusions of minority populations—in other words, of nonwhites. We want to argue instead that in addition to making an argument for diversity, we need to put more emphasis on the analysis of white ethnicity and the destabilization of white identity, specifically white supremacist ideology and practice. As David Roediger (1994) notes:

> Whiteness describes, from Little Big Horn to Simi Valley, not a culture but the absence of culture. It is the empty and therefore terrifying attempt to build an identity based on what one isn't and on whom one can hold back. (137)

One would think that the choice against whiteness would be morally self-evident. However, precisely because whiteness is so pervasive and yet built on "what one isn't," it remains difficult to identify, challenge, and separate from our daily lives.

Our critique of whiteness is not an all-out assault on white people. Our central argument is that we must create a new public sphere where the practice of whiteness is not only identified and analyzed but also contested and destroyed when it subverts the opportunities of those who are not white. For choosing against whiteness is the hope and promise of the future. One of the tasks ahead for those of us who wish to reclaim the dignity offered by true justice is to revive democratic citizenship in an era of diminishing returns. It is to create critical citizens who are no longer content in occupying furtive spaces of private affirmation but who possess the will and the knowledge to turn these spaces into public spheres through the creation of new social movements aimed at the deconstruction of de jure and de facto white privilege.

Rather than stressing the importance of diversity and inclusion, as do most multiculturalists, we think that significantly more emphasis should be placed on the social and political construction of white supremacy and the dispensation of white hegemony. Whiteness needs to be recognized and acted upon by multicultural educators as a cultural disposition and an ideology linked to specific political, social, and historical arrangements.

In particular, a neoliberal democracy, performing under the banner of diversity yet actually in the hidden service of capital accumulation, often reconfirms the racist stereotypes already prescribed by European American nationalist myths of supremacy. In the pluralizing move to become a society of diverse voices, neoliberal democracy has often succumbed to a recolonization of multiculturalism. It has done this by failing to challenge ideological assumptions surrounding difference that are installed in its current positions regarding anti-affirmative action and welfare "reform" initiatives. In this sense, people of color are still excluded from full U.S. citizenship.

One of the most hated groups among the poor in the Southwest and southern California is Mexican migrant workers. Stereotyped as *"crimmegrantes,"* they have become the object of xenophobia par excellence. Ron Prince, one of the architects of Proposition 187, has remarked: "Illegal aliens are a category of criminal, not a category of ethnic group" (Gómez-Peña 1996, 67). The process of "Mexicanization" has struck fear into the hearts of the European Americans who view this inevitability as an obdurate political reality. And this fear is only exacerbated by the media and anti-immigration activists.

Latinos have responded to the heterophobic rhetoric that has dominated California's public debate over the last several years. Through *banda* music, *quebradita* dance, and the surge of rock *en Español*, Latinos are very consciously exercising culture as a form of resistance to the pejorative stereotypes imposed by white hegemonic institutionalized structures and practices. These fashion and music trends are an indication of the many signals that the Southwest and beyond will continue to experience a substantial Latinization of major American urban hubs. Latinos have substantially influenced mainstream European American culture, a reality that flies in the face of the frequent charge that the Latino community represents a passive target of assimilation. We consider it a mark of ingenuity and courage that Latinos/as have managed to develop creatively independent cultural alternatives—as well as oppositional strategies—to dominant cultural arrangements that fuel extant mythologies surrounding Latino populations. Martínez (1994), writing from the point of view of a Latino addressing European Americans, states:

> You must accept that the Latinos of California aren't going anywhere. . . . You must stop thinking and acting with the arrogance of a culture that sees itself as the arbiter of life in the city: your culture will become less and less dominant . . . And I must accept that you aren't going anywhere either. . . . You must allow yourself to be transformed even as we are being and have been transformed. It is a process that is at the heart of America's democracy. (39)

Often the terrain inhabited by groups of native and immigrant people results in a creative experiment and eventually involves some degree of culture contact where both subordinate and dominant groups are transformed. This is precisely the point that Martínez is making. Perhaps no other geopolitical space offers an opportunity to view this phenomenon of cultural and ideological confluence more saliently than metropolitan Los Angeles, which has become a metaphor for the new urban frontier—a place where renegades still run wild, gun in hand, and where (as the prevailing discourse requires) the "good" guys still wear white.

Throughout the history of public education, the official school charter has been to socialize the children of recent immigrants into Americans and future workers possessing the habits and attitudes required of an industrialized economy. Schools were openly a means of indoctrinating the children of subordinate social groups. Not surprisingly, Latinos living in the United States carried with them from Latin American countries the idea that education is a fundamental necessity. Moreover, contrary to current myths, Latinos—then and now—clearly recognize the importance of higher education. An appalling and undeserved misrepresentation of Latinos/as as intellectually indifferent has led to their being stigmatized as academically docile and intellectual passive. This false image contradicts an abundance of evidence that portrays a vigorous history of academic participation, school-based activism, and resistance to unequal treatment. Given the importance that Latinos attach to education, the need to maintain a critically informed and representative curriculum is significant. However, conventional pedagogical and curricular approaches fail to substantively engage activities and topics that are most pressing to a community that still experiences pronounced levels of racial discrimination, economic oppression, and popular misrepresentation—not to mention exclusion and demonization on the part of the wider educational community.

Contributing to the situation whereby racialized relations become normalized is the aversion of whites to critically examine the processes responsible for white identity. They remain historically unwilling to consider their own processes of self-identification and how these processes are linked to other racialized groups. Furthermore, there exists a motivated amnesia with respect to acknowledging that the United States has been built by downtrodden immigrants of all hues, by Native Americans, and by southern blacks. The very mortar that holds its cities and towns in place has been stirred by the hands of minority workers. To negate this vital multiethnic presence is not simply factually incorrect. It is a serious abdication of the democratic impulse that is fundamental to the principles on which this country claims to rest.

The powerful but hidden force of whiteness has provided the context for our distorted views of history. However, it is difficult to clearly define the character of whiteness because cultural practices considered to be white are historically produced and transformable (Frankenberg 1993). White culture is not monolithic, and its borders are malleable and porous. It is a historically specific confluence of economic, geopolitical, and ethnocultural processes. According to Alastair Bonnett (1996), whiteness is neither a discrete entity nor a fixed social category. White identity is an ensemble of sometimes contradictory discourses. Whiteness is always in a state of flux. Bonnett notes that "even if one ignores the transgressive youth or ethnic borderlands of Western identities, and focuses on the 'center' or 'heartlands' of 'whiteness,' one will discover racialized subjectivities, that, far from being settled and confident, exhibit a constantly reformulated panic over the meaning of 'whiteness' and the defining presence of 'nonwhiteness' within it" (106).

Whiteness is a sociohistorical form of consciousness, born at the nexus of capitalism, colonial rule, and the emergent relationships among dominant and subordinate groups. Where whiteness operates, the white bourgeois appropriates the right to speak on behalf of everyone who is nonwhite, while denying voice to these others in the name of civilized. Whiteness demarcates ideas, feelings, knowledge, social practices, cultural formations, and systems of intelligibility that are invested in by white people as "white." Whiteness is also a refusal to acknowledge how white people are implicated in relations of domination and subordination. Whiteness, then, as we mentioned before, can be considered as a form of social amnesia. Whiteness constitutes the selective tradition of dominant discourses about race, class, gender, and sexuality. Whiteness is not a unified, homogeneous culture but a *social position*. As Ignatiev (1998) comments:

> There is nothing positive about white identity. As James Baldwin said, "As long as you think you're white, there's no hope for you." Whiteness is not a culture. There is Irish culture and Italian culture and American culture; there is youth culture and drug culture and gear culture. There is no such thing as white culture. Shakespeare was *not* white; he was English. Mozart was not white; he was Austrian. Whiteness has nothing to do with culture and everything to do with social position. Without the privileges attached to it, there would be no white race, and fair skin would have the same significance as big feet. (199)

Whiteness in the United States can be understood largely through the social consequences it provides for those who are considered to be nonwhite. Such consequences can be seen in the criminal justice system, in prisons, in schools, and in the boardrooms of corporations such as Texaco. It can be defined in relation to immigration practices, social policies, and practices of sexism, racism, and nationalism.

Ignatiev (1998) writes that while poor whites have been historically exploited, many of these "slaves" believe that they are part of the "master class" because they partake of the privilege of white skin. In actual fact, whiteness has become a substitute for freedom and dignity in the case of the majority of European Americans who live in the United States. What identification with white privilege does is to reconnect whites to relations of exploitation. The answer to this plight, notes Ignatiev, is for whites to cease to exist as whites. Whites "must commit suicide as whites to come alive as workers or youth or women or artists or whatever other identity will let them stop being the miserable, petulant, subordinated creatures they now are and become freely associated, developing human beings" (200). He goes on to say:

> The task at hand is not to convince more whites to oppose "racism"; there are already enough "antiracists" to do the job. The task is to make it impossible for anyone to be white. What would white people have to do to accomplish this? They would have to break the laws of whiteness so flagrantly as to destroy the myth of white unanimity. They would have to respond to every manifestation of white supremacy as if it were directed against them. (202)

Whiteness is so pervasive in our social, political, and economic structure that people tend to be unaware of its powerful and damaging presence. López

(1996) cites an incident at a feminist legal conference in which participants were asked to pick two or three words to describe themselves. All of the women of color selected at least one racial term, but not one white woman selected a term referring to her race. This prompted Angela Harris to remark that only white people in this society have the luxury of having no color. An informal study conducted at Harvard Law School underscores Harris's remark. A student interviewer asked ten African Americans and ten white Americans how they identified themselves. Unlike the African Americans, most of the white Americans did not consciously factor in their "whiteness" as a crucial or even tangential part of their identity.

Given the elusiveness of whiteness, the educational left has failed to address the issue sufficiently. Consider the case of the insecurities that young whites harbor regarding their future during times of diminishing economic expectations. With their racist and divisive rhetoric, neoconservatives may be able to enjoy tremendous success in helping insecure young white populations develop white identity along racist lines. Consider these comments by David Stowe (1996):

> The only people nowadays who profess any kind of loyalty to whiteness *qua* whiteness (as opposed to whiteness as an incidental feature of some more specific identity), are Christian Identity types and Aryan Nation diehards. Anecdotal surveys reveal that few white Americans mention whiteness as a quality that they think much about or particularly value. In their day-to-day cultural preferences—food, music, clothing, sports, hairstyles—the great majority of American whites display no particular attachment to white things. There does seem to be a kind of emptiness at the core of whiteness. (74)

Decentering Whiteness

López (1996) argues that one is not born white but becomes white "by virtue of the social context in which one finds oneself, to be sure, but also by virtue of the choices one makes" (190). But how can one born into the culture of whiteness, one who is defined as white, undo that whiteness? López addresses this question in his formulation of whiteness. He locates whiteness in the overlapping of *chance* (e.g., features and ancestry that we have no control over, morphology); *context* (context-specific meanings that are attached to race, the social setting in which races are recognized, constructed, and contested); and *choice* (conscious choices with regard to the morphology and ancestries of social actors) in order to "alter the readability of their identity" (191).

In other words, López (1996) maintains that chance and context are not racially determinative. He notes:

> Racial choices must always be made from within specific contexts, where the context materially and ideologically circumscribes the range of available choices and also delimits the significance of the act. Nevertheless, these are racial choices, if sometimes only in their overtone or subtext, because they resonate in the complex of meanings associated with race. Given the thorough suffusion of race throughout society, in the daily dance of life we constantly make racially meaningful decisions. (193)

López outlines—productively, in our view—three steps in dismantling whiteness:

> First, Whites must overcome the omnipresent effects of transparency and of the naturalization of race in order to recognize the many racial aspects of their identity, paying particular attention to the daily acts that draw upon and in turn confirm their whiteness. Second, they must recognize and accept the personal and social consequences of breaking out of a White identity. Third, they must embark on a daily process of choosing against whiteness. (193)

We are acutely aware that people of color might find troubling the idea that white populations can simply reinvent themselves by making the simple choice of not being white. Of course, this is not what López and others appear to be saying. The choices one makes and the reinvention one aspires to as a race traitor are not "simple," nor are they easy choices for groups of whites to make. Yet from the perspective of some people of color, offering the choice to white people of opting out of their whiteness could seem to set up an easy path for those who do not want to assume responsibility for their privilege as white people. Indeed, there is certainly cause for concern. David Roediger (1994) captures some of this when he remarks: "whites cannot fully renounce whiteness even if they want to" (16). Whites are, after all, still accorded the privileges of being white even as they ideologically renounce their whiteness, often with the best of intentions. Yet the possibility that whites might seriously consider nonwhiteness and antiwhite struggle is too important to ignore, dismiss as wishful thinking, or associate with a fashionable form of code-switching. Choosing not to be white is not an easy option for white people, for it implies the recognition of a profound existential pain, a heightened sense of social criticism, and an unwavering commitment to social justice (McLaren 1997a; Roediger 1994).

Does this mean that white people can become black or brown? No. In discussing the position of the "new abolitionism" (the name is taken from the abolitionists who fought against slavery in the United States and refers to a movement calling on whites to renounce their possessive investment in whiteness), Ignatiev (1998) writes:

> Abolitionists realize that no "white," as an individual, can escape from the privileges of whiteness. But they also understand that when there comes into being a critical mass of people who look white but who do not act white, the white race will undergo fission, and former whites, born again, will be able to take part with others in building a new human community. (203)

The key, George Yudice (1995) maintains, is to center the struggle for social justice around resource distribution rather than identity:

> Shifting the focus of struggle from identity to resource distribution will also make it possible to engage such seemingly nonracial issues as the environment, the military, the military-industrial complex, foreign aid, and free-trade agreements as matters impacting local identities and thus requiring a global politics that works outside of the national frame. (280)

Revolutionary Multiculturalism

Given the axiomatic role of capitalism in the perpetuation of racism, whiteness, and, consequently, social injustice, we propose a reorientation of educators toward revolutionary, or critical, multiculturalism. Revolutionary multiculturalism recognizes that the objective structures in which we live and the material relations tied to production in which we are situated are all reflected in our everyday lives. In other words, our lived experiences are always mediated through ideological configurations of discourses, political economies of power and privilege, and the social division of labor. The following characteristics offer a brief summary of the major position of revolutionary multiculturalism:

1. Revolutionary multiculturalism is a socialist-feminist multiculturalism that challenges the historically sedimented processes through which race, class, and gender identities are produced within capitalist society. Therefore, revolutionary multiculturalism is not limited to transforming attitudinal discrimination. Racism is not simply understood as a "wrong way to think" in the sense that it is politically incorrect. Racism is a complex process and is implicated in social relations of production and their valorization and naturalization through systems of classification produced historically in religious, anthropological, and scientific texts. Revolutionary multiculturalism is dedicated to reconstituting the deep structures of political economy, culture, and power in contemporary social arrangements. It is not about *reforming* capitalist democracy but rather *transforming* it by cutting it at its joints and then rebuilding the social order from the vantage point of the oppressed.

2. Revolutionary multiculturalism, as we envision it, is not a general theory but rather uses general categories that can capture the lived experiences of oppressed groups so that explanatory concepts can be developed and explanations mustered that have a historical concreteness. Too much theory preempts the development of knowledge and forecloses empirical speculation; too little theory, however, ends up on the cutting-room floor of banal, descriptive analysis that makes insufficient links to the social media and forces of which our categories for description are but ideal abstract expressions.

3. Revolutionary multiculturalism acknowledges the importance of identity politics but puts such politics in perspective. Identity politics—that is, social movements based on feminism, or Afrocentrism, or ecology, or gay or lesbian issues—are important (even those that are single-issue movements) as a self-defense against heteronomous control by the capitalist class. But such movements should be seen in terms of formulating a concrete multicultural universal that arches toward an organic whole. Rather than keep the larger movement against the social injustices of capitalism and a common class enemy fragmented, identity politics are valuable as transitional phases toward a multicultural universality (Katsiaficas 1998).

4. A revolutionary multicultural pedagogy will creatively respond to the needs of marginalized groups of learners, and it will prepare educators to consciously assist in reconciling pervasive social and economic inequities

(Darder 1992; Moraes 1996). The struggle for liberation on the basis of race and gender must not remain detached from anticapitalist struggle. More directly, the decentering of whiteness and the privileges it enjoys within the ideological mystifications of capitalism can serve as the basis of a new revolutionary multiculturalism (McLaren 1997a).

For Ignatiev (1998), the school system is a major institution of white supremacy that "is doing more harm than the Nazis and the Klan and all the other 'racist' groups combined by directing millions of black children into low-wage jobs, the military, and prison" (200). Consequently, school practices need to address more than ever before the objective, material conditions of the workplace and labor relations in order to prevent the further perpetuation of the neoliberal corporatist state.

5. A revolutionary multiculturalism links inequality on the basis of race, class, and gender to the vicissitudes of U.S. transnational capitalism and its neocolonial clientele and to the alienation and racism that overwhelmingly characterize everyday cultural practices. It is committed to freeing society from the alienation and exploitation endemic to a market-based system of profit. Revolutionary multiculturalism is not premised on creating diversity and inclusion—although it recognizes that such an effort is immensely important. Revolutionary multiculturalism does not begin with bringing the margins into the center but rather with criticizing the existing center of power—the power that inheres in white supremacist capitalist patriarchy. On this issue Paulo Freire (1998) writes:

> The criticism of capitalism I put forth, from an ethical point of view, derives as much from the educator as it does from the activist, which I seek to continue to be in my own way. My activism can never become dissociated from my theoretical work; on the contrary, the former has its tactics and strategies formulated on the latter. The moment we recognize that food production around the world could be sufficient to feed twice its population, it is desolating to realize the numbers of those who come into the world but do not stay, or those who do but are forced into early departure by hunger.
>
> My struggle against capitalism is founded on that—its intrinsic perversity, its antisolidarity nature.
>
> The argument has been destroyed of scarcity as a production problem that capitalism would not be able to respond to and that would represent an obstacle to the preservation of this system. Capitalism is effective in this and other aspects, but it has shown its other face—absolute insensitivity to the ethical dimension of existence. (88)

Revolutionary multiculturalism is not only about teaching about forms of social inequality but also about helping to transform that inequality. It is about reconstructing a society in which diversity, equality, and social and economic justice become organic parts of the life forms we invent for ourselves in our pursuit of democratic public life. But revolutionary multiculturalism goes further than this. It is international in scope and is part of a worldwide struggle for social emancipation from capital accumulation and its ideology of white patriarchal supremacy.

6. The ethics of revolutionary multiculturalism are not premised on a universally valid way of being human but rather fluctuate from rage against oppression to a joyous celebration and love of life (Welch 1999). According to Sharon Welch,

> Multicultural education is deeply disturbing, as disturbing to the myths of a common culture as it is to the myths of a revolutionary vanguard. It is also profoundly rewarding and exhilarating, a rush of creative energy that takes us out of the paralyzing trap of endlessly denouncing and analyzing forms of injustice and oppression. We can do so much more. The first step is to recognize that social cohesion is created by contact, by working with other people, and does not require uniformity or total agreement. The second step is focusing on the power we have and using it to create realtionships of mutuality and respect. Universal human solidarity is not our birthright, not a gift, not an essence, but a task. (117)

7. Schools in the United States should provide students with a language of criticism and a language of hope. They should prepare students to conceptualize fully the relationship between their private dreams and the collective dreams of the larger social order. Yet in doing so teachers cannot retreat to an extrahistorical, Archimedean vantage-point and must cancel their pretention to "neutral" analysis. Analysis itself is a political practice that is always mediated by the positionality of those undertaking it. How analysis imparts ballast to conditions of exploitation or supplies validation for it is a challenge that must be addressed rather than avoided. Students must further be capable of analyzing the social and material conditions in which dreams are given birth, realized, diminished, or destroyed. More important, students need to be able to recognize which dreams and which dreamers are dangerous to the larger society and why this is the case. Schools need to foster collective dreaming, a dreaming that speaks to the creation of social justice for all groups and the eventual elimination of classism, racism, sexism, and homophobia. This can only occur if schools help students analyze the ways in which their views or perceptions have been ideologically formed within the exploitative forces of globalized capitalism. Schools also need to help to foster a critical praxis that can eventually transform the conditions that are responsible for the exploitation of the subordinate classes. Schools need to help citizens resist the American business plutocracy, which pursues speculative international financial markets at the expense of international democracy.

One might argue that current school reform efforts are already addressing such issues of social justice. However, such measures most often provide only limited insurance against intractable sociopolitical conflicts. Most are forms of concessionary state policies, forms of state-mandated accords (Teeple 1995). Such reforms, in other words, are only limited concessions to people who continue to have no control over their lives. They are temporary reprieves. Reforms are always provisional and conditional and simply serve to postpone resolutions to class conflicts. As Teeple (1995) notes, reforms both resist the capitalist mode of production and maintain existing capitalist social relations.

They impose amelioration of the worst effects of capitalism, but they do not fundamentally transform the contradictions of contemporary capitalism. However, revolutionary multiculturalism acknowledges that reforms, while admittedly temporary and insufficient, are often necessary first steps in the struggle for social justice.

We must, nevertheless, go far beyond the current school reform movement. We must continue to wage new struggles of liberation, creating new identities—both global and local—along the way. We must begin to rethink identity more in terms of what we can do for each other (a question of ethics) rather than in terms of who we are (a question of epistemology). Both questions are important, certainly, but we believe that coalition-building requires us to begin our struggle with an ethical commitment to each other while at the same time understanding that both the 'self' and 'other' are forged out of historically determinate social relations of production. Only by committing ourselves to the "other"—to our "brother and sister outsiders"—can we discover the "other within." And only by discovering the "outsider within" can we discover who we are in our hearts. We cannot discover who we are separately from our common struggle with, against, and beyond each other, for only through such a struggle can we recognize that there exist no boundaries separating ourselves from others. We are all bound together in our humanity and in our struggle for peace and justice.

STUDY QUESTIONS

1. Since its inception, what has been the general aim of multicultural education and how does this chapter depart from, or perhaps modify, the conventional scope of multiculturalism? What are the conceptual and practical limitations of traditional multiculturalism, if any? What are the conceptual and practical limitations of the arguments presented in this chapter, if any?

2. In what ways and for what reasons does the chapter advocate a more sophisticated and complex linkage between multicultural education and related campaigns for social justice? Provide examples of the role multicultural education may yet serve in the pursuit of social justice.

3. The chapter offers several examples of historical information not typically available in conventional textbooks. Give some examples that you found particularly interesting and explain why. To the extent possible, describe how this information was instructive to your understanding of critical/revolutionary multiculturalism.

4. How does the absence of a critical/revolutionary multicultural agenda contribute to a cultural landscape that permits inequities to proceed unabated? According to a critical/revolutionary multicultural framework, what responsibility does an individual have to contest unequal relations of power? In particular, what are some areas in which whites can substantially contribute to the destabilization of white privilige and to the struggle for social justice?

5. The chapter examines the usefulness of deconstructing "whiteness" in shaping a reconceptualized notion of multiculturalism. How is whiteness defined and examined? What do the authors mean by "social amnesia" in relation to whiteness? How does social amnesia contribute to the preservation of whiteness?

6. Critical/revolutionary multiculturalism advocates an extreme personal commitment to the abolition of social inequalities and to the formation of a new human community through challenging capitalist social relations. How can one become committed to "others" without embracing a paternalistic or self-serving missionary attitude? In light of the chapter's general call for personal action, what concrete steps can you take to defend the interests of "others" (i.e., marginalized groups), while also contesting the privileged status of the ruling elite?

7. What type of society can we begin to envision and work toward that challenges the exploitative premises of so-called "capitalist democracy"? Can socialism be rescued as a viable alternative to capitalism? What would a democratic socialist society look like?

KEY CONCEPTS

Color-blindness

Connection between racism, capitalism, and multicultural education

Conscientization

Critical/revolutionary multiculturalism

Decentering whiteness

Hegemony

Liberal and neoliberal multiculturalism

Marginalized communities

Multicultural left

Neoliberal global capitalism

Whiteness as a privileged social position

REFERENCES

Acuña, R. 1972. *Occupied America: A history of Chicanos*. New York: HarperCollins.

Allen, T. 1994. *The Invention of the White Race, Volume One: Racial Oppression and Social Control*. London and New york: Verso.

Allen, T. 1997. *The Invention of the White Race, Volume Two: The Origin of Racial Oppression in Anglo-America*. London and New York: Verso.

Bonnett, A. 1996. Anti-racism and the critique of white identities. *New Community*, 22(1): 97–110.

Brenner, R. 1998. The economics of global turbulence. *New Left Review*, 229: 1–262.

Callinicos, A. 1993. *Race and class*. London: Bookmarks.

Darder, A. 1992. *Culture and Power in the Classroom*. South Hadley, MA: Bergin and Garvey.

Frankenberg, R. 1993. *The social construction of whiteness: White women, race matters*. Minneapolis: University of Minnesota Press.

Freire, P. 1970. *Pedagogy of the oppressed*. New York: Continuum.

Freire, P. 1998. *Pedagogy of the heart*. New York: Continuum.

Gates, J. 1998. Twenty-first century capitalism: To humanize, ownerize. *Humanist* 58(4): 9–14.

Grant, Car, Ed. 1999. *Multicultural Research: A Reflective Engagement with Race, Class, and Sexual Orientation*. London: Falmer Press.

Gómez-Peña, G. 1996. *The new world border*. San Francisco: City Lights Bookstore.

Gutiérrez, R. 1996. The erotic zone: Sexual transgression on the U.S.-Mexican border. In *Mapping multiculturalism*, ed. A. Gordon and C. Newfield, 253–262. Minneapolis: University of Minnesota Press.

Harris, C. I. 1993. Whiteness as property. *Harvard Law Review* 106(8): 1709–1791.

Ignatiev, N. 1998. The new abolitionists. *Transition*, 73: 199–203.

Jencks, Christopher. 1992. *Rethinking social policy: Race, poverty, and the underclass*. New York: HarperCollins.

Katsiaficas, G. 1998. The latent universal within identity politics. In *The promise of multiculturalism*, ed. G. Katsiaficas and T. Teodros, 72–81. New York: Routledge.

Kincheoe, J., and S. Steinberg. 1997. Changing multiculturalism. Philadelphia: Open University Press.

La Belle, T. J., and C. R. Ward. 1994. *Multiculturalism and education: Diversity and its impact on schools and society*. New York: State University of New York Press.

López, I. F. H. 1996. *White by law*. New York: New York University Press.

Loewen, J. W. 1995. *Lies my teacher told me: Everything your American history textbook got wrong*. New York: Touchstone.

Marable, M. 1998. The left. *Social Policy*, 28(93): 4-9.

Martínez, R. 1994. The shock of the new anti-immigrant fever is at a fever pitch, but the real issue is this: Will the old (Anglo) join the new (Latino) LA., and learn to dance the *quebradita*. *Los Angeles Times Magazine*, January, p. 12.

May, Stephen, Ed. 1999. *Critical Multiculturalism: Rethinking Multicultural and Antiracist Education*. London: Falmer Press.

McLaren, P. 1995. *Critical pedagogy and predatory culture*. New York: Routledge.

McLaren, P. 1997a. *Revolutionary multiculturalism: Pedagogies of dissent for the new millennium*. Boulder, Colo.: Westview Press.

McLaren, P. 1997b. Multiculturalismo crítico. São Paulo: Cortéz.

McLaren, P. 1999. Traumatizing capital. In *Critical education in the new information age*, ed. M. Castells, R. Flecha, Paulo Freire, H. A. Giroux, D. Macedo, and P. Willis. Boulder, Colo.: Rowman and Littlefield, pp. 1–36.

McLaren, P. 1998b. The pedagogy of Che Guevara. *Cultural Circles*, vol. 3, Ricardo Romo and Raymund Paredes, eds.

Moraes, M. 1996. *Bilingual Education: A Dialogue with the Bakhtin Circle*. Albany: SUNY Press.

Paredes, R. 1978. The Origins of anti-Mexican sentiment in the United States. In *New directions in Chicano scholarship*, 139–165. San Diego: University of California.

Parenti, M. 1998. *America besieged*. San Francisco: City Lights Books.

Perea, J. F. 1995. *Los olvidados*: On the making of invisible people. *New York University Law Review*, 70(4): 965–991.

Robertson, W. 1777. *The history of America*. New York: J. Harper.

Roediger, D. 1994. *Towards the abolition of whiteness*. New York: Verso.

Scott, J. 1998. "Before the White Race was Invented." *Against the Current,* vol. 72, pp. 46–49.

Sleeter, C. E., and C. A. Grant. 1994. *Making choices for multicultural education: Five approaches to race, class, gender*. Columbus, Ohio: Merrill.

Sleeter, C. E., and P. L. McLaren, eds. 1995. *Multicultural education, critical pedagogy, and the politics of difference*. Albany: State University of New York Press.

Stowe, D. W. 1996. Uncolored people: The rise of whiteness studies. *Lingua Franca* 6(6): 68–77.

Teeple, G. 1995. *Globalization and the decline of social reform*. New Jersey: Humanities Press.

Valle, V., and R. D. Torres. 1995. The idea of *Mestizaje* and the "race" problematic: Racialized media discourse in post-Fordist landscape. In *Culture and difference: Critical perspectives on the bicultural experience in the United States,* ed. A. Darder, 139-153. Westport, Conn.: Bergin and Garvey.

Welch, S. 1999. *Sweet dreams in America: Making ethics and spirituality work*. New York: Routledge.

West, C. 1998. I'm ofay, you're ofay. *Transition,* 73: 176–198.

Yudice, G. 1995. Neither impugning nor disavowing whiteness does a viable politics make: The limits of identity politics. In *After political correctness: The humanities and society in the 1990s,* ed. C. Newfield and R. Strickland, Boulder, Colo.: Westview Press. 255–285.

Henry A. Giroux

*A*t a time when culture has become a heated and contested terrain, especially cultural spheres such as higher and public education, both right- and left-wing theorists have attempted in different ways to abstract culture from politics to put forward their own ideological agendas. This chapter argues that culture is an important terrain of struggle and that it is impossible to link learning to social change if culture is abstracted from the realm of politics. The chapter provides a strong critique of conservative and liberal theorists such as Harold Bloom and Richard Rorty, and an extensive critique of left theorists such as Todd Gitlin. The chapter concludes by arguing for a cultural politics in which schools are viewed as crucial public spheres and teachers as engaged intellectuals.

CHAPTER 3

The War Against Cultural Politics

Beyond Conservative and Neo-Enlightenment Left "Oppositions": A Critique

Henry A. Giroux
Penn State University

Attack on Education

These are hard times for educators and advocates of democratic schooling. Besieged by the growing forces of vocationalism, commerce, and neoconservative cultural warriors, prospective and existing classroom teachers are caught in an ideological cross fire regarding their civic and political responsibilities. Asked to define themselves through either the language of the marketplace or a discourse of objectivity and neutrality that separates the political from the cultural and social, educators are increasingly being pressured to become either servants of corporate power or disengaged specialists wedded to the imperatives of a resurgent and debasing academic professionalism.

What is surprising about the current attack on education, especially in light of the growing corporatization and privatization at all levels of schooling, is the refusal on the part of many theorists to rethink the role academics might play in defending the university as a crucial democratic public. Lost in these debates is a view of the university that demands reinvigorated notions of civic courage and actions that address what it means to make the teaching more political and civic-oriented in a time of growing conservatism, racism, and corporatism. Even more surprising is the common ground shared by a growing number of progressives and conservatives who attempt to reduce pedagogy to the technical formalism and hermetic task of simply teaching the text (test, method, etc.) or narrowly define politics and pedagogy within a dichotomy that pits the alleged "real" material issues of class and labor against a fragmenting and marginalizing concern with the politics of culture, textuality, and difference.

Conservative and Liberal Criticism of Cultural Politics

The right-wing attack on culture as a site of pedagogical and political struggle is evident in the work of traditionalists such as Harold Bloom and liberals such as Richard Rorty, both of whom bemoan the death of romance, inspiration, and hope as casualties of the language of power, politics, and multiculturalism. For Bloom, literary criticism has been replaced in the academy by cultural criticism and the result is nothing less than the death of criticism. Bloom cannot bear the politics of what he calls "identity clubs"; he argues that "multiculturalism is a lie, a mask for mediocrity for the thought-control academic police, the Gestapo of our campuses."[1] Bloom wants to situate culture exclusively in the sphere of beauty and aesthetic transcendence, unhampered and uncorrupted by politics, the struggle over public memory, or the democratic imperative for self- and social criticism. For Bloom, cultural politics is an outgrowth of cultural guilt, a holdover from the sixties that begets what he calls "the School of Resentment."[2] But there is more at stake in delegitimatizing the investigation of the relationship between culture and power for Bloom and his fellow conservatives. Eager to speak for disenfranchised groups, conservatives claim that cultural politics demeans the oppressed and has nothing to do with their problems. It neither liberates nor informs, they maintain, but rather contributes to an ongoing decline in standards and civility by prioritizing visual culture over print culture, popular culture over high culture. For Bloom, replacing *Julius Caesar* with *The Color Purple* is indicative of the lowering of such standards and the "danger of cultural collapse."[3] By conflating cultural politics with popular culture and the decline of academic standards, Bloom conveniently cloaks the contempt he harbors for minorities of race, class, and color and their "uncivil" demands for inclusion in the curricula of higher education and the history and political life of the nation.

Although Richard Rorty does not reject the political as a meaningful category of public life, he does abstract it from culture and in so doing legitimates a conservative reading of pedagogy and the aesthetic. According to Rorty, you cannot "find inspirational value in a text at the same time as you are viewing it as a . . . mechanism of cultural production."[4] Rorty steadfastly believes in the rigid division between understanding and hope, mind and heart, thought and action. He rejects the work of critical theorists such as Stuart Hall, Larry Grossberg, Paulo Freire, and others who believe that hope is a practice of witnessing, an act of moral imagination and political passion that helps educators and other

---

[1] Harold Bloom, "They Have the Numbers; We HAVE the Heights," *Boston Review* (April/May 1998): 27.

[2] Harold Bloom, *The Western Canon* (New York: Riverhead Books, 1994), 29. Bloom's position is rooted in a nostalgia for the good old days when universities taught the select few who qualified as talented writers and readers willing to carry on an aesthetic tradition purged of the contamination of politics, ideology, and power. Unfortunately, for Bloom, the universities are now filled with the stars of the School of Resentment, who debase themselves by teaching social selflessness.

[3] Bloom, "They Have the Numbers," 28.

[4] Richard Rorty, "The Inspirational Value of Great Works of Literature," *Raritan* 16:1(1996): 13.

cultural workers to think otherwise in order to act otherwise. Moreover, Rorty shares with Bloom, though for different reasons, the fall-from-grace narrative that seems to be the lament of so many well-established white male academics.

Rorty not only is scornful about situating texts within the broader politics of representation and understanding pedagogy as a political practice, he is equally resentful of a cultural left that refuses to "talk about money," legislation, or welfare reform and squanders its intellectual and critical resources on "such academic disciplines as women's history, black history, gay studies, Hispanic-American studies, and migrant studies"[5]

For Rorty, the cultural left needs to transform itself into a reformed economic left that addresses "concrete" political issues such as reforming campaign finance laws, abolishing the local financing of public education, and fighting for universal health insurance. These are laudable goals for any left, but for Rorty, they cannot be addressed by means of a cultural politics that complicates and burdens political resistance through a language that speaks to how power works within popular culture or engages politics through the connected registers of race, gender, and sexuality. Nor can such goals be addressed by expanding the political field to include various social movements organized around issues such as AIDS, sexuality, environmentalism, feminism, and antiracist struggles. Similarly, Rorty, along with his liberal cohorts such as Stanley Fish, believes that the university and public schools are not a viable public arena in which to wage nondoctrinaire political struggles. For Rorty, the political does not include sites that trade in pedagogy, knowledge, and the production of identities that mediate the relationship between the self and the larger society. Culture is not a sphere in which political struggles can be effectively conducted over broad visions of social justice. Within the narrow confines of this language, cultural politics is dismissed either as a self-serving and narrow politics of difference or as victim politics.

If Rorty is to be believed, the left can get itself out of its alleged political impasse only by giving up on theory (which has produced a few good books but has done nothing to change the country) and shedding its "semi-conscious anti-Americanism, which it carried over from the rage of the late '60s."[6] Criticism that focuses on race, gender, sexuality, popular culture, schooling, or any other merely cultural issue represents not only a bad form of identity politics but contains an unwarranted (unpatriotic?) "doubt about our country and our culture" and should be replaced with "proposals for legislative change."[7] Rorty wants a progressive politics that is color-blind and concrete, a politics for which the question of difference is largely irrelevant to a resurgent materialism that defines itself as the antithesis of the cultural. In Rorty's version of politics, the pedagogical is reduced to old-time labor organizing, which primarily benefited white men and failed to question the exclusions at its basis. In the end,

---

[5]Richard Rorty, "The Dark Side of the American Left," *Chronicle of Higher Education*, 3 April 1998, B5.
[6] Rorty, " Dark Side," B6. This argument is repeated in greater detail in Rorty's *Achieving Our Country: Leftist Thought in 20th-Century America* (Cambridge: Harvard University Press, 1998).
[7]Richard Rorty, "First Projects, Then Principles," *Nation*, 22 December 1997, 19.

Rorty provides a caricature of the cultural left, misrepresents how social movements have worked to expand the arena of democratic struggle,[8] and ignores the centrality of culture as a pedagogical force for making politics meaningful as a basis for making it an object of both critique and transformation. Moreover, liberals such as Rorty conveniently forget the specific historical conditions and forms of oppression that gave rise to the "new left" and new social movements that Stuart Hall makes central to his arguments against a facile return to the totalizing politics of class struggle, that is, a politics that defines itself as so all-encompassing in its view of the world that it dismisses any other explanation. Hall insightfully reminds us that in order to think politics in the sixties, progressives had to confront the legacy of Stalinism, the bureaucracy of the Cold War, and the stiflingly racist and sexist hierarchies within traditional left organizations.[9] Class was not the only form of domination, and it was to their credit that some "New Left" theorists made visible the diverse and often interconnected forms of oppression organized against women, racial minorities, homosexuals, the aged, the disabled, and others.

Cultural Politics and the Neo-Enlightenment Left

The attack on culture as a terrain of politics not only is evident in the works of conservatives such as Harold Bloom and liberals such as Richard Rorty, but it also is gaining ground in the writings of a number of renegades from the New Left, the most notable of whom are Todd Gitlin, Michael Tomasky, and Jim Sleeper.[10] Unlike Bloom and Rorty, Gitlin and his ideological cohorts speak from the vantage point of left politics but display a similar contempt for cultural politics, popular culture, cultural pedagogy, and differences based on race, ethnicity, gender, and sexual orientation. In what follows, I highlight some of the recurrent arguments made by this group. I will also focus on the work of Todd Gitlin, one of its most prolific and public representatives.

For Gitlin, contemporary cultural struggles, especially those taken up by social movements organized around sexuality, gender, race, the politics of representation, and, more broadly, multiculturalism, are nothing more than a weak substitute for "real world" politics, notably one that focuses on class, labor, and economic inequality.[11] According to Gitlin, social movements that reject the primacy of class give politics a bad name; they serve primarily to splinter the left into identity sects, fail "to address questions of economic equity and redistribution,"[12] and offer no unifying vision of the common good capable of challenging corporate power and right-wing ideologues.

---

[8]For a brilliant rejoinder to this type of historical amnesia, see Robin D. G. Kelley, *Yo' Mama's Disfunktional! Fighting the Culture Wars in America* (Boston: Beacon Press, 1998).

[9]Kuan-Hsing Chen, "The Formation of a Diasporic Intellectual: An Interview with Stuart Hall," in *Stuart Hall: Critical Dialogues in Cultural Studies,* ed. David Morley and Kuan-Hsing Chen (New York: Routledge, 1996), 484–503.

[10]See Todd Gitlin, *Twilight of Our Common Dreams* (New York: Metropolitan Books, 1995); Michael Tomasky, *Left for Dead: The Life, Death and Possible Resurrection of Progressive Politics in America* (New York: Free Press, 1996); Jim Sleeper, The Closest of Strangers *(New York: W. W. Norton, 1990).*

[11]Gitlin's most sustained development of this argument can be found in his, *Twilight of Our Common Dreams* (New York: Metropolitan Books, 1995).

[12]Judith Butler, "Merely Cultural," *Social Text* 15:52–53 (fall/winter 1997): 266.

Gitlin's critique of social movements rests on a number of omissions and evasions. First, in presupposing that class is a transcendent and universal category that can unite the left, Gitlin fails to acknowledge a history in which class politics was used to demean and domesticate issues raised by those groups oppressed under the sign of race, gender, and sexual orientation. Marked by the assumption that race and gender considerations could not contribute to a general notion of emancipation, the legacy of class-based politics is distinguished by a history of subordination and exclusion toward marginalized social movements. Moreover, it was precisely because of the subordination and smothering of difference that social groups organized to articulate their respective goals, histories, and interests outside of the orthodoxy of class politics. Judith Butler is right in arguing, "How quickly we forget that new social movements based on democratic principles became articulated against a hegemonic Left as well as a complicitous liberal center and a truly threatening right wing."[13] Moreover, not only does Gitlin limit social agency to the pristine category of class, he can imagine class only as a unified, pregiven subject position, rather than as a shifting, negotiated space marked by historical, symbolic, and social mediations, including the complex negotiations of race and gender. Within this discourse, the history of class-based sectarianism is forgotten, the category of class is essentialized, and politics is so narrowly defined as to freeze the open-ended and shifting relationship between culture and power.[14]

Second, in reducing all social movements to the most essentialistic and rigid forms of identity politics, Gitlin fails to understand how class is actually lived through the everyday relations of race and gender. In Gitlin's discourse, social movements are defined as narrowly particularistic; hence, it is impossible for him to "conceive of social movements as essential to a class-based politics."[15] For instance, historian Robin Kelley insightfully points out the failure of Gitlin and others to recognize how Act UP, the movement to fight discrimination against gays and lesbians, through its varied demonstrations and media-blitz campaigns, made AIDS visible as a deadly disease that is now taking its greatest toll among poor black women.[16] Nor is there any recognition of how the feminist movement made visible the dynamics of sexual abuse, particularly as it raged through the communities of poor black and white households. Nor is there any understanding of how a whole generation of young people might be educated to recognize the racist ideologies that permeate advertising, films, and other aspects of media culture that flood daily life.

Third, Gitlin's appeal to majority principles slips easily into the reactionary tactic of blaming minorities for the current white backlash, going so far as to argue that because the followers of identity politics (struggles organized around the specific interests of gender, race, age, and sexuality) abandoned a concern for materialist issues, they opened up the door for an all-out

---

[13]Ibid., 268.

[14]For an insightful analysis of this position, see Lawrence Grossberg, "Cultural Studies: What's in a Name?" in *Bringing It All Back Home: Essays on Cultural Studies* (Durham: Duke University Press, 1997), 245–271.

[15]Kelley, *Yo' Mama's Disfunktional!* 113–114.

[16]Ibid.

attack by right-wing conservatives on labor and the poor. At the same time, identity politics bears the burden in Gitlin's discourse for allowing the right to attack "racialized rhetoric as a way of diverting attention from the economic restructuring that has been hurting most Americans."[17] Thoughtlessly aligning himself with the right, Gitlin seems unwilling to acknowledge how the historical legacy of slavery, imperialism, urban ghettoization, segregation, the extermination of Native Americans, the war against immigrants, and the discrimination against Jews as it has been rewritten back into the discourse of American history may upset a majority population that finds it more convenient to blame subordinate groups for their problems than to acknowledge their own complicity.

Against this form of historical amnesia, the call to patriotism, majority values, and unity shares an ignoble relationship to a past in which such principles were rooted in the ideology of white supremacy, the presumption that the public sphere was exclusively white, and the prioritizing of a "racially cleansed notion of class."[18] If identity politics poses a threat to the endearing (because transcendent and universal) category that class represents to some critics, as Robin Kelley argues, it may be because such critics fail to understand how class is actually lived through race, sexual orientation, and gender, or it may be that the return to a form of class warfare against corporate power represents simply another form of identity politics—an identity-based campaign that stems from the anxiety and revulsion of white males who cannot imagine participating in movements led by African Americans, women, Latinos, or gays and lesbians speaking for the whole, or even embracing radical humanism.[19]

Finally, Gitlin's materialism finds its antithesis in a version of cultural studies that is pure caricature. According to Gitlin, cultural studies is a form of populism intent on finding resistance in the most mundane of cultural practices, ignoring the ever-deepening economic inequities, and dispensing entirely with material relations of power. Banal in its refusal to discriminate between a culture of excellence and consumer culture, cultural studies becomes a symbol of bad faith and political irresponsibility. For theorists in cultural studies, Gitlin argues, it is irrelevant that African Americans suffer gross material injustice because what really matters is that "they have rap."[20] It seems that for Gitlin, cultural studies should "free itself of the burden of imagining itself to be a political practice"[21] since the locus of much of its work is the university—a bankrupt site for intellectuals to address the most pressing questions of our age. Rather than take responsibility for what British cultural theorist Stuart Hall calls "translating knowledge into the practice of culture,"[22] academics, according to Gitlin, should put "real politics" ahead of cultural

[17]Iris Marion Young, "The Complexities of Coalition," *Dissent* (winter 1997): 67.

[18]Butler, "Merely Cultural," 268.

[19]Robin D. G. Kelley, *Yo' Mama's Disfunktional! Fighting the Culture Wars in America* (Boston: Beacon Press, 1998).

[20]Todd Gitlin, "The Anti-Political Populism of Cultural Studies," *Dissent* (spring 1997): 81.

[21]Ibid., 82.

[22]Stuart Hall, "The Emergence of Cultural Studies and the Crisis of the Humanities," *October* 53 (summer 1990): 18.

matters, "not mistake the academy for the larger world," [and] put their efforts into organizing "groups, coalitions, and movements."[23]

Gitlin's model of politics is characteristic of a resurgent economism rooted in a notion of class struggle in which it is argued that "we can do class or culture, but not both."[24] Within this view, social movements are dismissed as merely cultural, and the cultural is no longer acknowledged as a serious terrain of political struggle. Unfortunately, this critique not only fails to recognize how issues of race, gender, age, sexual orientation, and class are intertwined, it also refuses to acknowledge the pedagogical function of culture in constructing identities, mobilizing desires, and shaping moral values. Questions of agency or resistance in Gitlin's version of cultural studies are dismissed as retrograde forms of populism, while cultural pedagogy is traded for an anti-intellectual and antitheoretical incitement to organizing and pamphleteering.

What is disturbing about this view is that it not only separates culture from politics, but it also leaves no room for capturing the contradictions within dominant institutions that open up political and social possibilities for contesting domination, doing critical work within the schools and other public spheres, or furthering the capacity of students and others to question oppressive forms of authority and the operations of power.

Rethinking the Relationship Between Culture and Politics

Unfortunately, the current onslaught on cultural politics by conservatives and the neo-Enlightenment left tends to disregard the substantive role of culture, particularly popular culture, in pedagogy and learning, especially for young people. There is no sense in this position of the enormous influence Hollywood films, television, comics, magazines, video games, and Internet culture exert in teaching young people about themselves and their relationship to the larger society. Moreover, neither group addresses the role that academics and public school teachers might assume as public intellectuals mindful of the part that culture plays in shaping public memory, moral awareness, and political agency; similarly, neither group addresses the significance of higher and public education as important cultural sites that function as public spheres essential to sustaining a vibrant democracy.

In its best moments, the debate over the politics of culture has reinvigorated the dialogue about the role that public and higher education might play in creating a pluralized public culture essential for animating basic precepts of democratic public life, that is, educating students to be critical and active citizens. At the same time, the right- and left-wing orthodox versions of the debate have failed to consider more fundamental issues about the importance of culture as a teaching force that goes far beyond institutionalized schooling. With the rise of new media technologies and the global reach of the highly concentrated culture industries, the scope and impact of the educational force of culture in shaping and refiguring all aspects of daily life appear unprecedented.

---

[23]Gitlin, "Anti-Political Populism." *Dissent* (spring 1997): 82.
[24]Ellen Willis, "We Need a Radical Left," *Nation,* 29 June 1998, 19.

Yet the current debates have generally ignored the powerful pedagogical influence of popular culture, along with the implications it has for shaping curricula, questioning notions of high-status knowledge, and redefining the relationship between the culture of schooling and the cultures of everyday life. Consequently, the political, ethical, and social significance of the role that popular culture plays as the primary pedagogical medium for young people remains largely unexamined. For instance, there is little recognition by either conservatives or progressives of the importance of using Hollywood films such as *Schindler's List* to examine important historical events or incorporating Disney's animated cartoons in the curriculum to examine how gender roles are constructed within these films and what they suggest about the roles that young people should take, question, or resist in a patriarchal society. Nor do conservatives or liberals who disavow cultural politics and pedagogy exhibit any understanding of the importance of expanding literacy in the schools beyond the culture of the book to teach students how to use the new electronic technologies that characterize the digital age.

Informal learning for many young people is directly linked to their watching CD-ROMs, videos, films, television, and computers. Students need to learn how to read these new cultural texts critically, but they should also learn how to create their own cultural texts by mastering the technical skills needed to produce television scripts, use video cameras, write programs for computers, and produce television documentaries. For instance, a growing number of alternative school programs have developed very successful media literacy programs. These programs combine basic literacy aimed at reading and writing with literacy classes aimed at learning the basics of video production and television programming. These programs allow kids to tell their own stories, learn to write scripts, and get involved in community action programs.[25] They also challenge the assumption that popular cultural texts cannot be as profoundly important as traditional sources of learning in teaching about important issues framed through, for example, the social lens of poverty, racial conflict, and gender discrimination. Within these approaches, hands-on learning, basic literacy skills, and more advanced classroom studies are combined with the skills and knowledge needed to both produce and critically examine the new media technologies. This is not so much a matter of pitting popular culture against traditional curricula sources as it is of using both in a mutually informative way.

As culture, especially popular culture, becomes the most powerful educational force in shaping the perceptions of young people about themselves and their relationships to others, educators must ask new kinds of questions: How might teachers address education anew, given the new forms of cultural pedagogy that have arisen outside of traditional schooling? In light of such changes, how do educators respond to value-based questions regarding the purposes that schools should serve, what types of knowledge are of the most worth, and

---

[25]See the excellent story on video literacy and schooling in Ellen Pall, "Video Verite," *New York Times*, 3 January 1999, Education Life Section, 34–36, 38.

what does it mean to claim authority in a world where borders are constantly shifting? How might pedagogy be understood as a political and moral practice rather than a technical strategy? And what relation should public and higher education have to young people as they develop a sense of agency, particularly with respect to the obligations of critical citizenship and public life in a radically transformed cultural and global landscape?

As citizenship becomes more privatized and youth are increasingly educated to become consumers rather than critical social subjects, it becomes all the more imperative for educators to rethink how the educational force of the culture works to both secure and exclude particular identities and values. In opposition to Harold Bloom, Richard Rorty, and Todd Gitlin, educators need to foreground their role as public intellectuals and affirm the importance of such critical work in expanding the possibilities for democratic public life, especially as it addresses the education of youth within rather than outside of the relations of politics and culture. What exactly does this suggest?

Assuming the role of public intellectuals, educators might begin by establishing the pedagogical conditions for students to be able to develop a sense of perspective and hope in order to recognize that the way things are is not the way they have always been or must necessarily be in the future. More specifically, it suggests that educators develop educational practices that promote a language of critical imagination, one that both insists on and enables students to consider the structure, movement, and opportunities in the contemporary order of things and how they might act to prevent the barbaric while developing those aspects of public life that point to its best and as yet unrealized possibilities. This is a language of educated hope and democratic possibilities, which asserts that schools play a vital role in developing the political and moral consciousness of its citizens. It is also grounded in a notion of educational leadership that does not begin with the question of raising test scores or educating students to be experts, but with a moral and political vision of what it means to educate to govern, lead a humane life, and address the social welfare of those less fortunate than themselves. This is a notion of leadership that dreams in order to change the world rather than simply manage it. Teachers who take on the role of public intellectuals can also teach students what might be called a language of social criticism. This is a language that refuses to treat knowledge as something to be consumed passively, taken up merely to test, or legitimated outside of an ethical discourse. Central to such a language is the goal of creating those pedagogical conditions that enable students to develop the discipline, ability, and opportunity to think in oppositional terms, to critically analyze the assumptions and interests that authorize the very questions asked within the authoritative language of the school or classroom. This is a language that breaks into common sense and critically engages a variety of cultural texts and public forms. It is a language that learns how to address social injustices and break the tyranny of the present.

Another possible requirement for teachers who assume the position of public intellectuals is the need to develop new ways to engage history to develop a critical watch over the relationship between historical events and the ways in which those events are produced and recalled through the narratives in which they unfold. This suggests that educators teach students to be skilled in the language of public memory. Public memory rejects the notion of knowledge as merely an inheritance with transmission as its only form of practice. Public memory sees knowledge as a social and historical construction that is always the object of struggle. Rather than be preoccupied with the ordinary, public memory is concerned with what is distinctive and extraordinary; it is concerned not with societies that are quiet, that reduce learning to reverence, procedure, and whispers but with forms of public life that are noisy, that are engaged in dialogue and vociferous speech.

In addition, educators as public intellectuals need to expand and apply the principles of diversity, dialogue, compassion, and tolerance in their classrooms to strengthen rather than weaken the relationship between learning and empowerment on the one hand and democracy and schooling on the other. Bigotry, not difference, is the enemy of democracy, and it is difficult, if not impossible, for students to believe in democracy without recognizing cultural and political diversity as a primary condition for learning multiple literacies, experiencing the vitality of diverse public cultures, and refusing the comfort of monolithic cultures defined by racist exclusions.

In a world marked by increasing poverty, unemployment, and diminished social opportunities, educators must vindicate the crucial connection between culture and politics in defending public and higher education as sites of democratic learning and struggle. Essential to such a task is providing students with the knowledge, skills, and values they will need to address some of the most urgent questions of our time. Educating for critical citizenship and civic courage, in part, means redefining the role of academics as engaged public intellectuals and border crossers who can come together to explore the crucial role that culture plays in revising and strengthening the fabric of public life. Culture is a strategic pedagogical and political terrain whose force as a "crucial site and weapon of power in the modern world"[26] can be extended to broader public discourses and practices about the meaning of democracy, citizenship, and social justice. One of the most important functions of a vibrant democratic culture is to provide the institutional and symbolic resources necessary for young people to develop their capacity to think critically, to participate in power relations and policy decisions that affect their lives, and to transform those racial, social, and economic inequities that impede democratic social relations.

STUDY QUESTIONS

1. Why do you think there is a war against cultural politics, especially in higher and public education?

---

[26]Lawrence Grossberg, "Toward a Genealogy of the State of Cultural Studies," *Disciplinarity and Dissent in Cultural Studies*, eds. Gary Nelson and Dilip Parameshwar Gaonkar, (New York: Routledge, 1996), 142.

2. Compare and contrast the ways in which right- and left-wing theorists have attempted to abstract culture from politics to promote their own ideological agendas.
3. Do you agree or disagree with the author's position that culture is an important terrain of struggle and that it is impossible to link learning to social change if culture is abstracted from the realm of politics? Why?
4. What linkages do you see between racialized politics and multiculturalism?
5. What do you think the author means by his concluding argument for a cultural politics in which schools would be viewed as crucial public spheres and teachers as involved intellectuals who engage popular culture in the classroom?

KEY CONCEPTS

Color-blind politics

Conservative ideology

Corporatization and privatization of schooling

Cultural abstraction

Cultural pedagogy

Cultural politics

Identity politics

Neo-Enlightenment left ideology

Popular culture

Politics of inclusion

Racialized politics

Status and power

Universities as democratic publics

Warren A. Nord

*M*any people's strongest sense of identity comes from their religious traditions. This is especially true for members of those religious subcultures that define themselves in opposition to the dominant secular culture of the United States. Yet the multicultural movement has almost entirely ignored them. A part of this chapter's agenda will be to explain this fact. A larger goal will be to argue that many of the usual multicultural arguments can be used to support the inclusion of religious voices in the curriculum. There is also a constitutional argument for including religious voices that is not available to other advocates of multiculturalism. Finally, the author argues that what is at issue is in part a broader set of concerns relating to the role of religion in modern intellectual life to which most educators are insensitive.

CHAPTER 4

Multiculturalism and Religion

Warren A. Nord
University of North Carolina at Chapel Hill

While multiculturalists sometimes acknowledge, in passing, America's religious subcultures, the multicultural movement has essentially ignored religion. This is, perhaps, unsurprising, as most educators ignore religion (though, as we shall see, there is more to the explanation than this). I will argue that multiculturalism—at least in several of its most important and, to my way of thinking, acceptable varieties—requires sensitivity to religion at least as much as to race, ethnicity, class, and gender. Of course, any discussion of the role of religion in the curriculum requires some attention to constitutional considerations—leading us, in this case, to some perhaps surprising conclusions.

Religion and Culture

Historically, religions have provided the central symbols and myths, rituals and institutions, concepts and categories that have shaped people's ways of thinking about the world and their lives. Indeed, for most of human history, religious ways of thinking and living were integrated into all aspects of culture: politics and economics, art and literature, physical nature and human nature, morality and sexuality, war and peace were all understood, in large part, religiously, and for a millennium, Western civilization could be called Christendom (Smith 1964). As the West has become increasingly secular over the past several centuries, however, religion has been more and more segregated from the dominant "modern" culture and confined to "subcultural" enclaves. And yet it is now clear that once-common predictions of the death of God and religion were premature. Religion continues to possess a measure of cultural and intellectual vitality, even in the modern, secular West.

1. *Religious identity.* Millions of Americans continue to find the most profound sources of meaning in their lives in their religious traditions and define themselves not in terms of ethnicity, gender, or nationality but in terms of religion. Their primary identities are as Christians or Jews or Muslims, rather than as blacks or women or Americans. Not only do the vast majority of Americans believe in God, most pray regularly, and almost half

63

attend a religious service in any given week. Financial giving to religious institutions vastly exceeds giving to institutions defined in terms of race, ethnicity, or gender. Fifty-five percent of Americans claim that religion is "very important" in their lives, and 40 percent claim to value their relationship with God above all other relationships. Even if these statistics exaggerate the extent of our religiosity—and they probably do—many, if not most, Americans are strikingly religious people.

2. *Religious pluralism.* We are increasingly pluralistic, religiously. While most Americans (over 80 percent) identify themselves as Christian, there are significant Jewish, Muslim, Buddhist, and Hindu minorities. Depending on the survey, there are now or will soon be more Muslims in the United States than Episcopalians or Jews. One state, Hawaii, has a non-Christian majority (Buddhism). While many Americans profess no orthodox religious tradition, they nonetheless adhere to a somewhat amorphous spirituality (sometimes called "New Age" religion). Among Christians, the differences among Pentecostals, Catholics, Baptists, and Episcopalians may be as important as their similarities; indeed, within a denomination, striking differences can exist between liberals and conservatives. The old Protestant cultural establishment was long ago disestablished, and concern is now growing that no American *unum* can bind together the discordant *pluribus* of contemporary religious pluralism (Guinness, 1993).

3. *The reach of religion.* The theologian Max Stackhouse (1987) once wrote that any god worth worshipping will have implications for what we think about the world and how we live our lives (x). For example, the Western religions have historically held that God created the world and that nature is the handiwork of God, that we have souls and there is an afterlife, that we are obligated in our lives to serve God and do justice to humankind, that history has a purpose and that truth is revealed in Scripture. If the dominant culture is increasingly secular, and if many religious folk limit their religious practice to Friday evening or Sunday morning, it remains true that within religious subcultures, the implications of religious commitment extend through all of life, from how one understands the origins of the universe to how one spends one's money, from the rituals of birth to the meaning of death.

4. *The importance of religion.* Religious beliefs and practices are not primarily matters of antiquarian or theoretical interest only to theologians, historians, and sociologists. Religions have historically addressed the big questions of salvation and the meaning of life. On almost anyone's account, the implications of God's existence or nonexistence are momentous.

5. *The historical depth of religious culture.* Religious identities and "subcultures" are grounded in long-standing and deeply textured traditions, shaped by millennia of practice, reflection, and scholarship. There is a danger in emphasizing too much the ancient roots of religion, however, for, as I have said, religion retains a powerful vitality in the contemporary world. Indeed, there is a vast contemporary literature of religious commentary (conservative and liberal, devotional and scholarly) on all aspects of life.

6. *The distinctiveness of religious culture.* It is not just the vitality of religion that we must notice but also the extent to which virtually all religious traditions define themselves in categories that distinguish them from—and often set themselves against—the dominant ideals and institutions of modernity. Religious cultures are, to some considerable extent, "adversary cultures," probably much more so than are subcultures grounded in race, ethnicity, and gender. True, the more liberal the religion, the more it has accommodated itself to modernity; still, most mainline and liberal religions are defined by beliefs about God and history, morality and justice that are strikingly at odds with the dominant secular culture.

7. *The oppression of religious subcultures.* The tensions between religion and the dominant culture are so marked and the victory of the dominant culture over religion is so complete in many of the institutional domains of life, including education, that it now makes sense to talk about the oppression of religious subcultures. This may strike some readers as an exaggeration, so let me say a little more about it.

Oppression

Over the past few years, I have reviewed eighty-two widely used high school textbooks in history, economics, home economics, literature, health, and the sciences for their treatment of religion (Nord 1995, ch. 4; Nord and Haynes 1998, passim). Only the history textbooks and those literature anthologies that include historical literature (and many do not) say anything about religion, and even they fall silent as they approach the last century or two. In the other texts, students can learn all about nature and psychology, values and sexuality, justice and economics without ever having to consider what difference religion might make in understanding the subject at hand.

Or consider the new national content standards for kindergarten-through-twelfth-grade education. How does God measure up to American standards? Only the history and civics standards pay much attention to religion, and the history standards relegate it essentially to the past. In other areas of the curriculum, including literature, economics, and the sciences, there is no mention of God or religion whatever (Nord and Haynes 1998, passim).

The conventional wisdom of public education is that students can learn everything they need to know about any nonhistorical subject in the curriculum without learning anything about religion. As a result, the great majority of students earn their high school diplomas (indeed, their undergraduate, professional, and graduate degrees) without ever having to confront a live religious idea.

The problem is not simply that religion is ignored, however. It is that we teach students to think about virtually all aspects of the world in secular ways that stand in some tension (and often some conflict) with religious alternatives.

Take, for example, economics. The new national standards in economics, and each of the ten economics textbooks I have reviewed, teach students to think about the economic world in terms of neoclassical economic theory: economics is a value-free science; people are self-interested utility-maximizers;

choices should be made according to cost-benefit analyses; and the world of economics is properly understood as an arena of competition for scarce resources. None of this is compatible with any religious tradition (Nord and Haynes 1998, ch. 5). Appallingly, the national economics standards recommend that only neoclassical theory be taught, lest teachers and students be confused by the alternatives (National Council on Economic Education 1997, viii). (I should note that the texts and standards ignore not just religion, they essentially ignore those areas of our economic life of most concern within religious traditions—ideals of stewardship and justice, the need for charity and human dignity, and the dangers of consumerism and extreme individualism.)

Of course, the biology texts teach neo-Darwinian evolution and fail to consider any of the theological alternatives, conservative or liberal. Religiously, the important thing to keep in mind is that neo-Darwinism denies the religious claim that evolution is teleological, the working out of God's purposes, and, as such, it conflicts with much liberal theology, not just with fundamentalism. More generally, modern science and science texts systematically drain nature of any religious significance—a matter of considerable relevance in, for example, the environmental movement, where it is often claimed that nature is in some sense sacred. While science texts do not argue that there is no God behind the forces of nature, they do clearly convey the idea that scientific method is fully adequate for understanding nature—and, consequently, that religion is irrelevant (Nord and Haynes 1998, ch. 7).

Even in history texts, which are of all textbooks the most sensitive to religion, the governing framework for understanding history is exclusively secular. Neither history texts nor the national history standards pay any attention to the idea that history may have a religious meaning, that it acquires its shape from God's actions, as Judaism, Christianity, and Islam have each affirmed to be the case (Nord and Haynes 1998, ch. 4).

That is, we teach students to think about virtually all aspects of the world in exclusively secular categories—and if religion is included in the discussion (as in history texts), it too is interpreted in secular categories. The problem is not so much with particular claims about nature or history or morality but with the philosophical categories and language used to make sense of those claims. Public education nurtures a secular mentality; it segregates religion from our intellectual life and, hence, marginalizes it to the realms of irrelevance and irrationality (Nord 1995, ch. 4–5).

Worse, all of this is done completely uncritically. That is, students are given no idea whatever that there are also religious ways of interpreting history, nature, economics, psychology, morality, and sexuality that carve up the world quite differently and often stand in tension with the secular interpretations they learn to accept as a matter of faith, as it were.

It is striking that many liberals can be deeply offended by a single, once-in-a-lifetime nonsectarian graduation prayer but are oblivious to the fact that public schools systematically and uncritically teach children to think about virtually everything in secular categories—often undermining foundational religious beliefs and values in the process.

One of the reasons it is hard for liberals to see this is that they are all too aware of a not-so-distant history in which most American students were taught Protestant truths (sometimes against their wills); they also know that many religious conservatives would love to take over school boards and reinstate prayer and the old orthodoxies in the schools.

Indeed, there are places in America where students are unconstitutionally led in prayer and conservative majorities on school boards censor textbooks. But such places are relatively few, and the effects of such policies are typically superficial. If graduation prayers are still heard, if Christmas is still celebrated, religion has long since disappeared from the textbooks and curricula of public schools.

Why Is Religion Ignored by the Multiculturalists?   Given the deep sense of religious identity that many people feel, the vitality of religious culture, its breadth, its historical and philosophical depth, the significance of the claims it makes for the meaning of life, and its distinctiveness, why is it ignored by the multiculturalists?

A part of the answer, of course, is that most educators, not just multiculturalists, ignore religion. Education mirrors the dominant intellectual culture, which has become deeply secular.

I have told the story of the secularization of modern culture and American education at some length elsewhere (Nord 1995, 15–97). Here, I will simply sketch what I take to be three important subplots in that story. First, the framers of the Constitution believed that in the pluralistic religious culture of the new United States, government must be built on common ground; the divisiveness of religion was one reason they chose to disestablish religion. Similarly, it was the task of the early public or common schools of the nineteenth century to unite an increasingly individualistic and pluralistic culture; schools should teach what we hold in common, not what divides us. Because religion was divisive, schools began to marginalize it—not in one fell swoop, but gradually. Americanism, by contrast, would unite us, and in an immigrant nation, educators gave it many of the tasks given to religion in earlier times and more homogeneous cultures.

Second, our civilization—and our educational institutions—grew more secular as material wealth and happiness in this world became the goals of life, rather than salvation in a world to come. By the end of the nineteenth century, the purposes of schooling had become in large part economic—to nurture the practical knowledge that would enable individuals and the country to compete and thrive economically.

Third, the extraordinary success of modern science and social science in creating new technologies and new ways of making sense of the world led to a devaluation of traditional religion. Physicists and biologists saw no need to appeal to God in explaining the workings of nature; nor did psychologists or economists find the evidence of Scripture relevant in explaining human nature or the economy.

As a result, by the end of the nineteenth century (and fifty years before the Supreme Court first addressed the place of religion in public schools), religion had largely disappeared from textbooks and the curriculum. True, a ceremonial husk of religion—school prayers, devotionals, and Bible-reading—survived in some places (and occasionally up until the present day). Still, religion has long been gone from the heart of education, from the understanding of life and the world conveyed in textbooks and the curriculum.

Of course, the multicultural movement has been largely a movement of the cultural left, and in the usual alignment of combatants in our culture wars, the left finds among its foes the religious right. In the early days of multiculturalism, James Banks suggested that multiculturalists "limit the boundaries of multicultural education" to "those groups which are victims of discrimination because of their unique cultural characteristics" (quoted in Fullinwider, 1996, 16). Adopting this approach, many multiculturalists defined themselves in opposition to the white, male, Eurocentric, and (vaguely) Protestant view of the world that had dominated American education for so long and that had been oppressive in matters of race, ethnicity, and gender.

Of course, over the last few decades, religious conservatism has enjoyed a resurgence; indeed, mainline churches have steadily lost members, while conservative churches have gained them. With the growth of the Moral Majority, Focus on the Family, the Eagle Forum, and the Christian Coalition, many of the most vocal religious voices in battle over public schooling have been heard from the right.

Not surprisingly then, with a heritage of Protestant schools and with the efforts of religious conservatives to restore prayer, creationism, and "traditional values" to public schools (if not dismantle the schools through voucher programs), multiculturalism has shown little sympathy for religion.

But if it is not surprising, it is, nonetheless, unfortunate.

Religion, Pluralism, and Vouchers

I take it that one central purpose of the multicultural movement is to sustain cultural diversity and pluralism against the forces of cultural oppression and assimilation. Obviously, several strategies exist for doing this, one of which is to encourage private schooling and vouchers.

In the light of the secular domination of public education, many religious folks, like the philosopher Richard Baer (1985), ask whether Americans are willing "to let people think for themselves; to preserve their particular religious, social, and moral traditions; and to take charge of the education of their own children?" (34–35). The problem, he suggests, is that "liberal educators often tend to see pluralism in terms of the individual student's right to free expression and freedom to read and learn what he or she wants. But surely this is naive, for pluralism almost certainly will not survive if it is dependent on individuals making isolated value choices. If we have learned anything from sociology, it is that values are related to communities and that, therefore, enabling structures are necessary if a tradition is to survive and flourish" (33). The legal scholar Sanford Levinson (1993) agrees: "If one genuinely supports pluralism, diversity, and multiculturalism, then one cannot be indifferent to the fact that such a society is possible only when each group has a genuine ability to maintain itself" (75). That is, public policy must nurture communities of diverse values if pluralism is to be robust. One way of nurturing such communities is through private schooling and vouchers, and arguments for vouchers are as often made on religious as on economic lines.

(While arguments for vouchers typically come from the right, it is important to keep in mind that there is a left-liberal social justice argument that vouchers enable poor people to act on their constitutional right to educate their children in accord with their beliefs. Indeed, there is some irony in the usual political alignments here: while conservatives often acknowledge the existence of rights, they typically stop short of using the government to provide the means for citizens to act on those rights; liberals, by contrast, often argue that rights are meaningless without the financial means to act on them. Think of abortion, for example. In the case of vouchers, however, liberals and conservatives adopt each others' usual position.)

Not surprisingly, many fundamentalist Christians and Orthodox Jews favor private schooling and vouchers, believing, no doubt correctly, that the religious meaning and distinctiveness of their subcultures will be undermined by public education. And while Catholics have become rather more assimilated into the dominant culture, the Roman Catholic Church still favors vouchers as a way of respecting the fundamental right of parents to educate their children in accord with their consciences and their religious tradition.

The usual response to such "separatist" or "particularist" multiculturalism is that if pluralism is to be a viable ideal, students must learn to appreciate and respect it, neither of which is likely to happen in private religious schools (or so the argument goes).

For example, Amy Gutmann (1987) argues that to "reap the benefits" of pluralism "children must be exposed to ways of life different from [that of] their parents and—in the course of their exposure—must embrace certain values, such as mutual respect among persons, that make social diversity both possible and desirable. There is no reason to assume that placing educational authority exclusively in the hands of parents is the best way of achieving these ends" (33). Similarly, Richard Walzer (1983) has argued that for most children, "parental choice almost certainly means less diversity, less tension, less opportunity for personal change than they would find in schools to which they were politically assigned. Their schools would be more like their homes" (219). Or as another (anonymous) critic put it, in many private schools, "children themselves do not sample at will from the tempting feast of options the voucher system makes available; they are bound to the one dish preselected by their parents" ("Educating our children" 1985, 3).

While I believe that parents should have the right to educate their children in private schools (as the Supreme Court has made clear) and that vouchers should be held constitutional (when the court finally rules on them), I am not convinced that vouchers are good public policy—though we must take very seriously the reasons so many religious parents object to public education (Nord 1995, ch. 12).

My primary question, however, is what position public schools should take regarding religion and multiculturalism.

Public Schools: Rights and Respect

The idea of a "pluralistic" (as opposed to a "particularistic") multiculturalism is often grounded in a conception of America defined, in part, by moral and political ideals of liberty: individuals and subcultures must be free to define and sustain themselves—at least within certain broad limits. For the ideals of liberty and pluralism to possess vitality, however, their preconditions must be nourished; among them are a common respect for the rights of others, an appreciation of cultural diversity, and a prohibition on the use of governmental institutions to silence minority subcultures.

Public education has an extraordinarily powerful role to play with regard to these preconditions. It is important that students learn to respect the rights of others and appreciate the pluralism of our culture. One of the most important ways of doing this is by taking those subcultures seriously, making room for them in the curricular conversation. Indeed, children have a right to have their subcultures included in the stories that are told and the history that is studied. If a subculture's most fundamental beliefs about the world are not given voice in the curriculum, its members are, in effect, disenfranchised much as if they could not vote. *Public* education must take *the public* seriously.

Arguments based in liberty and rights can lead to cultural fragmentation, of course, but the idea of respect can bind us together. Indeed, there is a sense in which a conception of ourselves (whether locally or nationally) as a community can commit us to multiculturalism. K. Anthony Appiah (1996) has argued that multiculturalism is necessary to "reduce the misunderstandings across subcultures." It is "a way of making sure we care enough about people across ethnic divides to keep those ethnic divides from destroying us." Consequently, it must be "a central part of the function of our educational system to equip all of us to share the public space with people of multiple identities and distinct subcultures" (84).

We are, at least in our better moments, communities of caring, bound together (to some considerable extent) by history, personal relationships, and an overlapping consensus of moral values. Or perhaps it is better to say that by virtue of the contingencies of history, we find ourselves thrown together in a common social enterprise: living together with our deepest differences. It has been, quite properly, the role of the public schools, the *common schools*, to nurture a sense of community—one that binds us together while respecting differences.

Indeed, if there is to be social peace, if the landscape of American education is not to be a battleground of warring ideologies and subcultures, of majority and minority ideas and ideals, we must build schools on common ground, and the only way to do this is to agree to treat each other with respect (even while we disagree about matters of great importance), talk civilly with each other, learn about each other, and establish the trust that is necessary to live together with our deepest differences.

It is now widely (if not universally) held by educators that some such arguments apply in the cases of race, ethnicity, and gender. The exclusion of minority and women's history and literature from the curriculum was unjust; it relegated many children to second-class status, and massive efforts have been made over the last several decades to integrate public schools culturally, rebuilding them on common (rather than segregated) ground.

While it has not always been so, hardly any subculture is now so ignored, even oppressed, in public schools as are religious subcultures. In part, this is a matter of respecting and taking seriously children from minority religious cultures whose beliefs and values are different from those of the majority religion. Even more fundamental, however, is the fact that public schools do not take any religion seriously in the curriculum; at best, the study of religion is relegated to the distant past.

As I have already noted, the strongest reactions again public education come from religious conservatives who feel betrayed and oppressed. Indeed, the danger is considerable that public education could be crippled or even destroyed, as the voucher movement gains strength, fueled by their hostility (and if the Supreme Court rules vouchers constitutional—as it might—their influence will surely grow).

What I wish to suggest is that those same multicultural arguments for respect, diversity, community, and common ground apply also to religion and religious subcultures. As a matter of justice, public education must allow religious voices into the curricular conversation.

Rather surprisingly, in the midst of our culture wars over religion and public education, a good deal of common ground has already been staked out—though far from everyone appreciates this. A number of national documents, articulating what might be called a "New Consensus" regarding religion and public education, have been signed by a wide range of organizations, including the American Jewish Congress, the Islamic Society of North America, the National Association of Evangelicals, the National Education Association, the American Federation of Teachers, the American Association of School Administrators, and the American School Boards Association. The fundamental principles of this consensus are: the importance of religious liberty for all Americans; that public schools may neither promote nor inhibit religion; that the study of religion is essential to a good education; and that religion must be ← *how?* taught neutrally (rather than in a sectarian way, as a matter of indoctrination or proselytizing). (These documents are reproduced and discussed in Haynes 1994; also see Nord and Haynes 1998, ch. 1–2.)

For Charles Haynes (1994), who has done more than anyone to nurture this national consensus and help local school districts find common ground, the starting point must be a deeper appreciation of "rights, responsibilities, and respect" in which "all perspectives have a right to be heard, and each citizen has an obligation to protect the freedom of conscience of all others" (1:6). It is his experience that when we talk civilly and listen to each other, trust can be established and we can share a conception of public education that binds us together rather than separates us. But it is necessary that we take each other seriously in both formulating school policies and shaping the curriculum. We certainly need to recognize, Haynes argues, that "avoidance of religion and exclusion of religious perspectives is anything but neutral or fair. . . . All sides need to recognize that the current battles about 'world views' cannot be resolved either by excluding all religious perspectives or by establishing one religion (or world view) over all others" (1:3).

To preserve peace, sustain community, and take each other seriously, public schools should nurture mutual understanding and encourage respect and civil discussion among members of different cultures, secular and religious. Needless to say, public schools cannot silence particular ideologies or subcultures if they are to be just.

Public Schools: The First Amendment and Neutrality

The "New Consensus" is grounded, in part, in the religion clauses of the First Amendment—"Congress shall make no law respecting an establishment of religion or prohibiting the free exercise thereof." The purpose of the religion clauses of the First Amendment was to protect religious liberty from the federal government, but in the 1940s, the Supreme Court began to apply the First Amendment to the states and, therefore, to public education, as well. Public schools must respect the religious liberty of students.

Within certain broad limits, Americans are to be free from governmental interference in practicing (or exercising) their religion, in living by the dictates of their religious traditions. The Supreme Court has, on occasion, used the free exercise clause to rule laws unconstitutional or to carve out exemptions from constitutional laws, when this was necessary to protect the religious beliefs and practices of people—often members of religious minorities such as Jehovah's Witnesses, the Amish, or the Santerians. (It is usually religious minorities that require protection from laws made by the dominant culture.)

The establishment clause, by contrast, protects liberty by prohibiting the establishment of religion. It is widely held that this clause requires the "separation of church and state"—which, in turn, is often taken to mean that public schools can have nothing to do with religion. It was in *Everson v. Board of Education* (1947) that Justice Hugo Black read President Thomas Jefferson's metaphor of a "wall of separation" between church and state into the Supreme Court's interpretation of the First Amendment, but in that ruling, Black went on to parse the meaning of the clause in terms of neutrality, a somewhat different notion. According to the Court, the establishment clause requires two kinds of neutrality: neutrality among religions and neutrality between religion and nonreligion. The state cannot favor one religion over another; neither can it favor religion (in general) over nonreligion. The state, Black wrote, must be "neutral in its relations with groups of religious believers and non-believers." Of course, neutrality is a two-edged sword, as Black made clear: "State power is no more to be used so as to handicap religions than it is to favor them" (300 U.S. 1, 18).

Public schools may neither practice religion nor proselytize (neither would be religiously neutral), but the Court has also clearly held that it is permissible to teach about the Bible and religion in public schools so long as this is done "objectively as part of a secular program of education," as Justice Tom Clark put it for the Court in *Abington Township v. Schempp* (374 U.S. 203, 225 [1963]). That is, religion must be taught neutrally. No member of the Supreme Court has ever held that students cannot be taught about religion in public schools. This is uncontroversial.

What neutrality means, however, is a somewhat more subtle matter about which neither the Court nor educators have been particularly perceptive. It is clear that government and public schools cannot favor one religion over another. The more difficult question has to do with neutrality between religion and nonreligion. In *Schempp,* Justice Clark wrote that schools could not establish a "religion of secularism," preferring "those who believe in no religion over those who do believe" (374 U.S. 203, 225). And in a concurring opinion, Justice Arthur Goldberg warned that an "untutored devotion to the concept of neutrality" can lead to a "pervasive devotion to the secular and a passive, or even active, hostility to the religious" (374 U.S. 203, 306).

Of course, this is just what has happened. An "untutored" conception of neutrality has led educators to conflate secular education with religiously neutral education. The courts, in turn, have required a smoking gun, an overt hostility to religion, as evidence that neutrality has been violated, when the hostility has been philosophically rather more subtle, though no less substantial for that. No doubt many of the particular claims made by scientists and secular ideologues can be reconciled with much religion. It is at the level of philosophical presuppositions that they are more often in tension, for they assume conflicting conceptions of causality and meaning, evidence and rationality, and when the adequacy of secular categories for making full sense of the subject at hand is uncritically conveyed, the conflict is even more striking.

The only way of being neutral when all ground is contested ground is by being fair to the alternatives and withholding judgment. That is, given the Court's long-standing liberal or "separationist" reading of the establishment clause, public schools must require the study of religion if they require the study of disciplines that cumulatively lead to a "pervasive devotion to the secular" and, consequently, a "passive" hostility to religion.

Consider a multicultural analogy. Until the last several decades, textbooks and curricula routinely ignored women's history and minority literature. We are now (almost) all sensitive to the fact that this was not a benign neglect but rather a form of discrimination, and it would now be utterly naive to hold that the old texts and curricula were neutral in matters of race or gender. Of course (as multiculturalists are well aware), the problem was not just that minority and women's history and literature were ignored; it was that conflicting, distinctively male and white ways of thinking and acting, and patterns of culture were taught to children.

Similarly, it is anything but neutral to ignore religion, much less teach secular and scientific ways of thinking and living that conflict (albeit often at the philosophical level) with religious alternatives. Such violations of neutrality are, because of the establishment clause, unconstitutional. The purpose of the establishment clause should be to promote what the legal scholar Douglas Laycock (1990) has called "substantive neutrality." Such neutrality requires government "to minimize the extent to which it either encourages or discourages religious belief or disbelief, practice or nonpractice, observance or nonobservance." Religion "should proceed as unaffected by government as possible" (1001–1002). In regard to the curriculum, "government must be scrupulously even handed, treating the range of religious and nonreligious views as neutrally as possible" (Laycock 1996, 348). I take it from this that because public schools teach students ways of thinking about the world that stand in some tension (or open conflict) with religion, they must also teach students about religion in some depth (Nord 1995, ch. 5–7).

And, of course, they must teach students about a variety of religions; as we have seen, neutrality also means that public schools cannot promote or privilege a particular religion over others.

Public Schools and Liberal Education

Another kind of multicultural argument also is now widely accepted. Students should learn something about other cultures and history, not primarily as a matter of justice or community and certainly not for constitutional reasons, but because we (as individuals and as a society) cannot make informed and responsible judgments about our lives and social policies without understanding the larger, increasingly interdependent world of which we are part.

No doubt we might approach other cultures or subcultures with the idea of learning about our enemies, but I trust I am not naive in attributing a rather more benign motivation to educators. We have a good deal to learn from non-Western cultures and from those neglected and oppressed subcultures that have been part of Western and American history and culture; our lives will be richer, our decisions more reasonable, and social progress more likely as we broaden our understanding of human nature, history, and culture, and explore various cultural experiments in living.

Education—at least a liberal education—compels us to take seriously cultures other than our own; it is, by its very nature, open and critical. Indeed, it might be argued that we socialize or indoctrinate students (rather than educate them) when we (uncritically) limit their study to a single tradition or culture or world view when there are live alternatives. Students become educated as they are able to think critically and comparatively about alternatives.

We sometimes think that a liberal education requires students to take a variety of subjects: a little history, a little math and science, a little literature, and so on. No doubt this is part of what constitutes a liberal education, but it is naive to think that this is all there is to it. Indeed, a part of the problem is that we do not actually teach subjects (which are open to a variety of interpretations) so much as we teach particular interpretations that often harden into disciplines.

It is one thing, for example, to teach the subject of literature by including material and interpretations drawn from a variety of traditions, cultures, and subcultures; it is another thing to teach only the traditional canon and ways of thinking about literature that go with it. If students in literature courses read no minority or women's literature and learn nothing about alternative ways of thinking about what it means to be canonical, they will not have been liberally educated.

A liberal education requires that students be exposed to the major contending ways of interpreting the most important subjects. As the multicultural movement has made clear, traditional ways of teaching history and literature have ignored whole domains of culture and uncritically taught traditional, often illiberal, ways of thinking about them.

This problem cuts deeper than is often acknowledged, however, with regard to religion. For example, we do not teach the subject of economics; we teach the discipline of economics; that is, we teach students to think about economics (society, values, and human nature) like secular neoclassical economists. We do not teach students about nature as a subject that might be interpreted in religious as well as secular categories; rather, we teach students to think about nature as scientists do, using the scientific method. Indeed, we teach students to think about history and health and sexuality and morality in exclusively secular categories, ignoring the religious alternatives that are at the heart of many religious traditions. As we have seen, public schooling takes sides; it encourages students to think (and feel) about the world in secular rather than religious ways.

This is not just a problem of justice and community and constitutional neutrality. There is a fundamental educational problem as well. Such "education" is deeply illiberal: it actively undermines the ability of students to think critically about the world by systematically limiting the range of alternatives available to them.

If religion were a "dead" alternative, there might be no obligation to take it seriously, but in spite of the secularity of our culture, religion continues to possess a great deal of vitality. Religious ideas and ideals shape our hopes and our fears, our literature and our morality, our politics and our wars (both military and cultural). Religions continue to ask—and provide answers to—those existential questions on which any educated person must reflect. Theologians and religious thinkers—conservative and liberal, Western and non-Western—continue to provide alternatives to secular ways of thinking about the world. As the great scholar of world religions Ninian Smart (1987) puts it, scientific humanism is often "in living contact and conflict with traditionally religious belief-systems. Rivals should be treated together. If they are not, then we are taking steps to entrench some determinate viewpoint into our educational system, and genuine pluralism is in this way eroded" (9).

What do they know of England who only England know? What do they know of nature who only science know? What do they know of economics who only neoclassical theory know? In the end, we may decide that science and secular scholarship provide us with the truth. Maybe. But my argument is about what it means to be educated. By itself, science and secular ways of thinking cannot make an educated person. A good liberal education should expose students to the major ways our culture has devised for understanding what is most important, and some of those ways of thinking and living are religious.

It might be argued in response that educators have an obligation to guide the thinking of students and, after all, modern science and secular scholarship yield truth; they are more reasonable than the religious alternatives. We can, after all, safely ignore superstition and positions grounded in faith.

But, of course, we disagree about what is reasonable. We disagree deeply about how to acquire the truth about sexuality and politics and economics and the origins of the world, and if the dominant interpretations in our intellectual life are secular, there continue to be religious alternatives. In fact, what appears to be a secular consensus among scholars is artificial and misleading because theologians and religious writers are not allowed to vote. They are not allowed into the main quad of the academy or public schools but are exiled to divinity schools and seminaries, think tanks and denominational bureaucracies; their votes are not counted when we decide what interpretations to teach our students. The truth of the matter is that we disagree deeply about the truth, and the only way we can get a consensus is by excluding the dissenters.

Gerald Graff (1992) has rightly argued that "the best solution to today's conflicts over culture is to teach the conflicts themselves, making them part of our object of study and using them as a new kind of organizing principle to give the curriculum the clarity and focus that almost all sides now agree it lacks" (12).

Students are not well educated if they have heard the voices on only one side of a disagreement; if students are to be liberally educated, they must be taught the conflicts—including, I might add, those conflicts relating to multiculturalism itself. After all, we disagree deeply about multiculturalism. It is not permissible to teach students only the traditional Western canon; nor is it permissible to teach them any particular multicultural view of the world uncritically. At some point in their educations, students must learn to appreciate what is at issue in the multiculturalism debate. The purpose of education is not to teach the truth when we disagree but rather the conflict; it is not to initiate students uncritically into a particular way of seeing the world (be it liberal or conservative, religious or secular, traditional or multicultural, modern or postmodern) but rather into a conversation about the truth in which all the (major) sides are given voice.

Tensions

The various multicultural arguments I have considered are compatible, indeed reinforcing, in this respect: they each require that education be open in a way in which it has traditionally been closed. They each take fairness to be a major educational virtue; we must take each other, and our respective traditions, seriously.

There is a potential tension among the arguments that merits attention, however brief.

It is widely held that to be educated, students need not just learn about a variety of traditions, cultures, and subcultures. They also should acquire some sense of how to judge them, of how to assess which alternatives are more or less reasonable.

The multicultural movement has often resisted this conclusion, however. For example, the National Council for Social Studies (1991) has prescribed a curriculum in which students are taught "to feel positively about their identities" and "develop a high regard for their original languages and cultures" (8). Indeed, students should learn that every ethnic group has "worth and dignity." Comparative approaches to ethnic experiences must be "descriptive and analytical, not normative or judgmental," and teachers "should avoid, as much as possible, labeling any perspective 'right' or 'wrong'" (13). The importance of self-esteem dictates that all cultures and subcultures be respected neutrally.

This has at least two problems, however. First, cultures are not just different, they have conflicting beliefs and values. Can we respect at one and the same time American feminism and the overt sexism of many Third World cultures or fundamentalist and gay subcultures?

Second, the idea of a completely uncritical tolerance or affirmation of the worth and dignity of all cultures and subcultures is morally problematic. Nazi culture deserves no such tolerance, nor should the apartheid culture of South Africa be affirmed.

Robert Fullinwider (1996) puts it this way: "students should learn to respect what is respectable and learn to appreciate what is *worthy* of appreciation." The "real" question, of course, is: "What standards of discrimination should we use to identify the respectable and the worthy in matters of culture?" In promoting "a broad-mindedness and generosity of judgment, multiculturalism must avoid a vacuous relativism" (14; emphasis added).

One reason that multiculturalists have resisted such comparative judgments is that many subcultures have suffered oppression as a result of them. But Fullinwider (1994) argues, rightly I believe, that multiculturalists should want students "to avoid smug, arrogant judgments . . . [and] the obtuseness of those who hear and do not understand, see and do not perceive, and who, in their obtuseness, unfairly denigrate or disparage other people's accomplishments and traditions." The problem is that in response, they "recommend an uncritical attitude toward cultural difference when they should be describing instead the virtues of an open mind" (7).

Of course, the fact that we properly teach students the evil of Nazi culture and antebellum slave culture does not mean that one culture (even ours) is better than all others or that there are not many different cultures that merit (more or less) equal respect.

Nor does it mean that members of various cultures do not merit respect. We may disagree deeply about the values of different subcultures, all the while treating each other with respect as individuals, talking civilly with each other. We may legitimately disagree about homosexuality, while agreeing that gay bashing is reprehensible and not to be permitted.

Nor does it mean that judgments about the relative merits of contending cultures and subcultures are easily made; they are matters of considerable complexity. Indeed, because we naturally assume our own culture to be superior, we need the impetus of the multicultural movement to force us to think more critically about the shortcomings of our own culture and merits of others (whatever our final judgments might be).

There is another reason why multiculturalists often reject an evaluative approach to alternative cultures; many of them are committed to some form of postmodernism and to a rejection of all "metanarratives" that might be used to ground comparative cultural assessments. The result is sometimes a thorough-going cultural relativism.

This, too, is one of the possibilities that needs to be included in the conversation—at least for older, more mature students, but it should not be taught to any students uncritically, for it is also deeply controversial.

My own inclination is to argue for the importance of nurturing in students the capacity for reflective and informed judgments, leavened by a deep sense of humility in dealing with difficult and controversial matters (in which they have something of a vested interest). In matters of religion, however, educators are necessarily constrained by the First Amendment, which trumps all other considerations. Public schools cannot in any official way promote or denigrate any particular religion, or religion generally, whatever the critical purposes of a liberal education might be. Neutrality must be the governing virtue. In this regard, religious traditions and subcultures must be treated differently from secular cultures and subcultures.

Practical Problems

How should teachers approach Christmas (or Passover or Ramadan) in a third grade classroom? What should they say about creationism in a high school biology class? Needless to say, how we teach the conflicts and how we take religion seriously are matters of considerable complexity and controversy—though it is easy to overstate the difficulties. As I noted above, there is something of a "New Consensus" about the role of religion in the curriculum.

Still, much needs to be said about how religion fits into the curriculum and the pedagogy of "teaching about religion." In *Taking Religion Seriously Across the Curriculum* (1995), Charles Haynes and I have developed a fairly detailed proposal for taking religion seriously across the curriculum, and I refer readers to it. Here, I simply note that if the challenge is to be met, a number of significant reforms are necessary.

First, teachers and administrators must have a much better sense than most now do of the civic and constitutional ground rules for dealing with religion in public schools generally and in the curriculum in particular. This means that schools of education must begin to take religion seriously.

Second, teachers need to study how religion relates to the subjects they teach. Understandably, many members of minority religious traditions are wary of proposals to include religion in the curriculum, fearing that most teachers, well-intentioned though they be, will through ignorance convey distorted and prejudiced conceptions of most religious traditions.

Third, we need a new generation of textbooks that take religion seriously. Some evidence exists that history and social studies texts have improved at least a little over the last decade, though they still have a long way to go, but most texts ignore religion completely, even though they teach material that is deeply controversial on religious grounds.

Fourth, all school districts need to have policies that make clear the legitimate role of religion in the classroom and in the curriculum. Unless teachers and administrators are protected, they will not feel safe in dealing with potentially controversial matters—such as religion—in the classroom.

Some educators will find it unrealistic to expect such reforms; some will find these proposals too controversial. Of course several decades ago, teachers, textbooks, and curricula said little about women and minority cultures—and multiculturalism has proven to be controversial. But things do change.

Educators will be particularly shortsighted if they ignore the case for religion. It is important to remember that it is also controversial to leave religion out of the curriculum. Indeed, because public schools do not take religion seriously, many religious parents have deserted them and, if the Supreme Court upholds vouchers, as it may do, the exodus will be much greater.

In the long run, the least controversial position is the one that takes everyone seriously. If public schools are to survive our culture wars, they must be built on common ground, and there can be no common ground when religious voices are left out of the curricular conversation.

CONCLUSION

There are, of course, a variety of multicultural positions. I have drawn on several of them for arguments for enlarging the curricular conversation to include religious voices.

Like most educators, however, multiculturalists have ignored religion. Given the alignment of combatants in our current culture wars this is, perhaps, unsurprising, but it is a betrayal of principles nonetheless. If public education is to be built on common ground, if it is to be inclusive, if it is to nurture respect for diversity and community, then religious voices must be included in the curriculum. If public education is to be religiously neutral, as the establishment clause of the First Amendment to the Constitution requires, then a variety of religious as well as secular voices must be included in the conversation. And finally, if public education is to be truly educational, if students are to receive a liberal (rather than parochial) education, they must be exposed to the religious voices in our multicultural marketplace that challenge the secular conventional wisdom of modern education.

STUDY QUESTIONS

1. In a country where presidents invoke the blessings of God and no political candidate could admit to being an atheist, what sense does it make to talk about the oppression of religion?

2. Virtually all of the religious opposition to public education and multiculturalism has come from conservatives. What might religious liberals find objectionable in the curriculum?

3. Is it true the science courses cannot be neutral by simply ignoring religion? Can it be argued that the scientific method is, by its nature, not religiously neutral?

4. How analogous are the cases for racial and religious integration of the curriculum?

5. Some people believe that religion is a matter of faith and does not belong in public schools, which should be reserved for subjects that are open to rational judgment. Can religion be rational? Can science be a matter of faith? Are cultural values matters of faith or reason?

6. What in your school's policies or curricula might be insensitive to members of minority religions?

KEY CONCEPTS

Pluralism and religious pluralism

Vouchers

Rights and respect

Establishment of religion

"New Consensus"

Neutrality among religions

Neutrality between religion and nonreligion

Subjects versus disciplines

Liberal versus illiberal education

Teaching the conflicts

Fairness

REFERENCES

Appiah, K. Anthony. 1996. Culture, subculture, multiculturalism: educational options. In *Public education in a multicultural society: Policy, theory, critique*, ed. Robert K. Fullinwider, 65–89. New York: Cambridge University Press.

Baer, Richard. 1985. *Censorship and the public schools.* Milwaukee: Catholic League for Religious and Civil Rights.

Educating our children: Whose responsibility? 1985. Unsigned article in *Philosophy and Public Policy* 5:1–5.

Fullinwider, Robert K. 1996. "Multicultural education: concepts, policies, and controversies." In *Public education in a multicultural society: Policy, theory, critique*, ed. Robert K. Fullinwider, 3–23. New York: Cambridge University Press.

Guinness, Os. 1993. *The American hour: A time of reckoning and the once and future role of faith.* New York: Free Press.

Graff, Gerald. 1992. *Beyond the culture wars.* New York: W. W. Norton.

Gutmann, Amy. 1987. *Democratic education.* Princeton, N.J.: Princeton University Press.

Haynes, Charles C. 1994. *Finding common ground: A First Amendment guide to religion and public education.* Nashville: Freedom Forum First Amendment Center at Vanderbilt University.

Laycock, Douglas. 1990. Formal, substantive, and disaggregated neutrality toward religion. *DePaul Law Review* 39:993–1018.

———. 1996. Religious liberty and liberty. *Journal of Contemporary Legal Issues* 7:313–356.

Levinson, Sanford. 1993. Chapter 18 (untitled). In *American Jews and the separationist faith,* ed. David G. Dalin. Washington, D.C.: Ethics and Public Policy Center.

National Council on Economic Education. 1997. *National content standards in economics.* New York: National Council on Economic Education.

National Council for the Social Studies. 1991. *Curriculum guidelines for multicultural education.* Washington, D.C.: National Council for the Social Studies.

Nord, Warren A. 1995. *Religion and American education: Rethinking a national dilemma.* Chapel Hill: University of North Carolina Press.

Nord, Warren A., and Charles C. Haynes. 1998. *Taking religion seriously across the curriculum.* Alexandria, Va.: Association for Supervision and Curriculum Development.

Smart, Ninian. 1987. *Religion and the Western mind.* New York: Macmillan.

Smith, Wilfred Cantwell. 1964. *The meaning and end of religion.* New York: Mentor Books.

Stackhouse, Max. 1987. *Public theology and political economy.* Grand Rapids, Mich.: Eerdmans.

Walzer, Richard. 1983. *Spheres of justice.* New York: Basic Books.

Sabrina W. M. Laine   Margaret Sutton

*T*he United States is not alone among nations in its struggle to come to terms with an ethnically and linguistically diverse citizenry. Although the circumstances of each society are historically unique, common threads run through the stories of nation building in modern, pluralistic states. This chapter compares the cases of Australia and Canada to that of the United States. While all three countries are Anglo-settler states that have subjugated native populations, and all have experienced rapidly increasing ethnic and linguistic diversity since the end of World War II, there are striking differences among the three. Each has a distinct "defining minority," a group whose oppression has critically shaped the development of multicultural questions, beliefs, and public actions. We maintain that the defining minority of Australia is Asian emigrants; of Canada, the Francophone population; and of the United States, African Americans. As a result, Canada and Australia have been more proactive and thoughtful about language use and language policy than has the U.S. By contrast, multicultural debate in the United States has never strayed far from issues of personal freedom and rights. One of the most striking differences between multiculturalism in the United States and that in Australia and Canada is that the latter two nations have developed federal policies of multiculturalism that have been enacted into law and supported by funded mandates; no such federal policy exists in the United States. Relating the history of multicultural debate and policy action in each of the three countries, the chapter asks why this is so.

CHAPTER 5

The Politics
of Multiculturalism

A Three-Country Comparison

Sabrina W. M. Laine
North Central Regional Education Laboratories

Margaret Sutton
Indiana University, Bloomington

Over the past four decades, the topic of multiculturalism—its pros and cons, its promises and threats—has become one of the most vehemently contested issues of educational debate in the United States. Critics of multicultural curricula that emphasize ethnicity question whether racism has actually decreased or increased as a result of such programs. They point to a new divisiveness perceived in society. Such critics believe that the best way to avoid hostility is to ignore people's ethnic origins. According to Gitlin (1995), "It is the identity obsessions, all of them, each fueling the others which give the question of multiculturalism its venom" (11). The valorization of ethnic or cultural identity, in the view of Schlesinger (1992), "belittles *unum* and glorifies *pluribus*" (17). In contrast, multicultural education supporters such as Walzer (1994) believe that promotion of multiculturalism is critical for creating a national framework within which individuals can develop their own cultural heritage, thus fostering a climate of acceptance toward others.

Importance of a National Policy

The United States is not the only country in which

> ... racial hysteria and racial anxiety ride the underside of the public discourse on schooling and society as rapid demographic changes alter the racial and ethnic landscape.... (McCarthy 1998, xii)

On the contrary, in their examination of global trends in education reform, Davies and Guppy (1997) found that Anglo democracies have responded to ethnic, religious, and language minorities by instituting policies of cultural diversity. Among such nations, however, the United States may be alone in its lack of a federal policy that explicitly addresses multiculturalism.

While the existence of a national multicultural policy in itself is no guarantee of social justice or interethnic harmony, it may well be a necessary ingredient in the struggle to reach these goals. In the United States, the absence of leadership from the federal government around issues of culture, national identity, ethnicity, and economic opportunity has left educators—arguably the primary transmitters of American culture—without a common vision of what it means to be a multicultural American. While it may be true, as Glazer asserts, that "We are multiculturalists now" (1997), our elected officials have not stepped up to the challenge of forging the debate into a policy affirming commonly held values and beliefs. As a result, teachers and students are frequently caught in the cross fire, as the debate around the role of multiculturalism in our schools continues to rage.

What would it mean for the U.S. government to play a leading role in accommodating different cultural identities with regard to how children are educated, how people are treated by government institutions, and the extent to which similar or equal opportunities exist for cultural or ethnic minorities (Gutmann and Taylor 1992)? As one approach to answering such a question, this chapter looks at the multicultural policies of two countries, Canada and Australia, that are similar to the United States in relevant ways. Both nations, like the United States, are predominantly Anglo-settler states, with minority indigenous populations, and substantial and changing influxes of non-Anglo emigrants. All are federal states that leave a large degree of authority over education in provincial or state hands, while the federal government defines citizenship and rights. However, both Australia and Canada, unlike the United States, have established national policies of multiculturalism. The federal commitments to multicultural policy are underscored in both countries by the establishment of ministerial posts associated with multiculturalism—in Australia, a minister for Immigration and Multicultural Affairs, and in Canada, a Secretary of State with portfolios for Multiculturalism and Women's Affairs.

Through a comparative analysis of the development of multicultural policies in Canada and Australia and of language and cultural policies in the United States, we intend to make three major points. We will demonstrate that the U.S. approach to racial, ethnic, and linguistic pluralism is not the only model available for contemporary societies striving to come to terms with cultural pluralism. We will argue that aspects of political culture in the United States have prevented serious consideration of a national multicultural policy, such as those that exist in Canada and Australia. Finally, we will show how federal multicultural policies in Canada and Australia have shifted the terms of public debate away from an exclusive focus on assimilation of difference toward a discourse of effective respect for differences. A similar shift in the

United States, we believe, might enable motion toward a less divided and antagonistic society.

Policies, Multiculturalism, and Comparison

Public policy can take a wide range of forms, from broad statements of goals to more specific statements of intention (Pressman and Widavsky 1984). Policy can be expressed in speeches, official statements, court decisions, laws and regulations, all of which embody the authority to define goals and priorities and to command means. Policy also provides a framework for taking action and lends legitimacy to implementation and evaluation purposes (Ray and Poonwassie 1992). The outcomes of a policy depend critically on the resources allocated to its support and the institutional arrangements mobilized in its implementation.

At the most basic level, all public policies specify priorities and procedures for distributing goods and services to the members of a society. As Bhola (1975) has observed, the intent of policy is "to *direct* and to *harness* social power for social outcomes" (1). In so doing, policies express the allocation of values by a decision-making body (Ball 1990). All states in the United States, for example, have policies defining how the revenues that support schools are to be raised and distributed. The extent to which educational resources are assigned locally versus centrally will reflect the relative importance placed on equity versus, for example, the autonomy of local communities.

Multicultural policies, whether in education or other realms of society, are those public statements and programs that recognize the ethnically, racially, and culturally pluralistic nature of the modern nation-state. In any given society, multicultural policy can exist over a wide array of social, cultural, economic, and educational programs, when such programs are intended to increase the participation of diverse racial and ethnic groups in mainstream society. Examples of multicultural policies that might be government-initiated include:

1. Official recognition in law by all public bodies of the cultural attributes of ethnic groups;
2. Public support for autonomous cultural institutions;
3. The use of public space—the media, for example—to accommodate all cultural groups;
4. Teaching multiple cultures in public schools; and
5. Elimination of the link between poverty, lack of education, and ethnicity. (Raz 1994).

As these examples show, multicultural policy can certainly focus on the education system, but it is not limited exclusively to the schools.

Indeed, as the cases of Canada and Australia will show, powerful supports for multiculturalism exist in the wider social and cultural realm of modern nations. In the United States, many educators and social researchers claim that the integration of multiculturalism in one segment of the public sector—public education—does not go far enough toward realizing an equalization of power among ethnic groups. According to Bullivant (1984), multiculturalism as it is currently taught in schools neglects sources of cultural differentiation in relations of power, dominance, and subordination, as well as noncultural sources of ethnic stratification. Transformative multicultural education (Banks 1993) and education that is both multicultural and social reconstructionist (Grant and Sleeter 1989) are examples of the most far-reaching and comprehensive approaches to multiculturalism as a framework for teaching tolerance and appreciation of cultural diversity, as well as a mechanism intended to foster the redistribution of economic, political, and cultural power from the dominant group to the subordinate ethnic group. However, even the most visionary participants in the debate on multiculturalism in the United States have not been successful in influencing policy makers to take new steps to address economic, political, and cultural inequality.

This comparative presentation of multicultural policies (or the lack thereof, in the case of the United States) fulfills a major purpose of comparative case studies as defined by Ragin (1987). Ragin argues that what distinguishes comparative studies from other forms of social science is the emphasis placed on understanding social phenomenon in their "macro-social context." When comparative studies analyze specific events, they consider overarching features of societies, such as economic form, demographic composition, or political system, as causal factors. In this chapter, for example, we will consider the contribution that a parliamentary versus a presidential system might make to enactment of multicultural policy. Comparative studies are also inescapably historical because "macro-social" phenomena exist and change over time. In this analysis, we will be especially concerned with understanding the "defining minority" groups in the debates about multiculturalism in each country, and how differences in "defining minorities" have led to differences in multicultural policy.

The comparison of policies and approaches to multiculturalism in Australia, Canada, and the United States illustrates the wide range of public actions that can and have been taken by nations to address contemporary issues of ethnic and cultural pluralism. Along the way, we hope that the account of these policies will stimulate multiculturalists in the United States to think in new ways about the processes available for fostering cultural pluralism and the policies that might support its development.

Multicultural Dynamics in the Three Case Countries

Despite their similarities, substantial historical and political differences exist among the three nations being considered here. For example, while all three were settled in part by indentured servants, only in the United States did slavery build a new country, while in Australia, convicts forged roads and farms. Canada, unlike the United States and Australia, has always included a politically distinct Francophone community whose existence critically defines Canadian multiculturalism. Canada and Australia are parliamentary democracies. Their judicial systems have historically been based in common law, though the Canadian system was radically reshaped by the Constitution Act of 1982. The United States, by contrast, has for over two hundred years been a constitutional democracy headed by a president.

These and other differences in institutions and histories among the three countries are manifest today in the unique political cultures of each, which in turn encompass different policies and approaches to multiculturalism. This section provides an overview of the historical development of cultural pluralism and multicultural policies in the three countries.

Australia   In 1788, the first one thousand British colonists, two-thirds of them convicts, settled in what is now the city of Sydney. The Aboriginal population of the continent at the time of conquest and colonization is estimated to have been between 300,000 and 750,000 (Allan and Hill 1995, 763). By 1901, the year of federation into the Commonwealth of Australia, more than 3 million colonists lived in the seven states of Australia. Through war, disease, and destruction of habitat, the Aboriginal population had declined to under one hundred thousand.

Before and after federation, Australia developed a political culture unique among colonial nations. On the one hand, the culture has been characterized by strong egalitarian sentiments and a liberal system of social supports, such as universal medical care and public allowances for single-parent families. This culture of generosity and equality, however, developed in an ethnically restricted society. One of the first acts of the new Commonwealth of Australia government was to implement the "white Australia policy," based on racially restrictive immigration laws designed to exclude Asians. The Immigration Restriction Act of 1901 and the Naturalisation Act of 1903 created the backbone of the white Australia policy. These laws were specifically anti-Asian, aimed at preventing a repeat of the Chinese migration to Australian goldfields in the 1860s. Racially restrictive immigration remained firmly in place until the mid-1960s; it was not until 1973 that the white Australia policy was fully abandoned (Miller 1985; Foster 1988; Allan and Hill, 1995).

Although the white Australia policy was directed outward, preventing an influx of nonwhite settlers, officially sanctioned racism has also characterized public policy toward Aborigines, which lay almost entirely with state governments until the late 1960s. As happened to the native populations of Canada and the United States, Aboriginal land rights were massively abrogated in the course of conquest and settlement. In Australia, however, permanent reserves were not established by treaty. Rather, state governments established "missions" for the settlement of indigent Aborigines. Assimilation through intermarriage with Anglos was widely promoted well into the twentieth century (Miller 1985, 172). In 1967, a federal Council for Aboriginal Affairs was established following a national referendum empowering the federal government to legislate in regard to Aborigines and, for the first time in the history of the country's colonization, to include the Aboriginal population in the census record. The movement for land rights and self-determination among Aborigines has grown stronger each year since and has registered some success.

Relations between Aborigines and non-Aboriginal Australians continue to command attention of those concerned with multiculturalism in Australia. However, multicultural policies that have developed since the 1970s did not come about initially in response to Aboriginal demands but rather to the influx of "nontraditional" immigrants from Asia and Latin America. This emigration was the proximate cause behind the development of multicultural policies.

Table 5.1 shows the most recent estimates of the Australian population by relevant ethnic or cultural definitions. Figures are drawn from the 1996 census.

In Australia, the notion of multiculturalism is firmly wedded to the post–World War II immigration of "nontraditional" settlers who have come to be known as "NESB" people—persons of non-English-speaking background. In 1973, the Whitlam government ended the white Australia policy by enacting immigration laws in which "race, skin color and nationality were no longer legitimate criteria for the selection and admission of migrants to Australia" (Foster 1988, 7). In the same year, the first public use of the term *multiculturalism* by a government official occurred in a speech by the Labor government Immigration minister, Al Grassby (Luketic, Breda, and Ackerman 1996, 3). Several other statements by and reports to the Labor government of 1972–1975 expressed the understanding that non-English-speaking immigrants to Australia were substantially more likely to be poor than the majority population and that attitudinal barriers of ethnocentrism compounded the probability of economic disadvantage (Foster 1988, 114).

Five years after Grassby's speech, multiculturalism became a salient policy issue through the 1978 *Migrant Services and Programs* report sponsored and issued by the Conservative government of Malcolm Fraser. This report came to be known as the Galbally Report, after its chairperson. Section 9 of the Galbally Report is entitled "Multiculturalism" and affirms the value of multiculturalism as a social goal:

> Provided that ethnic identity . . . is interwoven into the fabric of our nationhood by the process of multicultural interaction. . . . The knowledge that people are identified with their cultural background and ethnic group enables them to

TABLE 5.1 Australian Demographics

	Number	Percent of total
Total population	17,892,423	100
Aborigines and Torres Strait people	352,970	2
Born outside Australia	3,908,213	22
Born outside Australia but not from the U.K., U.S., New Zealand, Canada, or South Africa	2,362,379	13

Source: *Census Australia* (1996)

take their place in their new society with confidence if their ethnicity has been accepted by the community. (104)

The Galbally Report also alerted the public and the federal government to the inadequacy of services for migrants in areas such as legal rights, employment, health, and income security. It highlighted communication as the primary cultural barrier and recommended acceptance of ethnic languages as the first step in improving ethnic-group relations and social mobilization.

Several of the recommendations of the Galbally Report became law. New federal support was provided to English language education programs for adult immigrants in the NESB group and to bilingual education for children. This support extended to bilingual education for Aboriginal children whose needs were conflated with those of emigrants (Lo Bianco 1988, 26). Although not without critics, the federal government by 1991 had funded nearly two hundred thousand enrollments in schools run by ethnic organizations (Allan and Hill 1995, 769). Through bilingual and language maintenance programs, multicultural policy was intended to promote a national acceptance of diversity and the equal interaction of minority ethnic groups within Australian society.

In addition to language programs, three other recommendations of the Galbally Report were realized through law and appropriation. The development of multicultural education was funded through the federal government, as was the establishment of the Australian Institute of Multicultural Affairs and ethnic radio and television under the government-funded Special Broadcasting Service (Foster 1988, 118). Beginning in 1979, federal grants were made to schools in support of multicultural education programs, including bilingual education and ethnic schools. English as a Second Language (ESL) programs have been supported both in and outside of schools. State governments took up the charge to promote multicultural education. Allan and Hill (1995) point out that "by the early 1980s all Australian states had adopted multicultural education policies" (768). The impact of these curricula on majority attitudes and on minority economic and social opportunities, however, remains questionable (768).

In addition to support for immigrant cultures and languages through formal schooling, Australia provides an unique example of multicultural policy enacted through broadcasting policy. In 1980, the Special Broadcasting Service (SBS) was established with a mandate to promote multicultural broadcasting. It has since become one of the most visible expressions of the federal multicultural policy, as well as the second national television network. A unique feature of SBS programming is the prevalence of imported programs from countries of immigrant origins, glossed with English subtitles. Luketic and colleagues (1996) underscore the important contribution that SBS makes to promoting multiculturalism in Australia:

> Subtitling further quells arguments which claim the erosion of English language dominance in broadcasting through multilingual programming; instead it facilitates understanding and tolerance across cultures. Thus, rather

than disconnect ethnic audiences from the broader Australian community, SBS has undertaken the valuable work of better integrating ethnic Australia by making transparent the culture and information networks of the various communities. (15)

All of the programs and services committed to multiculturalism in the late 1970s came under the budget axe in the lean years of the mid-1980s. Despite a substantial reaffirmation of the Galbally Report principles in the Jupp Report of 1986, federal funding for multicultural programs declined dramatically in that year. The Australian Institute of Multicultural Affairs was closed; funding for multicultural education and ESL all but disappeared. One of the few federal multicultural programs to survive the 1980s relatively intact was ethnic broadcasting through the SBS.

In the late 1980s, multiculturalism reemerged at the federal level in the national policy on languages, which was endorsed by the prime minister and funded by the cabinet in 1987. Lo Bianco characterizes the policy as a "third phase" of multicultural policy in Australia, one that carries into the 1990s. The first phase, highlighted by Labor government reports in the early 1970s, focused on equality and inequality in the labor market and society, identifying language deficiencies as a primary cause. The second phase, characterized by the Galbally Report, was culturalist. That is, it viewed differences among ethnic groups as essentially cultural, downplaying power differences. With the advent of the language policy and extending into the present, multicultural policy in Australia has come to be based on explicit national self-interest. There is, Lo Bianco (1988) argues, an increasing move toward multiculturalism in the service of economic gain (28). An example is the promotion of second-language programs in Asian languages on the grounds of economic competitiveness (Allan and Hill 1995).

Canada   Being closer to Europe than is Australia, North America saw a longer buildup of European settlements. French and British fishermen worked the shores of what is now Maritime Canada in the mid-sixteenth century. The advent of the fur trade in the early years of the seventeenth century led to the first French settlement on the Saint Lawrence River. To the south, English settlements grew steadily in number; their leaders began to assert claim to land occupied by the French. In 1763, the French-Indian War in the New World and the Seven Year War in the Old World ended with the Treaty of Paris, which ceded all French territory in North America to the British crown. New France, now Québec, with approximately seventy thousand French inhabitants, became a British colony. When the thirteen U.S. colonies declared independence from Britain in 1776, British loyalists streamed north into what would become Canada, with a British legal system uniformly imposed by the Constitution Act of 1791. The Constitution Act of 1841 provided the legal framework for the Dominion of Canada, which federated in 1867 (see Creighton 1957).

Throughout the period of colonization, French and British colonizers uprooted and fought with native populations, siding at times with one tribe or band against another. As in the United States, Native Canadian and Inuit populations were displaced to restricted landholdings, called "reserves." Also as in the United States, many of the affairs of Canada's "status" Indians, as defined by the Indian Act of 1867, came under the direct jurisdiction of the federal, rather than provincial governments. In practice, the federal and provincial governments often worked together in the matter of education.

Historically, the separation of indigenous children from their parents has been a primary strategy aimed at the destruction of native cultures and assimilation of native people into the dominant culture of the colonizing forces. As noted by an early Indian commissioner for the province of British Columbia, the removal of Native Canadian children from their families and communities to residential schools was required to

> . . . interfere materially with irregular habits and customs incident to life in the wigwam, the destruction of which is so necessary ere the much desired higher life can be obtained.[1]

Although these policies created generations of personal pain and cultural displacement, they did not, in the end, result in the obliteration of native cultures— not in Canada, nor in Australia or the United States.

Prior to confederation, immigrants to Canada came primarily from the United States and the British Isles. In the late nineteenth century, westward expansion became the goal of Canada's government, and immigrants from all over Europe were urged to take advantage of "the last best west" (Creighton 1957, 387). Between 1901 and 1911, the population of Canada rose from just over 5 million to more than 7 million. In that year, Canadians of British and French descent totaled 83 percent of the population, down from 92 percent in 1871, the year of the first census. In addition to native people, Canada now included a sizable minority of non-English- and non-French-speaking Europeans, including Germans, Scandinavians, Ukrainians, Russians, Austrians, Italians, and Poles. Many of the new European migrants settled in ethnic clusters in the Prairie Provinces (413).

On the west coast, especially in British Columbia, immigrants of the late nineteenth and early twentieth century included Chinese gold-miner and railroad workers and Japanese who engaged in fishing, farming, and small business. In 1923, following similar actions in the United States and Australia, Canada passed a law restricting Asian immigration. Despite such efforts, however, by the early years of this century, identifiable Asian communities with school-aged children were established in British Columbia. Nearly twenty-five hundred Japanese-Canadian children were enrolled in the province's schools in 1925; five years later, enrollments peaked at over four thousand (Ashworth 1979, 99). In towns across the province, struggles over access to schooling were, if not the most violent, perhaps the most revealing incidents of the depths of

---

[1]From the 1876 annual report of I. W. Powell, Indian Commissioner in Victoria, quoted in Ashworth (1979, 11–12).

racial antipathy within the white communities. Between 1901 and 1925, there was repeated public agitation by non-Asian residents of Victoria and Vancouver to segregate Chinese and Japanese children from the general school population on grounds of morals, hygiene, and general style of life. In 1907, the Victoria schools resisted efforts by young Chinese emigrants, ages 9 to 16, to enroll. In contrast, public pressure to exclude the more numerous Japanese children from public schooling was generally opposed by school officials in Vancouver and Victoria, and so proved unsuccessful (99). During World War II, however, the Japanese-Canadian population of British Columbia suffered the same fate as Japanese Americans in the United States: loss of home and livelihood, and relocation to prison camps in the interior.

Twenty years after World War II, multiculturalism as a concept and policy emerged in Canada. Although the Canadian experience bears certain similarities to those of Australia and the United States, the development of French–English bilingualism, which preceded multiculturalism, uniquely marks the Canadian multicultural context and subsequent policies. In terms of our discussion, Francophone Canadians are the "defining minority" of multicultural policy in Canada. In 1963, Prime Minister Lester Pearson created the Royal Commission on Bilingualism and Biculturalism. The mandate of the commission was to recommend

> . . . the measures to be taken in order that the Canadian Confederation may develop according to the principle of equality between its two founding peoples, taking into account the contribution of other ethnic groups to the enrichment of Canada. (quoted in Rocher 1984, 42)

The recommendations of the commission and the acknowledgment of more than a century of inconsistent recognition of the rights of Francophone Canadians outside of Quebec led in 1969 to the Official Languages Act, which recognized the equal currency of English and French in government business. Thereafter, all discussions of multiculturalism in Canada have included implicit and explicit recognition of the primacy of French and English, the languages of the two "charter" groups of Canada.

As in Australia, the first official reference to multiculturalism came in a speech by a government minister. In the Canadian case, it was Prime Minister Pierre Trudeau addressing parliament in 1971. The occasion was the introduction of the fourth volume of the Report of the Royal Commission, which had been completed a year earlier. This volume specifically addressed linguistic and cultural affairs of the non-Anglo, non-French populations of Canada. The prime minister submitted the fourth volume to parliament with the discourse that was to define Canada's new policy of multiculturalism within bilingualism:

> . . . although there are two official languages, there is no official culture, nor does any ethnic group take precedence over any other. No citizen or group of citizens is other than Canadian, and all should be treated fairly. The Royal Commission was guided by the belief that adherence to one's ethnic group is influenced not so much by one's origin or mother tongue as by one's sense of belonging to the group, and by what the Commission calls the group's "collec-

tive will to exist." The government shares this belief. . . . A policy of multicul-turalism within a bilingual framework commends itself as the most suitable means of assuring the cultural freedom of Canadians.[2]

The concept of "multiculturalism within bilingualism" raised opposition among almost all ethnic groups in Canada. For Francophones, multicultural-ism diluted the hard-fought gains of French Canadians in securing rights to the use of the French language outside of Québec. The policy, for many, repre-sented "a large step backwards" (Rocher 1984, 46).

Native Canadians responded to the policy statement with a proclamation entitled *Indian Control of Indian Education* (National Indian Brotherhood 1972). The statement called for greater control by and accountability to Indian bands of the schools that educate Indian children. It also called urgently for educa-tion in native languages (141). Immigrant linguistic minorities urged recogni-tion for a support of their own "heritage" languages, above and beyond those of the two official languages. With 16 percent of Canadians in 1996 reporting a mother tongue other than English or French, compared to 23 percent report-ing French, the role of "heritage" languages has become highly visible in Canadian debates about multicultural policies. At the same time, claims for protection of "heritage" languages have been seen as problematic to Fran-cophones, who have argued for special language rights for French as one of the "charter" languages.

Within this context of debate, the Canadian "multiculturalism within bilingualism" policy went forward, backed by $200 million in funding between 1971 and 1987 "for specific initiatives in language and cultural maintenance" (Fleras and Elliott 1992, 74). In 1972, a directorate for multicul-turalism was created within the Department of the Secretary of State; a Min-istry of Multiculturalism was created in 1973. A council now called the Canadian Ethnocultural Council was established in 1973 to bring together as an advisory group to government a coalition of thirty-seven national ethnic organizations (74).

The meaning of "charter groups" in the Canadian context took on a new flavor with the passage of the Constitution Act of 1982. The act included the Canadian Charter of Rights and Freedoms, which provides substantial support and protection for both of the official or "charter" languages, including the right to education in either language no matter where in Canada one lives. The charter has had other, far-reaching impacts on the trajectory of multicultural-ism in Canada. Ratification of the charter has entailed new negotiations between the federal government and Native Canadians, resulting among other outcomes in the devolution of authority over schooling. For example, the four-teen Native Canadian bands and tribal councils that were party to the Yukon First Nations Self-Government Act of 1994 are granted legislative authority to provide "programs and services for citizens of the first nation in relation to

---

[2]Pierre Elliott Trudeau, House of Commons debates, 8 October 1971. Reproduced in Palmer (1975, 136).

their spiritual and cultural beliefs and practices" (Department of Justice of Canada). In the western provinces that have sizable First Nations populations, including Saskatchewan, Manitoba, and British Columbia, provincial education authorities have interpreted the federal policies of bilingualism and multiculturalism as support for bilingual education in Aboriginal languages and English, and for educational programs aimed at cultural maintenance for First Nations children (Mallea 1989, 60–62; Moodley 1995, 804).

In 1988, the Parliament of Canada passed the Canadian Multiculturalism Act, which reinforced the intent of government to "preserve and enhance the use of languages other than English and French, while strengthening the status and use of the official languages of Canada" (Department of Justice of Canada). The preamble acknowledges that Canada is a signatory to the International Convention on the Elimination of All Forms of Racial Discrimination and states that the government

> ... recognizes the diversity of Canadians as regards race, national or ethnic origin, colour and religion as a fundamental characteristic of Canadian society and is committed to a policy of multiculturalism designed to preserve and enhance the multicultural heritage of Canadians while working to achieve the equality of all Canadians in the economic, social, cultural and political life of Canada (ch. C-18.7)

The act entails an annual report to the Minister of Multiculturalism and provides ideological support for long-standing practices at the provincial level to provide educational and cultural support for "heritage" as well as official language groups. One outcome of the act is the continuing vitality of "heritage" language programs in schools across Canada (Moodley 1995, 804).

Canadian multicultural policies, like the country itself, carry the distinctive marks of bilingualism and ideological tolerance. In their 1992 monograph, Fleras and Elliott observe that the multicultural policy is viewed by the populace as "quintessentially Canadian":

> Our commitment to multicultural policies is viewed by many at home and abroad as a dimension of our national identity that purportedly sets us apart from the United States. Rightly or wrongly, we have internalized a set of images about ourselves as a tolerant and open people, and look askance at the American melting pot as less enlightened than the Canadian mosaic. (69)

Before and since the implementation of the Multiculturalism Act, the public discourse on multiculturalism in Canada has evoked the image of a mosaic, in which diversity composes the national picture. Like all metaphors, it only approximates reality, but the reality nonetheless differs from the extreme individualism that characterizes U.S. perspectives.

United States   Ideologies of white or European racial superiority without question have influenced the history of interactions between colonizers and indigenous people in all three of the case countries but perhaps nowhere so clearly and painfully as in the United States, where the struggles of African Americans for full political and economic rights have centrally defined the politics of culture. Black Americans, "America's permanent dilemma" (Glazer

TABLE 5.2 Canadian Demographics

	Number	Percent of total
Total population	28,528,125	100
Aborigines	799,005	3
Francophones	6,636,660	23
Anglophones	16,890,615	59
Speakers of non-official languages	4,598,285	16

Source: Statistics Canada (1996)   These are selected sub-population numbers.

1997, 90), are the defining minority in the politics of U.S. multiculturalism. Racialist beliefs, however, have also determined the cultural frameworks in which immigrants who are not white have created communities and forged individual lives. The cultural expression and civic participation of "nonwhite" emigrants, including those from Asia, have been historically restricted; demands for inclusion by Asian immigrants have contributed to the dynamics of multiculturalism. The largest language minority, Hispanics, have often been viewed through racialist lenses, while language stands out as a defining issue.

Seeking religious and political asylum, European immigrants were the first to settle in what currently constitutes the United States of America. Many European immigrants settled in ethnic neighborhoods, until through assimilation and improved political and economic conditions they have become the majority culture in the United States. Unlike white ethnic groups, African Americans primarily came to the United States as slaves during the seventeenth and eighteenth centuries. Andrew Billingsley (1968) states four main reasons that black immigrants were different from any other groups: (1) Blacks came with norms and values that were different from those of the European immigrants and their American masters; (2) they were made up of many different tribes, with different languages, cultures, and traditions; (3) in the beginning, they came without women; and (4) they came as slaves. In 1865, the Southern states in the United States enacted "black codes," that limited voting rights, working rights, and education opportunities for blacks. They could not own land, work in commerce, or get an education past the sixth grade. While the first Civil Rights Act of 1866 abolished the black codes and the Thirteenth and Fourteenth Amendments to the Constitution freed the slaves and guaranteed them rights regardless of race, color, or creed, racial isolation and discrimination against blacks continued well into the twentieth century. Even since the abolishment of slavery, the cultural discontinuities and socioeconomic oppression experienced by African Americans in the twentieth century continue to define issues of race and ethnicity in social, political and cultural policy in the United States.

The seemingly unending stream of European immigrants to North America eventually overpowered the indigenous cultures that thrived on this continent well before the arrival of the earliest white settlers. While many tribes of Native Americans had their own alphabets and most had governing bodies, they were treated as savages by the white settlers and forced off their lands inch by inch as the European expansion moved westward (Brown 1971). It was not until the 1960s that the demand for self-determination by Native Americans began to be recognized by the U.S. government. President John Kennedy's secretary of the Interior, Stewart Udall, appointed a Taskforce on Indian Affairs, which recommended in 1961 that Native Americans be given full citizenship and self-sufficiency. Education became a central issue in the struggle for self-determination with the release of a 1969 Senate committee report titled *Indian Education: A National Tragedy—A National Challenge.* The congressional debates that resulted from the report led to the Indian Education Act of 1972, which created the Office of Indian Education. In 1975, the Indian Self-Determination and Education Assistance Act gave tribes the power to contract with the federal government to run their own education and health programs. Despite these improvements in Native American self-determination, there was no accompanying economic policy to improve the self-sufficiency of Native Americans isolated on reservations, nor was there a larger strategic plan to address Native American culture in the existing cultural framework in the United States.

Like Native Americans, Hispanics have been part of the U.S. cultural fabric from the beginning. Following the Mexican-American War in 1848, discrimination against Mexicans increased. In most of the American Southwest, property restrictions, voting restrictions, and laws limiting the rights of Mexican Americans were imposed by U.S. settlers. In addition, discrimination against migrant workers from Mexico and Central America has further defined Hispanic cultural policy in the United States.

Both Hispanics and Asian immigrants fought to protect their civil rights under the Fourteenth Amendment, primarily in the federal courts. Unequal access to education has been the source of ongoing discrimination against these groups. Asians first came to the United States as invited guest workers to build the transcontinental railroad and work in the mining industries. When the work ended, Asian immigrants became unwelcome, and harsh limits were placed on emigration from Asian countries. In addition, laws such as the California Land Laws of 1913 and 1920 prevented first-generation Japanese Americans from owning land or even farming it. While Title IV of the Civil Rights Act of 1964 required school districts to provide bilingual education for children unable to understand English, it was not enforced with much rigor in the Southwest or California before the Supreme Court decision in *Lau v. Nichols* (414 U.S. 563) in 1974. The *Lau* decision obligated schools to: (1) identify students using a language other than English as a primary language; (2) provide special services when necessary for these students; and (3) employ instructors who speak languages spoken by the children having language difficulties.

In *The Rise of the Unmeltable Ethnics,* Novak (1971) predicts an end to the success of the great American melting pot strategy in which new and old emigrants shed their ethnic identities to become members of a new, yet often undefined, American culture. Written well before the second largest emigration wave in U.S. history, Novak's premonition does not address the impact of race and color on the melting pot theory, focusing instead on issues of social class, gender, religion, and culture. According to Novak, identification with an ethnic

TABLE 5.3 United States Demographics

	Number	Percent of total
Total population	270,933,000	100
Blacks	34,525,000	12.7
Native Americans, Eskimos and Aleuts	2,369,000	0.9
People of Hispanic origin*	30,769,000	11.4
Asians and Pacific Islanders	10,504,000	3.9
Whites	223,535,000	82.5

*"Hispanic origin" is a category which includes both blacks and whites.
Source: U.S. Census Bureau, 1999

group is a source of values, ideas, and perceptions that give shape to personal action and its significance. Novak contends that historically, America has assimilated individuals, but it has not successfully assimilated groups. It is the individual's identification with group ethnicity, Novak argues, that inspires the struggle for power and privilege in society.

Today, 81 percent of all new legal and illegal immigrants to the United States are from Latin America, the Caribbean, and Asia, contrasting with pre-World War II, when 70 percent came from Europe (Suárez-Orozco and Suárez-Orozco 1995). Throughout U.S. history, immigrants have been met with hostility by the already resident population. However, conflicts around European ethnicities have not had the tenacity of conflict over skin color.

The 1996 Republican Party platform on immigration was heavily influenced by California's Proposition 187, a statewide ballot initiative that called for denying social services to illegal immigrants. According to Tim Weiner, the feeling among the general public was that "emigration is out of control; our borders have fallen" (Suárez-Orozco and Suárez-Orozco 1995, 23). Traditional explanations for an increase in xenophobic sentiment are often based on the Marxist-Weberian model in which ethnicity becomes a basis for social differentiation in times of economic hardship. The economic recession of the early 1990s disproportionately affected states with large immigrant populations such as California, Texas, and Florida, and thus the social costs of immigration became political fodder for politicians looking for salient campaign issues. Immigrants from Southern, Eastern, and Central Europe at the turn of the century were subject to similar xenophobic ideology officially set forth in the Immigration Act of 1924. This act discriminated against these groups on the basis of their "inferior intellect," established through early forays into the pseudoscience of eugenics (Suárez-Orozco and Suárez-Orozco 1995).

Federal welfare legislation proposed in 1996 stripped even legal immigrants of some social programs, and a measure modeled on California's Proposition 187 would have allowed states to keep the children of illegal immigrants out of their schools (*Economist* 1997). Although the proposed legislation did not pass, public fear of ethnic minorities continues to center on their perceived lack of contribution to the local economy and their unwillingness to assimilate.

While the civil rights movement highlighted the need for greater minority group participation in American society, its impetus did not originate in the federal government or stem from a federally sponsored policy report. Instead, many of the demands put forth by civil rights leaders in the 1960s and early 1970s were eventually codified or mandated as executive orders of the president. In addition, the United States can point to the Constitution, court decisions, and legislative acts as examples of policies that promote the multicultural perspective (Ramsey, Vold, and Williams 1989).

According to Eugene García (1994), former director of the Office of Bilingual Education and Minority Languages Affairs in the U.S. Department of Education, rationales for changes in national education policy are often related to crisis intervention. García believes the evolution of national policy for linguistically and culturally diverse peoples in the United States is driven by some of this same rationale. Primary legislation addressing the needs of linguistically and culturally diverse groups, such as Title I and Title VII of the Elementary and Secondary Education Act, were limited responses to perceived national crises in U.S. education. Policies affecting these groups have suffered from limited resources and sporadic support at the national level (U.S. House of Representatives 1974).

Although it has been the subject of heated controversy, federal support for bilingual education is as close as the United States comes to a federal multicultural policy. As in Canada and Australia, laws and programs supporting language education have changed in their focus and ideology since they were first implemented in the late 1960s. Federal support for bilingual education began under Title VII of the Elementary and Secondary Education Act in 1968. Proposing modest fiscal outlays, the initial bill received substantial bipartisan support (Ovando and Collier 1998, 40). Appropriations increased through the 1970s and were cut almost in half during the years of Ronald Reagan's administration. The basic rationale and aims have also changed over time. By the late 1970s, Title VII included modest support for English-speaking children to participate in bilingual education, a small step toward multiculturalism. In the conservative backlash of the 1980s and into the 1990s, however, federal support for bilingual education has been encompassed by the rhetoric of academic competition and excellence (43–44).

In terms, however, of the needs and interests of the defining minority in the United States, federal action has been confined to remediation and protection, rather than support and development. Federal actions in support of African Americans in the courts, Congress, and the White House have aimed to open up individual opportunities. Beginning with the *Brown v. Board of Education* decision of 1954, which ruled that separate schools could never be equal, and continuing with the 1968 education act, the United States has a long and significant history of efforts to neutralize the effects of racism within the educational system. What is lacking, however, is an effort to capture in policy a national consensus on the meaning and value of being a multicultural nation. As a nation, we in the United States continue to view culture and multiculturalism as the property of individuals rather than society as a whole.

Federal Policies and Multiculturalism

The previous section has shown, in broad overview, the differing ethnolinguistic politics of culture among the three case countries. Despite the temporal, and some might argue, moral authority of their claims, the cultural politics of indigenous populations of Australia, Canada, and the United States are little encompassed in the larger public discourse on multiculturalism. In the United States, the enduring legacy of slavery and racism has uniquely marked public discourse on multiculturalism. Canadian debate, in contrast, is defined specifically by the politics of bilingualism. For Australia, multiculturalism is treated largely as an issue of immigration and language.

It is, or should be, humbling to promoters of multiculturalism in the United States to reflect on the multicultural policies of Australia and Canada. Despite its longer history of activism in support of multiculturalism, the United States has no laws of such overarching authority. Despite a broader and deeper weight of case law supporting the rights of ethnic and linguistic minorities, the United States has reached no official consensus on the value and meaning of multiculturalism as has Canada and Australia. The real puzzle here, from a comparative perspective, is not why such policies exist in other places but why they do not in the United States.

Multiculturalism is poorly understood by the American public and thus easily caricatured by opponents as a strategy to undermine our common culture and an attempt to politicize education, in particular, with fashionable "politically correct" attitudes. Current examples of multiculturalism in education in the United States run the gamut from promoting a simplistic, historically suspect brand of identity politics to the most radical examples of antiracist education. In addition, current examples of multiculturalism in practice offer no overarching ideology for uniting ethnic minority groups around shared interests. There may be a need, therefore, to bring together a wider range of participants to the discussion on what it means to build a multicultural society for the twenty-first century. The need for renewing dialogue on multiculturalism is particularly pressing as the current debate seems to polarize groups around ideological extremes while there may in fact be a great deal of common ground.

Two additional avenues explaining the multicultural policy void in the United States suggest themselves: the legal-juridical, and the political-cultural contexts. It is tempting—and perhaps not entirely untrue—to argue that parliamentary systems can be more accommodating of multiculturalism than presidential systems. Implicit to parliamentary democracies is the acceptance of the people choosing a group that in turn chooses a leader. It is conceivable that this political process naturalizes an acceptance of group identities that is evidently lacking in the United States. At a more pragmatic level, however, the legal rather than the political system of the United States constantly reinforces individual over group identities. The laws of the United States have evolved under constitutional authority for over two hundred years, in contrast to the judicial systems of Canada and Australia, which have historically rested in common law. The U.S. Constitution—especially the Bill of Rights—is a powerful mechanism for upholding the equality of individuals. It contains only the thinnest of grounds, however, for supporting the value of group identities. The legal system of Canada, of course, now combines constitutional with common law, making it a most intriguing hybrid and one well worth study by its neighbor to the south.

The political individualism of the U.S. Constitution has over time interacted with and reinforced the very "American" (in the U.S. sense) quality of laissez-faire economic individualism. The extreme individualism of the political culture of the United States makes it difficult to even talk meaningfully about multiculturalism. Culture, like capital, is viewed as a property of individuals that can either enhance or retard their personal progress. In fact, for those of the dominant group, culture is largely invisible and irrelevant as a fact of individual life.

What the United States has, if not in abundance, then at least in countable measure, are laws and policies that aim to nullify any deleterious effects of "having a culture." What the United States does not, as a nation, possess is a common awareness of the centrality of cultures to human life. According to Walzer (1994), the value Americans place on individualism is the greatest enemy of multiculturalism. As individuals focus on the private pursuit of happiness through the exercise of basic American values, such as freedom and choice, they disengage from cultural association and identity. Walzer believes that "if we want the mutual reinforcements of community and individuality to work effectively for everyone, we will have to act politically to make them effective" (189). Such work would embody the principle of "communitarian ethics" outlined by Bull and colleagues (1992) in their discussion of the ethics of multiculturalism and bilingualism.

There is room, in other words, for an active political strategy to mobilize, organize, and, under some circumstances, subsidize groups to engage in civil discourse around the replacement of old emphases on individualism with a new commitment to multiculturalism through community activism. President Bill Clinton's initiative on race has begun such a dialogue, but after almost two years, there still does not appear to be consensus on what the outcomes should be. Unlike the promotion of multicultural policy by leadership in Canada and Australia, the president's initiative on race continues to focus the U.S. discussion on ethnic group differences rather than how the rich history of cultural diversity in the United States adds value to society.

Dewey (1916) tells us that democracy is the struggle that happens when we attempt to make dialogue. Currently, our diversity has shed light primarily on how little different cultural and ethnic groups know about each other, which illustrates the challenge posed by reassociating with each other in conversation around a common national identity. Affirmative action programs that remedy underemployment, child subsidies, family-friendly tax credits, charter schools designed and run by teachers and parents, and locally owned community revitalization projects are examples of indirect government intervention promoting the value of community and multiculturalism over individualism. The creation of a new, common culture that truly values the contributions diversity can make to its development will require the political commitment that only dialogue between the critics and proponents of multiculturalism can produce. As Giroux (1996) argues, our first challenge is to find common ground for such dialogue.

STUDY QUESTIONS

1. What has been similar and different about the legal status of the native populations of Australia, Canada, and the United States?
2. What is the relationship between immigration policies and multiculturalism in the three countries?
3. How have the different "defining minorities" in the three countries created differences in debates and actions related to multiculturalism?
4. What are the similarities and differences between the federal multicultural policies of Australia and Canada?
5. What seem to be the practical impacts of federal multicultural policies such as those of Australia and Canada?
6. In your view, why has a federal multicultural policy not been constructed in the United States? Do you believe that this might occur in the future?
7. If you could design a federal multicultural policy for the United States (or another country), what would be its main points?

KEY CONCEPTS

Federalism

Immigration policy

Language policy

Cultural policy

Multicultural policy

Bilingualism

Defining minorities

Parliamentary system

Common law

Constitution

REFERENCES

Allan, R., and B. Hill. 1995. Multicultural education in Australia: Historical developments and current status. In *Handbook of research on multicultural education*, ed. J. A. Banks and C. A. M. Banks, (763–777. New York: Macmillan.

Ashworth, M. 1979. *The forces which shaped them: A history of the education of minority group children in British Columbia*. Vancouver, B.C.: New Star Books Ltd.

Ball, J. 1990. *Politics and policymaking in education*. London: Routledge.

Banks, J. 1993. Multicultural education: Progress and prospects. *Phi Delta Kappan* 75 (1)(September):21–28.

Bhola, H. S. 1975. The design of (educational) policy: Directing and harnessing social power for social organization. *Viewpoints: Bulletin of the School of Education, Indiana University* 51 (3)(May):1–16.

Bibby, W. 1987. Bilingualism and multiculturalism: A national reading. In *Ethnic demography and ecology*, ed. L. Driedger, 158–169. Toronto: Copp Clark Publications.

Billingsley, A. 1968. *Black families in white America.* Englewood Cliffs, N.J.: Prentice-Hall.

Brown, J. 1971. *Old frontiers.* New York: Arno Press.

Bull, B. L., R. T. Fruehling, and V. Chattergy. 1992. *The ethics of multicultural and bilingual education.* New York: Teachers College Press.

Bullivant, B. 1984. *Pluralism: Cultural maintenance and evolution.* Avon, England: Multilingual Matters.

Burnaby, B. 1988. Language in native education in Canada. In *International handbook of bilingualism and bilingual education*, ed. C. B. Paulston, 141–162. New York: Greenwood Press.

Census Australia. 1996. Available from *www.abs.gov.au/websitedbs/d3310108infsf/ASCG/.* Internet. Accessed 30 January 1999.

Challenge of change, The. *Instructor* January 1993, 34–41.

Creighton, D. 1957. *Dominion of the north: A history of Canada.* Toronto: Macmillan Company of Canada, Ltd.

Davies, S., and N. Guppy. 1997. Globalization and education reforms in Anglo-American democracies. *Comparative Education Review* 41(4):435–459.

Dewey, J. 1916. *Democracy and education: An introduction to the philosophy of education.* New York: The MacMillan Company.

Department of Justice of Canada. n.d. *Consolidated statutes.* Available from *http://canada.justice.gc.ca/STABLE/EN/Laws/Chap/index.html.* Internet. Accessed 27 January 1999.

Economist. Immigration: Turn of the Tide (Sept. 27, 1997) vol. 22.

Fleras, A., and J. L. Elliott. 1992. *The challenge of diversity: Multiculturism in Canada.* Scarborough, Ont.: Nelson, Canada.

Foster, L. E. 1988. *Diversity and multicultural education: A sociological perspective.* Sydney: Allen & Unwin.

Galbally, F. 1978, May. *Migrant services and programs: Report of the review of post-arrival programs and services for migrants.* Canberra: Australian Government Publishing Service.

García, E. 1994, March. The impact of linguistic and cultural diversity on *America's schools: A need for new policy.* Paper presented at the annual meeting of the American Educational Research Association, New Orleans.

Genevese, F. 1988. The Canadian second language immersion program. In *International handbook of bilingualism and bilingual education*, ed. C. B. Paulston, 163–184. New York: Greenwood Press.

Giroux, H. 1996. *Living dangerously: Multiculturalism and the politics of difference.* New York: Peter Lang.

Gitlin, T. 1995. *The twilight of common dreams.* New York: Metropolitan Books.

Glazer, N. 1997. *We are all multiculturalists now.* Cambridge: Harvard University Press.

Grant, C., and C. Sleeter. 1989. *Turning on learning: Five approaches for multicultural teaching plans for race, class, gender, and disability.* Columbus, Ohio: Merrill.

Gutmann, A., and C. Taylor. 1992. *Multiculturalism and the politics of recognition.* Princeton: Princeton University Press.

Lo Bianco, J. 1988. Multiculturalism and the national policy on languages. *Journal of Intercultural Studies* 9(1):25–38.

Luketic, J., M. Breda, and D. Ackerman. 1996. Television: Black and white or color. Comparing Canadian and Australian multicultural broadcasting initiatives. *Pacific Waves.* Available from *http://edward.cprost.sfu.ca/438/mltcult.html@beginnings.* Internet. Accessed 12 January 1999.

Mallea, J. R. 1989. *Schooling in a plural Canada*. Clevedon, U.K.: Multilingual Matters Ltd.

Martel, A. 1984. Minority-majority relations in second language education and the new Canadian Charter of Rights and Freedoms. *Educational Research Quarterly*. Special issue, *Culture, language, education*, ed. C. Ovando. 8(4):113–121.

McCarthy, C. 1998. *The uses of culture: Education and the limits of ethnic affiliation*. New York: Routledge.

McLellan, J. and A. Richmond. 1994. Multiculturalism in crisis: A postmodern perspective on Canada. *Ethnic and Racial Studies* 17(4):662–683.

Miller, J. 1985. *Koori: A will to win*. North Ryde, New South Wales: Angus & Robertson Publishers.

Moodley, K. A. 1985. *Multicultural education in Canada: Historical development and current status. Handbook of research on multicultural education*, ed. J. E. Banks and C. A. M. Banks, 801–820. New York: Macmillan.

National Indian Brotherhood. 1972. *Indian control of Indian education*. Policy paper presented to the Minister of Indian Affairs and Northern Development, Ottawa. Reprinted in J. R. Mallea and J. C. Yound, eds., *Cultural diversity and Canadian education: Issues and innovations* (Ottawa: Carleton University Press 1984), 131–149.

Novak, M. 1971. *The rise of the unmeltable ethnics*. New York: Macmillan.

Office of Multicultural Affairs. 1989. *National agenda for a multicultural Australia*. Canberra: Australian Government Printing Office.

Ovando, C. J., and V. P. Collier, 1998. *Bilingual and ESL classrooms: Teaching in multicultural contexts*. Boston: McGraw-Hill.

Palmer, H., ed. 1975. *Immigration and the rise of multiculturalism*. Vancouver, B.C.: Copp Clark Ltd.

Pressman, J., and L. Widavsky. 1984. *Implementation*. Berkeley: University of California Press.

Ragin, C. 1987. *The comparative method*. Berkeley: University of California Press.

Ramsey, P., E. Vold, and L. Williams. 1989. *Multicultural education: A sourcebook*. New York: Garland Publishing.

Ray, D., and D. Poonwassie. 1992. *Education and cultural differences*. New York: Garland Publishing.

Raz, J. 1994. Multiculturalism: A liberal perspective. *Dissent* 41 (winter):69.

Rocher, G. 1984. The ambiguities of a bilingual and multicultural Canada. *Cultural Diversity and Canadian Education*, ed. J. R. Mallea and J. C. Young, 41–47. Ottawa: Carleton University Press.

Schlesinger, A. 1992. *The disuniting of America*. New York: Norton.

Smolicz, J. 1981. Cultural pluralism and educational policy: In search of stable multiculturalism. *Australian Journal of Education* 25(2):121–145.

Sowell, T. 1993. *Inside American education*. New York: Free Press.

Statistics Canada. 1996. *1996 Census*. Available from *http://www.statcan.ca/english/census96/list.htm*. Internet. Accessed 27 January 1999.

Suárez-Orozco, C., and M. Suárez-Orozco. 1995. *Transformations: Immigration, family life, and achievement motivation among Latino adolescents*. Stanford, Calif.: Stanford University Press.

Takaki, R. 1993. *A different mirror: A history of multicultural America*, 417. Boston: Little, Brown.

U.S. House of Representatives. 1996. *A compilation of federal education laws as amended through December 31, 1974*. Washington, D.C.: U.S. Government Printing Office.

U.S. Census Bureau. 1999. *Population estimates, November 1998*. Available from *http://www.census.gov*. Internet. Accessed 2 February 1999.

Walzer, M. 1994. Multiculturalism and individualism. *Dissent* 2(27):185–191.

PART TWO

Teachers and Students Caught in the Cross Fire: Language Politics, U.S.-Mexico Border Realities, "Model Minorities," and Reaching Out to Minority Communities

James Crawford

*W*ith virtually no pedagogical experience to draw upon, the Bilingual Education Act of 1968 authorized a radical departure from traditional approaches to educating language-minority students. Nevertheless, it enjoyed broad support, passing the U.S. Congress without a single dissenting vote. Thirty years later, now that the research has established the benefits of well-designed bilingual programs, the pedagogy faces such a relentless attack that its future seems in doubt. What accounts for the erosion of bilingual education's political base and public sympathy? In exploring answers to this question, the chapter will analyze the peculiar tradition of language rights—or lack thereof—in the United States. It will show why bilingual education came to be dominated by a paradigm of ethnic assimilation rather than of self-determination. It will explain how the field's institutionalization has isolated it from a natural constituency: language-minority parents and communities. Finally, it will analyze prospects for the program's survival in a period of political adversity.

CHAPTER 6

Language Politics in the United States

The Paradox of Bilingual Education[*]

James Crawford
Independent Scholar

Enacted at the apex of the Great Society, the Bilingual Education Act was passed by Congress and signed into law by President Lyndon B. Johnson without a single voice raised in dissent. Americans have spent the past thirty years debating what it was meant to accomplish. Was this 1968 law intended primarily to assimilate limited-English-proficient (LEP) children more efficiently, to teach them English as rapidly as possible, to encourage bilingualism and biliteracy, to remedy academic underachievement and high dropout rates, to raise the self-esteem of minority students, to promote social equality, or to pursue all of these goals simultaneously? The bill's legislative history provides no definitive answer.

It is hardly an idle question. Whether to continue teaching LEP students in two languages is now a matter of public debate throughout the United States. Since the mid-1980s, critics have won increasing support for the contention that this experiment, while well-intentioned, has failed to meet expectations. Now, in the late 1990s, policy makers are seriously considering demands to limit or even dismantle the program. California voters have already chosen the latter course. Proposition 227, a ballot initiative approved in June 1998, eliminates most native-language instruction in a state with 40 percent of the nation's LEP students.[1] The future of bilingual education is suddenly in doubt.

Ironically, research provides considerably more support for bilingual approaches today than it did in 1968, when few program models existed and

---

[1]Proposition 227 was adopted on a vote of 61 percent to 39 percent. Immediately thereafter, the Mexican American Legal Defense and Educational Fund; Multicultural Education, Training and Advocacy, Inc.; American Civil Liberties Union; and other advocates filed suit to block the initiative statute on civil rights and constitutional grounds. A federal district judge in San Francisco declined, however, to order a preliminary injunction. Although the lawsuit continued, Proposition 227 took effect as scheduled on August 2, 1998.

[*]Copyright © 1998 by James Crawford. All rights reserved.

almost none had been evaluated. What seemed reasonable in theory—that investing in children's native-language development should ultimately pay cognitive and academic dividends—has now been borne out in pedagogical practice. Not that success has been universal for all approaches labeled "bilingual." Nor has research proved conclusively, beyond a reasonable doubt, their superiority over English-only methodologies for all children in all contexts. By a more reasonable standard, however, a preponderance of the evidence favors the conclusion that well-designed bilingual programs can produce high levels of school achievement over the long term, at no cost to English acquisition, among students from disempowered groups (see, e.g., Ramírez, Yven, and Ramey 1991; Willig 1985; Greene 1998).

Pedagogically speaking, these research findings are excellent news. They confirm that developing fluent bilingualism and cultivating academic excellence are complementary, rather than contradictory, goals. Sacrificing LEP students' native language is unnecessary to teach them effectively in English. Moreover, the findings suggest that while language is not the only barrier to school success for these children, approaches that stress native-language instruction can be helpful in overcoming other obstacles such as poverty, family illiteracy, and social stigmas associated with minority status. These challenges are formidable, to be sure, requiring schools to replicate effective program models, adapt them to local conditions, train and retrain teachers, develop curriculum and materials, involve parents, and pay attention to a host of other practical details. Yet they are hardly insuperable—given a public commitment to improve programs for English learners.

Politically speaking, however, the research findings are less encouraging. They support an educational rationale for bilingual instruction that is both complex and counterintuitive to members of the public. They also imply a sociopolitical goal that few Americans are inclined to endorse: the legitimation of "bilingualism" in public contexts. Indeed, since the mid-1980s, many U.S. voters have reacted defensively against the racial, cultural, and language diversity brought by rising levels of immigration. A nationwide campaign for "the legal protection of English" has led to the passage of nineteen state laws designating English as the sole language of government.[2] Immigrant children's progress in acquiring English is now regarded as a matter of urgency, not only by many Anglo-Americans but also by a significant number of immigrant parents, hence the growing popularity of nostrums like "structured immersion" and "sheltered English," whose enthusiasts promise short-cuts to English proficiency. Conversely, bilingual approaches that feature a more gradual transition to the mainstream are vulnerable to legislative restrictions. In addition to Proposition 227, bills have been proposed in various states and localities, as well as the U.S. Congress, to impose arbitrary time limits on a child's enrollment in bilingual education (or, in some cases, in *any* special program to address limited English proficiency).

[2]Three states had done so previously. In 1998, after a ten-year battle, Arizona's Article XXVIII was struck down by the state's supreme court as a violation of the First Amendment. This left a total of twenty-one states with active laws designating English as the official language.

To understand how we arrived at this juncture, it is necessary to analyze the historical roots of today's language attitudes. Ethnic diversity is hardly a recent phenomenon in this country. Nor is bilingual education. How have Americans thought about and coped with these issues previously? How have current policies on language-minority education evolved? How are future ones likely to be determined?

Deconstructing Title VII

Let's begin by considering our original question. Was the Bilingual Education Act (also known as Title VII of the Elementary and Secondary Education Act) intended as an

- *antipoverty initiative* to overcome the educational disadvantages of language-minority students—that is, to remedy the problem of limited English proficiency?
- *antidiscrimination measure* to open up the curriculum for LEP students—that is, to guarantee their right to equal educational opportunity?
- *experiment in multicultural education* to foster bilingualism—that is, to develop linguistic and cultural resources other than those of the dominant society?

These alternatives correspond to Ruíz's (1984) "orientations in language planning": ways of framing language issues and the language policies adopted in response. *Language-as-problem* focuses on social liabilities, such as limited proficiency in the majority tongue and its academic consequences. From this perspective, Title VII was a way to ease LEP children's transition to the mainstream by teaching them English, raising their self-esteem, and thereby enabling them to progress in school. *Language-as-right* emphasizes questions of social equality, or lack thereof, such as whether members of minority groups enjoy unimpeded access to public institutions. In this view, Title VII was designed to overcome language barriers, make school meaningful for LEP students, and give them a chance to succeed. *Language-as-resource* takes a human capital approach, stressing the social value of conserving and developing minority-language skills. Seen through this prism, Title VII was intended to promote fluency in two languages, exploit cultural diversity to meet national needs, and encourage ethnic tolerance.

Ruíz's orientations can help to illuminate the assumptions and implications of alternative language policies. For example, language-as-problem, by focusing on students' *language disability* is consistent with a quick-exit pedagogy (bilingual or otherwise) that places the rapid acquisition of English ahead of other academic goals. By contrast, language-as-resource, by focusing on students' *language ability* in a minority tongue, tends to support a late-exit enrichment model that continues native-language instruction after students are proficient in English.

As ex post facto descriptions, however, Ruíz's categories are less useful in explaining causality—that is, in analyzing the political and ideological factors that go into language policy decisions. Orientations in language planning, elaborated in "pure" form and focusing on sociolinguistic issues, may accurately summarize the policy alternatives as understood by experts in the field. Yet rarely do they correspond to the interests of contending factions or to the actual terms of political debate, which are never pure; usually they extend well beyond the realm of language. In short, orientations toward language per se are rarely determinant in policy decisions about language. This becomes evident in tracing the legislative history of Title VII.

Political momentum was strong from the outset, as thirty-seven different bilingual education bills were introduced in the Ninetieth Congress. Throughout 1967, a series of House and Senate hearings showcased the educational problems of LEP children and elicited virtually unanimous support for a solution involving bilingual instruction. Disagreements were confined to secondary issues, such as whether to cover all LEP students or just Spanish speakers. The witness lists included academic researchers, language educators, school administrators, teachers, psychologists, social workers, elected officials, and representatives of Hispanic, Asian American, and Native American organizations.[3] Some experts recommended bilingual education as a remedy for LEP students' "linguistic handicap" and resulting "educational problems." Others focused on the bill's potential to develop needed language resources, Spanish skills in particular. Many witnesses cited both objectives, describing them as educationally compatible. (Although the theme of language-as-right was barely detectable in deliberations over Title VII, that would soon change with a spate of litigation brought by language-minority parents.) José Cárdenas, a veteran educator from San Antonio, recalls that neither he nor his fellow experts worried about a contradiction between the "transition" and "maintenance" goals of bilingual instruction (Crawford 1992). These terms—yet to be coined in 1967—were the product of political, not pedagogical, necessity.

The most substantive, albeit brief, debate on the goals of the bill came on the Senate floor (*Congressional Record* 1967). Joseph Montoya of New Mexico urged his colleagues: "We must take advantage of the language pluralism that exists in the Southwest. But it must be constructive pluralism. Comprehensive bilingual education programs are, to my way of thinking, one way we can give to all [Spanish-speaking students] the best of both worlds in terms of language, culture, and cooperation in daily life" (35053). Frank Lausche of Ohio was less enthusiastic about "the Federal Government pouring in . . . money" to help maintain minority tongues. A native speaker of Slovenian, he recalled, "I went to a grammar school where they taught English. They did not teach me Slovenian in order to learn English [sic]." He also worried about the precedent: "What are we to do if there is a Hungarian neighborhood in Toledo that finds it wants Hungarian taught in its schools?" (34702). The bill's chief sponsor, Ralph Yarborough of Texas, sought to finesse the differences by emphasizing transition while leaving the door ajar for maintenance:

> It is not the purpose of this bill to create pockets of different languages throughout the country. It is the main purpose of the bill to bring millions of

[3]Thernstrom (1980), a critic of bilingual education, claims: "The chairmen of the House and Senate committees did not call witnesses—in the sense of experts on the educational and political questions raised by the legislation—but (with few exceptions) lobbyists. Ethnic activists—mostly Hispanics—came to testify on the bill's necessity" (6). In fact, only twenty-six of the 144 witnesses were lobbyists for community and advocacy groups; about half had Hispanic surnames.

school children into the mainstream of American life and make them literate in the national language of the country in which they live: namely, English. Not to stamp out the mother tongue and not to make their mother tongue the dominant language, but just to try to make these children fully literate in English, so that the children can move into the mainstream of American life. (34703)

This explanation appeared to satisfy Senator Lausche, who asked "whether all of us should not be expert in at least 2 languages—perhaps 3" and recommended "a knowledge of Latin" to everyone (34703). No further questions were raised, and the Bilingual Education Act passed as part of an omnibus education measure.[4]

Ambiguity served Senator Yarborough's purposes. In 1967, the political universe was perfectly aligned to create an antipoverty program serving Hispanic Americans, whose needs had thus far received little attention from the Great Society. Mexican American educators and the National Education Association (1966) had recently highlighted the plight of Spanish-speaking students, "the invisible minority." Yarborough, a populist Democrat, enlisted in the "bilingual movement" at the NEA's Tucson Conference in the fall of 1966. Senator George Murphy, a conservative California Republican, also endorsed the idea, noting that Governor Ronald Reagan had recently signed legislation repealing his state's mandate for English-only instruction. Still, there was no time to lose. Urban riots and a costly war in Southeast Asia were beginning to spoil the Johnson administration's appetite for social spending. Indeed, Yarborough had to twist arms to get its support for a new "title" of the Elementary and Secondary Education Act. (The administration initially favored funding bilingual approaches through existing programs.) Who knew when this opportunity would come again? Why risk it by raising sensitive matters like assimilation and pluralism? Better to pass a bilingual education bill today and clarify its goals at some future date.

As political strategy, Senator Yarborough's approach is hard to fault. As policy making, it left many loose ends. In particular, the unresolved question of goals would haunt Title VII for years to come. Reflecting on the legislative process long after the fact, many of the key players (including Yarborough) agreed that the law was conceived as an experiment not in language policy but in education policy, designed to tackle a problem of underachievement in which language happened to play a role (Croghan 1997). Conscious or not, the federal government's intervention on behalf of bilingual instruction was unprecedented and far-reaching. What did it mean? The program's administrators, members of Congress, school personnel, academic researchers, and the parents of LEP children all cherished their own interpretations.

The Office of Education included the following advice in its 1971 instructions for Title VII grant applicants: "It must be remembered that the ultimate goal of bilingual education is a student who functions well in two languages on any occasion." This was hardly the consensus view on Capitol Hill. Congressional committee members made it clear that "we were in there to overcome [students']

---

[4]There was no separate recorded vote on bilingual education in either the House or the Senate.

'bilingual problem,'" Albar Peña, the program's first director, recalled two decades later. "There was an obsession that if they were not English-speaking at the end of the first grade that the world would come to an end" (quoted in Crawford 1992, 85). Appropriations for Title VII nevertheless remained modest—only $7.5 million in 1969. Although funding increased to $45 million by 1974, it was enough to support a mere 211 local programs (Crawford 1995).

As state legislatures began repealing English-only school laws and authorizing native-language instruction, they showed a similar ambivalence. In 1971, Massachusetts became the first state to require "transitional bilingual education" under certain circumstances—and the first to use the term—but its definition of the program omitted any mention of goals (*Mass. Gen. Laws*, Title XII, chap. 71A). A similar law, adopted two years later in Illinois, articulated the purpose of transitional programs: "to meet the needs of [LEP] children and facilitate their integration into the regular public school curriculum" (*Ill. Ann. Stat.*, chap. 122, art. 14C). By the mid-1970s, more than a dozen states had enacted bilingual education statutes; none drew sharp lines of demarcation between transition and maintenance.

Educators, for their part, continued to see the two goals as compatible. According to the American Institutes for Research (AIR) report (Danoff et al. 1977–1978), a nationwide study of Title VII's impact, 86 percent of local bilingual programs retained Spanish-speaking children even after they were deemed fluent in English. On the other hand, 50 percent of "bilingual" teachers lacked proficiency in the native languages of their students—casting doubts on whether Title VII was doing much to promote fluent bilingualism. Amid the furor over the first finding, however, the second was largely ignored. Critics charged the Office of Education with flouting both the melting-pot tradition and the intent of Congress by failing to "mainstream" children as quickly as possible (Epstein 1977). The language-as-resource approach was condemned as diametrically opposed to the goal of assimilation. In addition, AIR's mediocre report card for Title VII—"no consistent significant impact" on achievement—led opponents to question the program's effectiveness. This marked the first serious opposition to the bilingual experiment. Under the leadership of Senator S. I. Hayakawa of California, it would soon expand into an English-only movement seeking to restrict most uses of minority tongues by government (Crawford 1992).

In reaction to the controversy, Congress voted in 1978 to restrict federal support to transitional bilingual education programs. Henceforth, the native language could be used only "to the extent necessary to allow a child to achieve competence in the English language" (Public Law 95-561). While this statutory restriction was eased in 1984, for another decade only a tiny portion of federal funds flowed to maintenance—now known as "developmental bilingual education." Nevertheless, critics successfully portrayed Title VII as a program that emphasized the native language and "ethnic pride" at the expense of English. Led by the Reagan administration's secretary of education, William J. Bennett, they advocated "local flexibility" for districts to try English-only alternatives such as "structured immersion" (Bennett 1985). In response, defenders insisted that bilingual education was the most efficient solution to the problems of limited English proficiency and academic underachievement.

Thus, during the 1987–1988 reauthorization of Title VII, the debate involved means, not ends. Both sides embraced the language-as-problem orientation, which proved to be consistent with diametrically opposed policies for educating LEP students. Congress struck a compromise, diverting up to 25 percent of annual appropriations from bilingual to "special alternative instructional programs." Only a tiny share was made available for developmental programs, despite their promising academic outcomes and success in cultivating bilingualism.

Language-as-resource, while gaining hegemony among educational researchers and practitioners, was marginalized politically by the new terms of the debate. With any form of native-language instruction now condemned as a distraction from English—in effect, Title VII's critics portrayed transitional bilingual education as a language-maintenance approach—the program's defenders tended to downplay its potential to develop bilingual skills. One exception was the Miami-based Spanish American League against Discrimination (SALAD). Troubled by Bennett's assimilationist rhetoric, in 1985 the group countered with the slogan "English Plus." While English is essential in the United States, SALAD argued, to succeed in a global economy, children need to learn more than one language and developmental bilingual education can be an effective means to that end. This philosophy was soon put into service as a programmatic alternative to the broader English-only campaign (Combs 1992). Again, however, its appeal has been limited mainly to language educators. English Plus has found few legislative champions outside of the Latino and Asian American caucuses (e.g., Serrano 1997).[5]

The Impact of Lau v. Nichols

Meanwhile, bilingual education had also become a civil rights issue. For militant Chicanos in particular, it emerged as a key demand—in no small part because of the suppression of Spanish in schools throughout the Southwest, a symbol of racial oppression. For La Raza Unida Party, which won control of the Crystal City, Texas, school board in 1970, bilingual education became a matter of self-determination, an assertion of ethnic pride, and a pedagogical approach to which high hopes were attached (Shockley 1974). Wherever language minorities were concentrated, school officials began to feel community pressure to adopt bilingual methods. Several districts became the target of lawsuits by parents who argued that failure to address students' language needs meant failure to provide them an equal opportunity to learn. As Mexican American students staged boycotts to protest their treatment by the schools in cities like Los Angeles, bilingual education was frequently among their demands.

In 1970, the U.S. Department of Health, Education, and Welfare responded with a memorandum on school districts' obligations toward LEP students. Under the Civil Rights Act of 1964, it warned, "sink or swim" was no longer permissible. Public schools would now have to take "affirmative steps" to help

---

[5]This situation may be changing, as Republicans begin to make overtures to Hispanic voters. A new English Plus resolution was introduced in 1998 by John McCain of Arizona and nine other Republican senators.

students overcome language barriers. Moreover, they would have to provide such assistance without segregating children on dead-end tracks of remedial education.

Few districts paid much attention. In San Francisco, for example, administrators insisted that by giving LEP students the *identical* education offered to all students—that is, instruction via the English language—schools were discharging their obligation to provide an *equal* education for all. Federal district and appeals courts agreed, rejecting a lawsuit brought on behalf of Chinese-speaking students and permitting sink-or-swim instruction. While this position may seem myopic today, in the early 1970s it was widely shared. The issue of desegregation had so dominated the civil rights struggle that any suggestion of "separate but equal" education was suspect even to progressives. Unlike African Americans fighting exclusion, the language-minority plaintiffs in the San Francisco case sought to establish the principle that children with different needs are entitled to different treatment by the schools. They cited the words of Justice Felix Frankfurter a generation earlier: "There is no greater inequality than the equal treatment of unequals" (Steinman 1971).

The U.S. Supreme Court embraced the parents' reasoning in a unanimous opinion. Its ruling in *Lau v. Nichols* (414 U.S. 563 [1974]), while limited in scope, remains the major legal precedent on language rights in the United States—or, more precisely, on the obligation of government to provide appropriate language accommodations to safeguard (other) fundamental rights. Writing for the court, Justice William O. Douglas reasoned that

> there is no equality of treatment merely by providing students with the same facilities, textbooks, teachers, and curriculum; for students who do not understand English are effectively foreclosed from any meaningful education. Basic English skills are at the very core of what these public schools teach. Imposition of a requirement that, before a child can effectively participate in the educational program, he must already have acquired those basic skills is to make a mockery of public education. We know that those who do not understand English are certain to find their classroom experiences wholly incomprehensible and in no way meaningful. (565)

The decision stopped short of mandating bilingual education, leaving the door open to other pedagogical treatments for students' "language deficiency":

> No specific remedy is urged upon us. Teaching English to the students of Chinese ancestry who do not speak the language is one choice. Giving instructions to this group in Chinese is another. There may be others. Petitioner asks only that the Board of Education be directed to apply its expertise to the problem and rectify the situation. (563)

As interpreted by the U.S. Office of Education, however, *Lau v. Nichols* soon became a mandate for bilingual education: the remedy of choice whenever a school district was found to be violating the civil rights of LEP students. Aggressive enforcement of the so-called Lau Remedies from 1975 to 1981 imposed bilingual education on nearly five hundred school districts, mostly in the Southwest, through consent agreements known as Lau Plans. This period of federal oversight—or federal "heavy-handedness," in the view of many local officials—had contradictory results.

For the first time, large numbers of school districts were induced to pay attention to the language needs of LEP students and to serve them through bilingual education. Before the mid-1970s, few had done either of these things—which required a thorough transformation of business as usual—without the carrot of federal or state subsidies. Now came the stick, as the federal Office for Civil Rights patrolled school systems with significant language-minority enrollments. Districts required to adopt Lau Plans, along with others that acted to pre-empt federal intervention, tended to accept the new pedagogy grudgingly at first. Over time, however, most came to regard bilingual instruction as, if not a panacea, at least a substantial improvement over "sink or swim." As pedagogical outcomes improved, community support usually increased.

Yet prescriptiveness also bred resistance. Bilingual education suddenly became a point of conflict between federal authorities and local school boards, a cause célèbre for opponents of Big Government—in short, a natural issue for conservatives of the period. First, the Lau Remedies were attacked as illegitimate because, as quasi-formal "guidelines," they had been issued without an opportunity for public scrutiny or comment. A federal court agreed. Labeling the rule-making process illegal, it ordered the Carter administration to develop formal Lau Regulations. When the new rules finally appeared, shortly before the 1980 election, they were greeted with near-unanimous opposition from the education community (other than the National Association for Bilingual Education and its affiliates).[6] Ronald Reagan, who had made attacks on federal red tape a major campaign theme, withdrew the Lau Regulations shortly after winning the presidency.[7] As a result, since 1981 the Office for Civil Rights has declined to articulate a preference for any pedagogical approach.[8]

Second, the Lau Remedies placed a new burden of proof on the federal government. Mandating bilingual instruction, rather than merely encouraging local school districts to try it, created pressure to offer "conclusive" evidence of its pedagogical benefits. A U.S. Department of Education review of the research literature, initiated by the Carter administration, found mixed results at best. Baker and de Kanter (1983) concluded that "no consistent evidence

---

[6]Among interest groups, the National Education Association was the only major exception.

[7]In a statement canceling the Lau Regulations, Terrel Bell, the new secretary of education, called them "harsh, inflexible, burdensome, unworkable, and incredibly costly" (quoted in Crawford 1995, 53).

[8]The civil rights agency has relied instead on the *Castañeda* standard for determining whether school districts are meeting their obligations toward LEP students (Crawford 1996). This three-part test was developed by a federal appeals court in interpreting the Equal Educational Opportunities Act of 1974. Reaffirming the *Lau v. Nichols* decision, the law requires school districts to take "appropriate action to overcome language barriers that impede equal participation by its students in its instructional programs" (Sec. 1703[f]). More than vague "good faith" efforts are required, the court ruled in *Castañeda v. Pickard* (648 F. 2d 989 [5th Cir. 1981]). A program serving LEP students must meet the following criteria:

It must be based on "a sound educational theory," endorsed by one or more experts.

It must be "implemented effectively," with adequate resources and personnel.

After a trial period, it must be evaluated as effective in overcoming language handicaps.

supports the effectiveness of [transition bilingual education (TBE)]. . . . An occasional, inexplicable success is not enough reason to make TBE the law of the land" (50-51). The report also speculated that alternative, all-English approaches might be promising. Yet the Baker-de Kanter study itself came under criticism for its methodology (e.g., Willig 1985). Many of the studies under review involved programs that were poorly designed and implemented, quick-exit models rather than the developmental approaches later found to be superior (Ramírez et al. 1991). The authors' claims for the promise of "structured immersion" were based on studies of Canadian programs (bilingual ones, at that) tailored to the needs of students who had little in common with language-minority students in the United States. Despite the study's limited credibility among researchers, however, it received considerable play in the news media. The debate lent credence to the argument, raised by Secretary of Education William Bennett (among others), that the experts are "divided" and thus the scientific evidence on bilingual education remains too "inconclusive" to support Title VII policy.

Hence the political paradox of bilingual education. It might well have remained a marginal experiment had it not been imposed on school districts via the Lau Remedies and assorted court orders. Today's most successful instructional models for LEP students might never have been developed; at best, they would likely be confined to a tiny number of schools. At the same time, however, federal and state mandates for bilingual education provoked a backlash and a fierce debate over the program's effectiveness. Critics charged that, however "well-intentioned," Title VII had failed to fulfill its promises—citing the persistence of high failure and dropout rates among Latino students in particular. Thus, its value as a civil rights remedy has come into question.

Increasingly, English-only advocates have appropriated the language-as-right approach for their own purposes. Chávez (1991) argues that if bilingual education segregates LEP children from the mainstream and discourages them from learning English, then it must limit their educational opportunities. Proposition 227, the so-called English for the Children (1997) initiative, made a similar pitch to California voters:

(a) WHEREAS the English language is the national public language of the United States of America and of the state of California, is spoken by the vast majority of California residents, and is also the leading world language for science, technology, and business, thereby being the language of economic opportunity; and

(b) WHEREAS immigrant parents are eager to have their children acquire a good knowledge of English, thereby allowing them to fully participate in the American Dream of economic and social advancement; and

(c) WHEREAS the government and the public schools of California have a moral obligation and a constitutional duty to provide all of California's children, regardless of their ethnicity or national origins, with the skills necessary to become productive members of our society, and of these skills, literacy in the English language is among the most important; and

(d) WHEREAS the public schools of California currently do a poor job of educating immigrant children, wasting financial resources on costly experimental language programs whose failure over the past two decades is demonstrated by the current high drop-out and low English literacy levels of many immigrant children; and

(e) WHEREAS young immigrant children can easily acquire full fluency in a new language, such as English, if they are heavily exposed to that language in the classroom at early age.

(f) THEREFORE it is resolved that: all children in California public schools shall be taught English as rapidly and effectively as possible. (Sec. 300)

Most fair-minded Americans would agree with most of these premises (although paragraphs [d] and [e] would receive few endorsements from experts in second-language acquisition). LEP children are surely entitled to "be taught English . . . as effectively as possible." Whether that also means "as rapidly as possible" is another matter. Still, no one disputes that English proficiency is crucial both to their academic success and to their "economic and social advancement" in the United States.

The question becomes one of means: How should these goals be pursued? Proposition 227 requires that "all children in California public schools shall be taught English by being taught *in* English." The initiative statute prohibits most uses of native-language instruction for LEP students and prescribes programs of "sheltered English immersion during a temporary transition period not normally intended to exceed one year" (English for the Children 1997, Sec. 305; emphasis added).[9]

Will this sweeping mandate serve the interests and safeguard the rights of English learners? Or will it do precisely the opposite? Laypersons are being asked to decide such questions not only in California but in other states as well—judgments that require sorting through complex and contradictory information. One might as well ask the electorate to mandate a treatment for AIDS or to select the design of the next space station.[10] How schools should teach LEP students has become a highly technical issue. It has also become a highly political one, which invites simplistic and demagogic answers.

Again, the paradox: In its path to acceptance, bilingual education followed the course of numerous reforms of the 1960s. Conceived as an innovative approach to a social problem, it was taken up as a demand by ethnic militants and parents' organizations, supported with federal funds, accepted by school boards, studied by researchers, embraced by practitioners, and sustained by a corps of experts, lawyers, and bureaucrats. In short, it became institutionalized. At the same time, however, these currents were eroding its political support. To the extent that bilingual education has become the domain of professionals, it is less of an activist cause, less of a community concern, less of a social movement.

---

[9]At parents' request, "waivers" of the English-only rule may be allowed for older LEP children and those with "special needs" but would be subject to many restrictions. Teachers, administrators, and school board members who failed to provide English-only instruction may be sued and held "personally liable" for financial damages (English for the Children 1997, Sec. 311 and 320).

[10]These examples are not entirely far-fetched, considering California's attachment to government-by-initiative. In early 1998, there were five measures certified for the June ballot and forty others being circulated for the November ballot, ranging from a proposal to legalize casino gambling to an effort to ban the sale of horse meat for human consumption (Kershner 1998).

Government agencies, educators' associations, and school districts have done little to explain the pedagogy to outsiders, including parents—many of whom are new to the United States and have no memory of earlier struggles for bilingual education. The broader public, never clear about the rationale for native-language instruction, is increasingly skeptical of its results. With the rise of English-only activity, assimilationist rhetoric has won a growing acceptance. Now it is making inroads into language-minority communities. Polled by the *Los Angeles Times* on whether they would favor a ballot initiative to "require all public school instruction to be conducted in English and for students not fluent in English to be placed in a short-term English immersion program," 84 percent of Latinos answered in the affirmative, as compared with just 80 percent of all voters (Barabak 1997).[11]

There is no question that the parents of LEP students continue to feel strongly about the civil rights goals of bilingual education. Yet it is also clear that in the 1990s, language-minority communities are less vocal on its behalf than in the 1970s. Defending the program's effectiveness has become largely a job for professionals. Whether bilingual instruction provides an antidote for school failure, whether it teaches English effectively, whether it safeguards children's rights under *Lau*—these questions are usually left to specialists who can explain the complexities of educational research. Few members of the public seem interested in such explanations, which contradict cherished myths on how languages are learned and how immigrant ancestors "made it" without special help.

Moreover, the voters exhibit a growing impatience with government programs that benefit immigrants and racial minorities. By approving Proposition 187 in 1994, Californians instructed school officials to hunt down and expel the children of "illegal aliens." With Proposition 209 two years later, they chose to outlaw all forms of affirmative action. In 1998, disregarding the advice of professionals in the field, they voted to outlaw bilingual education. Meanwhile, Latino and Asian American politicians, who once rallied liberal supporters behind programs serving immigrants, now sense ambiguous feelings among their own constituents. Hence their wariness about countering attacks like Proposition 227.

Thus the political viability of bilingual education becomes increasingly tenuous to the extent it relies on expert opinion. This is true not only because experts are routinely divided on pedagogical matters. In addition, many researchers today are sensitive to the charge that their work has become "politicized"; so they are more guarded in expressing support for bilingual approaches than they were in the 1980s. A recent report by the National Research Council strived for even-handedness, noting the benefits of both native-language and English-only instruction, even though the panel comprised several prominent enthusiasts of "additive bilingualism" (August and

---

[11] In fairness, it should be noted that this question poorly summarized the provisions of the "English for the Children" initiative, such as neglecting to mention its ban on bilingual education programs. Later polls showed contradictory results—for example, Spanish-language media in Los Angeles found that 88 percent of parents with children enrolled in bilingual programs were satisfied with the results. The major exit poll on June 2, 1998, concluded that Latinos had rejected Proposition 227 by 63 percent to 37 percent (Los Angeles Times–CNN Poll 1998). Yet even this level of support is substantially higher than in the past.

Hakuta 1997).[12] Bilingual teachers and administrators continue to champion their programs without equivocation. Yet such views are easily dismissed as expressions of narrow self-interest—a perennial line of attack by conservative critics (see, e.g., Thernstrom 1980, Chávez 1991).

Without a broader and firmer political base, the future of bilingual education would appear uncertain, to say the least. Where is the needed support to be found? The most obvious undeveloped sources are language-minority families and communities. What has kept them from playing a larger advocacy role? Several factors have already been noted: professionalization of bilingual programs, poor communication by the schools, timidity among elected officials, and immigrants' inexperience in a new political system. Most important perhaps is the peculiar tradition of language rights—or lack thereof—in the United States.

Language Rights, American Style

In most of the world, language rights are understood in two ways: "(1) the right of freedom from discrimination on the basis of language; and (2) the right to use your language(s) in the activities of communal life" (Macías 1979, 41). International treaties to which the United States is a signatory, such as the United Nations Charter and the International Declaration of Human Rights, recognize either one or both varieties. Such treaty obligations make these language rights a part of U.S. law—at least, theoretically. Nevertheless, they remain largely foreign to our legal traditions.

Americans have frequently addressed the language needs of its citizens on political, economic, or moral grounds. During the nineteenth century, for example, a dozen states and territories authorized bilingual education in public schools; elsewhere it was often provided without official sanction (Kloss 1977). Yet there were no constitutional obstacles to terminating such policies and mandating English-only instruction, as most states chose to do during the World War I era. Some Hispanic advocates have argued that, under the 1848 Treaty of Guadalupe Hidalgo, Spanish-speakers are entitled to bilingual-bicultural education in the Southwest. In fact, the treaty makes no explicit mention of language rights, and such interpretations have been rejected by U.S. courts (e.g., *López Tijerina v. Henry* 389 U.S. 922[1969]).

Language rights exist in the United States only as a component of other rights, in particular the Fourteenth Amendment guarantee of "equal protection" under law without regard to race or national origin. *Lau v. Nichols* was decided on similar grounds, relying on Title VI of the Civil Rights Act of 1964. Taking another approach in *Meyer v. Nebraska* (262 U.S. 390 [1923]), the Supreme Court struck down restrictions on foreign-language instruction as an unconstitutional violation of "due process" guarantees.

---

[12]Several panel members had been part of the Stanford Working Group on Federal Programs for Limited-English-Proficient Students, which influenced the Clinton administration to expand support for developmental bilingual education (Hakuta et al. 1993).

> While this court has not attempted to define with exactness the liberty thus guaranteed . . . without doubt, it denotes not merely freedom from bodily restraint but also the right of the individual to contract, to engage in any of the common occupations of life, to acquire useful knowledge, to marry, establish a home and bring up children, to worship God according to the dictates of his own conscience, and generally to enjoy those privileges long recognized at common law as essential to the orderly pursuit of happiness by free men. The established doctrine is that this liberty may not be interfered with, under the guise of protecting the public interest, by legislative action which is arbitrary or without reasonable relation to some purpose within the competency of the state to effect. (402)

Among these implicit rights, the Court enumerated a German language teacher's "right thus to teach and the right of parents to engage him so to instruct their children" (402).

Significantly, despite the breadth of constitutional "liberties" it found to be guaranteed by implication, the *Meyer* court said nothing about *community rights* to use and maintain a language other than English. Its omission is consistent with the Anglo-American tradition of common law, which almost always endows rights to individuals rather than to groups. This has tended to discourage the recognition of language rights, which have limited meaning outside a collective context. For example, the *Lau* decision defines an LEP student's right to special assistance designed to overcome the language barrier and make academic instruction comprehensible—not an ethnic group's right to perpetuate its language via vernacular (i.e., native-language) education. Restricted in this way, Magnet (1990) argues, language rights are ultimately meaningless:

> The right to utilize a language is absolutely empty of content unless it implies a linguistic community which understands the speaker and with whom that speaker can communicate. . . . *Language rights are collective rights.* They are exercised by individuals only as part of a collectivity or a group. Legal protection of language rights, therefore, means protection of that linguistic community, that community of speakers and hearers, vis-à-vis the larger community which would impinge upon it or restrict its right as a group to exist. (293; emphasis added)

Canada's policy of official bilingualism incorporates this philosophy. In essence, according to a former commissioner of official languages, it guarantees the Francophone minority's "right not to assimilate, the right to maintain a certain difference" (Yalden 1981). Besides entitling citizens to federal government services in both English and French, Canada provides subsidies to numerous indigenous and immigrant minorities for the purpose of linguistic maintenance. The United States, by contrast, has tended to resist such policies in principle, if not always in practice. Except in matters of religion, it would be hard to cite any collective "right not to assimilate" ever guaranteed by federal or state governments. Nor was there any formal recognition of a "right" to mother-tongue schooling for any non-Anglophone group, immigrant or indigenous.

Nevertheless, American linguistic minorities have succeeded in maintaining distinct communities, sometimes for several generations, with varying degrees of toleration or accommodation from authorities. Bilingual and vernacular education were widely, if inconsistently, available from the colonial era until World War I. In 1900, contemporary surveys reported that six hundred thousand elementary school children, public and parochial, were receiving part or all of their instruction in the German language. This figure—which Kloss (1977) regards as overly conservative—was equivalent to 4 percent of the elementary school population at the time,[13] probably larger than the proportion of children in all bilingual classrooms today.[14]

This era of accommodation ended following World War I, a period when speaking languages other than English, especially German, came to be associated with disloyalty to the United States. Such wartime fears strengthened a campaign to "Americanize the immigrant," especially in linguistic matters. This in turn had a major impact on the schools. By 1923, thirty-four states had adopted laws banning native-language instruction and, in some cases, foreign-language teaching in the early grades (Leibowitz 1969). As a result, bilingual education largely disappeared until the early 1960s, when it was revived by Cuban exiles in Dade County, Florida.

The Once and Future Politics of Bilingualism

While a thorough historical analysis is beyond the scope of this chapter, for our purposes the key question is: What can be learned from early American "traditions" of bilingual education that might be relevant to its present political plight? In particular, what were its ideological and political foundations before the modern era?

First, it should be noted that bilingual and vernacular schools were often the product of practical necessity or local choice. Before the twentieth century, fully English-proficient teachers were often unavailable in large expanses of the rural Midwest, New Mexico, southern California, Louisiana, and northern New England. Where language minorities commanded local majorities, they usually controlled their own education systems. The first public schools in the state of Texas, established by the municipality of New Braunfels in the 1850s, operated mostly in German (Kloss 1977). At about the same time, the Cherokee Nation of Oklahoma established a system of twenty-one bilingual schools and two academies, achieving higher literacy rates in English and Cherokee than the neighboring states of Arkansas and Texas could manage in English alone (U.S. Senate 1969).

---

[13]Kloss (1977) argues that 1 million—or 7 percent—would be a more reasonable figure.

[14]Unfortunately, today's data in this area have barely improved since 1900. Based on reports from forty-eight states and the District of Columbia, the U.S. Department of Education estimates that 3,018,042 students in public and private elementary and secondary schools were limited-English-proficient in 1994–1995 (Macías and Kelly 1996). These counts vary in reliability, especially for private school enrollments. Information about the educational services provided to LEP children is especially fragmentary. California, the one state that conducts a thorough school-by-school language census each year, reports that only 30 percent of LEP students were enrolled in fully bilingual classrooms in 1994–1995. Extrapolated nationwide, that proportion would yield an estimate of 905,413 U.S. students in bilingual education—or less than 2 percent of the total elementary and secondary enrollment of 46,930,614.

Bilingual education also gained a foothold in major cities including St. Louis, Indianapolis, Milwaukee, and Cincinnati, which ran extensive German-English programs for several decades. School systems made conscious decisions to accommodate the wishes of immigrant parents. More than 5 million Germans arrived between 1830 and 1890, and most settled in the Ohio and Mississippi river valleys. Notwithstanding their religious, cultural, and political diversity, these immigrants were united on the value of German-language instruction as the key to a treasured heritage. For parents, language maintenance was usually the chief goal of bilingual instruction.

More important, school officials saw themselves in competition with parochial schools for immigrant students. Providing minority-language instruction became a way to entice parents to support the "common school." It was also conceived as a way to bring these groups into the mainstream of American life. William Torrey Harris, school superintendent in St. Louis and later U.S. commissioner of education, saw no contradiction in fostering bilingualism and assimilation simultaneously. Like other educational leaders—and unlike most immigrant parents—he saw the primary goal of bilingual education as teaching American culture, including the English language, as efficiently as possible. His rationale, however, was more political than pedagogical. "If separate nationalities keep their own [Lutheran and Catholic] schools," Harris wrote in 1870, "it will result that the Anglo- and German-American youth will not intermingle and caste-distinctions will grow up." On the other hand, "if the German children can learn to read and write the language of the fatherland in the public schools, they will not need separate ones" (quoted in Schlossman 1983, 152).

Harris believed strongly in the public schools' mission to "Americanize the immigrant." Yet he differed from later promoters of this cause in his conviction that the process would proceed more efficiently by voluntary rather than coercive means. In St. Louis, his approach proved successful. After fifteen years of German bilingual programs, the percentage of German-American children attending the public schools had increased from 20 percent to 80 percent (Schlossman 1983).

By offering bilingual instruction in St. Louis and elsewhere, schools recognized no language rights in the strict sense. Nevertheless, they paid homage to a strong tradition in American education: parents' prerogative to have a say in their children's schooling. However vaguely defined in legal terms, the right of parental choice has been revered as a political principle. Thus it has served at times as a powerful rallying cry for diverse groups of parents, including language minorities. In 1889, when German Americans learned that Wisconsin and Illinois had imposed English-only instruction on parochial as well as public schools, they put aside factional concerns, organized to defeat the ruling Republican Party at the next election, and soon repealed the legislation (Crawford 1992). In the 1960s, when Mexican Americans demanded an end to sink-or-swim neglect, they marshaled sufficient moral and legal authority to win bilingual education subsidies, court orders, and civil rights enforcement.

Parent activism can only flourish, however, when armed with clarity of purpose. To the extent that the parents of LEP children are uncertain about the rationale for bilingual education and alienated from the professionals who control it, they will remain passive players in the public policy debate. A majority of these parents may continue to favor the program. But without mass goals and leadership to rally behind, there can be no "bilingual movement" to provide needed political support. Indeed, parents' passivity may be taken for acquiescence to antibilingual policies—as it was in California's approval of Proposition 227.

If current trends continue, the consequences could be drastic: Bilingual educators find themselves increasingly isolated and hard-pressed to resist attacks. LEP students have fewer options, as many school districts limit access to native-language instruction and others convert to English-only models altogether. The nation's thirty-year experiment with bilingual education, despite its success in many schools and its benefits to many children, is branded a failure in the public mind. A generation of experience and research is discarded, as the pedagogy is relegated to marginal status.

The question for bilingual educators and advocates in the late 1990s is whether they can regain the confidence, understanding, and allegiance of their core constituency—language-minority communities—in time to rewrite this grim scenario.

STUDY QUESTIONS

1. What are the goals of bilingual education for various stakeholders? Which are primary and which are secondary? How successfully are they being met in practice and why? On what basis do you make these judgments?
2. What are the factors today that encourage public skepticism about teaching children in minority languages? To what extent do they reflect political concerns? Pedagogical concerns? Other concerns?
3. How have orientations toward U.S. language policy evolved as a result of Title VII, and what has been their impact? For example: How has "language-as-problem" affected the theory and practice of bilingual education? What contradictions in language rights have become evident in the public debate over the English-only movement? Why has the English Plus, language-as-resource strategy failed to appeal to significant numbers of Americans?
4. What accounts for the difference in the politics of bilingualism in the nineteenth century compared with the 1990s? What lessons can contemporary advocates draw from these differences?
5. Predict the future of bilingual education two decades from today. Will the field be stronger or weaker pedagogically? Will it stress the transition to English over the development of fluent bilingualism or vice versa? Will it continue to exist at all? Explain the early twenty-first century factors that led to these outcomes.

KEY CONCEPTS

Language attitudes

Language as a resource

Language-as-right

Language-as-problem

Societal bilingualism

Transitional versus maintenance bilingual education

English Plus

Equal educational opportunity

Nativism

Politicization of research

Individual versus collective rights

Parental choice

REFERENCES

August, Diane, and Kenji Hakuta, eds. 1997. *Improving schooling for language-minority students: A research agenda.* Washington, D.C.: National Academy Press.

Baker, Keith A., and Adriana A. de Kanter. 1983. The effectiveness of bilingual education. In *Bilingual Education,* ed. Keith A. Baker and Adriana A. de Kanter, 33–86. Lexington, Mass.: Lexington Books.

Barabak, Mark Z. 1997. Bilingual education gets little support. *Los Angeles Times,* 15 October, p. 1.

Bennett, William J. 1985. The Bilingual Education Act: A failed path. In *Language loyalties: A source book on the Official English controversy,* ed. James Crawford, 358–363, 1992. Chicago: University of Chicago Press.

Chávez, Linda. 1991. *Out of the barrio: Toward a new politics of Hispanic assimilation.* New York: Basic Books.

Combs, Mary Carol. 1992. English Plus: Responding to English Only. In *Language loyalties: A source book on the Official English controversy,* ed. James Crawford, 216–224. Chicago: University of Chicago Press.

Congressional Record. 1967. Debate on the Elementary and Secondary Education Amendments Act of 1967 (H.R. 7819), December 1, 5, pp. 34702–34703, 35053.

Crawford, James. 1992. *Hold your tongue: Bilingualism and the politics of "English Only."* Reading, Mass.: Addison-Wesley.

Crawford, James. 1995. *Bilingual education: History, politics, theory, and practice.* Los Angeles: Bilingual Educational Services.

Crawford, James. 1996. Summing up the *Lau* decision: Justice is never simple. In *Revisiting the* Lau *decision: 20 years later,* ed. Susan Sather, 81–86. Oakland, Calif.: ARC Associates.

Croghan, Michael Joseph. 1997. Title VII of 1968: Origins, orientations, and analysis. Ph.D. diss., University of Arizona.

Danoff, Malcolm N., et al. 1977–78. *Evaluation of the impact of ESEA Title VII Spanish/English bilingual education programs: vol. 1, Study design and interim findings,* and *vol. 3, Year two impact data, educational process, and in-depth analysis.* Arlington, Va.: American Institutes for Research.

English for the Children. 1997. *English language education for children in public schools.* California initiative statute (certified as Proposition 227 for the 2 June 1998, primary election).

Epstein, Noel, 1977. *Language, ethnicity, and the schools: Policy alternatives for bilingual-bicultural education.* Washington, D.C.: Institute for Educational Leadership.

Greene, Jay P. 1998. *A meta-analysis of the effectiveness of bilingual education.* Claremont, Calif.: Tomas Rivera Policy Institute.

Hakuta, Kenji, et al. 1993. *Federal education programs for limited-English-proficient students: A blueprint for the second generation.* Stanford, Calif.: Stanford Working Group.

Kershner, Vlae. 1998. Democracy gone awry. *San Francisco Chronicle,* 18 May, p. 1.

Kloss, Heinz. 1977. *The American bilingual tradition.* Rowley, Mass.: Newbury House.

Leibowitz, Arnold H. 1969. English literacy: Legal sanction for discrimination. *Notre Dame Lawyer* 45(7): 7–67.

Los Angeles Times - CNN Poll, "Profile of the Electorate," 4 June 1998. Available online: *http://www.latimes.com/HOME/NEWS/POLLS/exitpollsuper.htm.*

Macías, Reynaldo Flores. 1979. Choice of language as a human right: Public policy implications in the United States. In *Bilingual education and public policy,* ed. Raymond V. Padilla, 39–57. Ypsilanti: Department of Foreign Languages and Bilingual Studies, Eastern Michigan University.

Macías, Reynaldo F., and Candace Kelly. 1996. *Summary report of the survey of the states' limited English proficient students and available educational programs and services, 1994–1995.* Washington, D.C.: National Clearinghouse for Bilingual Education.

Magnet, Joseph. 1990. Language rights as collective rights. In *Perspectives on official English: The campaign for English as official language of the USA,* ed. Karen L. Adams and Daniel T. Brink, 293–299. Berlin: Mouton de Gruyter.

National Education Association. 1966. *The invisible minority: Report of the NEA-Tucson Survey.* Washington, D.C.: Author.

Ramírez, J. David, Sandra D. Yuen, and Dena R. Ramey. 1991. *Final report: Longitudinal study of structured immersion strategy, early-exit, and late-exit transitional bilingual education programs for language-minority children.* San Mateo, Calif.: Aguirre International.

Ruíz, Richard. 1984. Orientations in language planning. *NABE Journal* 8(2):15–34.

Schlossman, Steven L. 1983. Is there an American tradition of bilingual education? German in the public elementary schools, 1840–1919. *American Journal of Education* 91 (2): 139–186.

Serrano, José. 1997. English Plus resolution. H.Con.Res. 4, 105th Cong., 1st Sess.

Shockley, John Staples. 1974. *Chicano revolt in a Texas town.* Notre Dame, Ind.: University of Notre Dame Press.

Steinman, Edward H. 1971. *Kinney Kimmon Lau, et al., Appellants v. Alan H. Nichols, et al., Appellees: Appellants' reply brief.* U.S. Ninth Circuit Court of Appeals, 4 January.

Thernstrom, Abigail. 1980. *E pluribus plura*—Congress and bilingual education. *Public Interest* 60 (summer): 3–22.

U.S. Senate, Labor and Public Welfare Committee, Special Subcommittee on Indian Education. 1969. *Indian education: A national tragedy, a national challenge.* 91st Cong., 1st Sess.

Willig, Ann C. 1985. A meta-analysis of selected studies on the effectiveness of bilingual education. *Review of Educational Research* 55: 269–317.

Yalden, Maxwell F. 1981. The bilingual experience in Canada. In *The new bilingualism: An American dilemma,* ed. Martin Ridge. New Brunswick, N.J.: Transaction Books.

Jim Cummins

*T*he controversy over bilingual education in the United States involves both psychoeducational and sociopolitical considerations. The former relate to issues
regarding language learning by English language learners and the efficacy or otherwise of bilingual education in promoting English language proficiency and academic
achievement among such students. The latter relate to the resolution of power relations
between different groups in society, specifically issues such as the status of languages
other than English and cultures other than Anglo-American, the perceived threat of
societal fragmentation if maintenance of immigrants' language and culture is encouraged by societal institutions, and ultimately, the collective identity of U.S. society with
respect to who belongs and under what conditions. In the policy debate on bilingual
education, these two sets of issues have tended to be inextricably confounded. This
chapter tries to address the psychoeducational issues from the perspective of research
and theory to better inform policy decisions regarding what kinds of programs are in
the best interest of bilingual students and to permit the sociopolitical issues to be analyzed more clearly in isolation from psychoeducational considerations.

CHAPTER 7

Beyond Adversarial Discourse

Searching for Common Ground in the Education of Bilingual Students

Jim Cummins
University of Toronto

Seeds of Controversy

In June 1998, California voters reversed almost twenty-five years of educational policy in that state by passing Proposition 227 by a margin of 61 percent to 39 percent. Proposition 227 was aimed at eliminating the use of bilingual children's first language for instructional purposes except in very exceptional circumstances. The origins of this controversy go back twenty-five years to the 1974 ruling of the Supreme Court in the *Lau v. Nichols* case. According to the Court, the civil rights of non-English-speaking students were violated when the school in this case took no steps to help them acquire the language of instruction:

> . . . there is no equality of treatment merely by providing students with the same facilities, textbooks, teachers, and curriculum; for students who do not understand English are effectively foreclosed from any meaningful education. Basic English skills are at the very core of what these public schools teach. Imposition of a requirement that, before a child can effectively participate in the educational program, he must already have acquired those basic skills is to make a mockery of public education. We know that those who do not understand English are certain to find their classroom experiences wholly incomprehensible and in no way meaningful. (quoted in Crawford 1992a, 253)

The Court did not mandate bilingual education, but it did mandate that schools take effective measures to overcome the educational disadvantages resulting from a home-school language mismatch. The Office of Civil Rights, however, interpreted the Supreme Court's decision as effectively mandating transitional bilingual education unless a school district could prove that another approach would be equally or more effective. Transitional programs use the child's first language for some of the instructional time in the early stages of schooling as a bridge to the English-only mainstream classroom.

The Office of Civil Rights' interpretation of the Supreme Court decision sparked outrage among media commentators and educators in school districts that, for the most part, were totally unprepared to offer any form of bilingual instruction. The controversy has raged unabated since that time.

The debate leading up to the Proposition 227 referendum in California crystallized all of the arguments that had been advanced for and against bilingual education in the previous quarter century. Both sides claimed "equity" as their central guiding principle. Opponents of bilingual programs argued that limited-English-proficient students were being denied access to both English and academic advancement as a result of being instructed for part of the day through their first language. Exposure to English was being diluted, and as a result, it was not surprising that bilingual students continued to experience difficulty in academic aspects of English. Only maximum exposure to English (frequently termed "time-on-task") could remediate children's linguistic difficulties in that language on entry to school.

Proponents of bilingual education argued that first-language instruction in the early grades was necessary to ensure that students understood content instruction and experienced a successful start to their schooling. Reading and writing skills acquired initially through the first language provided a foundation upon which strong English language development could be built. Transfer of academic skills and knowledge across languages was evidenced consistently by the research literature on bilingual development. Thus, first-language proficiency could be promoted at no cost to children's academic development in English. Furthermore, the fact that teachers spoke the language of parents increased the likelihood of parental involvement and support for their children's learning. This, together with the reinforcement of children's sense of self as a result of the incorporation of their language and culture in the school program, contributed to long-term academic growth.

In the context of Proposition 227, bilingual advocates argued that bilingual education itself could not logically be regarded as a cause of continued high levels of academic failure among bilingual students since only 30 percent of limited-English-proficient students in California were in any form of bilingual education. Less than 18 percent were in classes taught by a certified bilingual teacher, with the other 12 percent in classes most likely taught by a monolingual English teacher and a bilingual aide (University of California 1997). Thus, they argued, educational failure among bilingual (particularly Latino) students is more logically attributed to the absence of genuine bilingual programs than to bilingual education in some absolute sense.

The educational arguments on both sides of the issue to a certain extent represent a surface structure for more deeply rooted ideological divisions. Opponents of bilingual education frequently characterized the use of languages other than English in schools as "un-American" and many also expressed concerns about the number of immigrants entering the United States and the consequent growth of cultural and linguistic diversity (Crawford 1992b). To them, the institutionalization of bilingual education by federal and state governments represented a "death wish" (Bethell 1979) that threatened to fragment the nation. This ideological opposition to bilingual education frequently resulted either in lukewarm implementation of bilingual education or outright attempts to sabotage the program (Wong Fillmore 1992).

Underlying the educational arguments of many bilingual education advocates was the conviction that a history of oppressive power relations was a significant contributing factor to bilingual students' underachievement. Traditionally, bilingual students had been punished for any use of their first language in the school context and were discriminated against in virtually all areas of education, from segregated schools to biased curriculum and assessment practices. Schools traditionally had communicated a sense of shame in regard to children's language and cultural background rather than a sense of affirmation and pride. Thus, some degree of genuine recognition or institutionalization of children's language and culture in the schools was a prerequisite to reversing this legacy of coercive power relations. This orientation was linked to the perceived desirability of adopting a pluralist rather than an assimilationist social policy in which the value of different cultures and groups was recognized and their contributions to American society respected (Ovando and Collier 1998). Implementation of multicultural education in schools was the logical expression of this pluralist orientation to social policy. In the case of bilingual students, promotion of pride in students' language and culture through bilingual programs was frequently regarded as an integral component of a broader philosophy of multicultural education.

My goal in this chapter is to examine the research and theory on bilingual education so that the policy options can be evaluated independently of the ideological convictions that propel both sides of the debate. The crucially important issue of what types of educational interventions are most likely to reverse the underachievement of many bilingual students has degenerated into the adversarial rhetoric of courtroom lawyers with each side trying to "spin" the interpretation of research to fit its strongly held beliefs.

My own research and theoretical arguments have figured prominently in this debate, and I will attempt to clarify the implications of this work in this chapter. I have argued that the research on bilingual education both in North America and around the world is highly consistent in what it shows. I have also suggested that the research data can be largely accounted for by three theoretical principles that permit accurate predictions regarding student outcomes from any well-implemented bilingual program. I am therefore disturbed to see what I have written sometimes misunderstood and misapplied by advocates of bilingual education and almost invariably distorted beyond recognition by opponents of bilingual education.

While I believe that the research is strongly supportive of the value of bilingual education, I have also argued (e.g., Cummins 1981a, 1996) that bilingual education by itself is no panacea. The reasons some groups of bilingual and culturally diverse students experience long-term persistent underachievement have much more to do with issues of status and power than with linguistic factors in isolation. Thus, educational interventions that challenge the low status that has been assigned to a linguistic or cultural group are much more likely to be successful than those that reinforce this status. It follows that a major criterion for judging the likely efficacy of any form of bilingual education or all-English program is the extent to which it generates a sense of empowerment among culturally diverse students and communities by challenging the devaluation of students' identities in the wider society.

In principle, the incorporation of students' primary language into the instructional program should operate to challenge the devaluation of the community in the wider society and thus contribute to students' academic engagement. Strong promotion of students' primary language literacy skills not only develops a conceptual foundation for academic growth but also communicates clearly to students the value of the cultural and linguistic resources they bring to school. However, only a small proportion of bilingual programs (specifically two-way bilingual immersion and developmental, or late-exit, programs) aspire to develop students' first-language literacy skills; thus, it is primarily these programs that would be expected to succeed in reversing the underachievement of bilingual students.

In the first section, I restate what the empirical research is clearly saying and outline the theoretical principles that permit us to explain these findings and predict the outcomes of various types of programs for bilingual students. Then I attempt to move beyond the divisive discourse of courtroom lawyers to search for areas of agreement in the perspectives and interpretations of both opponents and advocates of bilingual education. I believe that many such areas of agreement exist and focusing on them might provide a starting point for reconstructing a viable research-based approach to reversing a legacy of school failure.

Research Findings on Language Learning and Bilingual Education

The research is unambiguous in relation to three issues: (1) the distinction between conversational and academic skills in a language; (2) the positive effects of bilingualism on children's awareness of language and cognitive functioning; and (3) the close relationship between bilingual students' academic development in their first and second languages (L1 and L2) in situations where students are encouraged to develop both languages.

Conversational and Academic Proficiency   Research studies since the early 1980s have shown that immigrant students can quickly acquire considerable fluency in the target language when they are exposed to it in the environment and at school, but despite this rapid growth in conversational fluency, it generally takes a minimum of about five years (and frequently much longer) for them to catch up to native speakers in academic aspects of the language (Collier 1987; Cummins 1981b; Klesmer 1994). The Ramírez report data illustrate the pattern (Ramírez 1992): after four years of instruction, grade 3 students in both structured immersion (English-only) and early-exit bilingual programs were still far from grade norms in English achievement. Grade 6 students in late-exit programs who had consistently received about 40 percent of their instruction through their primary language were beginning to approach grade norms (see also Beykont 1994).

During this period, especially for younger students, conversational fluency in the home language tends to erode. This is frequently exacerbated by the temptation for teachers to encourage students to give up their first language and switch to English as their primary language of communication; however, the research evidence suggests that this retards rather than expedites academic progress in English (Dolson 1985).

The major implication of these data is that we should be looking for interventions that will sustain bilingual students' long-term academic progress rather than expecting any short-term, "quick fix" solution to students' academic underachievement in English.

The Positive Effects of Additive Bilingualism   Well over one hundred empirical studies have been carried out during the past thirty or so years that have reported a positive association between additive bilingualism and students' linguistic, cognitive, or academic growth. The term *additive bilingualism* refers to the form of bilingualism that results when students add a second language to their intellectual tool kit while continuing to develop conceptually and academically in their first language (e.g., Cummins 1978a; Lasagabaster Herrarte 1997, in press; Mohanty 1994; Ricciardelli 1992).

The educational implication of these research studies is that the development of literacy in two or more languages entails linguistic and academic benefits for individual students in addition to preparing them for a working environment in both domestic and international contexts that is increasingly characterized by diversity and where knowledge of additional languages represents a significant human resource.

Interdependence of First and Second Languages   The principle of first and second languages has been stated as follows (Cummins 1981a):

> To the extent that instruction in Lx is effective in promoting proficiency in Lx, transfer of this proficiency to Ly will occur provided there is adequate exposure to Ly (either in school or environment) and adequate motivation to learn Ly.

The term *common underlying proficiency (CUP)* has also been used to refer to the cognitive/academic proficiency that underlies academic performance in both languages.

Consider the following research data that support this principle:

> In virtually every bilingual program that has ever been evaluated, whether intended for linguistic-majority or -minority students, spending instructional time teaching through the minority language entails no academic costs for students' academic development in the majority language. This is borne out in the review of research carried out by Rossell and Baker (1996) as well as by the thirty chapters describing an extremely large number of bilingual programs in countries around the globe in the volume edited by Cummins and Corson (1998). Countless research studies have documented a moderately strong correlation between bilingual students' first- and second-language literacy skills in situations where students have the opportunity to develop literacy in both languages (for a detailed review of these studies, see Cummins 1991b). It is worth noting, as Genesee (1979) points out, that these findings also apply to the relationships among very dissimilar languages in

addition to languages that are more closely related, although the strength of relationship is often reduced (e.g., Japanese/English, Chinese/English, Basque/Spanish; see Cummins et al. 1984; Cummins 1983; Gabina et al. 1986; Sierra and Olaziregi 1989, 1991).

Fitzgerald's (1995) comprehensive review of U.S. research on cognitive reading processes among English as a Second Language (ESL) learners concluded that this research consistently supported the common underlying proficiency model:

> . . . considerable evidence emerged to support the CUP model. United States ESL readers used knowledge of their native language as they read in English. This supports a prominent current view that native-language development can enhance ESL reading. (181)

The research data show clearly that within a bilingual program, instructional time can be focused on developing students' literacy skills in their primary language without adverse effects on the development of their literacy skills in English. Furthermore, the relationship between first- and second-language literacy skills suggests that effective development of primary-language literacy skills can provide a conceptual foundation for long-term growth in English literacy skills.

Misconceptions and Distortions

The research data are very specific in what they are saying: to reiterate, superficial conversational fluency is not a good indicator of long-term academic growth in English. Thus, premature exit from a bilingual program into a typical mainstream program is likely to result in underachievement in both languages. Bilingual students will usually require most of the elementary school years to bridge the gap between themselves and native speakers of English; this is, in part, due to the obvious fact that native speakers are naturally also progressing in their command of academic English year by year. Bilingual students' prospects for long-term academic growth in English will not be reduced in any way as a result of spending part of the instructional day developing academic skills in the primary language. In fact, the research suggests that students may experience some linguistic and cognitive benefits as a result of developing literacy in both languages.

Misconceptions Among Some Bilingual Program Advocates   These psychoeducational data do not show, nor do they claim to show, that all forms of bilingual education are more effective than all forms of all-English instruction. In fact, many bilingual education advocates have argued for more than twenty years that quick-exit transitional bilingual education is an inferior model based on an inadequate theoretical assumption (what I have termed the *linguistic mismatch* assumption) (Cummins 1981a). Any adequate bilingual program should strive to develop, to the extent possible, literacy in both languages; transitional bilingual programs, however, almost by definition, aspire to monolingualism rather than bilingualism. Such programs also generally do little to address the causes of bilingual students' underachievement, which, as sketched above, are rooted in the subordination of the community in the wider society.

The psychoeducational data also say nothing about the language in which reading instruction should be introduced. A survey I conducted of bilingual programs in Ireland (which catered both to Irish L1 and English L1 students) showed that teachers were equally divided with respect to whether reading should be taught first in L1 or L2, or both simultaneously (Cummins 1978b), and it appears likely that under different circumstances, all three of these approaches are viable. For Spanish-speaking students, the much greater regularity of phoneme/grapheme correspondence in Spanish in comparison to English might suggest that this is a more logical language in which to introduce reading. Thus, one might expect those who strongly advocate direct instruction in phonics also to support initial reading instruction in the native language for these students. For my part, however, the promotion of literacy in bilingual students' two languages throughout elementary school is far more important than the specific language in which students are introduced to literacy.

A third misconception that may operate in a small number of bilingual programs is the notion that English academic instruction should be delayed for several grades until students' L1 literacy is well-established. This approach can work well for bilingual students, as the data from two-way bilingual immersion programs demonstrate (e.g., Dolson and Lindholm 1995; Christian et al. 1998; Porter 1990). However, in these cases, there is a coherent instructional program from kindergarten through grade 6 with L1 literacy instruction continued through elementary school as the proportion of English instruction increases. There is also direct contact with native speakers of English who are in the same classes. What is much less likely to work well is L1-only instruction (with some oral English) until grades 2 or 3 and then dropping students into all-English programs taught by mainstream teachers who may have had minimal professional development in strategies for supporting bilingual students' academic growth. To succeed well, a bilingual program should be a genuine bilingual program with coherence across grade levels and a strong English-language literacy development syllabus built into the overall plan (Cummins 1996). Ideally, teachers would work for two-way transfer across languages to amplify bilingual students' awareness of language (e.g., through drawing attention to cognate connections, student collaborative research projects focused on language, etc.). The interdependence principle does *not*, in itself, argue for initial literacy instruction either totally or primarily through the minority language, although in some situations this may be a viable option.[1]

---

[1]Critics of bilingual education have sometimes interpreted my work as advocating this kind of "L1-only" program. A January 1999 article in the *New York Times Magazine*, for example, outlined the rationale for bilingual education as follows:

> The idea of bilingual education is that students can learn a subject in their native tongue, and then "transfer" their skills to English once they have gained English proficiency. Some bilingual theorists, like the linguist Jim Cummins, argue that children should not switch to English until they have attained academic mastery in their native tongue, which takes at least five to six years—a staggering idea given the speed with which young children attain verbal fluency. (Traub 1999, 33)

As is clear from the preceding sections of this chapter, this is a complete misrepresentation of the implications of the research and theory. An effective bilingual program should have a strong emphasis on promotion of literacy in students' primary language together with at least an equally strong emphasis on literacy development in English. When implemented appropriately, literacy in each language will reinforce the development of literacy in the other.

The final misconception that sometimes characterizes the implementation of bilingual programs is the notion that bilingual education is a panacea that by itself will miraculously elevate student achievement levels. In fact, no program will promote bilingual students' academic achievement effectively unless there is a genuine *schoolwide* commitment to: (1) promote, to the extent possible, an additive form of bilingualism; (2) collaborate with culturally diverse parents and communities to involve them as partners in their children's education; and (3) instruct in ways that build on bilingual students' personal and cultural experience (i.e., their cognitive schemata) and that promote critical literacy; such instruction would focus on providing students with opportunities to generate new knowledge, create literature and art, and act on social realities (see Cummins and Sayers 1995 for a discussion of "transformative" pedagogy).

It is doubtlessly much easier to promote students' bilingualism, involve parents (who may speak little or no English), and build on students' background experience in the context of a genuine bilingual program than in a monolingual program. A shared language between teachers, students, and parents clearly facilitates communication. However, not all bilingual programs have been strongly committed to these goals, and the academic progress of students in these programs frequently reflects this lack of commitment.

Distortions by Opponents of Bilingual Programs   A few examples from Rossell and Baker (1996) will serve to illustrate the frequent distortions of the research on immersion and bilingual programs by opponents of bilingual education.

In the first place, Rossell and Baker characterize me (and virtually all others who have evaluated bilingual or immersion programs) as a supporter of transitional bilingual education despite the fact that I have argued strongly and consistently for twenty years *against* transitional bilingual education and its theoretical rationale.

They also attribute to me what they term "the facilitation theory," despite the fact that I have never used this term. As noted above, in attempting to account for the research on the relationship between the first and second languages, I have employed the term *interdependence* to signify the consistent positive relationship between L1 and L2 academic proficiency and the fact that instruction through a minority language for a considerable period of the day results in no adverse long-term effects on students' academic development in the majority language.

Rossell and Baker (1996) do acknowledge that I have advanced a "'developmental interdependence' hypothesis that states that the development of skills in a second language is facilitated by skills already developed in the first language" (27). They go on to state that they are in agreement with this principle:

> . . . even though *it is true that it is easier to teach a second language to individuals who are literate in their native tongue,* this tells us nothing about how non-literate individuals should be taught, nor the language in which they should be taught." (30; emphasis added)

As I have outlined above, I fully agree that neither the interdependence principle nor the research data showing that students taught bilingually suffer no adverse academic consequences in English demonstrate by themselves that bilingual instruction will lead to better long-term achievement. What the research data and theory do show and what Rossell and Baker apparently agree with is, to quote Rossell's commentary on the Ramírez report, "large deficits in English language instruction over several grades apparently make little or no difference in a student's achievement" (1992, 183). Expressed more positively, promoting literacy in students' primary language will provide a foundation for the development of literacy in English such that no deficits in English language development result as a consequence of spending less instructional time through English.[2]

Particularly interesting in this regard is Beykont's (1994) analysis of Site E grades 3 to 6 longitudinal data from the Ramírez (1992) study, which showed that academic progress in English reading was faster for students with high initial (grade 3) Spanish reading scores and slower for those with low scores. Beykont also observed a strong relationship between English and Spanish reading at the grade 3 level, a finding predicted by the interdependence hypothesis.

Interpretation of French Immersion Research   A final, more general, set of distortions in the Rossell and Baker article can be noted. They cite ten research studies that they claim show structured immersion to be superior to transitional bilingual education. Specifically, they claim that in comparisons of reading performance in transitional bilingual versus structured immersion programs, no difference was found in 17 percent and transitional bilingual education produced significantly inferior results in 83 percent of the studies. Seven of these studies were of French immersion programs in Canada. One (Malherbe 1946) was an extremely large-scale study of Afrikaans-English bilingual education in South Africa involving nineteen thousand students. The other two were carried out in the United States (Gersten 1985; Peña-Hughes and Solis 1980).

The Peña-Hughes and Solis program (labeled "structured immersion" by Rossell and Baker) involved an hour of Spanish language arts per day and was viewed as a form of bilingual education by the director of the program (Willig 1981/1982). I would see the genuine promotion of first-language literacy in this program as indicating a much more adequate model of bilingual education than

---

[2]Rossell and Baker's use of the term "facilitation hypothesis" to describe my theoretical constructs permits them to claim that the results of studies such as the large-scale evaluation of programs for minority Francophones in Manitoba conducted by Hébert (1976) are contrary to the "facilitation hypothesis" (28–29). Hébert's study showed that French L1 students taught primarily through French throughout their schooling were doing just as well in English as similar students taught primarily in English. This study not only refutes Rossell and Baker's "time-on-task" principle (as do all of the other evaluations they cite), but it also provides direct support for the interdependence principle. Rossell and Baker, however, argue that it is inconsistent with the "facilitation hypothesis" because the minority students instructed through the minority language did not do *better* in English than those with less instruction through English. Thus, in their version of the "facilitation hypothesis" (which they inaccurately attribute to me), minority students taught through their primary language should always perform better in English than students taught exclusively through English, regardless of the conditions or sociocultural context. This is a very different prediction than that which derives from the interdependence hypothesis, which is that the transfer of conceptual and linguistic knowledge across languages can compensate for the significantly reduced instructional time through the majority language.

the quick-exit transitional bilingual program to which it was being compared. Gersten's study involved an extremely small number of Asian-origin students (twelve immersion students and nine bilingual program students in the first cohort, and sixteen and seven, respectively, in the second) and hardly constitutes an adequate sample upon which to base national policy.

Malherbe's study concluded that students instructed bilingually did at least as well in each language as students instructed monolingually, despite much less instructional time through each language. Malherbe argues strongly for the benefits of bilingual education, and his data are clearly consistent with the interdependence principle.

So we come to the seven Canadian French immersion programs. First, it is important to note that these are all fully bilingual programs, taught by bilingual teachers, with the goal of promoting bilingualism and biliteracy. Typical French immersion programs in Canada are taught by fluently bilingual teachers and involve 100 percent French instruction in kindergarten and grade 1 with English language arts introduced in grade 2 and a gradual movement toward half the instructional time through each language by grades 5 and 6. It seems incongruous that Rossell and Baker use the success of such bilingual programs to argue for monolingual immersion programs taught largely by monolingual teachers with the goal of developing monolingualism. This is especially the case in view of the fact that two of the evaluations considered to demonstrate the superiority of monolingual English-only structured immersion programs were actually evaluations of *trilingual* programs (Hebrew, French, and English), which demonstrated clearly that such programs were highly feasible (Genesee and Lambert 1983; Genesee, Lambert, and Tucker 1977).

More bizarre, however, is the fact that Rossell and Baker's (1996) account of the outcomes of these programs is erroneous in the extreme. Consider the following quotation:

> Both the middle class and working class English-speaking students who were immersed in French in kindergarten and grade one were almost the equal of native French-speaking students until the curriculum became bilingual in grade two, at which point their French ability declined and continued to decline as English was increased. The 'time-on-task' principle—that is, the notion that the amount of time spent learning a subject is the greatest predictor of achievement in that subject—holds across classes in the Canadian programs. (22)

Rossell and Baker seem oblivious of the fact that the "time-on-task" principle is refuted by every evaluation of French immersion programs (and there are hundreds) by virtue of the fact that there is no relationship between the development of students' English proficiency and the amount of time spent in instruction through English in the program. Consistent with the interdependence principle, French immersion students who spend about two-thirds of their instructional time in elementary school through French perform as well in English as students who have had all of their instruction through English.

Rossell and Baker also seem oblivious to the fact that by the end of grade 1 French immersion students are still at very early stages in their acquisition of French. Despite good progress in learning French (particularly receptive skills) during the initial two years of the program, they are still far from native-like in virtually all aspects of proficiency—speaking, listening, reading, and writing. Most grade 1 and 2 French immersion students are still incapable of carrying on even an elementary conversation in French without major errors and insertions of English. To claim that two years of immersion in French in kindergarten and grade 1 results in almost native-like proficiency in French in a context where there is virtually no French exposure in the environment or in school outside the classroom flies in the face of a massive amount of research data.[3]

Similarly, it is bizarre to claim, as Baker and Rossell do, that the French proficiency of grade 6 immersion students is more poorly developed than that of grade 1 students and to attribute this to the fact that first-language instruction has been incorporated in the program. Significantly, Rossell and Baker cite no specific study to back up these claims. The validity of the claims can be assessed from Swain and Lapkin's (1982) overview of the French immersion research conducted in Ontario:

---

[3]The same pattern is reported by Christian et al. (1997) for English L1 students in U.S. two-way immersion programs. They report, for example, that in the River Glen program in San Jose, California, 60 percent of the English L1 students were rated as fluent in Spanish by the end of grade 1 (compared to 100 percent of the Spanish L1 students), but students had bridged the gap by grade 5, where 100 percent of the English-L1 students were rated as fluent. Students had also caught up to grade norms in Spanish reading by this stage.

In legal declarations submitted in the wake of the passage of Proposition 227 in California, which has attempted to eradicate bilingual education in favor of a one-year intensive English program, Professors Kenji Hakuta and Lily Wong Fillmore each reported data showing what level of English-language proficiency might be expected after one-year of intensive exposure. Wong Fillmore's study, conducted with 239 limited-English-proficient students showed that more than 60 percent of them fell into levels 1 and 2 of the Language Assessment Scales after one year of intensive exposure to English at school. These levels indicated minimal English proficiency on the five-point scale.

Hakuta (1998) examined data from the Westminister School District in Orange County, California, which has operated an all-English rather than bilingual education program. His conclusions are reproduced below:

37. Several things are noteworthy about Westminster's data, particularly the use of it to show that the district's all-English "program is successful in overcoming language barriers" (Westminster declaration; para. 13).

38. The average [limited-English-proficient] student in Westminster gains slightly more than one (1.1) language level per year of instruction. This means that if a student begins school in first grade at language level A (i.e., a non-English speaker unable to function in English at any level), she or he will require *nearly 3 years* to be at level D, which IPT test developers (IPT 1 Oral, Grades K–6, English forms C & D) designate as "limited English speaking," and an additional 2 *years* to become a fluent English speaker. Even on the face of it, Westminster's data appear to support the proposition that achieving English fluency requires approximately 5 years: A non-English speaker entering 1st grade will become "limited English proficient" in late 3rd/early 4th grade and will not become a fluent English speaker until around the end of 5th grade.

In short, the presuppositions of Proposition 227 (and of Rossell and Baker's claims regarding French immersion) are devoid of empirical support.

... by grade 1 or 2, the immersion students were scoring as well as about one-third of native French-speaking students in Montreal, and by grade 6 as well as one-half of the Montreal comparison group. (41–42)

These data refer to performance on a standardized achievement measure; Swain and Lapkin point out that there are major differences at all grade levels in the productive skills of speaking and writing (see also Swain 1978).

Lambert and Tucker (1972) similarly report highly significant differences between grade 1 immersion and native French-speaking students on a variety of vocabulary, grammatical, and expressive skills in French, despite the fact that no differences were found in some of the subskills of reading such as word discrimination. By the end of grade 4, however (after three years of English [L1] language arts instruction), the immersion students had caught up with the French native-speaker controls in vocabulary knowledge and listening comprehension, although differences still remained in speaking ability.

In short, the French immersion data are the *opposite* of what Rossell and Baker claim. There are very significant differences between the immersion students and native French-speaking controls at the end of grade 1 (after two years of monolingual total immersion), but the immersion students catch up in French listening and reading in the later grades of elementary school after the program becomes bilingual (and obviously after they have had several more years of learning French!).

Rossell and Baker's discussion of the French immersion data is presumably meant to imply that two years of "structured immersion" in English should be sufficient for limited-English-proficient students to come close to grade norms in English. The fact that the one large-scale "methodologically acceptable" study that investigated this issue (Ramírez 1992) found that early-grade students in "structured immersion" were very far from grade norms in English even after four years of immersion does not seem to disturb them.

The significance of these points is that the empirical basis of Rossell and Baker's entire argument rests, according to their own admission, on the performance in French of English-background students in the first two years of Canadian French immersion programs. Not only are a large majority of the programs they cite as evidence for "structured immersion" Canadian French immersion programs, but Rossell (1996) (in response to critiques from Kathy Escamilla and Susan Dicker) suggests that

> In the first two years, the program is one of total immersion, and evaluations conducted at that point are considered to be evaluations of "structured immersion." It is really not important that, in later years, the program becomes bilingual if the evaluation is being conducted while it is still and always has been a structured immersion program (383).

Rossell and Baker's argument thus rests on their claim that students in monolingual "structured immersion" programs (Canadian French immersion programs in kindergarten and grade 1) come close to grade norms while the program is monolingual in the second language but lose ground in comparison to native speakers when the program becomes bilingual in later grades. As we have seen, the data show exactly the opposite: there are major gaps between immersion students and native French speakers after the initial two years of monolingual second-language instruction but students catch up with native speakers after instruction in their first language (English) is introduced and the program has become fully bilingual.

Based on their own premises and interpretation of the data, it is clear that Rossell and Baker should be arguing *for* bilingual (and trilingual!) instruction rather than against it.

Reconciling Differences: Investing in Quality Education

It seems clear that if only because of the shortage of bilingual teachers, at least 70 percent of limited-English-proficient students will continue to be taught in English-only programs. However, for the 30 percent who might continue to be in some form of bilingual program, the perspectives of those who ostensibly oppose bilingual education are instructive in highlighting directions for implementing quality bilingual programs.

I look briefly at some of the arguments made by four of the most prominent opponents of bilingual education (Keith Baker, Charles Glenn, Rosalie Pedalino Porter, and Christine Rossell) and suggest that both their interpretation of the research data and their stated educational philosophies in relation to bilingual students provide ample overlap with the positions taken by advocates of bilingual education. With the possible exception of Rossell, all have endorsed high-quality "dual immersion" or "two-way bilingual immersion" programs as a highly effective way to promote both bilingualism and English academic achievement among bilingual students. This is exactly the type of optimal program that is implied by the theoretical principles outlined earlier in this chapter.

According to Porter (1990), a two-way or dual immersion program is "particularly appealing because it not only enhances the prestige of the minority language but also offers a rich opportunity for expanding genuine bilingualism to the majority population" (154). Such programs promise "mutual learning, enrichment, and respect" and "are also considered to be the best possible vehicles for integration of language minority students, since these students are grouped with English-speakers for natural and equal exchange of skills" (154). She goes on to argue that two-way programs are "the best opportunity for families that are seriously committed to genuine bilingualism for their children," and these programs "do not cost any more than the average single-language classes to maintain" (156). She points out, however, that probably the maximum proportion of language-minority students such programs could serve would be about 10 percent (157). Since only about 30 percent of limited-English-proficient students have been in any form of bilingual program in the 1997–1998 school year (University of California 1997) and a large proportion of those are in questionable forms of quick-exit transitional bilingual programs, aspiring toward a 10 percent coverage for dual immersion programs appears to be a worthwhile goal. As is evident from the quotations above, Porter does not appear at all concerned that in dual immersion programs, generally between 50 percent and 90 percent of instructional time in the early grades is devoted to instruction through the minority language, and language arts instruction in this language is continued throughout schooling, despite the fact that this appears to contradict the "time-on-task" principle that she advocates elsewhere in her book.

Keith Baker (1992) has similarly endorsed dual immersion programs, ironically in an extremely critical review of Porter's book *Forked Tongue*. He repudiates Porter's interpretation of dual immersion program evaluations in El Paso, Texas, and San Diego, California, as representing support for English-only immersion:

> She summarizes a report from El Paso (1987) as finding that an all-English immersion program was superior to bilingual education programs. The El Paso report has no such finding. What Porter describes as an all-English immersion program in El Paso is, in fact, a Spanish-English dual immersion program. The El Paso study supports the claims of bilingual education advocates that most bilingual education programs do not use enough of the native language. It does not support Porter's claims that they should use less.
>
> . . . Like El Paso, San Diego has an extensive two-language program. Like El Paso, there is evidence that the extensive bilingual education program worked better than the typical bilingual education program. . . . Like El Paso, the results of the San Diego study argue for more bilingual education programs, not fewer as Porter maintains. (6)

It is worth noting that the study by the El Paso Independent School District (1987, 1992) is one of those considered methodologically acceptable by Rossell and Baker (1996), so presumably Rossell also would regard dual immersion programs as a promising model to implement. This is particularly so in view of the fact that another "methodologically acceptable" study, Legarretta (1979), also reported that a 50 percent-L1, 50 percent-L2 model resulted in more English language acquisition than models with less L1 instruction. Yet another "methodologically acceptable" study (Peña-Hughes and Solis 1980) showed that a program with consistent first-language literacy instruction (for 25 percent of the school day) aimed at promoting students' Spanish literacy worked better than a program that did not aim to promote Spanish literacy.

It seems clear that Rossell and Baker could have constructed a far more convincing case for the efficacy of dual immersion or two-way bilingual immersion than the one they attempt to build for English-only "structured immersion." Nine of the ten studies they cite as supporting monolingual "structured immersion" are in fact bilingual (or trilingual) programs, and almost all of these were conducted outside the United States with students very different from those who are currently underachieving in U.S. schools. On the basis of their own review of the literature and Baker's published statements endorsing the El Paso and San Diego models, they would surely have to agree with Porter that dual immersion is a model with demonstrated success in promoting bilingual students' academic achievement and that this model should be promoted as vigorously as possible.

Charles Glenn's (1997) review of the National Research Council report on schooling for language-minority children similarly appears highly critical of bilingual education, at least on the surface. Glenn views as one of the central articles of faith of bilingual education that children must be taught to read first in the language that they speak at home. As noted above, I have argued for more than twenty years against this simplistic "linguistic mismatch" assumption underlying early bilingual programs in the United States. I fully agree with Glenn's concluding statement, which demonstrates his personal support for bilingual education as a means of developing children's bilingualism:

> What cannot be justified, however, is to continue substituting a preoccupation with the language of instruction for the essential concern that instruction be effective. Bilingual education, it has become clear, is not of itself a solution to the under-achievement of any group of poor children. It is time that those of us who support bilingual education—in my case, by sending five of my children to an inner-city bilingual school—insist upon honesty about its goals and its limits. Bilingual education is a way to teach children to be bilingual, but it possesses no magic answer to the challenge of educating children at risk. Bilingualism is a very good thing indeed, but what language-minority children need most is schools that expect and enable them to succeed through providing a demanding academic program, taught very well and without compromise, schools which respect the ways in which children differ but insist that these differences must not be barriers to equal opportunity. (15)

Glenn concurs with the National Research Council's (1997) recommendation of three components that should characterize any effective program:

- Some native-language instruction, especially initially
- For most students, a relatively early phasing in of English instruction
- Teachers specially trained in instructing English-language learners

To this list I would add the goal of genuinely promoting literacy in students' first language, where possible and to the extent possible, and continuation of first-language literacy development throughout elementary school. Glenn approvingly cites the common European (and Canadian) practice of providing immigrant students with the opportunity to continue to study their "heritage" language and culture as an elective, so presumably he would endorse the goal of first-language literacy development for bilingual students in the United States, at least for Spanish-speaking students where numbers and concentration make this goal administratively feasible.

Glenn (1997), however, is clearly concerned that, in his view, many bilingual programs segregate students and retain them too long outside the mainstream, with newcomers "simply dumped into a bilingual class of the appropriate age level" (7). In addition, he suggests that these programs may lack coherent, cognitively challenging opportunities for students to develop higher-order English literacy skills.

As noted earlier, these concerns may certainly be justified in the case of a proportion of poorly implemented bilingual programs; however, concerns about segregation, low teacher expectations, and cognitively undemanding "drill and practice" instruction equally characterize the English-only programs attended by about 70 percent of limited-English-proficient students. Segregation in schools is primarily a function of housing and neighborhood ghettoization and will exist regardless of the language of instruction. A major advantage of two-way bilingual programs, as noted above, is that they overcome segregation in a planned program that aims to enrich the learning opportunities of both minority- and majority-language students. However, even in segregated, low-income, inner-city contexts, the findings of Ramírez (1992) and Beykont (1994) show that well-implemented developmental (late-exit) bilingual programs can achieve remarkable success in promoting grade-level academic success for bilingual students.

A final point of agreement in relation to Glenn's (1997) analysis is his statement that "the under-achievement of Hispanics in the United States and of Turks and Moroccans in northwestern Europe, I suggested in my recent book, may have less to do with language differences than with their status in the society and how they come to terms with that status" (10). This emphasis on status and power relations as a cause of underachievement is consistent with the perspective sketched earlier in this chapter and elaborated in Cummins (1996), which attempts to work out how status and power differentials in the wider society are played out in the interactions between educators and students in school.

The distinction that Glenn draws between "language differences" and "status in society" implies an either/or logic that suggests that if underachievement is related to status and power differentials, then it has nothing to do with language. Clearly, this is absurd. As Glenn knows better than most, the subordinated status of colonized and stigmatized minority groups in countries around the world has been reinforced in the school by punishing students for speaking their home language and making them feel ashamed of their language, culture, and religion. In other words, the interactions that subordinated-group students experience in school have reinforced the inferior status that the minority community has experienced in the wider society.

It seems obvious that if one diagnoses that the roots of the problem of minority-student underachievement are to be found in the low status of the subordinated group in the wider society (as Glenn appears to do), then surely one would acknowledge that a significant rationale for promoting students' primary language in school through bilingual education is to challenge this subordinated status and the coercive power relations that gave rise to it. The evidence is overwhelming that strong promotion of literacy in the primary language will result in no adverse consequences for literacy in English (provided there is also an equally strong program for literacy promotion in English, which any well-implemented bilingual program will have). Promotion of literacy in the primary language for subordinated-group students is obviously not by itself a total solution, but it can certainly make an important contribution to academic achievement for many bilingual students.

CONCLUSION

I have suggested that when the adversarial screen of courtroom discourse is lifted, there is actually much that advocates and opponents of bilingual education can agree on. Opponents consistently acknowledge the value of bilingualism, and their endorsement of dual immersion or two-way bilingual programs ranges from implicit in the case of Rossell (through citing considerably more U.S. examples of successful dual immersion programs than successful structured immersion programs) to explicit and enthusiastic in the case of Porter and Baker. Glenn is also clearly a strong advocate of using bilingual education to develop students' bilingualism, although highly critical of the way in which many bilingual education programs in the United States have been implemented (as are virtually all academic advocates of bilingual education; see, for example, Krashen 1996; Wong Fillmore 1992).

The challenge for opponents and advocates is to create an ideological space to collaborate in planning quality programs for bilingual students in view of the fact that there appears to be consensus on the desirability of promoting students' individual bilingualism (and the linguistic resources of the nation) and, as acknowledged by Rossell in her analysis of the Ramírez report, clear evidence exists in virtually all the research data (reviewed by Rossell and Baker, and many others) that promotion of bilingual students' primary language, in itself, will not in any way impede the development of English academic proficiency.

Working together to disseminate information on the effectiveness of two-way bilingual immersion programs, as advocated by Porter, would be a good place to start. Another initiative would be to defuse the acrimony regarding the language-of-instruction issue by acknowledging that the deep structure of interactions between educators and students is a primary determinant of students' academic engagement or withdrawal; these interactions are much more likely to be effective in promoting student engagement when they challenge explicitly the low status that has been assigned to the subordinated group in the wider society (as implied by Glenn's analysis). Instructional models that explicitly challenge what Glenn terms the "demoralized underclass" status of the group are likely to vary with respect to the amount of first- and second-language instruction, depending on the context, parental wishes, and the availability of bilingual teachers; but all will have in common a deep structure that affirms the value of students' cultural and linguistic identity and offers students opportunities to develop powerful intellectual and linguistic tools to act on the social realities that affect their lives.

STUDY QUESTIONS

1. What are some of the reasons bilingual education has aroused such controversy in the United States?
2. List the arguments for and against bilingual education for students who are learning English as an additional language? Assess the validity of each argument you list.

3. What are the differences between Canadian French immersion programs and two-way bilingual (dual language) programs in the United States? Try to find out more about each of these programs (e.g., through the Internet or university library).

4. Is the "melting pot" still working in the United States? Why do you think it never seemed to work very well for African American and Latino/Latina students?

5. With increasing global interdependence and population mobility, knowledge of other languages and cultures is often seen as an important skill to promote through education. Do you think bilingual education might be a good way to teach foreign languages? If so, why? If not, why not? Do you know of any more successful way to teach a foreign language?

KEY CONCEPTS

Bilingualism

Bilingual education

Equity

Academic achievement

Language development

Language proficiency

Interdependence principle

Power relations

French immersion programs

Research methodology

REFERENCES

Baker, K. 1992. Review of *Forked tongue*. *Bilingual Basics* (winter/spring): 6–7.

Bethell, T. 1979. Against bilingual education. *Harper's*, February.

Beykont, Z. F. 1994. Academic progress of a nondominant group: A longitudinal study of Puerto Ricans in New York City's late-exit bilingual programs. Ph.D. diss., Harvard University Graduate School of Education.

Christian, D., C. L. Montone, K. J. Lindholm, and I. Carranza. 1997. *Profiles in two-way immersion education.* Washington, D.C.: Center for Applied Linguistics and Delta Systems.

Collier, V. P. 1987. Age and rate of acquisition of second language for academic purposes. *TESOL Quarterly* 21: 617–641.

Crawford, J., ed. 1992a. *Language loyalties: A source book on the Official English controversy.* Chicago: University of Chicago Press.

Crawford, J. 1992b. *Hold your tongue: Bilingualism and the politics of "English Only."* New York: Addison-Wesley.

Cummins, J. 1978a. Metalinguistic development of children in bilingual education pro-grams: Data from Irish and Canadian (Ukrainian-English) programs. In *Aspects of bilingualism,* ed. M. Paradis, 127–138. Columbia, S.C.: Hornbeam Press.

Cummins, J. 1978b. Immersion programmes: The Irish experience. *International Review of Education* 24: 273–282.

Cummins, J. 1981a. The role of primary language development in promoting educa-tional success for language minority students. In *Schooling and language minority stu-dents: A theoretical framework,* ed. California Department of Education, 3–49. Los Angeles: National Dissemination and Assessment Center.

Cummins, J. 1981b. Age on arrival and immigrant second language learning in Canada. A reassessment. *Applied Linguistics* 2: 132–149.

Cummins, J. 1983. *Policy report: Language and literacy learning in bilingual instruction.* Austin, Texas: Southwest Educational Development Laboratory.

Cummins, J. 1991b. Interdependence of first- and second-language proficiency in bilin-gual children. In *Language processing in bilingual children,* ed. E. Bialystok, 70–89. Cambridge: Cambridge University Press.

Cummins, J. 1996. *Negotiating identities: Education for empowerment in a diverse society.* Los Angeles: California Association for Bilingual Education.

Cummins, J. and D. Corson, eds. 1998. *Bilingual education.* Dordrecht, Netherlands: Kluwer Academic Publishers.

Cummins, J. and D. Sayers. 1995. *Brave new schools: Challenging cultural illiteracy through global learning networks.* New York: St. Martin's Press.

Cummins, J., M. Swain, K. Nakajima, J. Handscombe, D. Green, and C. Tran. 1984. Lin-guistic interdependence among Japanese immigrant students. In *Communicative competence approaches to language proficiency assessment: Research and application,* ed. C. Rivera, 60–81. Clevedon, England: Multilingual Matters.

Dolson, D. 1985. The effects of Spanish home language use on the scholastic performance of Hispanic pupils. *Journal of Multilingual and Multicultural Development* 6: 135–156.

Dolson, D., and K. Lindholm. 1995. World class education for children in California: A comparison of the two-way bilingual immersion and European Schools model. In *Multilingualism for all,* ed. T. Skutnabb-Kangas, 69–102. Amsterdam/Lisse, The Netherlands: Swets & Zeitlinger.

El Paso Independent School District. 1987. *Interim report of the five-year bilingual education pilot 1986–87 school year.* El Paso, Texas: Office for Research and Evaluation.

El Paso Independent School District. 1992. *Bilingual education evaluation.* El Paso, Texas: Office for Research and Evaluation.

Fitzgerald, J. 1995. English-as-a-second-language learners' cognitive reading processes: A review of research in the United States. *Review of Educational Research* 65: 145–190.

Gabina, J. J., et al. 1986. *EIFE. Influence of factors on the learning of Basque.* Gasteiz, The Basque Country, Spain: Central Publications Service of the Basque Country.

Genesee, F. 1979. Acquisition of reading skills in immersion programs. *Foreign Language Annals* 12: 71–77.

Genesee, F., and W. Lambert. 1983. Trilingual education for majority-language children. *Child Development* 54: 105–114.

Genesee, F., W. Lambert, and G. Tucker. 1977. An experiment in trilingual education. Unpublished manuscript. Montreal: McGill University.

Gersten, R. 1985. Structured immersion for language minority students: Results of a lon-gitudinal evaluation. *Educational Evaluation and Policy Analysis* 7: 187–196.

Glenn, C. L. 1997. *What does the National Research Council study tell us about educating lan-guage minority children?* Washington, D.C.: READ Institute.

Hakuta, K. 1998. Supplemental declaration of Kenji Hakuta. Legal declaration in appeal of Proposition 227. Available from *http://ourworld.compuserve.com/homepages/jwcrawford.* Internet (July 1998).

Hébert, R., et al. 1976. *Academic achievement, language of instruction, and the Franco-Manitoban student.* Winnipeg: Centre de Recherches, Colläge Universitaire de Saint Boniface.

Krashen, S. D. 1996. *Under attack: The case against bilingual education.* Culver City, Calif.: Language Education Associates.

Klesmer, H. 1994. Assessment and teacher perceptions of ESL student achievement. *English Quarterly* 26(3): 5–7.

Lambert, W. E. and G. R. Tucker. 1972. *Bilingual education of children: The St. Lambert Experiment.* Rowley, Mass.: Newbury House.

Lasagabaster Herrarte, D. 1997. *Creatividad conciencia metalinguistica: Incidencia en el aprendizaje del Ingles como L3.* Ph.D. diss. Universidad del Pais Vasco/Euskal Herriko Unibertsitatea.

Lasagabaster Herrarte, D. In press. The threshold hypothesis applied to three languages in contact at school. *International Journal of Bilingual Education and Bilingualism* 1.

Legaretta, D. 1979. The effects of program models on language acquisition by Spanish speaking children. *TESOL Quarterly* 13: 521–534.

Malherbe, E. G. 1946. *The bilingual school.* Johannesburg: Bilingual School Association.

Mohanty, A. K. 1994. *Bilingualism in a multilingual society: Psychological and pedagogical implications.* Mysore, India: Central Institute of Indian Languages.

National Research Council. 1997. *Improving schooling for language minority children: A research agenda.* Washington, D.C.: National Academy Press.

Ovando, C. J., and V. Collier. 1998. *Bilingual and ESL classrooms: Teaching in multicultural contexts* (2nd ed.). Boston: McGraw-Hill.

Peña-Hughes, E. and J. Solis. 1980. ABCs. Unpublished report. McAllen, Texas: McAllen Independent School District.

Porter, R. P. 1990. *Forked tongue: The politics of bilingual education.* New York: Basic Books.

Ramírez, J. D. 1992. Executive summary. *Bilingual Research Journal* 16: 1–62.

Ricciardelli, L. 1992. Bilingualism and cognitive development in relation to threshold theory. *Journal of Psycholinguistic Research* 21: 301–316.

Rossell, C. H. 1992. Nothing matters? a critique of the Ramírez et al. longitudinal study of instructional programs for language-minority children. *Bilingual Research Journal,* 16: 159–186.

Rossell, C. H. 1996. Letters from readers (reply to critiques from Kathy Escamilla and Susan Dicker). *Research in the Teaching of English* 30: 376–385.

Rossell, C. H. and K. Baker. 1996. The effectiveness of bilingual education. *Research in the Teaching of English* 30: 7–74.

Sierra, J., and I. Olaziregi. 1989. *EIFE 2. Influence of factors on the learning of Basque.* Gasteiz: Central Publications Service of the Basque Country.

Sierra, J., and I. Olaziregi. 1991. *EIFE 3. Influence of factors on the learning of Basque. Study of the models A, B and D in second year Basic General Education.* Gasteiz: Central Publications Service of the Basque Country.

Swain, M. 1978. French immersion: Early, late, or partial? *Canadian Modern Language Review* 34: 577–585.

Swain, M. and S. Lapkin. (1982). *Evaluating bilingual education.* Clevedon, England: Multilingual Matters.

Traub, J. 1999. The bilingual barrier. *New York Times Magazine,* 31 January p. 32–35.

University of California Linguistic Minority Research Institute Education Policy Center. 1997. *Review of research on instruction of limited English proficient students*. Davis: University of California Davis.

Willig, A. C. 1981/1982. The effectiveness of bilingual education: Review of a report. *NABE Journal* 6: 1–19.

Wong Fillmore, L. 1992. Against our best interest: The attempt to sabotage bilingual education. In *Language loyalties: A sourcebook on the Official English controversy* ed. J. Crawford. Chicago: University of Chicago Press.

Wong Fillmore, L. 1998. Supplemental declaration of Lily Wong Fillmore. Legal declaration in Appeal of Proposition 227. Available from *http://ourworld.compuserve.com/homepages/jwcrawford*. Internet (July 1998).

Carlos J. Ovando   Ricardo Pérez

*I*n this chapter, we examine the political football played with language immersion programs for language-minority students in the United States. We look at three now-defunct language immersion programs in El Paso, McAllen, and Uvalde, Texas. Such immersion programs at one time were touted by some educators and policy makers as the best way to educate language-minority students in the United States. Through interviews with individuals involved with programs in these three cities, we track some of the factors that contributed to the demise of the programs. We also examine a different two-way bilingual immersion program developed in the Pharr-San Juan-Alamo School District in Texas. This program, through meaningful and sustained parental, community, teacher, and administrative involvement, has avoided some of the pitfalls of the other three short-lived immersion programs. We conclude the chapter with implications for research and policy within the context of language immersion programs in multicultural societies.

CHAPTER 8

The Politics of Bilingual Immersion Programs[1]

Carlos J. Ovando
Indiana University, Bloomington

Ricardo Pérez
University of Texas, Pan American

The probability is overwhelming that when two groups with different cultural histories establish contacts that are regular rather than occasional or intermittent, one of the two groups will typically assume dominance over the other.
R. A. Schermerhorn, Comparative Ethnic Relations, 68

Hegemonic Tensions

Because of complex multicultural and multilingual factors, as well as many unfulfilled democratic ideals such as the integration of all persons into mainstream society regardless of their race, class, gender, or ethnic background, it is not surprising that hegemonic tensions have emerged in the United States among ethnolinguistic groups with unequal social, cultural, political, and economic power. The principle holds that those in power tend to determine whose cultures and languages will be affirmed in public life. In the United States, for example, the stage for linguistic hegemonic tensions was set during the colonial period, when the many indigenous and non-indigenous languages competed for their survival with English, the powerful language of the colonizer. As early as 1664, when Manhattan Island was obtained by the British, eighteen different European languages were already spoken there. In addition, some five hundred native languages were present in North America at the time (Crawford 1995). Despite this diversity, however, Hechinger (1978) notes that "the facts of history are quite clear; they cannot be rewritten or revised. Those facts show clearly that the founding fathers viewed the United States as a country with a unified history, with unified traditions, and with a common language" (130).

---

[1]An earlier version of this chapter was presented as a paper at the Third European Conference on Immersion Programmes in Barcelona, Spain, 25–28 September 1996.

He argues that from its beginnings, the United States was meant to be a nation ruled by English institutions, language, and cultural patterns. To accomplish this goal, the "melting pot ideology" was created. He attributes the failure of this process to integrate all Americans into the Anglo-Saxon cultural milieu to the highly discriminatory practices that did not allow all racial, linguistic, and cultural groups to "melt" (130). According to Hechinger, the source of the difficulty is not the melting pot concept per se but rather the reluctance of the dominant society to accept historically stigmatized racial and linguistic minorities who wanted to assimilate.

As American society today is becoming increasingly diverse ethnically, racially, linguistically, and economically, public debate has been renewed on the best way to induct the growing number of language-minority students into mainstream society. Some social observers argue that unless diversity is channeled into a common culture, language, and school curriculum, the country will become divided into myriad ethnic enclaves with very particular agendas that could threaten its unity and future (Schlesinger 1992; Salins 1997). Others suggest that it is not only possible but essential to maintain cultural and linguistic roots while concurrently sharing a set of pluralistic democratic principles and values, especially through bilingual education (Nieto 1996; Ovando 1990; Ovando and McCarty 1992; Cummins 1998).

Recent Background of Bilingual Education in the United States

At the beginning of the twentieth century, Americanization classes were held in many large urban centers. These classes were created especially to prepare immigrants for integration into mainstream society. Apart from such classes, which were often characterized by an ethnocentric stance in which U.S. cultural patterns were presented as more desirable than the immigrants' ancestral cultures and languages (Ovando and Collier 1998), the predominant approach in the United States for educating poor and frequently marginalized language-minority students until the 1960s was the sink-or-swim approach, also known as submersion. The position taken by most educators and policy makers then was that it was up to the language-minority students, not the schools, to make the necessary linguistic, cultural, and cognitive adjustments to be assimilated into American society. When many of these students did not prosper in the schools, their home cultures and languages were frequently singled out as the reason. In essence, the victim was blamed: school leaders generally did not assume responsibility for developing culturally and linguistically compatible classroom practices.

Subsequent generations of language-minority students, however—voluntary and involuntary immigrants, children of undocumented workers, refugee children, and Native Americans—would have the opportunity to participate in a national educational experiment that would alter dramatically the way they would be treated and perceived in our schools. In 1968, the passage of the federal Bilingual Education Act brought a promising yet controversial approach to educating language-minority students. For the first time in American educational history, the federal government was embarking on an educational experiment that sought to affirm the students' home cultures, languages, and prior experiences in such a way that they could start learning without first being proficient in English. It was controversial, however, because some social observers interpreted such a path as ill-advised. Noel Epstein (1977), for example, labeled it the "Columbus Complex," in reference to the explorer's adventure in uncharted waters. He also referred to the new experiment as a "death wish" on the part of the nation, for he saw bilingual education as an instrument of maintaining ethnolinguistic enclaves that someday would threaten the unity of the United States. Educators and linguists in the area of English as a Second Language (ESL) had developed over the years a substantial knowledge base in their field, and various forms of bilingual education had been experimented with in the United States since at least the early 1800s. However, it was not until the passage of the federal Bilingual Education Act that many elementary and some secondary bilingual and ESL programs were implemented throughout the United States to address the academic, linguistic, sociocultural, and emotional needs of students from culturally and linguistically diverse backgrounds. Guided initially more by goodwill and intuition than by specific pedagogical principles based on empirical research, the Bilingual Education Act set in motion a movement that has come very far since its inception.

Bilingual versus nonbilingual programs is not a black-and-white issue; programs fall on a continuum rather than into cubbyholes. In reality, there are many different programs developed to fit specific contexts. In general, however, they can be classified as follows:

Submersion programs: In these, there is no use of the native language, and no special instruction is provided to help learners acquire English.

Structured immersion programs: In these, there is no use of the native language, but students are given specialized ESL instruction designed to be appropriate to their level of English proficiency.

Partial immersion programs: These programs also provide specialized ESL instruction. However, a small amount of time (for example, one hour each day) may be set aside temporarily for instruction in the native language, but the goal is to move to English as quickly as possible.

Transitional bilingual programs: These programs provide extensive instruction in the native language as well as in English. However, once students attain a certain level of English proficiency, they are put into a monolingual English program. Early-exit transitional bilingual programs mainstream students after two years or by the second semester of the second grade. Late-exit transitional programs, on the other hand, delay moving students out until the fifth or sixth grade. Programs vary and may not always adhere to these guidelines.

Maintenance or developmental bilingual education programs: Extensive instruction is provided in the native language as well as English. Unlike students in transitional bilingual education, those in a maintenance or developmental program continue to receive part of their instruction in the native language even after they become proficient in English.

Two-way immersion programs: Speakers of both languages are placed together in a bilingual classroom to learn each other's languages and work academically in both languages. In a two-way program, language-majority students become bilingual and biliterate alongside language-minority students. For example, the English-speaking child learns Spanish, while the Spanish-speaking child learns English within the same classroom.

Quality bilingual education programs have been shown to be effective in the education of language-minority students. For example, Crawford (1995) writes,

> Bilingual approaches in the 1990s reflect the latest findings in linguistics and cognitive psychology. The past quarter century has brought enormous advances in curricula, methodologies, materials, and teacher training. No longer stigmatized as slow learners, language minority children are achieving at or near grade level by the time they leave well-designed bilingual programs, even in urban schools where failure was once the norm. (12)

Given the evidence for the effectiveness of well-implemented bilingual education programs (Krashen 1997; Ovando and Collier 1998; Ramírez, Yuen, and Ramey 1991; Rosier and Holm 1980), why have they not become more widely accepted, and why does this curricular approach continue to be so controversial throughout the United States? Bilingual education continues to be a societal irritant because it is more than just a useful pedagogical tool that addresses the learning needs of language-minority students. It also involves complex issues of political power, cultural identity, and social status. These issues, on the surface, seem quite remote from the day-to-day realities of bilingual and ESL classrooms across the United States. Yet these large sociopolitical and cultural issues are the bases on which bilingual education is either loved or hated (Ovando 1990, 341). Rather than being concerned about the best way to educate language-minority students, antibilingual educators and policy makers seem more concerned about how quickly these students learn English. They tend to assume that bilingual instruction *slows* the acquisition of English and assimilation into American mainstream life. Instead, they argue for immersion programs in English with no or minimal support in the home language. We believe that the principal reason there is renewed interest among some educators and policy makers in promoting such immersion programs has to do more with a proassimilationist ideology than with pedagogy. We feel, however, that these language immersion approaches do not fit well with the sociocultural and linguistic reality of marginalized language-minority students in the United States (see Hernández-Chávez 1984; Roberts 1995; Wink et al. 1995).

Immersion versus Bilingual Education in Texas

In the 1950s, Hispanic children in Texas were generally forced to sink or swim in an educational system that was imbued with discriminatory practices such as prohibiting the use of Spanish on school grounds as well as discouraging attachment to Hispanic culture. Submersion programs were activated in Texas soon after the 1948 court-ordered decreed integration of Hispanic students into the previously all-white school system. By attacking the sociocultural and linguistic heritage of these students and by not taking advantage of pedagogical principles that affirmed prior knowledge and experiences, these submersion practices were certainly a strong contributing factor in the failure of nearly half of the Hispanic population of this generation to graduate from high school (U.S. Commission, 1972, 12–42). The 1960s brought new hope with the implementation of bilingual programs. As programs developed, bilingual educators debated the issue of which bilingual education model was best suited to support the needs of English language learners. Based on a growing body of empirical studies on second language acquisition, most bilingual educators came to a consensus that a maintenance program offered the best approach for preparing proficient bilingual-bicultural citizens for the twenty-first century (Krashen 1997; Ovando and Collier 1998; Ramírez, Yuen, and Ramey 1991; Rosier and Holm 1980; Willig 1985). In a maintenance program, students continue to spend part of the school day studying in their native language even after they have achieved proficiency in English. These educators believed that today's high school graduates needed to be not only academically and technologically competent but also linguistically proficient in more than one language. Rather than *losing* their home language in school, language-minority students through maintenance bilingual education could retain it while acquiring English, with the result that they were fully biliterate upon completing high school. In the case of two-way maintenance programs, children who entered the school system as monolingual English speakers could also exit as bilingual individuals.

What appeared to be desirable to so many bilingual educators, however, did not appear logical to many Americans who were convinced that one language and one culture are the glue that unifies what had begun as a weak colonial confederation of immigrants into the United States. Despite the passage of the Bilingual Education Act in 1968, the political atmosphere in both the state of Texas and the nation as a whole during the late 1960s and 1970s was one of staunch resistance to the use of any language other than English in the classroom, with the exception of secondary foreign language programs for English-speaking students (Crawford 1995). Based on the emotions of the period, bilingual educators became convinced that the idealistic and pluralistic maintenance bilingual education model was doomed from the start, and they shifted their energies to support state legislative bills promoting transitional bilingual education as a compromise that was at least better than immersion programs in which the native language was not used or was used very little (Texas Education Code 1982). Even so, because of strong legislative resistance to any type of bilingual education in Texas, it proved to be extremely difficult to pass both the 1973 Bilingual School Act and the 1982 Senate Bill 477, Bilingual Education and Other Special Language Programs. Compromises had to be made, and other special language program models, such partial or structured immersion models, were given state approval in the 1981 Bilingual School Law (SB 477). Eight Texas school districts either were contacted by state education officials or were volunteered by school district officials, as permitted under the 1981 statute, to help test such immersion programs. These Texas immersion pilot programs operated from 1981 to 1987 (Crawford 1995, 145).

Comparisons of the effectiveness of existing transitional bilingual elementary education programs and immersion programs were thus predestined for public debate, media scrutiny, and scholarly review (Baker and de Kanter 1983; Willig 1985; Cziko 1992). Unlike the highly successful Canadian enrichment immersion programs, which targeted majority Anglophone students (Genesee 1991, 1985, and 1987), Texas immersion programs would target language-minority Hispanic school children, most of them poor. These children were to be taught content almost exclusively in the majority language, English (Hernández-Chávez 1984; Genesee 1985). To accomplish this, English language learners were identified and placed in special programs designed to provide English instruction at a level of comprehension to be understood by non-English speakers. While the classroom teacher might be bilingual, communicative interactions between instructor and language learner were in the majority language. Some of the state's structured immersion programs allowed native language use during the first six weeks of kindergarten, while the state's partial immersion programs usually offered one hour of Spanish per day.

McAllen, El Paso, and Uvalde Immersion Programs

McAllen Language Response Program   A 1983 *Wall Street Journal* story cited the McAllen Independent School District's Language Response Immersion Program as a fresh, new approach to teaching English to language-minority children. English mainstreaming of language-minority children as soon as possible was the key attraction over a transitional bilingual education program. McAllen educators, interviewed in the *Wall Street Journal,* acknowledged that they were directed to speak to the children in English and not in Spanish. According to one administrator, before the immersion program was implemented, "teachers were speaking too much Spanish, flip-flopping [code-switching] from one language to the other, [and] lacked guidance [on] when to transition to English, causing students to become illiterate in two languages" (Schorr 1983, 24). When the term "English as a second language" was first introduced in McAllen, community members complained that English was the number one language in the United States and therefore should not be referred to as a second language. As a result, the term "language response program" was substituted for "English as a second language." The McAllen Language Response Program was to be a five-year state-approved partial immersion program. Teachers could address the children in Spanish for about the first six weeks in kindergarten, but after that, they were to use English. Children were never forced to speak English and could continue to use their native language while addressing teachers, but they were to be answered in English by their bilingual classroom teachers. The curriculum was to include forty-five to sixty minutes of Spanish literacy and to extend through the fifth grade.

A research design was implemented to compare the district's immersion and transitional bilingual programs, and for this comparison, children were randomly selected and placed in four control and four experimental kindergarten classes. Had this immersion program proven to be successful, the plan was to totally discontinue the transitional bilingual program in favor of the immersion program (Ramírez, Wofron, and Morales 1985, 35). Suddenly, however, at the end of the second year of program implementation, a newly hired superintendent directed that the immersion project be discontinued in favor of the district's transitional bilingual education program (Solís 1996). The decision to discontinue the immersion project was largely political. The new superintendent simply felt that transitional bilingual education was better, and so the programmatic change was made. Area educators and residents perceived the partial immersion program to be a structured immersion program—that is, a completely nonbilingual program, and those misconceptions, possibly also fueled by the *Wall Street Journal* article, caused the immersion program to lose favor with the Hispanic community (Hughes 1996). Many Hispanic Texans shudder at the mere thought of returning to a submersion curriculum, remembering all of the personal indignities and punishments for speaking Spanish that they suffered as public school students, with resultant dropout rates of nearly 50 percent.

Immersion Program in the El Paso Independent School District   One of the most discussed partial immersion programs during the 1980s was the one implemented in the El Paso Independent School District. Similar to McAllen's partial immersion program, the El Paso district program allowed children to respond in Spanish, though English was preferred as the instructional language. The district chose this English-emphasis partial immersion approach as a way to solve several problems. The program moved the district toward compliance with Senate Bill 477, which mandated elementary bilingual education programs; it was also a pragmatic response to deficiencies in quantity and quality of instructional materials available in Spanish; finally, the program was generally acceptable to opponents of bilingual education, who predominated at most schools (Carreón 1998).

In the El Paso partial immersion program, teachers provided some instructional time in Spanish every day. In kindergarten, up to 50 percent of instructional time could be in Spanish, but in subsequent grades, it decreased to as little as 10 percent. This inclusion of Spanish instruction within the immersion program was an acknowledgment of the role of the native language in cognitive development. In fact, the Spanish component of instruction was called "native language cognitive development" (NLCD) rather than "Spanish language arts." This NLCD component was offered during the first period of the school day to provide a conceptual native language foundation for the subsequent sheltered language arts, math, science, and social studies lessons that were taught in English. English language arts in particular were integrated with the content of the NLCD component.

From about 1984 to 1994, this partial immersion program was the predominant approach to elementary language-minority education in the El Paso Independent School District, although some schools continued to use a transitional bilingual education approach. Longitudinal studies indicated that neither the transitional programs nor the English immersion programs were producing desired academic outcomes. As a result, a district task force used current research and an analysis of the local realities to develop a new Integrated Bilingual Education Program based on one common philosophy (Carreón 1998). This new program provides sufficient time for cognitive development in the native language, giving equal instructional time for both languages. At the same time, it uses the concept of integrated, thematic units of study for full cognitive development in an equitable multicultural environment. As will be seen in the final section of this chapter, the revised El Paso Integrated Bilingual Education Program shares an approach similar to that of the Pharr-San Juan-Alamo Independent School District's promising two-way immersion model.

Uvalde Bilingual Follow Through Program   The Uvalde program is one of the oldest structured immersion programs in Texas and is referenced extensively by advocates of structured immersion (e.g., Baker and de Kanter 1981; Gersten et al. 1984; Rossell 1989). Introduced in 1968 as a concession to political pressure put on the Texas Education Agency by strong antibilingual forces, school administrators placed instructional priority on being able to have Spanish-speaking children learn English as quickly as possible. While all kindergarten Spanish speakers were placed in a transitional bilingual program to abide by state law, their parents decided at the end of the year whether to continue their child's program placement in the transitional bilingual program (grades 1 through 3), the Bilingual Follow Through First to Third Grade Program (structured immersion), or the Regular Follow Through Program (mainstream English-only). Except for some limited use of Spanish during the first six weeks in the structured immersion Bilingual Follow Through Program, English was the exclusive classroom language of instruction (Ramírez, Wofron, and Morales 1985, 74). Uvalde chose to implement the direct instruction model (Becker et al.1981) for its structured immersion program. The direct instruction model relied on the DISTAR program, which was originally developed for low socioeconomic-status black and white urban student populations. This program came to be highly criticized throughout the United States by educators who felt that it had highly negative cultural deficit underpinnings (Erickson 1982).

By the mid-1980s, the Texas Education Agency, comparing achievement test scores in immersion and bilingual programs, became convinced that the immersion model was not producing good results, and the program was canceled. Despite its demise, however, proponents of structured immersion continue to refer to Uvalde as evidence that structured immersion works. So the game of political football with this immersion program continues to be played.

Texas Immersion and the "Early-Exit Fix"   Other Texas school districts also implemented immersion programs during the 1980s. Most of these programs had very weak or nonexistent parental program orientations and no permanent community involvement components. The districts based their premise for implementing immersion programs on the promotion of a "rapid approach" for language-minority students to learn English; the desire was to seek an alternative to transitional bilingual education, which had an underlying phi-losophy that many Texans questioned. While both immersion and transitional bilingual education programs use second-language acquisition methodology, the main differences between the approaches in Texas narrowed down to *how much* native culture and language was to be included in the curriculum, the degree of urgency in the rate at which English was to be acquired, and subtle but important attitudinal differences about the legitimacy of Spanish or other "foreign" languages in the public schools. In an immersion program, the atti-tude toward the minority language is more likely to be one of "temporary toler-ance." In contrast, in a bilingual program, the minority language is valued rather than tolerated (Brittain 1991; Skutnabb-Kangas and Cummins 1988).

The demise of the Texas immersion programs of the 1980s appears to have been caused largely by the quick-fix solution of moving students into main-stream or "regular" classes as early as possible. The Texas Education Agency Report (1988) concluded that early exiting of language-minority students from such programs had created a high occurrence of academic failure and the need for later remediation. On the other hand, late exiting of language-minority stu-dents, as was more likely to happen in a transition bilingual program, dimin-ished the need for later remediation. Unfortunately, on the continuum of language programs, many Texas transitional bilingual education programs are in reality more like immersion programs. For example, Spanish instruction may be used about 80 percent of the time at the kindergarten level but is dimin-ished considerably by the first grade so as to allow the early transition of lan-guage-minority students into mainstream second grade classes. Because the Texas Education Code mandates that identified language-minority students, with parents' consent, must spend at least two years in a bilingual classroom, school district administrators, under pressure to meet the demands of the state-imposed testing in English, choose to go with the minimum requirement of only two years of bilingual instruction. On closer inspection, these two-year early-exit transitional bilingual programs are really more like total English immersion (submersion) programs masquerading as transitional bilingual pro-grams. Thus, both immersion and early-exit transitional bilingual education programs are often guilty of the same flaw of "the early-exit fix."

Two-Way Immersion Model: Pharr-San Juan-Alamo Independent School District   A new type of immersion model called two-way immersion educa-tion takes a different view of bilingualism. A linguistically heterogeneous class-room is crucial to the two-way model. The language and culture of minority students are seen as assets, not deficits, and the language-majority children learn a second language that will ultimately increase their employability in the Southwestern United States, considering the contiguity in the region of two cultures and two major world languages. The native Spanish speakers and the native English speakers learn to work cooperatively with each other in the two-way classroom environment. An embrace rather than rejection of cultural diversity becomes the established school norm, and both languages are valued equally. This emphasis on cultural diversity reflects bilingual educators' belief that today's students must be bilingual and biliterate, as well as competent in math, science, and technology. Structured immersion programs and early-exit transitional bilingual programs no longer fit into today's shrinking global village as do late-exit transitional, maintenance, and two-way enrichment bilingual programs (Brittain 1991).

Two-way immersion models vary in the amount of classroom instructional time given to each of the two languages. Some designs provide a higher daily dosage of native-language instruction than second-language, while others do the opposite; some balance the time evenly. For example, a 50 percent native language and 50 percent second language, two-way partial immersion curriculum model is being implemented in three elementary schools in the Pharr-San Juan-Alamo Independent School District in southern Texas. This pilot study will add one grade level per year and is being carefully monitored by a team of university researchers and local school administrative personnel. Classroom teachers were trained in first and second language theory, communicative/natural ESL methods, whole language, cooperative education, learning centers, developmentally appropriate practices, thematic units, and two-way educational philosophy. In contrast to many of the state's immersion programs during the 1980s, community and parental involvement components have been built into this curriculum model. School principals and administrators, classroom teachers, community members, and university personnel worked collegially to conceptualize the design. Early inclusion of diverse personnel reflects the importance given to the promotion of program ownership among the group members. Administrative and supervisory staff are developing classroom observation instruments, with direct input from two-way classroom teachers, to help identify appropriate two-way instructional classroom strategies for heterogeneous classes of monolingual language-majority and -minority students. The supervisor's observation checklist in Appendix A of this chapter conveys an idea of the instructional flavor of such two-way classrooms. The curriculum model in Appendix B outlines by grade level the types of heterogeneous instructional groups that are used and the approach to the use of the two languages for content instruction. The curriculum model, classroom observation instruments, and teacher training needs are continuously being fine-tuned to maximize the affective, linguistic, and cognitive needs of language learners. Because the two-way model destigmatizes the educational process for language-minority children and provides for linguistically and cognitively rich classroom environments, it is gaining favor among bilingual educators (Christian et al. 1997). To date, transitional bilingual programs have tended to enroll mostly non-English-speaking students of lower socioeconomic status. Placing such students in homogenous classroom settings tends to create social and ethnic tensions in Southwestern schools between English-dominant Hispanic students (mostly from middle-class homes) and Spanish-dominant Hispanic students (mostly from poor homes). In contrast, the two-way bilingual education model allows for all socioeconomic and linguistic groups to function cooperatively on a level educational playing field in school. Notwithstanding the positive aspects of two-way bilingual immersion education, however, the political tug of war continues between those who want English-only instruction and quick assimilation for language-minority students and those who wish to affirm the primary languages and cultures of students within a context of democratic pluralism.

CONCLUSION

In the two-way immersion model, speakers of English and speakers of a different language are placed together in a classroom to learn each other's languages and to establish successful cross-cultural communication skills. Unlike Hechinger, who sees a nation dependent exclusively on English-language traditions and values, we think that complex multicultural and multilingual societies such as the United States can move into the twenty-first century with reason and understanding to affirm the power and beauty of and the functional need for language diversity. The United States cannot afford to continue to be seen by other nations as the world's champion of monolingualism.

We know, of course, that this vision of multilingual competency will not automatically evolve into reality; its realization will depend on educational and political activism. The United States can take two possible paths. One is the language-affirming path of two-way bilingual education just described. The other is to continue the predominant path of the 1980s and 1990s by resisting the use of the home language for English language learners (see Crawford's chapter in this anthology for a discussion of Proposition 227, an antibilingual measure recently approved by California voters). A review of basic research on second-language acquisition (Masahiko and Ovando 1995) indicates, though, that if we continue on this path, we may be shortchanging language-minority students from developing their full potential. Assimilation and language acquisition do not take place through coercion (see Fishman 1991). Nor do they take place when children are deprived of their first language before they have mastered English. Rather, these processes occur in a classroom context that encourages minority students' cognitive, sociocultural, and linguistic development. As a nation, we need to be concerned primarily with providing a first-rate educational environment for English language learners, one that will enable them to participate meaningfully in a highly competitive, complex, and technological global society. We know that *both* quality-controlled, sustained native language support and ESL are necessary in developing language-minority students' full intellectual capacity.

STUDY QUESTIONS

1. What are the three goals of two-way bilingual education immersion programs? In what ways do you think this approach to schooling language-minority and -majority students would benefit society as a whole? Do you see any limitations to this approach?

2. Why do you think there is relentless opposition to bilingual education in the United States but not to the teaching of foreign languages in the public schools, colleges, and universities? Why is the field so politicized?

3. How much of the fear surrounding bilingual and multicultural education do you think is about immigration and class issues? To what extent are antibilingual and antimulticultural policies veiled forms of racism and xenophobia? To what extent are they legitimate concerns about the need to quickly assimilate new immigrants into the U.S. culture and the English language so they can participate in the American dream?

4. Explain the rationale for educating children bilingually. What does research suggest about the efficacy of quality-controlled bilingual programs?

5. Define the "melting pot" ideology and explain why, despite its discriminatory practices, it continues to shape language and multicultural policies at the state and national levels.

6. Why do you think that the story of bilingualism in U.S. society is not well-known? What were some important events in our nation's history that have shaped our attitudes toward minority languages and cultures?

7. What caused the demise of the Texas immersion programs in the 1980s? What lessons could we have learned?

APPENDIX A: PHARR-SAN JUAN-ALAMO ISD

Two-Way Partial Immersion Classroom Observation Checklist

Name of teacher: _____

Observer: _____

School: _____

Date: _____

y=yes n=no s=somewhat

_____ Print-rich environment in English and Spanish

_____ books for shared reading

_____ books for guided reading

_____ books for read aloud

_____ poetry

_____ children's writing

_____ object labeled in English and Spanish

_____ Separation of languages

_____ blue and red color coding

_____ monolingual instructional delivery:

_____ teacher _____ paraprofessional

_____ monolingual noninstructional (social) delivery:

_____ teacher _____ paraprofessional

_____ use of visuals or concrete objects to ensure comprehensible input

_____ Materials adequately displayed

_____ materials in logical and sequential order

___ materials on edge of shelves
___ materials in clean and attractive condition
___ materials color-coded
___ exercises complete and self-contained
___ Library/reading corner
   Spanish ___
   English ___
Grade level: _____
Total number of children _____
NES _____ NSS _____
Time in _____ Time out _____
___ The prepared environment is child-centered, conducive to learning, attractive
   ___ areas clearly delineated
      ___ practical life
      ___ art/expression
      ___ sensorial
      ___ language: Sp. ___ Eng. ___
      ___ math
      ___ science/social studies
   ___ materials easily accessible to children/ good traffic flow
   ___ teacher materials neatly organized and stored
   ___ furniture (shelves, tables, and chairs) appropriate size and height
   ___ water source
   ___ natural light
   ___ plants
   ___ visiting animals
   ___ large group space
   ___ individual work spaces:
      floor work ___
      table work ___
___ Evidence of holistic reading and writing instruction
   ___ daily news/model writing
   ___ phonics presented in context
   ___ webbing/brainstorming
   ___ reproduction or innovations
   ___ wall stories
   ___ interactive journals
   ___ cooperative learning
   ___ student portfolios
   ___ other
___ Overall, this is a developmentally appropriate teaching/learning environment conducive to bilingual development.
General comments: _____
_____
Suggestions: _____
_____

APPENDIX B: TWO-WAY PARTIAL IMMERSION CURRICULUM MODEL

Grade Level	Heterogenous Instructional Grouping	Separation of Languages for Content-Area Instruction	Computer Focus	Instructional Staff	L2 Literacy Reinforcement
PK	Subject areas: *Whole group [*except language arts] engaged in learning centers in bilingual pairs	Language arts (Spanish: LEP) / (English: LSP) Learning center activities in English and/or Spanish (DAP and whole language)	Initial computer literacy	Bilingual certified or ESL certified	Major focus (ESL or SSL)
K	Subject areas: *Whole group [*except language arts] engaged in learning centers in bilingual pairs	Language arts (Spanish: LEP) / (English: LSP) Learning center activities in English and/or Spanish (DAP and whole language)	Bilingual linguistic and cognitive development via content instruction	Bilingual certified or ESL certified	Major focus (ESL or SSL)
1st	Subject areas: *Whole group [*except language arts] engaged in learning centers in bilingual pairs	Language arts (Spanish: LEP) / (English: LSP) Mathematics (English and/or Spanish) Social studies and science (Spanish) Reading and music (English/Spanish) Learning center activities in English and/or Spanish (DAP and whole language)	Bilingual linguistic and cognitive development via content instruction	Bilingual certified or ESL certified	Major focus (ESL or SSL)
2nd	Subject areas: Whole group engaged in learning centers in bilingual pairs	Language arts, mathematics Language arts and social studies (Spanish) Reading and music (English/Spanish) Learning center activities in English and/or Spanish (DAP and whole language)	Bilingual linguistic and cognitive development via content instruction	Bilingual certified or ESL certified	Major focus (ESL or SSL)
3rd	Subject areas: Whole group engaged in learning centers in bilingual pairs	Language arts, mathematics Language arts and social studies (Spanish) Reading and music (English/Spanish) Learning center activities in English and/or Spanish (DAP and whole language)	Bilingual linguistic and cognitive development via content instruction	Bilingual certified or ESL certified	Moderate focus (ESL or SSL)
4th	Subject areas: Whole group engaged in learning centers in bilingual pairs	Language arts, mathematics Language arts and social studies (Spanish) Reading and music (English/Spanish) Learning center activities in English and/or Spanish (DAP and whole language)	Bilingual linguistic and cognitive development via content instruction	Bilingual certified or ESL certified	Moderate focus (ESL or SSL)
5th	Subject areas: Whole group engaged in learning centers in bilingual pairs	Language arts, mathematics Language arts and social studies (Spanish) Reading and music (English/Spanish) Learning center activities in English and/or Spanish (DAP and whole language)	Bilingual linguistic and cognitive development via content instruction	Bilingual certified or ESL certified	Moderate focus (ESL or SSL)

Source: Drs. Leo Gómez and Ricardo J. Pérez, University of Texas, Pan American 1995

KEY CONCEPTS

Anglo conformity

Assimilation

Bilingual Education Act of 1968

Death wish

Ethnic enclave

Melting pot

Maintenance or developmental bilingual education

Partial immersion

Second language acquisition

Sink or swim or submersion

Structured immersion

Transitional bilingual education

Two-way immersion bilingual education

REFERENCES

Baker, K. A. and A. A. de Kanter. 1981. *Effectiveness of bilingual education: A review of the literature.* Washington D.C.: U.S. Department of Education, Office of Planning, Budget, and Evaluation.

Becker, W. C., S. Engelmann, D. Carnine, and W. R. Rine. 1981. Direct instructional model. In *Making schools more effective: New directions from Follow Through,* ed. W. R. Rhine, 95–154. New York: Academic Press.

Brittain, F. Pittman. 1991. Effects of a maintenance bilingual bicultural program on fully English proficient students. *Journal of Educational Issues of Language-Minority Students* 8: 125–146.

Carreón, A. 1998. Personal communication. 3 January.

Christian, D., C. L. Montone, K. J. Lindholm, and I. Carranza. 1997. *Profiles in two-way immersion education.* McHenry, Ill.: Center for Applied Linguistics and Delta Systems.

Crawford, J. 1995. *Bilingual education: History, politics, theory and practice,* 3rd ed. Los Angeles, Calif.: Bilingual Education Services.

Cummins, J. 1998. Foreword. In *Bilingual and ESL classrooms: Teaching in multicultural contexts,* ed. C. J. Ovando and V. P. Collier, 2nd ed., ix–xi. Boston: McGraw-Hill.

Cziko, G. A. 1992. The evaluation of bilingual education: From necessity and probability to possibility. *Educational Researcher* 21(2): 10–15.

Epstein, N. 1977. *Language, ethnicity, and the schools: Policy alternatives for bilingual-bicultural education.* Washington, D.C.: Institute for Educational Leadership, George Washington University.

Erickson, F. 1982. *Kana'i Pono (Striving for Excellence.)* Honolulu: Kamehameha Educational Research Institute. Video.

Fishman, J. A. 1991. *Reversing language shift.* Clevedon, England: Multilingual Matters.

Genesee, F. 1985. Second language learning through immersion: A review of U.S. programs. *Review of Educational Research* 55(4): 541–561.

Genesee, F. 1987. *Learning through two languages: Studies of immersion and bilingual education.* Boston: Heinle and Heinle.

Genesee, F. 1991. Pedagogical implications of second language immersion. Paper presented at the Spanish Association of Applied Linguistics, San Sebastian, Spain, 10 April.

Gertsen, R., R. Taylor, J. Woodward, and W. A. T. White. 1984. Structured English immersion for Hispanic students in the U.S.: Findings from the fourteen year evaluation of the Uvalde, Texas, Program. Paper presented at the Annual Meeting of the American Educational Research Association, New Orleans. ERIC Document Reproduction Service No. ED 247 058.

Hechinger, F. M. 1978. Political issues in education: Reflections and directions. In *Political issues in education,* ed. W. I. Israel, 127–135. Washington, D.C.: Council of Chief State School Officers.

Hernández-Chávez, E. 1984. The inadequacy of English immersion education as an educational approach for language-minority students in the United States. In *Studies on immersion education: A collection for United States educators,* by California State Department of Education, 144–183. Sacramento: California Department of Education.

Hughes, E. 1996. Personal communication. 24 June.

Krashen, S. D. 1997. *Under attack: The case against bilingual education.* Culver City, Calif.: Language Education Associates.

Masahiko, M., and C. J. Ovando. 1995. Language issues in multicultural contexts. In *Handbook of research on multicultural education,* ed. J. A. Banks and C. A. M. Banks, 427–444. New York: Macmillan.

Nieto, S. 2000. *Affirming diversity: The sociocultural context of multicultural education,* 3rd ed. New York: Longman.

Ovando, C. J. 1990. Politics and pedagogy: The case of bilingual education. *Harvard Educational Review* 60(3): 341–356.

Ovando, C. J. and V. P. Collier. 1998. *Bilingual and ESL classrooms: Teaching in multicultural contexts,* 2nd ed. Boston: McGraw-Hill.

Ovando, C. J., and L. P. McCarty. 1992. Multiculturalism in U.S. society and education: Why an irritant and paradox? Paper presented at the World Council for Curriculum and Instruction, Seventh Triennial World Conference, Cairo, Egypt, 25 July to 2 August.

Ramírez, J. D., R. Wofron, and F. Morales. 1985. Description of immersion strategy programs in the United States. Arlington, Va.: SRA Technologies. ERIC Document Reproduction Service No. ED 206 352.

Ramírez, J. D., S. Yuen, and D. R. Ramey. 1991. Final report: Longitudinal study of structured immersion strategy, early-exit, and late-exit transitional bilingual education programs for language-minority children. *NABE Journal* 8: 15–34.

Roberts, C. A. 1995. Bilingual education program models: A framework for understanding. *Bilingual Research Journal* 19(3&4): 369–377.

Rosie, P., and W. Holm. 1980. *The Rock Point experience: A longitudinal study of Navajo school program.* Washington, D.C.: Center for Applied Linguistics.

Rossell, C. H. 1989. The effectiveness of educational alternatives for limited English proficient children. Paper presented at the Public Policy Conference on Bilingual Education, Washington, D.C., 13 April.

Salins, P. D. 1997. *Assimilation American style.* New York: Basic Books.

Schlesinger, A. M., Jr. 1992. *The disuniting of America: Reflections on a multicultural society.* New York: W. W. Norton.

Schermerhorn, R. A. 1970. *Comparative ethnic relations.* New York: Random House.

Schorr, B. 1983. Grade school project helps Hispanic pupils learn English quickly—but Texas test's avoidance of a bilingual approach is a source of controversy. *Wall Street Journal* 30 November, pp. 1, 24.

Skutnabb-Kangas, T., and J. Cummins, eds. 1988. *Minority education: From shame to struggle.* Clevedon, England: Multilingual Matters.

Solís, J. 1996. Personal communication. 7 August.

Texas Education Agency. 1988. *Program evaluation report: Bilingual/ESL education.* Austin: Publication Distribution Office.

Texas Education Code. 1982. *University of Texas Law School Bulletin* 7: 163–168.

U.S. Commission on Civil Rights. 1971. *Report II: The Unfinished Education.* Washington, D.C.: U. S. Government Printing Office.

Willig, A. C. 1985. A meta-analysis of selected studies on the effectiveness of bilingual education. *Review of Educational Researcher* 55(3): 269–317.

Wink, J., C. Bender, I. Bravo, L. Putney, R. Reberg, and S. Whitehead. 1995. California: A picture of diverse language groups and ESL/bilingual programs. *Bilingual Research Journal* 19(3&4): 641–659.

Margarita Calderón   *Argelia Carreón*

*T*he U.S.-Mexico border is a place to study inter- and intraconflict and possibilities
between teachers, their administrators, and communities. Border conflicts, moreover, go beyond the two-thousand-mile-long dividing line between the United States
and Mexico. They extend into large urban centers throughout the nation where large
numbers of Latino students flow in and out of schools. Border pedagogy must not only
create new knowledge but also address how inequalities, power, and human suffering
are rooted in basic institutional structures. This chapter examines an initiative of a
group of binational researchers, teachers, and school administrators to begin to create a
new border pedagogy. This new initiative addresses the intersociopolitical and pedagogical possibilities bilingual teachers and teachers working with language-minority
students face every day.*

CHAPTER 9

In Search of a New Border Pedagogy

Sociocultural Conflicts Facing Bilingual Teachers and Students Along the U.S.-Mexico Border

Margarita Calderón
Johns Hopkins University

Argelia Carreón
Success for All Foundation

The Future Is at the Border

The U.S.-Mexico border is more than just a geographic boundary. It connotes opportunity, struggle, fragmentation, tradition, and hope for the future. With respect to education, it is a place of extremes. On the one hand, the schools along the border that have the largest numbers of bilingual teachers and language-minority students have a history of academic and linguistic underachievement. On the other hand, international, binational, and two-way bilingual schools are emerging there that hold great promise academically in addition to serving as sociocultural models for the future.

The largest twin cities on the Texas-Mexico border, El Paso and Juárez, are viewed as a single entity by the more than 2 million people who live there. Every day, they exchange their cultures and economies, their difficulties and vitalities. Each has a past entwined with the other's. Sometimes they do not admit it, but they share the future, too (Sharp 1994).

The future is linked through environmental, health, and infrastructure requirements superimposed by the North American Free Trade Agreement (NAFTA). *La Frontera* has been interdependently linked for the past four hundred years as the two cultures and two countries emerge. Today, nearly three in five Americans live in households in which Spanish is spoken. Students from *La Frontera* families are often defined by the characteristic they share—a lack of fluency in English. But such a definition masks their diversity and underestimates the challenge facing the schools (García 1996). Attempting to assimilate students into a "mainstream culture" does not work, because the "mainstream culture" along the border is very different from what the schools have erroneously attempted to establish all these years. Schools have responded to the bicultural and bilingualism issues along the border by attempting to accelerate this assimilation into the American mainstream. Their mission has been to Americanize immigrants and even fourth-generation Mexican Americans by replacing their native language with English. Because schools have not learned to appreciate and capitalize on the diversity of their students, a cycle of underachievement and low status for Spanish and the Mexican culture has been perpetuated.

Need for a Border Pedagogy

The need for a "border pedagogy" becomes evident when we consider the forces that are shaping the future of towns and cities along the border. This two-thousand-mile-long line, however, is essentially imaginary. "Some say it stretches into parts of Houston, San Antonio, Chicago, and Miami, or that it can be found in North Denver, East L.A., Oakland, and San Francisco's Mission District—approximately the same outpost boundaries that marked the height of the Spanish expansion north from Mexico during the 17th and 18th centuries" (Sharp 1994, 28). Forty percent of New York City's new student population in 1977 were from Mexico. Manhattan is now known in many circles as "Manhatitlán" because many of the immigrants come from the Tenochtitlán area of central Mexico. There are thousands of Hispanic-Latino students along the extended border and its corridors. Therefore, a border pedagogy is critical not only for the twin cities but also for addressing the needs of students throughout the Latino corridor.

- What should this border pedagogy look like?
- How can schools break the cycle of low performance?
- How can principals and teachers reinvent the norms, structures, and school cultures so that they reflect the needs of the community culture?
- What type of staff development processes help cultivate relations so that differences are respected yet become part of the norms and structures of the school culture?

We use the term *border pedagogy* in this chapter to integrate two levels of meaning. On the one hand, it is used as a marker for the physical border with Mexico and the corridor through which Latinos migrate back and forth between the United States and Mexico. We also borrow Giroux's (1992) and Giroux's and McLaren's (1994) definitions. Giroux (1992) defines *border pedagogy* as an "explicitly stated agenda of progressive education." He reminds us that "a border pedagogy must take up the dual task of not only creating new objects of knowledge but also addressing how inequalities, power, and human suffering are rooted in basic institutional structures" (33). Estrada and McClaren (1993) define borders as "sites of interlinguistic play and liminal identities where many realities come together" (28). They see the borderization of the United States as a process in which "borders are widening, creating cultural sites of instability—sites that are not Anglo and not not-Anglo; not Chicano and not not-Chicano . . . where cultures can collide creatively or destructively" (28). Yet we feel that those liminal identities are the forces that will thrust people on the border onto the threshold of an exciting future. These are the people who are changing American society. Their futures will have an impact on the schooling practices of both countries (Calderón 1996a).

Central to the notion of a border pedagogy is the role that principals, teachers, and teacher educators might play in fostering or restricting the social and cultural transformations needed in border schools. In a recent study of seven border schools with 75 percent to 95 percent Hispanic student populations, principals and teachers continued to ignore the identity of their students as they set out to "reform" their schools. They restructured their schools and continued using the dominant pedagogy instead of switching to a pedagogy that questions the omissions and tensions of decades of teaching the "invisible" minority (in this case, majority). Since half of the principals in that study were Hispanic themselves, born and raised in the area, we can get a sense of how solidly the borders have been built around their notions of schooling in the past few decades. It will take tremendous intellectual and emotional energy to examine and situate their own histories and voices (Nash and Calderón 1996). Racism and the boundaries of power marginalize and continually oppress even those who rise to power.

At the other extreme, we have principals in Juárez schools who have adopted a deep-seated reconstructivist approach to creating new schools. These principals have teamed up with principals in El Paso who are also seeking interventions through understanding, continuous study, and contact with teachers and students from both sides of the border. They see the school as part of a wider social, economic, and political agenda and are willing to listen to the voices of students, teachers, and parents in their school community. They have created a community of educators with similar goals and adventurous spirits as they set out to rediscover the new Southwest frontier, *La Nueva Frontera.*

The principals, as primary agents of the new border schools, have as much unlearning as learning to do. Their initial university preparation was targeted at reproducing the institutional agendas of the past, and their present in-service preparation focuses on the norms of reformational mandates. The globalization of free market economies, however, blurs borders and calls for a more linguistically and technologically sophisticated labor force.

As NAFTA opens the border for economic interdependence, quality education becomes ever more imperative. Although a planned strategy is not yet in place, interest in second-language study for economic purposes is increasing (Sharp 1994). Interpreters and translators have more work than ever. Large companies are now seeking employees with both bilingual and business/managerial skills. Such people have an edge over others without language capability. The same is happening in schools. Bilingual teachers are in great demand. In fact,

Texas, like many other states, is having to import Spanish-speaking teachers to meet the supply and demand.

While the academic success of language-minority students is becoming a new priority in education, the beliefs about and attitudes toward these students are slow in changing. Educators and the community have a choice whether to accept these students as an invaluable resource and the key to our future or to continue with policies and practices that reinforce the inequities that widen the gap between language-majority and -minority students. As we enter the twenty-first century, this minority will be at least 25 percent of the newly entering workforce in the United States (Collier 1995, 41). In border communities, where it is common to have at least one-third of the student population in grades prekindergarten through 12 enrolled in bilingual or English as a Second Language (ESL) programs, and where the makeup of these communities is more than 70 percent minority, the workforce will reflect the makeup of each community.

> From a purely economic point of view, failure to pursue educational equity for minority youth is a form of slow suicide. The internationalization of the economy will require an increasing economic competitiveness. The U.S. lead in this area continues to diminish as we lose ground in technology and manufacturing and in the development of a competent and competitive workforce. Just as twenty-five years ago no one could have projected the diversity of computer-related careers that exist today, it is impossible to project the diversity of careers that will be available during the 21st century. We must transcend the common practices of focusing on basic skills and marketable skills for minority students without providing the thinking and learning skills that will help them to adapt to the 21st century career environment. (Cawelti 1993, 12).

For border communities, the choice is clear: we must examine the research and discover that the changes needed for language-minority students to succeed academically and for teachers and schools to facilitate their success will benefit all students. Yet most schools are still not convinced that bilingual education is a desirable goal.

The constant attack on bilingual education continues in the face of mounting research on the intellectual benefits of bilingualism. The power of language is multiplied by the number of languages that a person speaks. Current longitudinal research results indicate that in the long term, students schooled in quality late-exit and two-way bilingual education programs match or outperform monolingual English-speaking students (Collier 1995).

The adverse conditions for the education of language-minority students vary in intensity in communities along the border and throughout the United States. Even under the most positive circumstances, negative attitudes still affect the school and its community. It is often difficult for the layperson to understand that the best and most effective route to academic success and the acquisition of English is a balanced instructional approach that makes extensive use of both the native language and English. Through quality instruction in two languages, educators transform the image of language-minority students from being limited in English to being "linguistically gifted people." Schools that believe in this philosophy succeed in presenting the benefits of bilingual education to the community, and all profit from the intellectual power of bilingualism. However, in most schools, only the bilingual teachers are expected to be the advocates for bilingual education.

Whether school officials, teachers, or teacher educators, we need to ask ourselves these questions:

If we have the research, knowledge base, and technology to implement quality bilingual education, what is it that keeps some schools from doing so?

What conflicts do teachers and school principals face that prevent them from shifting from a deficit model to an enrichment model for bilingual education?

What types of educational reform should be investigated and how?

As schools move forward into comprehensive reform, they will most certainly come face to face with such conflicts. The conflicts will first emerge between teachers, administrators, and students as they begin to peel back the layers of past biases and racism. The status of Spanish and English, instructional approaches, program models, language proficiency of teachers, the preparation of the teachers, the principal's beliefs and leadership role, and parental knowledge about the program are but a few of the conflicts that schools typically face in the midst of change. These conflicts are further discussed below in an attempt to highlight what needs to be addressed in a border pedagogy.

Conflicts Facing Bilingual Teachers, Administrators, and Students

Throughout our careers, we have found that conflicts can arise from simple misunderstandings or misinterpretations between educators at all levels. Or they can arise from years of power struggles, racism, or prejudice. Conflict usually emerges from a fear of change. Most of these conflicts stem from perceptions about Spanish—and all its ramifications. The conflict with Spanish leads to other conflicts, which can be categorized as follows: Spanish coexisting with English; Spanish as the medium of instruction; degree of proficiency; principals' and administrators' agendas; parents' and communities' prejudiced views; students' experiences; and conflicting messages from staff development programs and school reform practices.

Conflicts with Spanish Coexisting with English   One of the major questions facing bilingual educators is the status of the minority language, which along the U.S.-Mexico border is predominantly Spanish. Educators as well as parents often struggle with the role that Spanish plays, especially in bilingual education. In spite of program requirements and research results, the perception that academic success is accelerated by providing more English and less Spanish instruction is often held by parents, the community, and many educators. This attitude accompanies a lack of value accorded to the Spanish language, which is often considered inferior and associated with low socioeconomic status.

Americans in general fear languages (Cummins 1993) and Spanish in particular. It is usually the language of the new immigrant, who is seen as the intruder encroaching upon the diminishing resources of this country and preventing the eradication of a foreign tongue on U.S. soil. Consequently, the use of Spanish along with English in bilingual education evokes deep-seated fears and prejudices that may have been fostered in the past but are no longer relevant in today's social, economic, and educational contexts. Nevertheless, the majority of principals and teachers in schools with large populations of Latino students still hold strongly to the old beliefs and traditions. Their schools reflect a reductionist approach and a deficit model of education for all their Latino students.

The negative feelings toward Spanish are shared by many Latinos. Because of their experiences in border schools, they have grown up with less than positive feelings about their ancestral language and culture. Some who became educators found themselves attempting to compensate for their inner conflicts through their educational philosophies and approaches. Some tried too hard to change the system and got burned or burned out. Some tried their best to exemplify the American ideal by negating and eliminating all that was Mexican or Spanish. Unfortunately, these inner conflicts are handed down to younger generations in their classrooms or schools.

In spite of this environment, Spanish and English coexist in the communities of *La Frontera*. It is common to find signs and advertisements in English and Spanish in communities on both sides of the U.S.-Mexico border. New market opportunities help the business community be more open to the use of both languages. Profits do not discriminate! Employment ads increasingly seek applicants who are bilingual and often biliterate. However, aside from the business sector, the rest of the community has not kept pace with this shift. Border community leaders still make statements that expose their long-held beliefs about language—their xenophobia. Recently, a city official asked, "How much longer does our community need bilingual education? Haven't those kids learned English yet?"

Conflicts with Spanish as the Medium of Instruction   The shortage of bilingual teachers constitutes a major obstacle for implementing quality bilingual programs. Even if the teachers are available, school administrators are reluctant to transfer nonbilingual teachers out of their schools. This perpetuates the piecemeal approach to bilingual instruction. Students may have a fully qualified bilingual teacher for only one or two grades. This situation creates illogical configurations in schools such as bilingual grades 1 and 3 but no bilingual kindergarten or grades 2, 4, or 5.

Even among bilingual teachers, conflicts occur as the result of differences in philosophy on matters such as the extent to which the first language should be used and how English should be taught. Bilingual teachers feel the pressure to "get the kids into English as quickly as possible" and "sacrifice Spanish" so they can "teach to the test in English." The "teaching" of English then becomes a drilling exercise in which the holistic essence of learning English is lost, along with the students' love for learning.

A new elementary principal recently reported that when she began observing the ESL classes in her school to find out what they were doing, she found that there were no teaching plans; each teacher used a hodgepodge of materials—some dating from 1972—and most teachers used Spanish 60 percent or more of the time. The Spanish was usually employed to translate English exercises in workbooks.

Four principals from elementary schools with over 50 percent Latino student populations and at least 30 percent limited-English-proficient students reported that they did not know if their "bilingual program was transitional, maintenance, or what." There was no clarification from the district about what to teach in English or what to teach in Spanish and for what length of time. We have visited schools throughout the nation, and this situation seems to be the norm in many.

The time-on-language conflicts are exacerbated when bilingual and nonbilingual teachers turn their philosophical differences into an "us versus them" cold war. Divisions are drawn, and the bilingual program becomes the stepchild of the school. At that point, no administrator dares to interfere. And for the last decade or so, this cold war has been the normal climate of the school.

Conflicts with Spanish Proficiency   The bilingual teacher's bilingual competency also affects the quality of the program and the perceptions of parents and colleagues. Most facilities have varying degrees of bilingual proficiency. Some bilingual teachers were schooled in a Latino country and the United States; some took Spanish only through college courses; some studied abroad one or two summers, some are learning Spanish as they teach; and some refuse to learn it even though the majority of their students speak it. Some teachers were schooled mainly in Latino countries and still struggle with English. A lack of proficiency leads to insecurity about one's teaching. Many bilingual teachers are afraid to open their doors to instructional innovations and collegial activities for fear of being found out.

Understandably, proficiency in two languages leads to success not just for students but also in the professional endeavors of teachers. It is not unusual to find that the teachers in the school who are on the cutting edge of knowledge and activity are the proficient bilingual teachers. There is also research showing that teacher fluency in the students' first language is linked to better student achievement in English and Spanish (McGroarty 1986). We have found from our studies that the more teachers continue to learn two languages, the more their teaching improves (Calderón 1997a; Calderón, Hertz-Lazarowitz, and Slavin 1997c).

Proficiency plays a big role in the employment of two languages during instruction. Many bilingual teachers still struggle with code-switching (using some words in English and others in Spanish in the same sentence). Some grew up code-switching because that was the social norm; others do it because they did not have quality bilingual instruction themselves. As bilingual programs flourished in the seventies, many code-switchers became teachers. Others were "prepared" in teacher preparation programs to use "preview-review" methods in which a concept is introduced in English and then translated into Spanish. These habits are hard to break. Teachers say it is easier to translate and then move on to another part of the lesson. Through classroom ethnographies, it becomes obvious that code-switching and preview-review methods serve only to help students tune out the target language of instruction and to model fragmented bilingualism.

The Principal's Conflicts   Perhaps the greatest silent conflicts are suffered by the school's administrator. Caught in the "us versus them" conflict and in the conflict between what is pedagogically sound and what is politically expected, a principal often chooses to sustain the status quo. Peer pressure from other principals in the same district often sways the irresolute principal in the direction of the latest fad instead of a critical pedagogy and research-based program.

Some school conflicts stem from the way programs are funded for language-minority students. Although bilingual funds are supposed to provide services and resources above and beyond the amount of money generated per student, administrators sometimes divert these funds to provide the core materials and staff services. While the intent of bilingual funding is to bridge the equity gap, in such cases it supplants general funds, thereby leaving even more money than before to the other students. Thus, the imbalance of access is ensured year after year.

Bilingual and ESL teachers who are aware of the needs and consequences of such action often find themselves at odds with administrators and in conflict with other teachers. When new textbooks or instructional materials are distributed in such schools, the bilingual or ESL teachers get their materials only if enough are left after the mainstream teachers get theirs. In the interest of their students, some teachers quickly protest, while others merely do without. Sometimes bilingual or ESL teachers do not realize that they are missing materials sent specifically for their students because these materials were distributed to the mainstream teachers.

High school administrators have great difficulty dealing with the needs of language-minority students. High schools face the challenge of little English and little time. The clock is ticking away and working against new arrivals who need time to learn English while also meeting the performance standards of the high school curricula. On the one hand, some administrators have students entering high school with no English first attend a one-year program devoted to English instruction, so that when they attend content classes, they will fit in without any accommodations. While this may seem reasonable, it denies the students access to the full curriculum the first year and probably further delays the fulfillment of graduation requirements. On the other hand, to avoid personnel conflicts, administrators often place first-year students in high school math classes with teachers who lack the appropriate training in language acquisition and second-language methodology for teaching content subjects. Administrative actions such as these have devastating consequences for language-minority students. They create an unaccepting environment for students and teachers and undermine the potential for academic success. School accountability for literacy and academic achievement is often circumvented by the lack of district, state, and national testing programs that provide assessment instruments in languages other than English and thereby negate the value of instruction via other languages.

Conflicts of Parents and Communities   Many border communities find that new arrivals are seen as a threat to the established immigrant or second-generation population. There are fewer jobs to go around for low-skilled workers and more students with special language needs to educate, which usually translates into higher taxes and lower incomes. The need for bilingual and ESL teachers increases as the need for mainstream monolingual teachers tends to decrease. These and other demands on the community often polarize groups.

Parents enrolling young children in school express divergent views of the benefits of education. Whereas some monolingual English-speaking parents seek schools in which their children will have the opportunity to learn Spanish and profit from the social, intellectual, and economic benefits of speaking two languages, others fear that learning another language will interfere with their children's immediate academic success. They do not see this as an opportunity to prepare for high school and university foreign language requirements or for the demands of a global economy.

Some Latino parents have beliefs and expectations that are different from those generally held by the schools. The demographic makeup of most border cities creates school communities with large groups of language-minority students who require separate classes for bilingual education, which limits their interaction with the mainstream. It is under these circumstances that Spanish-speaking parents and other minorities tend to question the benefits of bilingual education. These parents understandably want the best for their children, and the best for them is to learn English. They often say, "Pero maestra, mi hija ya sabe español. Lo que necesita es aprender inglés." (But teacher, my daughter already speaks Spanish. What she needs is to learn English.) This sets the stage for one of the greatest challenges at the school: trying to change the parents' way of conceptualizing the perceived problem.

Culturally diverse students can be "empowered" or "disabled" (Cummins 1994). They can be educationally disadvantaged, or they can benefit from the cognitive and intellectual flexibility that results from their interactions with schooling. The effect of schooling on these students will be determined by the effort made by schools to understand the students' background and to provide for their needs. The extent to which schools incorporate the minority students' language and culture sets the stage for empowerment. A pedagogy that motivates students to use language actively to generate their own knowledge promotes self-efficacy. The school further embraces its responsibilities by encouraging the participation of the minority community as an integral component of the children's education. When professionals conducting student assessment become advocates for minority students by studying the academic difficulty experienced by students as a function of the school context, instead of a problem inherent in the students, the danger of labeling culturally and linguistically diverse students as disabled is minimized (Cummins 1994).

These four factors can be viewed as characteristics of effective schooling and measures of appropriate bilingual or English as a Second Language programs. More important, they are the determiners of the potential for academic and socioemotional strength of each individual student. It is a well-known fact that the desire for safety and a feeling of security is a basic human need. What safe haven does a school offer when strange noises and mysterious ways confront a youngster and learning is limited to what can be inferred or misunderstood? How does a high school student feel when asked to read an unknown poem in English? When students do not see themselves in comfortable surroundings, when they do not see themselves reflected in the content and books used for instruction, schooling is seen as something done to them and not as a process for personal growth.

Along the border and among language minorities across the country, the self-identity of language-minority students remains liminal. Some seek to become more acceptable and feel more white by selecting English first names to accompany their Spanish last names. Others, like the Tere renamed Terry by her first grade teacher in a skit by the well-known Chicano author and lecturer Carmen Tafoya, suffer the humiliation of finding out that any exuberance they bring to school and openness to learning soon are stifled when the door is closed on the pride and self-assurance of a language and culture that has nurtured them to this point. As Tere, now Terry, says, "No importa Mis." Yes, it no longer matters to many children and youth in our schools who must find other places where they will be accepted. The question is, where and by whom will that sense of belonging be provided? When such students feel that their identity is not important, gangs serve as a welcoming alternative. It is difficult to compete with a group culture that embraces its members with the promise: " I'll die for you. I'll kill for you."

Conflicts with School Reform and Staff Relations   Perhaps the biggest conflict a school leader confronts is the lack of a unifying and supportive philosophy at the school based on knowledge of research, policy, pedagogy, and teaching-learning needs. Pervasive lack of knowledge on the part of a school staff, coupled with superficial attention to relationships, promotes the negative and counterproductive attitudes that create the conflicts in the first place. This dominant "culture of a school" tends to stabilize reform efforts so that nothing fundamentally changes, particularly its people. The problem of the knowledge base from which the teaching profession operates remains a serious one. In many respects, the knowledge base in education has advanced greatly during the past five years, but such advances remain terribly slow to find their way into classroom practice and school reform efforts.

Since site-based management is the most prevalent reform initiated to provide the knowledge base for improving student achievement and school accountability, schools must look to themselves for the answers to past injustices. They also need to embrace research-based methods and not spend so much time debating which latest instructional trend to use. As schools take stock of their needs and establish goals and plans for improvement, they must use new structures for self-study and continuous renewal to meet these challenges and address common conflicts. Although school reform means different things to different schools, it does imply a search for professional growth and changes in the approach to staff development.

Historically, staff development programs have tended to disempower teachers or to create wider gaps between bilingual and nonbilingual teachers. This fragmentation and alienation have had an extremely negative impact on bilingual teachers. Bilingual or minority teachers have generally been sent to the back of the "mainstream bus" of school reform and staff development. Others always get to make decisions for themselves and their students. These actions have engendered in bilingual teachers at best a superficial interest in school innovations and restructuring efforts and at worst a deep-rooted sense of disempowerment. Their isolation has caused many teachers to settle comfortably into their own ways of teaching. They come to in-service meetings but go back to their classrooms reassured that no one will hold them accountable for changing old habits. When we ask these teachers why they are not trying the new methods or techniques, they simply respond that it is too much work! Sometimes they come up with other excuses, such as "There are no materials in Spanish" or "It doesn't work with my students."

Conflicts with Traditional Staff Development Practices   The conflict between comfort and continuous learning in bilingual contexts stems from years of ineffective staff development practices. Staff development has meant bringing in a motivational speaker for a couple of hours—the more expensive, the better—or consultants who provide "lots of helpful hints and techniques and some showy materials" in one-shot workshops; or a series of workshops in English, without adequate materials in both languages. There is rarely follow-up to these workshops, and bilingual teachers report that opportunities for collegial learning and problem solving are almost nonexistent.

An exhaustive meta-analysis of effective programs for Latino students (Fashola et al. 1996) showed that throughout the country, bilingual teachers' classroom performance has rarely been considered, analyzed, or held accountable. Administrators and teacher evaluators report that they barely know how to judge good bilingual instruction, much less how to give teachers feedback for improvement. Therefore, bilingual teachers are left to their own devices to implement instructional strategies behind closed doors. They go along with the fads for a while; occasionally, they try something new; but they seldom change their fundamental practice.

In essence, the conflicts created by the staff development practices prevalent at schools have these characteristics: they focus too much on skill and on giving teachers bags of tricks; they are typically transmission models where teachers are fed information; they ignore the context and diversity of classrooms; they are one-size-fits-all workshops where all grade-level teachers receive the same "training"; they do not address the need to develop positive human relations and collegial working relations; and teachers' learning communities in which teachers can construct their own learning are nonexistent.

Conflict as Opportunity   Whatever the conflict, it must be seen as an opportunity to address a need or meet a challenge. If schools are to prepare students to be competent and innovative problem solvers, educators must establish structures for decision making and continuous self-improvement that address conflict within this framework. The next section, which describes promising practices, illustrates some ways in which successful schools turn from a deficit model to a talent development model. By tapping the talents of parents, students, teachers, and administrators, a new school without boundaries is built.

A New Border Pedagogy and a Talent Development Model

School reform and site-based decision making has enabled schools in border cities to experiment with new ways of schooling language-minority students. At the elementary level, two-way bilingual programs have become the vehicle for positive change. This more holistic view of bilingual program implementation does away with artificial bureaucratic and racist arguments about when to move students from Spanish into English or when students should exit the bilingual program. Instead, teams of teachers and administrators focus on implementing student-centered programs that are integrated with whole-school efforts to improve and enrich instruction for all students.

A New Border Pedagogy for Students   A new border pedagogy must take into consideration that the students we are preparing along the U.S.-Mexico border must be able to manage complexity, find and use resources, and continually learn new technologies and occupations. The need for an emphasis on global and binational education has brought out the need for cultural literacy and multiliteracies. In contrast to the low-skilled assembly lines of the past and today's *maquiladoras* (assembly plants), tomorrow's work sites will require employees to frame problems; design their own tasks; plan, construct, and use new technologies; evaluate outcomes; and cooperate in finding novel solutions to problems.

Since border-city students live in bicultural or binational communities, they must also understand and evaluate multidimensional issues that will continue to affect their bilingual society. As Luke (1994) reminds us, the twenty-first century citizen will work in media-, text-, and symbol-saturated environments. For millions of students, these will be bilingual or multilingual environments.

English proficiency and academic success are the target of bilingual programs, and it is the responsibility of the whole school community to provide the best means of attaining that objective. The philosophy of the school is to use the native language in developing literacy skills and attaining academic knowledge and skills (Collier 1995; Cummins 1993; Krashen 1996; García 1996). There is no question that bilingual education works; rather, the question is how well bilingual education is being implemented to ensure that students benefit from the intellectual power of biliteracy.

A border pedagogy for students that builds on the language and culture of the community and celebrates its diversity creates an opportunity for learning and questioning without judging the worth of the individual or demeaning that background. Teens can find a safe haven in religious groups in high school, such as Youth for Christ, the Fellowship of Christian Athletes, Young Life, Youth Alive, or Friends in Christ. Because they value and respect the student's background, these groups are becoming more popular in border-area high schools than secular groups such as the student council, the French club, or Odyssey of the Mind (Villalva 1998). In the primary grades, it is just as easy and more effective to begin the school year by redesigning the traditional unit on "Me" or "I am special" to explore the ethnic, cultural, and language background of the class. The collaborative knowledge helps students make connections with the real world and the place they can create in it for themselves. It is particularly important for older students to explore their cultural heritage and analyze knowledge and the world around them from different perspectives to find connections and opportunities for self-realization.

Although it is common knowledge that each individual perceives the world differently, it is often difficult to internalize this notion. In an effort to give El Paso high school students in their first year of schooling in the United States an opportunity to learn about their new country and see their place among its people, the English for Speakers of Other Languages program includes a course entitled "One People, Many Cultures." This course meets the need described by Cortés (1986) for students to view universal human qualities as the basis for building bridges between people of different backgrounds, while at the same time understanding the real and meaningful group variations in cultural, racial, ethnic, and social experience. Through such a process of viewing ourselves "juxtaposed against other different individuals as a way of better understanding and illuminating ourselves," cultural awareness is facilitated (Kibler 1996, 239).

Schools that actively seek culturally relevant and language-appropriate materials and develop curriculum to meet the needs of language-minority students find that a little effort will yield guidelines for the selection of materials, appropriate literature, and a multitude of other resources. An example of such guidelines for using cultural experiences in the classroom are those developed by Ngoe-Diep Thi Nguyen and John Kibler (1993):

> Teachers maximize learning by using cultural experiences in the classroom where students can compare and contrast subject matter of similar themes, genres, or historical significance.

> Teachers use content-based instruction that is grounded in diverse, real-life purposes and contexts, and raise students' awareness of the complexity and interconnectedness of human knowledge.

> In their classrooms, teachers and students treat cross-cultural conflict as a natural part of communication that can be resolved and create experiences that challenge a student's own cultural assumptions (250).

Sources of information, rationale, and implementation procedures are also readily found in the literature. At a 1996 seminar for bilingual education teachers from El Paso, Texas, Kathy Escamilla (1996) proposed that the study of Mexican American history and culture should be part of the core curriculum for all children in the United States, but especially for those who are Mexican American or Chicano. The Hispanic population clearly makes up a significant portion of this nation, and 63 percent of this group is Mexican American; thus, knowledge of the contributions, struggles, history, and contemporary life of this group is critical to the self-awareness and understanding of the critical sociopolitical issues facing this country. Escamilla also provides titles of history textbooks and literature to achieve this goal.

Walter Secada and Yolanda De La Cruz (1996) address the teaching of mathematics in a culturally relevant and linguistically appropriate manner. Kibler, Escamilla, and Secada are only a few valuable sources, but these exemplify the wealth of information and resources available to educators seeking culturally relevant instruction.

A New Border Pedagogy for Teachers   The new border pedagogy requires that teachers combine a profound knowledge of subject matter with a wide repertoire of teaching strategies; state-of-the-art knowledge about learning theory, cognition, pedagogy, curriculum, technology, and assessment; ample knowledge of the students' language, sociocultural, and developmental background; and proficiency in two languages. Teaching for a new border pedagogy goes beyond the standard teacher-proof curriculum, traditional bilingual teaching, and the typical staff development program. Bilingual teachers and administrators must now undertake tasks they have never before been called on to accomplish. They will need a strong support system to sustain their motivation, sense of experimentation, and success. The support system must be constructed to give teachers profound learning opportunities, support, freedom within a well-structured program, and resources to do their job well.

With the new border pedagogy, teaching is seen as a professional craft. Teachers are "expected to analyze or diagnose situational factors and adapt working strategies to the true needs . . . of their clients" (Mitchell and Kerchner 1983, 218). In the situation of the border and extended border, the clients are truly diverse. The deliberative teacher engages in self-reflection and analysis, makes carefully considered choices about instruction based on the needs of students, and assumes responsibility for the curriculum (Zumwalt 1988). Professionals not only know whether and when to choose particular courses of action according to general principles, but they can also evaluate complex situations in which many variables intersect. Practice is monitored by peers according to standards of the profession and the standards reflect the interactive, complete nature of the work. This also implies greater interaction with other professionals. In the case of bilingual and ESL teachers, collegiality also means interdependence among themselves and the mainstream teachers.

The new border pedagogy and talent development model fosters the teachers' proficiency in the first language of the students and uses the students' native language to promote academic excellence in two languages. The dual-language or two-way bilingual programs foster a positive self-concept, pride in two languages and two cultures, and multicultural understanding among teachers and students. Two-way bilingual programs provide an important role for mainstream and bilingual teachers in the instruction of all students in the school.

Promising Practices for Parents and Community and School Partnerships

Innovative communities accept the dynamic nature and cultural diversity of their citizens as an opportunity to create effective models for the enhancement of education for both language-minority and language-majority students. Two-way/dual-language bilingual education programs give the minority language equal status with English by integrating students from both groups in the same class, usually in equal numbers. A process needs to be implemented along with a two-way program to help the participants move from coercive to collaborative relations of power. When this process is effectively organized between dominant and subordinate groups, both groups are empowered.

Parents who saw the advantages of using two languages expressed an interest in Spanish instruction for their children and were the catalyst for the introduction of the Accelerated Two-Way Bilingual Education Program at Rivera Elementary School in El Paso, Texas, in 1991. In contrast, the same program was started at the same time at Rusk Elementary as a result of teachers' interest in integrating students from mainstream and bilingual education. Other schools in the area have since initiated two-way bilingual programs in an attempt to integrate students and improve academic achievement for all within a multicultural context. In 1997, the same interest was expressed by parents at Mesita School, which led to the initiation of a gifted two-way bilingual program in grades 1 through 3. Hillside School is in the process of implementing and researching the first combined Success for All Two-Way Bilingual Program in the nation. Aside from El Paso Independent School District, all the school districts within the city of El Paso are in the process of implementing diverse two-way programs (Calderón 1997b; Slavin and Fashola 1998).

When it comes to parental and community partnerships, a school needs to consider these elements of educational reform and begin actively seeking the involvement of parents and other community people representing the linguistic diversity of the community; developing an awareness that all students can benefit from linguistic strengths; and redefining linguistic diversity as an asset rather than a deficit. This means that bilingual and multicultural programs for all students have to be comprehensively defined and strongly supported (Nieto 1993).

As schools consider such changes and apply an inquiry process, they will embark on the search for a border pedagogy and find unique answers to questions such as the ones raised earlier:

> How can relations be cultivated so that there is respect for differences, yet these differences can become part of the norms and structures of the school culture?

> How can principals and teachers reinvent the norms, structures, and school cultures so that they reflect the needs of the community culture?

As schools and support groups have made efforts to include parents in the educational process, many successful practices and models for parental involvement have evolved. One of the most common strategies has been the creation of a parent resource center, a special place at the school where parents are welcomed to interact with other parents, work on school projects, and hold meetings and classes in arts and crafts; literacy; hands-on math, science, and social studies projects at home; ESL; drug and gang prevention and intervention; or any pertinent topic. This is a common practice at schools required to have a comprehensive parent involvement plan under Title I of the Improving America's School Act. Other well-known models are the Mother-Daughter and Father-Son programs, "Padres con Poder" (Empowered Parents), and family literacy initiatives, such as Read to Your Babies/Léale a Sus Bebés.

The Success for All (SFA) (Slavin and Fashola 1998) schools have perhaps the most comprehensive family support program for each grade level in both Spanish and English. In SFA schools, parents are an essential part of the formula for success. A family support team helps families to feel respected and welcomed in the school and to become active supporters of their children's education. These teams conduct welcome visits for new families, organize many attractive programs in the school, and implement programs such as "Raising Readers/Creando Lectores, and Books and Breakfast/Libros y Desayunos" in which parents learn strategies to use in reading with their own children in their primary language or in facilitating literacy by enjoying stories with their children. The teams also intervene in cases of absenteeism by helping families to get their children to school; and they help with problems involving behavior, nutrition, adequate sleep, and the need for glasses. They also provide workshops for parents to teach them how to fulfill numerous roles within the school and take part in the decision-making process.

Family support teams, parent advisory councils, home visits, and regular community meetings serve as structures to improve parent-school communication and build understanding and respect between parents and the school, as well as to provide opportunities for parents to interact with each other. Welcoming strategies are incorporated to encourage parents to participate, especially those who lack English. Translation services are often provided, or if Spanish is the only non-English language spoken, meetings or conferences are conducted bilingually. Professional teacher conferences often include a parent strand, and parent conferences are increasingly conducted by parent groups, such as the state and local Migrant Students Parent Conference and the annual Texas Parent Engagement Conference.

Schools can continue to improve their efforts to involve parents as partners in education by providing flexible schedules for meetings and simple refreshments as a token of hospitality. School-sponsored transportation and child care increase attendance at meetings and events, especially when these are held at convenient locations selected by the parents. Such accommodations help remove logistical barriers. Attitudinal issues related to self-concept may be addressed by recognizing that migrant and immigrant families value education and by providing sessions on the expectations, roles, and responsibilities of parents (Sosa 1996).

Promising Practices for Professional Development and School Reform   A talent development model is built on the premise that the purpose of staff development is to create a new culture of transformative reform. Effecting fundamental change is clearly the mission of staff development efforts in multicultural and binational settings. The transformation begins with continuous professional development and a structure that facilitates the implementation of a dynamic program constantly under review and improvement. These structures are often called teachers' learning communities (TLCs).

TLCs are structured times during the workday when teachers get together to share accomplishments for the week; do problem solving; exchange instructional strategies; brag about their students' products; learn to analyze student progress; and discover what they need to learn. TLCs enable teachers to co-construct knowledge and meaning from their craft. They are sometimes called "study groups," "collegial groups," "communities of practice," or "grade-level meetings." A TLC by any other name is basically a community of teachers working together toward success in teaching and student learning. It is an opportunity for teachers to collaboratively examine, question, do profound study, experiment and implement, evaluate and change.

Our research on the implementation of the TLCs has found that they allow teachers to develop personal and professional expertise through their collective talents. The purpose and focus of TLCs thus far have been as diverse as school contexts, contingent on the climate and mission of the school or institution. Five purposes have been documented for TLC activity: (1) to improve or adjust existing instructional programs; (2) to integrate complex instructional processes; (3) to construct new programs; (4) to cope with structural barriers in schools ; and (5) to develop the border pedagogy. Descriptions of these studies can be found elsewhere (Calderón 1990–1991, 1991, 1994, 1996b, 1996c, and 1998a, b).

A Border Pedagogy in Progress

The border pedagogy is still in the process of developing through binational research and implementation projects. Researchers and educators are collaborating in novel approaches to problem solving and collaborative learning. In essence, the new way of looking at instruction, professional development, and school reform is being approached through multidisciplinary research and learning communities.

All the schools in the nation will soon experience what the border is currently experiencing. As they attempt reforms, our recommendation is that they first set up TLCs where everyone can learn about first and second language acquisition, the research-based exemplary programs that have been proven to work, and ways to continuously refine their own professional development. The knowledge base exists today. There is no room for excuses any more!

STUDY QUESTIONS

1. Analyze one of the conflicts facing bilingual teachers, administrators, students, parents and communities, school reform, staff relations, or traditional staff development practices, and describe possible opportunities for change.
2. What are the factors that promote or inhibit the participation of parents in the activities of the school community and the decision-making process in the formal education of their children?
3. Hold a study group session with a few classmates to discuss what border pedagogy means to individuals in the group and develop a definition that incorporates the beliefs of the group. Present it to the class or another group for review.
4. How do TLCs contribute to professional development?
5. What have schools done "wrong" in implementing bilingual programs so far? Make a list.
6. Describe the interdependence among the communities on the Texas-Mexico border and explain its possible impact on U.S. schools along the border.
7. In two or three paragraphs, summarize how we can equalize educational success for all students and all teachers.

KEY CONCEPTS

Talent development model

Teacher professional development

Staff development

Learning communities

Border pedagogy

Bilingual education conflicts

School reform

REFERENCES

Calderón, M. 1990–1991. Cooperative learning builds communities of teachers. *Journal of Teacher Education and Practice* 6(2): 75–79.

Calderón, M. 1991. Benefits of cooperative learning for Hispanic students. *Texas Research Journal* 2: 39–57.

Calderón, M. 1994. Mentoring, peer-coaching, and support systems for first-year minority/bilingual teachers. In *Cultural diversity in schools: From rhetoric to practice*, ed. R. A. De Villar, C. J. Faltis, and J. Cummins, 117–144. New York: State University of New York Press.

Calderón, M. 1996a. Bilingual, bicultural, and binational cooperative learning communities for students and teachers. In *Children of la frontera*, ed. J. L. Flores and E. García, 203–228). Charleston, W.V.: ERIC/CRESS.

Calderón, M. 1996b. La construcción de comunidades de aprendizaje para alumnos, maestros y directivos. *Sembrando: Revista de Educación de Jalisco* 1(3): 5–7.

Calderón, M. 1996c. ¿Qué es el aprendizaje cooperativo? *Sembrando: Revista de Educación de Jalisco*, 1(3): 12–14.

Calderón, M. 1997a. *Staff development in multilingual multicultural schools.* ERIC Digest EDO-UD-97-5. New York: ERIC Clearinghouse on Urban Education.

Calderón, M. 1997b. *Preparing teachers and administrators to better serve the needs of Latino students.* Proceedings from the 1996 ETS Invitational Conference. Princeton, N.J.: Educational Testing Service.

Calderón, M. 1998a. *Creating a border pedagogy.* Proceedings from Border Researchers' Learning Community, vol. 1–111. Baltimore: Center for Research on the Education of Students Placed at Risk.

Calderón, M. 1998b. Adolescent sons and daughters of immigrants: How schools can respond. In *Youth experience and development: Social influences and educational challenges,* ed. K. M. Borman and B. Schneider, 65–87. Chicago: National Society for the Study of Education.

Calderón, M., R. Hertz-Lazarowitz, and R. E. Slavin. 1997. *Effects of bilingual cooperative integrated reading and composition on students transitioning from Spanish to English reading.* Report 10. Baltimore: Center for Research on the Education of Students Placed at Risk.

Cawelti, G. 1993. *Challenges and achievements of American education.* Alexandria, Va.: Association for Supervision and Curriculum Development.

Collier, V. 1995. *Promoting academic success for ESL students: Understanding second language acquisition for school.* Princeton, N.J.: NJTESOL-BE.

Cortés, C. 1986. The education of language minority students: A contextual interaction model. In *Beyond language: Social and cultural factors in schooling language minority students,* ed. California Department of Education, 3–34. Los Angeles: California State University, Evaluation, Dissemination and Assessment Center.

Cummins, J. 1993. Empowerment through biliteracy. In *The power of two languages,* ed. J. Villamil Tinajero and A. Ada, 9–25. New York: Macmillan/McGraw-Hill.

Cummins, J. 1994. The socioacademic achievement model in the context of coercive and collaborative relations of power. In *Cultural diversity in schools: From rhetoric to practice,* ed. R. DeVillar, C. Faltis, and J. Cummins, 363–390. New York: State University of New York Press.

Escamilla, K. 1996. Incorporating Mexican American history and culture into the social studies classroom. In *Children of la frontera,* ed. J. L. Flores and E. García, 269–284. Charleston, W.V.: ERIC/CRESS.

Estrada, K., and P. McLaren. 1993. A dialogue on multiculturalism and democracy. *Educational Researcher* (April): 27–33.

Fashola, O. S., R. E. Slavin, M. Calderón, and R. Durán. 1996. *Effective programs for Latino students in elementary and middle schools. Hispanic Dropout Project.* Washington, D.C.: U.S. Department of Education, Office of Educational Research and Improvement.

García, E. 1996. Foreword to *Children of la frontera,* ed. J. D. Flores and E. García, ix–xiv. Charleston, W.V.: ERIC/CRESS.

Giroux, H. 1992. *Border crossings: Cultural workers and the politics of education.* New York: Routledge.

Giroux, H. A., and P. McLaren, eds. 1994. *Between borders: Pedagogy and the politics of cultural studies.* New York: Routledge.

Kibler, J. M. 1996. Latino voices in children's literature: Instructional approaches for developing cultural understanding in the classroom. In *Children of la frontera,* ed. J. D. Flores and E. García, 239–268. Charleston, W.V.: ERIC/CRESS.

Krashen, S. 1996. *Under attack: The case against bilingual education.* Culver City, Calif.: Language Education Associates.

Luke, G. 1994. *The educational implications for NAFTA (transcript of the United States Coalition for Education for All).* Washington, D.C.: Mexican Cultural Institute.

McGroarty, M. 1986. Educators' responses to sociocultural diversity: Implications for practice. In *Beyond language: Social and cultural factors in schooling language minority students,* ed. California Department of Education, 299–343. Los Angeles: California State University Evaluation, Dissemination and Assessment Center.

Mitchell, D. E., and C. T. Kershner. 1983. Unionization and shaping of teacher work. *Teacher Education Quarterly* 10(4).

Nash, J., and M. Calderón. 1996. Principals' attempts at establishing teaming communities in low-performance schools. Paper presented at the American Educational Research Association, New York, April.

Nieto, S. 1992. We speak in many tongues: Language diversity and multicultural education. In *Multicultural education for the 21st century,* ed. C. Díaz, 112–136. Washington, D.C.: National Education Association.

Nguyen, N.-D. T., and J. Kibler. 1993. The refugee experience: Its impact on student adjustment and schooling. *Linguathon* 9(3): 12–14.

Sharp, J. 1994. *Forces of change: Shaping the future of Texas.* Austin, Texas: State Comptroller Office.

Secada, W., and Y. De La Cruz. 1996. Teaching mathematics for understanding to bilingual students. In *Children of la frontera,* ed. J. D. Flores and E. García, 285–310. Charleston, W.V.: ERIC/CRESS.

Slavin, R., and O. S. Fashola. 1998. *Show me the evidence! Proven and promising programs for American schools.* Thousand Oaks, Calif.: Corwin Press.

Sosa, A. 1996. Twenty years after *Lau:* In pursuit of equity, not just a language response program. In *Revisiting the* Lau *decision: 20 years after,* ed. ARC, 34–42. Oakland, Calif.: ARC Associates.

Zumwalt, M. 1988. Teacher competencies: Who, what, where, and why? *Contemporary Education* 59(4).

Villalva, M. 1998. Teens keep the faith. *El Paso Times,* 2 January, p. 133.

Masahiko Minami

*B*ecause *of rapid social diversification, due in large part to rising immigration from Asian countries such as China, Korea, Taiwan, and Japan, educational settings are becoming increasingly multicultural, particularly in urban areas in the United States. This chapter examines the experiences of adolescents from East Asian backgrounds in U.S. high schools. In open-ended interviews, which were conducted at public and private high schools in the industrial Northeast of the United States, Asian students spoke openly about their experiences in classrooms with teachers and with other students. The chapter discloses that Asian students are sensitive about being understood and that teachers and policy makers therefore need to create classrooms that maximize the participation of students who may have different representation styles. In light of the Asian students' experiences and understandings, the chapter also discusses the issue of "model minorities" in the United States.*

CHAPTER 10

Crossing Borders

The Politics of Schooling Asian Students*

Masahiko Minami
San Francisco State University

Cross-Cultural Miscommunications

Although sociologists have long described the United States as a melting pot in which a variety of cultural experiences and backgrounds merge into something entirely new, cross-cultural miscommunications or misunderstandings between individuals are prevalent. One of the most prominent examples in contemporary popular culture is probably the musical *Miss Saigon,* an adaptation of Puccini's *Madame Butterfly.* Such miscommunications occur because people are likely to continue to see other cultures through their own cultural lens and rely on stereotypical misconceptions.

Recent demographic changes in the United States are leading to rapid social diversification. According to a report on the demographic changes from 1980 to 1990 summarized by the *New York Times* (1993), the number of U.S. residents for whom English is a foreign or second language jumped by nearly 40 percent, to 32 million. A notably sharp increase occurred in the number of Asian-language speakers, such as Koreans (127 percent), Chinese (98 percent), and Japanese (25 percent). This rapid expansion in the Asian population in the United States, however, is a rather recent trend. As Uchida (1971) describes in her autobiographic novel *Journey to Topaz,* before World War II, the Issei (the first generation of Japanese Americans) were, by law, not allowed to become U.S. citizens. Because of constant societal concerns about the "New Immigration," later waves of immigrants as well were almost always treated unfairly. As Crawford (1992) puts it, the Asian immigration trend became noticeable only after 1965, when "Congress abolished the national-origins quota system, a

*The research described in this chapter was made possible through a grant from the American Institute for Foreign Study Scholarship Foundation. I thank all the people who cooperated in the data collection, the students who gave time generously for the interviews, and the school personnel who helped make the necessary arrangements. My thanks also go to Thomas Shaw, Rosalind Michahelles, Rachel Sing, and Xiangming Chen for being stimulating collaborators.

189

racially restrictive policy that long favored northwestern Europeans and virtually excluded Asians" (3).

This sharp increase in immigration has brought about changes in bilingual
education. A large number of children whose first language is not English are
entering U.S. schools. How to educate these language-minority children is an
issue with a complex history. In its *Lau v. Nichols* (414 U.S. 563) decision in 1974
involving a class action suit brought by Chinese public school students against
the San Francisco Unified School District, the U.S. Supreme Court held that
public schools had to provide an education to meet the specific needs of limited-
English-proficient (LEP) children.[1] *Lau v. Nichols* has had an enormous impact
on bilingual education programs. In the early 1990s, the U.S. Department of
Education (1992) reported that approximately 2.3 million elementary and secondary school students were LEP children. The Stanford Working Group (1993),
however, estimated that the number of LEP children was much higher: 3.3 million between the ages of 5 and 17.

Much broader measures than those called for in the *Lau v. Nichols* decision,
however, need to be considered to modify U.S. classrooms for nonmainstream
students. In this sense, issues of cultural identity draw critical links between
bilingualism and discourse/participation styles in instructional settings.
Gumperz (1996) argues that the Eurocentric notion of society will soon be obso-
lete. When it comes to school populations in particular, the growing number of
linguistic minorities will surpass the number of monolingual English speakers in
the near future. As a consequence, students will inevitably encounter more than
one grammatical and cultural system in the process of socialization. Although
U.S. society is becoming increasingly both multilingual and multicultural, educators, unfortunately, are not well prepared to work effectively in such diverse
contexts. Deploring the fact that U.S. schools have made no systematic efforts to
cope with this issue, Gumperz (1996) stresses the need to introduce cultural content into school curricula: "Interlocutors should have at least some understanding of their audience's cultural background to make themselves understood"
(469). Understanding the socioculturally embedded nature of language learning
thus holds a significant meaning. Accordingly, we should modify classroom discourse patterns, interactional patterns, and participation structures.

This chapter specifically addresses the critical issue of understanding the
asymmetries of power derived from differences in such factors as race, ethnicity, culture, and language that shape U.S. school contexts. The chapter also
refers to issues associated with English as a Second Language (ESL) and bilin-

---

[1]Genesee (1994) claims that the term "limited English proficient" is unacceptable because it implies
deficiencies in children who live in language-minority households and make substantial use of a
minority language. The term, therefore, is likely to be associated with the "deficit hypothesis,"
which assumes that the parents in some sociocultural groups lack the skills necessary to promote
their children's academic success at school (Auerbach 1989; Brandt 1990). Although I use the term
"limited English proficient" in this chapter, I do not intend to imply any connections with the
deficit hypothesis. See Ovando and Collier (1998) and Crawford (1995) for expanded views on the
use of this term vis-à-vis "English language learner," the more positive term advocated by many
bilingual and ESL educators.

gual classrooms. More than half a million immigrants from nearly one hundred different countries and cultures enter the United States—a nation of immigrants—every year, most of them speaking languages other than English (Crawford 1989; Hakuta 1986). As language-minority children make their way into the schools, the schools need to prepare special programs such as ESL and bilingual programs. A central question is how to improve the quality of learning, instruction, and interaction that take place in ESL and bilingual classrooms. Unfortunately, there have been heated discussions not only among laypeople but also among policy makers for and against bilingual education (Ovando 1990). To make matters worse, there seems to be a general sentiment, particularly among policy makers across the United States, that people from countries with different languages should just learn English (Hakuta 1986; Huddy and Sears 1990). Education is thus deeply involved in politics, and this chapter consequently appeals for policy changes needed to correct inequalities that students from racial and ethnic minority backgrounds might face in the United States.

Although this chapter focuses on Asian immigrant students, it does not intend to contrast the experiences of Asian high school students from different cultural backgrounds. Similarities among Asians certainly exist. For example, when comparing mathematics learning in Japanese, Chinese (Taiwan), and U.S. elementary school classrooms, Stigler and Perry (1988) concluded that whereas Western educators tend to rely on nativism (i.e., children have inherently unique limitations), Asian educators are more comfortable with the principle of empiricism (i.e., all children have the potential, with proper effort, to attain almost anything). Similarly, other studies (Stevenson, Chen, and Lee 1993) reported that for Asian students, effort is more important than ability. Despite such similarities between classrooms of Japanese and Chinese students, however, these researchers warn about the danger of lumping Asians together in one category. Stigler and Perry (1988), for example, added that Chinese classrooms are more performance-oriented, whereas Japanese classrooms are more reflective. Likewise, investigating similarities and differences in preschool education, Tobin, Wu, and Davidson (1989) concluded that although Japan and China are both Asian societies in which group-oriented norms prevail, the two nations differ greatly in their standards of institutional child care. Thus, Asian cultures cannot be lumped together in one category; moreover, different Asian cultures apply distinct standards in socializing and educating children.

Cultural differences among Asians are also evident among adults. Redmond and Bunyi (1993), for example, gathered self-reports by Asian students residing in the United States and examined the relationship between the degree of stress caused by intercultural communication and how the students handled such stress. These researchers found that while students from Chinese, Korean, and Japanese backgrounds alike reported that they suffered from a greater amount of stress compared to students from South American backgrounds, Chinese students felt more competent in handling such stress than the other two Asian groups. Because Asians who live in the United States are from different groups, cultures, and ancestries, extrapolating from one Asian culture and its underlying values to another culture is inappropriate at best, and making sweeping generalizations about Asian cultures leads to erroneous conclusions and stereotyping at worst. The present study, therefore, acknowledges that some differences among Asians, which actually emerged in some of the comments of the students interviewed, are significant. The study, however, does not highlight those differences, because the main goal of this chapter is to present characteristic features of Asian high school students' perspectives on the interaction between teachers and students in U.S. classrooms. Understanding such features should be considered a prerequisite not only for those who are actively engaged in teaching but also for policy makers when they consider the schooling of Asian students. As seen in the *Lau v. Nichols* decision, if inequality in whatever form does exist, then reducing it involves policies that are supposed to provide students with equal opportunities for access to learning.

Method

Participants   Thirty Asian high school students (nine males and twenty-one females) volunteered to participate in this study.[2] There were fifteen students from a Chinese background (two from Hong Kong, twelve from mainland China, and one from Taiwan), fourteen from a Japanese background, and one from a Korean background. Many of them were children of recent immigrants who had been in the United States for no more than two years. Therefore, entering the classroom without adequate proficiency in the dominant language and having to adjust to a whole new set of dynamics and the relationship between teachers and students placed these students in a position similar to that of children starting school for the first time, except that they might start with a different set of information and expectations. Additionally, nineteen of the students attended public schools and eleven attended private high schools in a greater metropolitan area located in the industrial Northeast of the United States.

Procedure   To help facilitate open and honest discussion, the interviewers communicated with all but one of the students in their home languages—either Japanese or Chinese. The Korean student was interviewed in English because none of the interviewers spoke Korean. The interviews were based on a loosely structured set of questions designed to encourage the students to speak openly about their experiences in the classroom with teachers and with other students.[3] This conversational, open, or loosely structured mode of interviewing is sometimes called interactive interviewing (Modell and Brodsky

---

[2]The project initially intended to focus primarily on international students who were planning to stay in the United States for a certain period of time. Because of geographical reasons (i.e., the large population of children of recent immigrants in the northeastern United States), however, we decided to study students from Asian backgrounds in general. Additionally, please note that I will use "Asian students," "language-minority students," and "nonmainstream students" interchangeably hereafter in the results and discussion section.

[3]A preliminary pilot study of ten interviews helped to define which questions would be most productive.

1994), and it is considered an important method for generating personal memories. The average interview lasted about one hour.

Each interview was tape-recorded and transcribed verbatim for coding. This approach was used for two reasons. First, the dynamics of relationships in schools can sometimes silence students—minority students in particular—on critical issues; thus, their experiences and perspectives should be conveyed in their own words. In the oral interview, the process of self-construction is critical, although we must be aware that the interviewee may shape his or her experiences through interactions with the interviewer (Clark 1994). Second, although in this chapter I may interpret students' remarks in certain ways, unnecessary discrepancies in the interpretation of what the students stated should be avoided as much as possible.[4] For these reasons, the verbatim responses of students were coded, using text analysis software.

Results and Discussion

Cultural Discontinuity and Societal/Structural Inequality

The Significance of This Study Derived from Socialization   Culture, which consists of shared customs and values, shapes attitudes and encourages certain types of behaviors. From infancy, an individual is socialized in culturally specific ways, with the primary agent of socialization being the family and local community, which are under the influence of a certain culture. Cultural differences lead to differences in a variety of areas. As previously mentioned, for instance, differences between Eastern and Western learning styles are well documented. American culture—European American culture in particular—values originality and independence; it is believed that creativity will never emerge unless children are encouraged to acquire it early. In Chinese culture, in contrast, it is believed that children will never acquire skills unless they learn those skills early (Gardner 1989).

In multicultural U.S. society, cultural differences bring about complicated issues (Minami and Ovando 1995). Once a child has started schooling, the primary agent of socialization changes from the primary speech community to the secondary speech community, namely the school. Following the mainstream cultural norms and values, the school often tries to reshape the child's interaction style, particularly in the classroom. Because the interaction style that a child has acquired at home is likely to persist, his or her success at school may depend largely on whether the earlier and later patterns of socialization parallel each other (Scollon and Scollon 1981). As Kagitcibasi (1989) argues, furthermore, non-Western urban families are likely to evolve a hybrid structure in which certain values and practices consonant with Western views coexist

---

[4]For example, based on his experience as a European American male who interviewed Nisei (the second generation of Japanese Americans) who had been interned at a relocation center in California during World War II, Hansen (1994) advises that the interviewer be sensitive to subtle nuances that are easily overlooked, particularly in cross-cultural interactions.

with traditional, non-Western values. This explanation seems to hold true of nonmainstream families in the United States. Minami (1995), for example, found that some discourse dimensions of Japanese immigrant families in the United States are close to North American norms, some are close to Japanese norms, and others show a style that is somewhere in between North American and Japanese norms. Asian families in the United States, therefore, are subject to the influence of Western culture; more specifically, Asian Americans' interaction style is generally embedded in American cultural practices and testifies to their Americanization. At the same time, however, they are possibly inducting their children into a certain interaction style that is reflective of their native culture. Socialization into the new environment is complex, particularly in this pluralistic society. Unfortunately, however, policy makers and even teachers may not understand this complexity and its impact on educational settings. In this way, socialization—either explicitly or implicitly—connects to the politics of multiculturalism.

In light of this paradigm, interviewing Asian high school students has been an interesting and productive undertaking in many respects. These adolescents have gone through Asian patterns of early socialization at home and are experiencing a later pattern of socialization that does not necessarily parallel the early ones. The accounts by these adolescents of their interactions with mainstream European American teachers reveal some fundamental differences in socialization between the East and the West. For example, mainstream European Americans may tend to interpret Asian students' generally observant but passive participation style in the classroom as a simple sign of passivity and thus may consider Asians to be not so bright or even dull. Miyanaga (1991) writes:

> The difficulty and frustration that Japanese commonly experience in America comes from the fact that their passivity is an *active* expression of their values. To the Japanese, to be quiet and to listen is active, not passive. . . . In a classroom with American students, students from Japan rarely raise their hands or speak up. They have been trained, as American students have not, to wait for a sign of approval from the teacher. (96)

Perceptual differences with regard to what constitutes active and passive participation can be attributed to differences in socialization between mainstream Americans and Asians. In the present study, a student from a Chinese background proudly pointed out the same issue. Asians may thus consider being quiet and listening intently in the classroom to be active, not passive, participation (see also Mingming's remarks in the next section). In other words, as a result of early socialization, students from different cultures may have different ideas about how to participate in classroom activities. As can be seen in the contrast between active and passive participation, mainstream Americans may have difficulty understanding an Asian student's viewpoint. The complex contrast between the East and the West presented in this chapter further implies that habitual ways of communicating in one cultural setting may not necessarily work in another.

Dynamics of Classroom Participation   In addition to the contrast between active and passive participation, Asian students offered a variety of reasons to explain why they often did not feel much like speaking up in class—from simple reasons (such as not understanding the lecture and not liking the class) to more complicated discourse-related issues (such as topics changing too quickly and being hesitant about cutting in while others are talking). A major pedagogical characteristic of U.S. classrooms is their orientation toward discussion: teachers lead discussions; they do not "teach to test." In many Asian cultures, however, much emphasis is placed on the memorization of facts. The Asian students interviewed were fully aware of these differences:

> [In U.S. classrooms] there is a lot of discussion about the implications of the text, rather than just sticking to the text. (Ming, male, 22 years old, Chinese)[5]

> [In American culture] how to understand [something] is important, whereas [in Chinese culture] memorizing the facts is important. (Hepin, male, 17 years old, Chinese)[6]

> I'm the kind of person who doesn't say much. But I don't think that I'm not active. If I know the answer, I'll speak up. Sometimes I don't speak up because I'm afraid of making mistakes. I don't feel it's good to make mistakes. (Mingming, female, 14 years old, Chinese)[7]

> I fear to talk. Sometimes other people don't understand what I'm saying. They ask me to say it again. They say, "What?" or "Pardon?" I'm embarrassed. (Tae Son, male, 19 years old, Korean)[8]

The last two examples above are related to self-consciousness, the extreme form of which among adolescents is known as adolescent egocentrism (Elkind 1984). To a certain degree, a fear of not being understood inhibits any students'

---

[5]Ming came to the United States as a student at a prestigious private boarding school in the northeastern United States (although he had been a college student at a technical institute in northern China). He had been in the United States for six months at the time of the interview.

[6]Hepin came from Beijing to the United States one year before the interview. He came to join his parents, who had been here for three years before he came. When he was interviewed, Hepin was studying in the eleventh grade of a public school in a suburb of an industrial city in the northeastern United States.

[7]Mingming is the sister of Shishi (who will appear later). She had been in the United States for one and a half years at the time of the interview. Unlike her brother, however, she went first to a public school, where she had some negative experiences as a Chinese student. She later joined her brother in a private school near an industrial city located in the northeastern United States. When she was interviewed, both she and her brother lived with their parents.

[8]Tae Son came from an industrial city in South Korea a year before the interview. When he was interviewed, Tae Son attended a public school and lived with his mother and siblings in an affluent suburb of an industrial city in the northeastern United States. His family had close relatives in the same town. His father, who is in a medical profession, was still in Korea and traveled back and forth occasionally until he could find employment in the United States. Tae Son's mother did not speak English, so he and his older brother were responsible for taking care of family matters outside the home. His mother was not happy in the United States but believed that it would offer more opportunities for her children.

classroom participation; that is, not only Asian adolescents but also their European American counterparts are self-conscious. Most students are likely to feel embarrassed when they feel that attention is focused on them; they may even question the value of their entire experience. What makes this issue complicated, however, is that multiple factors interact in a complex fashion—not only the factor associated with age but also the factor associated with culture.

The discontinuity in socialization and subsequent differences in participation style, as illustrated above, have generally been considered to be the reasons minority students do not necessarily prosper in U.S. school settings. Previous studies (Cook-Gumperz and Gumperz 1982; Mehan 1991; Philips 1982; Scollon and Scollon 1981) have argued that because the interaction styles that minority children learn in their homes do not match the interaction styles expected in the school environment, problems in academic achievement tend to arise. This match-mismatch formulation has much in common with the theory of cultural discontinuities, which proposes that the lower school accomplishment of "minorities is caused by cultural conflicts or cultural discontinuities in teaching and learning situations" (Ogbu 1990, 521). Mainstream European Americans, for example, tend to believe that learning is a "two-way street"; that is, learning should be reciprocal, not based on a relationship in which the teacher possesses all the knowledge and the students possess none. In reality, there is more than one way to approach learning (Hemphill and Minami 1994; Minami and McCabe 1996). Not only minority students but also their teachers should be aware of this fact.

For minority students and the mainstream teachers who teach them, however, discovering the facts about each other poses a great challenge. Students from different cultural backgrounds are faced with having to discover how to participate in the mainstream classroom and how to be part of the group. To a certain extent, students may need to learn how to navigate in the classroom or at least understand what the rules are, because "not fully understanding what is being said" and "not being fully understood" are two sides of the same coin. In other words, minority students might need to be aware that mainstream teachers can have somewhat different interaction styles and hold different expectations for their students. These differences, however, can be confounding to minority students. Aside from the more obvious problems of sharing knowledge and participating in classroom activities, there are emotional consequences of being out of the loop of understanding. Students described their feelings about being isolated and excluded from the day-to-day life of their peers. Their dispirited attitudes often have a direct effect on their performance in school. To cope with these problems, teachers need to discover how best to draw on the strengths of minority students in their classes. It is a challenging task for most teachers to anticipate the learning styles and needs of the students entrusted to their care and to create the learning environment that is best suited to these needs.[9]

---

[9]According to Hemphill and Minami (1994), one of the techniques—particularly useful with Asian students—is to inform students in advance about some upcoming discussion topic and ask them to prepare a contribution that they might be able to make in class.

Despite such differences in interaction styles and expectations, establishing good rapport with their students is a priority for teachers. Minority students hope that the teacher will signal that they are welcome and even appreciated. Feeling understood and accepted is important to any student but particularly so for minority students. Such an attitude on the part of the teacher also means providing minority students with a comfortable and enjoyable environment. Thus, extending a hand of welcome will eventually have a great bearing on minority students' perceptions of the classroom.

Subject Issues and Learning Environments Some subjects are more difficult than others. Contrary to the "model minority" (Ogbu 1990, 1992) stereotype, which I will soon explain, Asian students' preferences for subjects are as rich and diverse as they are. One student likes physics; another likes painting; another is fascinated with photography; still another expresses a keen interest in history, especially American history. For some students, mathematics is less difficult because numbers are universal. In many cases, however, students' likes and dislikes are closely related to the classroom atmosphere:

> I like photography. I had never done anything other than taking pictures and having a photography shop develop those pictures. Although this is my first experience, it is very interesting for me to think about many things, such as taking pictures by myself, developing them, and printing them out. Also, I like the world history class in terms of atmosphere. The students in the world history class are one year younger than me, but the class is very active. They say a lot voluntarily, and I learn a lot. Although the class is about the history of the world, they do not stick to the textbook, but they take up current issues such as the presidential election campaign and ask who supports whom. Because of that, I learn a lot. And the atmosphere is good. (Masayo, female, 16 years old, Japanese)[10]

> I like the mathematics class. I like the teacher and students who are there. They are all very active and there are funny jokes, too. In addition to these things, mathematics is the subject which I know best among the subjects I am taking. (Sachiko, female, 17 years old, Japanese)[11]

Some Asian students may seek help from peers, tutors, and teachers. As discussed earlier, however, many seem reluctant to bother others and emphasize solving problems on their own: "I feel terrible when I have to ask the teacher" (Tae Son, Korean). Teachers can make learning easier for these students. Paying careful, friendly attention to minority students—not only as students but also as individuals—can do a lot to smooth their educational journey.

Having some basic knowledge or facts about the nonmainstream cultures from which these students come would also go a long way toward helping

---

[10]Masayo came from a city in central Japan one year before the interview. Although her aunt lived in the same city in the northeastern United States, she was staying with an American family. When she was interviewed, Masayo was attending a local public high school.
[11]Attending a public school in an affluent suburb of an industrial city in the northeastern United States, Sachiko came from a suburb of a major city in Japan one year before the interview.

nonmainstream students feel welcome and less isolated. Unfortunately, however, some teachers lack basic information on minority cultures:[12]

> I feel very proud as a Chinese. I don't feel Chinese culture is inferior to American culture. I think there is some discrimination in this country. Sometimes, people ask me, "Where are you from?" and before I reply, they say, "Are you from Japan?" When I tell them I am from China, they say, "Oh!" like this. This makes me very angry. Just because there are a lot of Japanese goods in this country, they think that every Asian is Japanese. Things like this are difficult to understand here. Even Taiwan has a higher position than China here. (Gaoxin, male, 19 years old, Chinese)[13]

> European [Americans] are all sophisticated. They come from a rich culture. They think that Asians are just from poor countries and uneducated. I feel it. I feel something, some responsibility. Because I guess that most Asians, or most Koreans, don't know about this and I'm here so I think I'll change it. I have to change it—both the people here and the people there. First, I have to get people here to know more about our culture or understand it. And our people, Koreans, have to know about this. I think there should be more interchange, more intermingling of cultures with each other. (Tae Son, Korean)

Lee (1996) examines the development of ethnic and racial identity among Asian American students within the context of race relations in a metropolitan public high school. The present study has revealed that Asian students not only take pride in their own cultural identity and heritage but simultaneously expect mainstream teachers and students to have a better understanding of Asian students. If this does not occur, minority students are likely to consider a lack of understanding or appreciation for their culture as outright discrimination. The following story was told by Setsuko, a 17-year-old female student from a Japanese background:[14]

---

[12]I would like to encourage mainstream teachers and students to read literature about Asian Americans' lives in the United States. For example, in *The Best Bad Thing,* Uchida (1983), a Nisei writer, assigns a variety of roles and characters to Japanese Americans. Through such literature, those who are from mainstream backgrounds can broaden their knowledge of Japanese culture, including what kinds of foods Japanese Americans eat daily, such as onigiri (oval-shaped rice balls). A wide variety of literature available about Asian life in the United States will surely facilitate mainstream students' and teachers' better understanding of Asian students; it will also help Asian students take pride in their cultural identity and heritage. As described earlier, Uchida's autobiographical novel *Journey to Topaz* (1971) shows how difficult Asian minorities' lives in the United States were and provides a more balanced view of U.S. history. Uchida vividly describes how Japanese Americans were forcibly evacuated from California during World War II and the severe circumstances and challenges they faced in an internment camp in Utah. In a similar manner, Yep's series of novels, such as *Child of the Owl* (1977), describe how strongly Chinese Americans retained their values and self-respect in the United States and, moreover, contributed to the progress in U.S. society.

[13]Gaoxin had been in the United States for only three months at the time of the interview. He came from Shenyian, a city in northern China, to join his father. Gaoxin was attending a public school in an affluent suburb of an industrial city in the northeastern United States.

[14]Setsuko came from Tokyo in the summer before the interview and first attended a high school in a working-class suburb of an industrial city in the northeastern United States. In December of that year, however, she moved to an affluent suburb of the city and was attending school there when she was interviewed.

I also had problems with teachers. When I first arrived there, I found that many residents in the town came from Southeast Asian countries, such as Vietnam and Cambodia. I think when I first went to the school, they thought I was from Vietnam or somewhere. For the first couple of weeks, I talked to them in a usual manner like I was simply a newcomer. But when I said, "I am Japanese," some teachers, who had not known that I am Japanese, said, "Oh, you are Jap." They hated Japanese. Students then began saying, "Jap." Since I am stubborn by nature, I often had fights. I did so because I thought I didn't do anything wrong. They told me not to enter the cafeteria. I forcibly entered the cafeteria. Teachers came and spoke to me as if I had caused all the problems. I couldn't make friends at all. So at first I was doing well, but when I said I am Japanese, many problems occurred and I don't think it is fair.

In relation to the empowerment of minorities, Asians are often considered "model minorities" in the United States. Ogbu (1990, 1992) classifies minorities into two groups, castelike or involuntary minorities, and immigrant or voluntary minorities. For example, whereas African Americans belong to an involuntary minority, Asians, such as Chinese, Koreans, and Japanese, are representative of voluntary or immigrant minorities. According to Ogbu, involuntary minorities try to preserve linguistic and cultural differences as symbolic of their ethnic identity and their separation from the oppressive mainstream culture.[15] In contrast, Ogbu argues that voluntary minorities generally believe that their lives in the United States are better than their lives in their native countries. They are therefore more likely to succeed than involuntary minorities, particularly in academic achievement. Voluntary minorities' positive appraisal of their situation is thus likely to have a positive influence on their overall performance.

Unfortunately, however, the monolithic view of Asian Americans as academic high achievers, which derives from the "model minority" stereotype, is oversimplified. As the remarks by Gaoxin, Tae Son, and Setsuko indicate, voluntary minorities at times feel the same way that involuntary minorities do. To begin with, they find no justification for the discrimination and prejudice they have experienced. Furthermore, they resent and tend to interpret such treatments as institutionalized. Moreover, in some schools, in the past, voluntary minority students were not allowed to speak their first language in school settings (Crawford 1989, 1992).[16] In such situations voluntary minorities may feel that they are treated as if they were castelike involuntary minorities. Therefore, regardless of their status, minority students (either voluntary or involuntary) may feel that they belong to subordinate groups and that they are looked down on or even rejected by peers as well as teachers from mainstream backgrounds. The concept of the "model minority" is one of the most interesting yet troubling issues in the field of multicultural education.

---

[15]Similar situations—diglossic situations (coexistence of languages of high prestige and low prestige) in particular—are found in other societies as well. For instance, Korean Japanese, descendants of Koreans who were brought into Japanese society through colonization, are discouraged from speaking the Korean language (and consequently lose their native tongue as if the eventual replacement of Korean by Japanese was a necessary step in Japanization), whereas a great number of Korean Americans in the United States believe that they can speak the Korean language fluently (Kim 1990).

[16]According to Crawford (1989), for example, "until 1973 it was a crime in Texas to use a language other than English as the medium of public instruction" (26).

Language Issues (ESL and Bilingual Classrooms)   Although they claim that they can fully understand a lecture or classroom discussion, some language-minority students suffer from not having the language proficiency to participate in class or to discuss issues with their peers. This situation can lead to language-minority students feeling isolated and embarrassed when they cannot respond to questions. For this reason, one subject that seemed to be a favorite of many of the students who were interviewed in this study was the ESL classroom. The popularity of ESL was due to the fact that this classroom offered many more opportunities for active participation by students who lacked proficiency in English. Moreover, because of self-consciousness, particularly among adolescents (Elkind 1984), students' favorite classroom tends to be the one in which they feel the least embarrassed:

> In the ESL class, we do not hesitate to talk, and it has a warm atmosphere. Also, it is in the ESL class that I can actively participate. I feel that I am not considered important in mainstream classrooms. (Kyoko, female, 17 years old, Japanese)[17]

> The ESL program is very good. It's like our foreign students' home. Whenever we are free, we come here. We are all foreign students. We understand each other better than we do Americans. American students look very happy every day. They don't understand our problems. So, I like to come to the ESL class. The teachers are very helpful. The school cannot force American students to talk with us more. If they don't like to talk to us, the school cannot force them to. I think [European] American students have some prejudice against Chinese students. Asians are not considered very important here. (Gaoxin, Chinese)

> I like ESL. I have friends there. (Noriko, female, 16 years old, Japanese)[18]

> I have lunch in the ESL room. It's good. Because if you go to the cafeteria, nobody is there. You feel lonely. But in the ESL room, it's different. You can talk about everything—what happened (in class). . . . [The ESL teacher] always helps us and talks to us, so I think that is the most wonderful part. (Emilia, female, 18 years old, Chinese [Hong Kong])[19]

Not all students, however, share the same positive feelings about ESL programs. As with many of their other classes, the degree of popularity of ESL and bilingual programs depends largely on the quality of the learning, instruction, and interaction that takes place in these classrooms:

[17]From Tokyo, Kyoko arrived with her brother in the summer before the interview to join their father, who was living in a large, diverse suburb of an industrial city in the northeastern United States. At the time of the interview, she was attending a public school there.

[18]Noriko came to the United States a year before the interview after completing junior high school in Japan. She was staying with a family (mother and daughter) in a large, diverse suburb of an industrial city in the northeastern United States and attending a public school there when she was interviewed.

[19]Emilia was living in an affluent suburb of an industrial city in the northeastern United States with an uncle and his European American wife. She was attending the town's large public high school. She arrived in the United States in the summer before the interview and spent some time with relatives in Canada. She had attended a private girls' school in Hong Kong, where she grew up and her family still lived (at the time of the interview). She was hoping to attend college in the United States or Canada.

I don't like ESL, or bilingual programs. I don't think it's challenging enough. There is no stimulation at all. You don't have to study very much. But if you study in the mainstream classroom, you feel pressure, and you want to be as good as others. In ESL, you don't have an objective and aspiration. (Shishi, male, 18 years old, Chinese)[20]

I don't think that the bilingual program is good. You do not learn much. Later on, you may enter ESL, which may be different from the bilingual program.[21] But the bilingual program is really not good. There is no pressure at all. Only those who didn't pass the placement test went to the bilingual program, and they do not learn much. (Mingming, Chinese)

From the above comments, it appears that Asian students do not necessarily participate more actively in either the ESL or the bilingual classroom simply because they are designed to assist LEP students. It seems that Asian students' "active participation" in class is more likely to increase in a classroom in which (1) the teacher provides good, solid instruction; (2) the teacher is sensitive to their needs; and (3) the teacher tries hard to engage them in the ongoing life and development of the classroom, school, and culture.

CONCLUSION

Assimilation and accommodation are psychological concepts (Piaget 1952). Assimilation indicates the incorporation of new information into an existing cognitive structure, whereas accommodation symbolizes a change in an existing cognitive structure to cope with new information. There is little doubt that few settings provide a better environment for studying processes of cultural assimilation and accommodation than a school. As can be seen in Eriksonian theory of identity versus role confusion among adolescents (Erikson 1968, 1973), adolescents are in their formative years, trying to determine their own sense of self. Exposure to a different culture, new relationships, and a new way of life contribute substantially to the students' developing world view and, at the same time, offers a keen sense of perspective that can foster a renewed pride in their cultural heritage.

---

[20]Shishi was in the twelfth grade of a private school near an industrial city in the northeastern United States. He came from Beijing one and a half years before the interview to join his parents.
[21]Bilingual and ESL programs have distinct differences. In a bilingual program, the students' first language is used as a medium as well as an object of instruction. First-language instruction for non-English-speaking children means that the curriculum of a bilingual program may be different from that of ESL programs, where the medium of instruction is English. To put it another way, teachers in bilingual programs present the content material of the standard curriculum using the native language of the students. In the ESL program, on the other hand, the emphasis is on helping students acquire enough proficiency in English to be able to function well in the mainstream or regular classroom. Other types of programs are also available; for example, dual-language immersion programs, which not only provide minority students with first-language instruction but simultaneously offer English-speaking children access to other languages, have recently received a great deal of attention from parents, researchers, and policy makers (Valdés, 1997).

The present study has indicated that U.S. classrooms, particularly bilingual and ESL classrooms, can do more than offer these students a haven in which they can relax and relieve some of the tension that they feel outside school. Thus, not all U.S. classrooms have failed to respond to the unique needs of language-minority students. Rather, some classrooms have had positive success in educating language-minority students, providing them with opportunities for active participation. The results obtained in this study, in fact, confirm previous studies of different populations. For example, Lucas, Henze, and Donato (1990) identified several important factors that are related to language-minority students' success in secondary schools:

1. Value is placed on the students' languages and cultures.
2. High expectations of language-minority students are made concrete.
3. School leaders make the education of language-minority students a priority.
4. Staff development is explicitly designed to help teachers and other staff serve language-minority students more effectively.
5. A variety of courses and programs for language-minority students is offered.
6. School staff members share a strong commitment to empower language-minority students through education. (324–325)

As Cummins (1986) emphasizes, the role of educators and policy makers should be to empower all minority students, including language-minority students such as the Asian students described in this chapter (see page 191). Cummins has long examined the pattern of minority students' academic success and failure and emphasized ways in which educators can promote the empowerment of minority students and their parents and communities, so that those children can become confident and capable in academic environments. Certainly, teachers themselves should be empowered as well to improve the quality of education programs.

The importance of minority students' empowerment is also clear in the writing of Freire[22] (1970a, 1970b), who suggests that the literacy process should be conceptualized as playing a central role in empowering those who are, in many ways, oppressed in a given social system, so that those people can fully participate in the system. Specifically, Freire argues for educational practice based on an authentic dialogue between teachers and learners as equally knowing subjects.

Finally, I would like to discuss "model minorities," which, generally referring to Asians, are associated with being "quiet, respectful of authority, and hardworking" (Lee 1996, 31). As this chapter has revealed, however, contrary to the static view of "model minorities," Asians are as diverse as other minorities. The issue of "model minorities" further bears a significant meaning in U.S. history. Hansen (1994) writes:

---

[22]I would like to express my condolences on the recent death of Paulo Freire, who has exerted an enormous influence on my work.

In the late 1950s and early 1960s when many Americans indulged themselves in a wave of self-congratulatory democratic liberalism, a profusion of articles appeared in mass-circulation magazines announcing that the Japanese American Evacuation [during World War II] had been for the Nikkei (Americans of Japanese ancestry) a "blessing in disguise," for it had broken up their ethnic enclaves, relocated them geographically to other parts of the country, and precipitated not only their assimilation into the larger society but also set them on a course leading to their status as America's "model minority." At the time I did not appreciate the perversity of the logic informing this line of thought and, unwittingly, became a temporal captive of it. (136)

The title of "model minority" (given to Japanese Americans) might be a result of those sad realities.[23] As a matter of fact, in one of the interviews conducted in this project, Setsuko (from a Japanese background) recalled that she had been called "Jap" not only by her peers but also by her teachers.

To conclude, this study has revealed that minority students are sensitive about being understood and that teachers, therefore, need to create classrooms that maximize participation by students who have acquired different interaction styles in their homes. I hope that the perspectives of the Asian students expressed in this study will have some value not only to teachers but also to policy makers and administrators as they think about and design learning environments for U.S. schools. A collection of the authentic expressions of the students' "lived experience" in this chapter should spawn thinking about how to make U.S. schools valuable to students from minority backgrounds.

STUDY QUESTIONS

1. Historical legal exclusion of Asians from the United States has been accompanied by unfamiliarity with Asian customs, traditions, and beliefs. What kind of social injustice is imbedded in U.S. governmental policies (local as well as federal)? Recall, for example, the *Lau v. Nichols* decision in 1974, a class action suit brought by Chinese public school students against the San Francisco Unified School District. What do you think about the role of government in education and the effect of policy on educational practice? Are there any examples of political decisions that have caused serious negative consequences in Asians' lives and education? For social justice, then, how can teachers and policy makers empower Asian students?

---

[23]In like manner, Spina and Tai (1998) state:

The "model minority" stereotype can be used by the dominant White culture to maintain its power while also maintaining its invisibility. By maintaining a "model minority" stereotype, the dominant White culture never needs to explicitly label non-"model minorities" negatively. . . . By seemingly complimenting the "model minority," the dominant White culture implicitly denigrates other minorities (including less successful Whites). (39)

2. Stereotypes are fixed ideas and opinions about people who are members of cultures other than one's own. What kinds of stereotypes do we have about Asian students? For example, do you think that all Asian students are high achievers in school? Do you believe that all Asian students are superior in mathematical abilities to students from other cultural backgrounds? Is the belief of the superior performance of Asian students a stereotypical misconception? Can you identify factors that are related to successful schooling outcomes with Asian students? More generally, how can we relate the notion of "model minorities" to the stereotypes you mention?

3. Cultural diversity has many implications in a multiethnic society such as the United States. For example, Asian individuals possibly have different values, beliefs, and norms from other cultural groups. These culture-specific views shape the individual's cultural identity. The static view of cultural identity, however, is sometimes erroneous. Lee (1996), for example, examines the development of ethnic and racial identity among Asian American students within the context of race relations in a metropolitan public high school. Contrary to the iconic conception of Asian Americans, Lee found a more flexible model of identity formation among Asian adolescents. In today's complex society, then, how can we encourage and promote multicultural learning in classrooms? What is the first step toward a more equitable education for Asian students?

4. Some Asian cultures stipulate that individuals listen empathically to others and expect others to reciprocate when they talk. Children in some Asian cultures might be accustomed to conversations consisting of frequent brief turns exchanged with their interlocutors. These styles might differ greatly from the Western styles of communication. How can we create classrooms that maximize participation by Asian students who might have different representation styles?

5. How can we raise awareness and sensitivity toward Asian students in U.S. classrooms? We might need to promote the empowerment of not only Asian students but also their parents and communities. Can you think of appropriate family programs that are designed to support Asian immigrant families so that they can actively participate in their children's education?

6. Historically, bilingual education has aroused strong emotions, both pro and con. In California alone, approximately 1.4 million children are in bilingual classrooms. A recent example illustrating this controversy is Proposition 227, which passed in California in June 1998. Under this initiative, students have only one year to master English before entering regular classrooms. Many educators are now concerned that this initiative might virtually eliminate bilingual education in the state's public schools, and teachers might need to resort to untried methodology. In the complexities of the issues surrounding bilingual education, how can we create an integrated classroom, not a separate one, both physically and psychologically?

KEY CONCEPTS

"Active" versus "passive" participation

Asian cultures

Cross-cultural miscommunications or misunderstandings

Cultural discontinuities

Cultural identity

Discourse/participation styles in instructional settings

Home-school continuum in socialization

"Model minority" stereotypes

Societal/structural inequality

REFERENCES

Auerbach, E. R. 1989. Toward a social-contextual approach to family literacy. *Harvard Educational Review* 59(2): 165–181.

Barringer, F. 1993. On 32 million tongues, English is alien. *The New York Times,* 28 April: A1, A10.

Brandt, D. 1990. *Literacy as involvement: The acts of writer, reader, and texts.* Carbondale: Southern Illinois University Press.

Clark, E. C. 1994. Reconstructing history. In *Interactive oral history interviewing,* ed. E. M. McMahan and K. L. Rogers, 19–30. Hillsdale, N.J.: Lawrence Erlbaum.

Cook-Gumperz, J., and J. J. Gumperz. 1982. Communicative competence in educational perspective. In *Communicating in the classroom,* ed. L. C. Wilkinson, 13–24. New York: Academic Press.

Crawford, J. 1989. *Bilingual education: History, politics, theory, and practice.* Trenton, N.J.: Crane Publishing.

Crawford, J. 1992. *Hold your tongue: Bilingualism and the politics of "English only."* Reading, Mass.: Addison-Wesley.

Crawford, J. 1995. *Bilingual education: History, politics, theory, and practice,* 3rd ed. Los Angeles: Bilingual Education Services.

Cummins, J. 1986. Empowering minority students: A framework for intervention. *Harvard Educational Review* 56(1): 18–36.

Elkind, D. 1984. *All grown up and no place to go.* Reading, Mass.: Addison-Wesley.

Erikson, E. H. 1968. *Identity: Youth and crisis.* New York: Norton.

Erikson, E. H. 1973. The wider identity. In *In search of common ground: Conversations with Erik H. Erikson and Huey P. Newton,* ed. K. T. Erikson, 44–70. New York: Norton.

Freire, P. 1970a. *Pedagogy of the oppressed.* New York: Seabury Press.

Freire, P. 1970b. The adult literacy process as cultural action for freedom. *Harvard Educational Review* 40(2): 205–225.

Gardner, H. 1989. *To open minds: Chinese clues to the dilemma of contemporary education.* New York: Basic Books.

Genesee, F., ed. 1994. *Educating second language children: The whole child, the whole curriculum, and the whole community.* New York: Cambridge University Press.

Gumperz, J. J. 1996. On teaching language in its social context. In *Social interaction, social context, and language: Essays in honor of Susan Ervin-Tripp*, ed. D. I. Slobin, J. Gerhardt, A. Kyratzis, and J. Guo, 469–493. Mahwah, N.J.: Lawrence Erlbaum.

Hakuta, K. 1986. *Mirror of language: The debate on bilingualism*. New York: Basic Books.

Hansen, A. A. 1994. A riot of voices: Racial and ethnic variables in interactive oral history interviewing. In *Interactive oral history interviewing*, ed. E. M. McMahan and K. L. Rogers, 107–139. Hillsdale, N.J.: Lawrence Erlbaum.

Hemphill, L., and M. Minami. 1994. U.S. classrooms: A sociolinguistic perspective. In *Teaching and the case method*, ed. L. B. Barnes, C. R. Christensen, and A. J. Hansen, 244–248. Boston: Harvard Business School Press.

Huddy, L., and D. O. Sears. 1990. Qualified public support for bilingual education: Some policy implications. In *English plus: Issues in bilingual education*, ed. C. B. Cazden and C. E. Snow, 119–134. Newbury Park, Calif.: Sage.

Kagitcibasi, C. 1989. Family and socialization in cross-cultural perspective: A model of change. *Nebraska symposium on motivation*, 135–200. Lincoln: University of Nebraska Press.

Kim, Y. D. 1990. *Zainichi choosenjin no kika* [Naturalization of Korean Japanese]. Tokyo: Akashi Shuppan.

Lee, S. J. 1996. *Unraveling the "model minority" stereotype: Listening to Asian American youth*. New York: Columbia University Teachers College Press.

Lucas, T., R. Henze, and R. Donato. 1990. Promoting the success of Latino language-minority students: An exploratory study of six high schools. *Harvard Educational Review* 60(3): 341–356.

Mehan, H. 1991. *Sociological foundations supporting the study of cultural diversity, research report: 1*. Santa Cruz, Calif.: National Center for Research on Cultural Diversity and Second Language Learning.

Minami, M. 1995. Long conversational turns or frequent turn exchanges: Cross-cultural comparison of parental narrative elicitation. *Journal of Asian Pacific Communication* 6(4): 213–230.

Minami, M., and A. McCabe. 1996. Compressed collections of experiences. In *Chameleon readers: Some problems cultural differences in narrative structure pose for multicultural literacy programs*, ed. A. McCabe, 72–97. New York: McGraw-Hill.

Minami, M., and C. J. Ovando. 1995. Language issues in multicultural contexts. In *Handbook of research on multicultural education*, ed. J. A. Banks and C. M. Banks, 427–444. New York: Macmillan.

Miyanaga, K. 1991. *The creative edge: Emerging individualism in Japan*. New Brunswick, N.J.: Transaction Publishers.

Modell, J., and C. Brodsky. 1994. Envisioning Homestead: Using photographs in interviewing (Homestead, Pennsylvania). In *Interactive oral history interviewing*, ed. E. M. McMahan and K. L. Rogers, 141–161. Hillsdale, N.J.: Lawrence Erlbaum.

Ogbu, J. U. 1990. Cultural model, identity, and literacy. In *Cultural psychology: Essays on comparative human development*, ed. J. W. Stigler, R. A. Shweder, and G. Herdt, 520–541. New York: Cambridge University Press.

Ogbu, J. U. 1992. Understanding cultural diversity and learning. *Educational Researcher* 21(8): 5–14.

Ovando, C. J. 1990. Politics and pedagogy: The case of bilingual education. *Harvard Educational Review* 60(3): 341–356.

Ovando, C. J., and V. P. Collier. 1998. *Bilingual and ESL classrooms: Teaching in multicultural contexts*, 2nd ed. Boston: McGraw-Hill.

Philips, S.U. 1982. *The invisible culture: Communication in classroom and community on the Warm Springs Indian Reservation.* New York: Longman.

Piaget, J. 1952. *The origins of intelligence in children.* New York: International Universities Press. Original work, 1936.

Redmond, M. V., and J. M. Bunyi. 1993. The relationship of intercultural communication competence with stress and the handling of stress as reported by international students. *International Journal of Intercultural Relations* 17: 235–254.

Scollon, R., and S. Scollon. 1981. *Narrative, literacy and face in interethnic communications.* Norwood, N.J.: Ablex.

Spina, S. U., and R. H. Tai. 1998. The politics of racial identity: A pedagogy of invisibility. *Educational Researcher* 27(1): 36–40, 48.

Stanford Working Group. 1993. *Federal Education programs for limited-English-proficient students: A blueprint for the second generation.* Palo Alto, Calif.: Stanford University.

Stevenson, H. W., C. Chen, and S.-Y. Lee. 1993. Mathematics achievement of Chinese, Japanese, and American children: Ten years later. *Science* 258: 53–58.

Stigler, J., and M. Perry. 1988. Mathematics learning in Japanese Chinese, and American classrooms. In *Children's mathematics,* ed. G. Saxe and M. Gearhart, 27–54. San Francisco: Jossey-Bass.

Tobin, J. J., D. Y .H. Wu, and D. H. Davidson. 1989. *Preschool in three cultures: Japan, China, and the United States.* New Haven, Conn.: Yale University Press.

U.S. Department of Education. 1992. *The condition of bilingual education: A report to the Congress and the President.* Washington, D.C.: U.S. Government Printing Office.

Uchida, Y. 1971. *Journey to Topaz: A story of the Japanese-American evacuation.* New York: Charles Scribner's Sons.

Uchida, Y. 1983. *The best bad thing.* New York: Atheneum.

Valdés, C. 1997. Dual-language immersion programs: A cautionary note concerning the education of language-minority students. *Harvard Educational Review* 67(3): 391–429.

Yep, L. 1977. *Child of the owl.* New York: Harper & Row.

Carolyn R. O'Grady   Beth Chappell

*C*ombining service with academic learning offers college students the opportunity to engage in a meaningful real-world experience while they critically reflect on the relationship between the college or university and the larger community of which it is a part. But profound issues surround the involvement of students from a predominantly white college in performing service in communities of color. This chapter explores the interaction of conflict, racial identity, interests, and power inherent in a service-learning pedagogy that links a mostly white higher education community with a racially and linguistically diverse local community.

CHAPTER 11

With, Not For

The Politics of Service Learning in Multicultural Communities

Carolyn R. O'Grady

Gustavus Adolphus College

Beth Chappell

High school English teacher in Minnesota

In 1968, in a speech to a group of North American college students working on service projects in Latin America, Ivan Illich (1990) declared, "You will not help anybody by your good intentions" (315). His challenge to those he called "U.S. idealists" was to stop calling what they did "service" and start facing how their very presence perpetuated the status quo of a more affluent group's domination over another less "developed" one.

Illich focused his talk on international cultural hegemony. His comments did not specifically examine the racial dynamics implicit when mostly white U.S. "do-gooders" (as he called them) volunteer time among communities of color. It is this racial dynamic that we wish to examine in this chapter. While Illich's talk was almost thirty years ago, his caution about good intentions echoes in our ears today as we examine what went wrong with a service-learning project that, despite all our best intentions, reinforced dominant racist ideology.

This chapter will describe the implementation of a service-learning project in which white college students in a required education class worked with Latinos in Minnesota. We will explore the political implications of this project in light of issues of paternalism and noblesse oblige that impinge when a white privileged group performs service in a community of color. Specifically, we will analyze this experience from a political perspective, focusing on the ways in which interests, conflict, and power were and were not acknowledged and addressed (Morgan 1986).

In keeping with the spirit of service learning, in which the academic and the experiential converge, we will tell this story in both traditionally academic and more personal ways. At times, you will read our combined academic voice as it provides context and background. You will also hear the voices of students describing their experience of the project, as well as personal reflections on what the instructor (Carolyn) intended the project to do and how one student in particular (Beth) responded to it. Throughout your reading of this chapter, we encourage you to notice whose voices you hear and whose you do not.

The Course and the Project

"Social Foundations of Education" is a required course that students at a private liberal arts college in Minnesota take before entering the teaching certification program. While the course covers a number of traditional foundations subjects, it is essentially a multicultural education course in which teaching in a diverse society is examined through exploration of important ideas and challenges current in schools today. A service-learning component was added in fall 1995, and the academic context of the course was redesigned so that education in the United States is examined in part through the lens of the Latino experience of it. Among the issues probed are racism toward immigrants, language, cultural differences and similarities between Latinos and Anglos, specific issues facing migrant workers in the United States, and the tension within education between assimilation and affirmation of cultural diversity.

The demographics in Minnesota are changing to include a growing number of Latinos (primarily Mexican Americans) who are choosing to settle here rather than work seasonally. This demographic shift is leading to economic and social pressures on small, rural communities and an increase in tension between Anglos who have lived here for generations and previously settled Latinos as well as new Latino residents. It has been difficult for some long-time white residents to see positive implications of this trend, even though in some cases these new residents have brought renewed vigor to what had been dying communities. The intention of the service-learning component of "Social Foundations of Education" was to offer education students the opportunity to gain insight into Latino culture as well as practical experience for teaching in a diverse classroom. It also was intended to offer the Latino community the opportunity to design and benefit from needed social and educational programs with the assistance of student servers.

Choosing from a number of community sites, students were placed at their site for two hours a week for a total of twenty hours over the semester. Sites included English as a Second Language (ESL) classrooms at nearby elementary and secondary schools and an adult basic education ESL program. At each of these sites, preservice teachers tutored children or adults in small groups or individually. Other sites included a public library at which preservice students designed a bilingual story hour and a youth center that provided after-school recreational drop-in time for Latino and white youth. The college students traveled about 25 miles round-trip to most sites. Only one site—the adult education program—was in the same community as the college.

During the service experience, students maintained a journal and wrote a number of papers on specific prompts related to their experience. In addition, class discussion included references to and descriptions of students' individual experiences at their site and the relevance of assigned readings to the service-learning project.

Carolyn's Voice: The Impetus for the Project   *As a white faculty member in an education department, I grapple constantly with how best to help my mostly white pre-service teachers explore issues of racial diversity in a concrete, experiential way. This concern is heightened by the fact that the liberal arts Lutheran college in which I teach is located in a fairly homogeneous rural area in the upper Midwest, far enough from an urban area to exclude easy contact with the diversity that a city can provide. I grew up in the West in a rural area in which cultural diversity was never mentioned. There is an Indian reservation not far from my hometown, and I knew many in my childhood, but cultural or racial differences between Native Americans and whites were never explored in informative or positive ways. I knew nothing about Latinos, even though parts of my home state were seasonally home to and dependent on large numbers of migrant workers, most of whom were Latino.*

As an adult, I have traveled extensively, lived and worked in racially diverse communities, and studied and practiced multicultural and critical teaching. These activities have provided academic and personal opportunities to explore my own racism and white privilege. While my upbringing helps me empathize with my white students who are grappling with their own racism for the first time, my commitment to social justice fuels my sense of urgency about creating opportunities for white students to look at what it means to be a white person or a person of color in U.S. society. My hope was that by incorporating a service project into my class, my students would have more contextualized, concrete learning with and about a racial group that is substantially changing the demographics in our area. This project also provided an avenue for pre-dominantly white students to explore issues of privilege, power, and oppression not only in education but also in their own backyard.

Beth's Voice: Who I Was When I Walked into the Classroom   *As a white undergraduate student at a primarily white college, I was both like and unlike many of the students who come to this college with a minimal exposure to diversity or the issues it encompasses. I grew up in a fairly diverse town and was familiar with seeing people of color in my community, but until I came to college, I had never considered what it meant to be white or to have skin color privilege (McIntosh 1990).*

My hometown of Willmar, Minnesota, is a small city two hours away from this small college and about three hours from Minnesota's largest metropolitan community. With about 23,000 people and growing, it is a business center for many of the rural communities surrounding it. Willmar has also recently become known in the state for its rapidly growing Latino community. As a result of this demographic shift, conflicts between whites and Latinos have exposed the violence and racism present in Willmar.

My memories of school dynamics dealing directly with different ethnicities began vividly in high school. The cliques at Willmar Senior High divided us by race and socioeconomic standing. It was and continues to be hard for me to accept being excluded from groups of color. This began in high school and came to a head when I was interested in joining the Black Student Organization at my college in my junior year but was not welcomed with open arms. It has been hard for me to accept that I may not be welcome because of my skin color. For some reason I do not fully understand, I never

*consciously looked at people of color and thought of them as lesser than myself or wanted
to exclude them because of skin color. It's not that I wasn't racist. For instance, when I
worked at a local fast-food restaurant one summer and waited on Latinos who had just
come from the welfare office with envelopes of twenty-dollar bills, I believed what others
said about "those people" taking advantage of the system. However, my conscience would
not allow me to accept or perpetuate my racist attitudes. I kept probing the implications of
my attitude, and I began to discuss the issue and ask questions of others about the welfare
system. I soon learned that "those people" could often make better money receiving welfare and staying home with their family than leaving home and working forty to sixty
hours a week. It was a pivotal moment for me. "Those people" in the drive-thru didn't
give a damn what I thought—they wanted to do the best thing for their family.*

*I remember my fear of entering the part of town that was dominated by low-income
Latino families, Elm Lane Trailer Park. This fear came from overhearing and believing
comments others made about this area. Elm Lane was a neighborhood (the operative
part of the word being "hood") that the police frequented. Eventually, the Willmar
police established a station on its outskirts. This was supposed to help the members of
Elm Lane and the community at large feel safer. A few years ago, Elm Lane was condemned and demolished. The Willmar City Council has since been developing different
parts of town with apartment complexes where the rent is income-based. Local banks
and other community organizations have pooled resources to cover down payments on
houses for the relocated families.*

*Other issues in Willmar have been lawsuits filed by Latinos against the police
department and the school. In 1994, the year after I graduated, a new high school
opened, replacing the old one. Security is tight there, and most students refer to this
school (although physically beautiful) as "the jail." Willmar, however, has an "alternative school" located at the Willmar Community College that enrolls many pregnant
teens, nontraditional students, and a rapidly growing number of Latinos. A majority of
the Latino students who were at Willmar High School have moved to the alternative
school. They say the new high school has not been a welcoming and helpful environment in which they can learn. As I've considered this, I've wondered, Is this because
they are outnumbered? Or is the curriculum not multicultural? Do they lack the adequate language training and support? The answer is probably a combination of all of
these. This has become a very controversial issue in the community and may be considered a classic example of what I now know to be institutional racism.*

*The controversy about race continues in my hometown. The process of understanding
my own racial identity continues (Hardiman and Jackson 1992). My experience in Carolyn's class deepened my understanding of racial issues concerning both individuals and
institutions. However, it also reinforced my discomfort with how students often group
only with others like themselves and how institutions actually reinforce that grouping.*

Service Learning, Multicultural Education,
and Critical Pedagogy

Teaching from a critical perspective requires educators to explore the intercon-
nections among power, culture, and the political nature of schooling. As
McLaren and Hammer describe it, critical teachers must "affirm the voices of

marginalized students, engage them critically, while at the same time assist them in transforming their communities into sites of struggle and resistance" (quoted in Sleeter 1996, 117). For a course such as "Social Foundations of Education," in which all or most of the students are white, voices of marginalized peoples must somehow be brought into the classroom so that dominant-group students learn to identify the social relations that lead to social inequity.

The task for Carolyn as instructor was to provide opportunities for students to begin thinking critically about their own social identities, about those whose voices were not present in the classroom, and about education as a social institution. As Sleeter and McLaren (1995) point out, students and teachers are often embedded, knowingly or not, in "a highly politicized field of power relations that partake of unjust race, class and gender affiliations" (6). White, middle-class students in particular often cannot see how their own interests are being met through the curriculum and school structure, which tends to emphasize middle-class, European American values, while the interests of more marginal groups are not met. For instance, Aparicio and Jose-Kampfner (1995) describe some of the educational costs for Latinos in public school, including issues of linguistic and cultural erasure, psychological and bodily punishment for speaking Spanish, low levels of motivation based on alienation, and inequitable placement policies. The result is systemic violence in schools that is "exerted on cultures, languages and people who are marked as 'different' from the hegemonic norm imposed by education" (96). The 50 percent dropout rate of Latinos in Willmar, Minnesota, is one more example of "the success of public schools in ousting students who resist being homogenized into prevailing monocultural dictates" (96). To even be at a private liberal arts college connotes a certain access to social power, even though most white students in the class did not personally *feel* very powerful. In the class that Beth was part of, student attitudes fell on a continuum of understanding about race and racism. Some students had much less awareness than Beth and considered the college to be exceptionally diverse because it offered them the first or one of the few times they had seen a person of color (5.6 percent of the student body in 1994–1995 were students of color). Other students in the class were much more comfortable with diversity than Beth was, having grown up in an urban area and attended inner-city schools (though this did not necessarily mean they understood white privilege or racial oppression).

To help surface the students' unexamined interests, conflicts, and power dynamics, the course incorporated strategies from social reconstructionist multicultural education and critical pedagogy. According to Sleeter and McLaren (1995), "Critical and multicultural pedagogy defamiliarize and make remarkable what is often passed off as the ordinary, the mundane, the routine, and the banal" (7). In particular, the "familiar" must be contested in such a way that students are able to reassess power relations in what have been taken-for-granted attitudes and experiences. Key to this deconstruction is a teaching process that encourages critical discourse, particularly in analyzing what is viewed as "truth" (Kitano 1997).

Using a combination of readings, reflections, classroom dialogue, and the service project, the goal of the "Social Foundations" course was to pose problems, explore power relations, and encourage student commitment to activism. Service-learning pedagogy, with its focus on real-world experience, is a natural complement to potentially more abstract critical classroom pedagogy. By engaging in significant and authentic work in the community outside of the classroom, students have the opportunity to critically examine social structures (Anderson and Guest 1994). Keith (1997) describes as most authentic the kind of learning that enables students to "recognize themselves, name their experiences, and learn how to change existing conditions for themselves as well as for others in the community" (137). The best service-learning projects are integrated into a student's academic curriculum, provide students an opportunity to develop skills and knowledge in real-life situations, and meet a real community need. They reinforce the connections between a school and the community of which it is a part and teach students how to work collaboratively with others to create change.

The emphasis on reflection within service learning stresses the dialogic nature of this approach. Students are not mere receptacles to be filled but must engage in an active way with their own experiences and with the social consequences of their service. As Kendall (1990) notes, "A good service learning program helps participants see their questions in the larger context of issues of social justice and social policy—rather than in the context of charity" (20). Therefore, service-learning programs, to be "good practice," must engage people in responsible action for the common good.

When constructed as a natural outgrowth of critical pedagogy, service-learning experiences extend students' ability to analyze social contradictions. When students can learn through service learning to analyze, critically reflect, and transform oppressive situations through action, they are engaged in a social reconstructionist multicultural education approach (Sleeter and Grant 1987). Students will learn to understand the intrinsically political nature of social institutions and to examine how people with conflicting interests may or may not have the social power to have their interests met.

Unfortunately, the service-learning project in the "Social Foundations" course did not live up to this potential. A significant drawback to our particular project was the extent to which action was possible given the power differential between preservice teachers and classroom teachers within an established institutional structure. In addition, as we will discuss shortly, the service-learning project may have reinforced the "us versus them" divisiveness between white college students and a community of color. The lack of true partnership between the college and the community of color and its implications will be explored in more detail in our conclusion.

Carolyn's Perceptions: What Students Learned and Didn't Learn   *In their journals and in class discussion, students seemed to find it easier to identify what was positive about the experience than what was negative (the time commitment was the only thing most students didn't like). In particular, students regularly mentioned three specific learnings that were important to them. First, it was hands-on experience, usually in a real classroom, something they all wanted as they began the academic process* *of becoming a teacher. When I asked them to discuss in writing why service learning should or should not be included in education, the majority felt the experience had enhanced their learning. As Jean wrote,*

> *One of the most valuable components of this class for me was the service learning experience. From this I have gained what I call exposure to reality. . . . The experience gave me an opportunity to be in an actual classroom and the chance to work with ESL students. By actually working and seeing for myself, all that I read was enhanced and ingrained into my mind. It was a chance to prove or disprove the information that the texts presented. Plus the process forced me to think beyond what was happening at the surface.*

Second, the knowledge they gained about educational issues for migrant workers—and the politics of second-language learning in particular—had a powerful impact on them. As Stephen noted,

> *Looking back on my years of schooling in Hibbing, I cannot remember a single time in which a classmate of mine could not keep up in his or her studies because he or she did not understand the English language. Now as a second-year college student studying to be an educator, it has been brought to my attention that not only does this occur frequently in the classroom—it is occurring right here in Minnesota! I am not talking about "inner city" schools in the metro area either.*

Mary was even more concrete in her increasing awareness of the politics of language.

> *Sometimes I feel like what the school is saying to these kids is that it is okay that you have a different language, but you have to learn ours. Almost like it is a disease—"You have Spanish, but we'll help you get over it." This isn't the school's fault and a program like this is better than nothing. Unfortunately, the way things are, students need opportunities like these in order to succeed in our country. I think something more affirmative would allow Spanish speakers to learn English, but also allow English speakers to learn Spanish. This would be like saying "Wow, you speak Spanish—I really value that and you, so maybe I can make the effort to learn more about you and the language you speak."*

Third, the chance to "make a difference" in a child's life was something that resonated for the students, particularly at those times when they felt they "saw" learning on the part of the child or adult they were tutoring. Unfortunately, this feeling often echoed a kind of missionary attitude, as when students wrote or talked about how "good" doing this made them feel because they were "helping" someone learn. Service to others very rightly can and should elicit good feelings about oneself, but often these feelings mask an attitude of superiority that students may not be aware they are expressing. Lisa described feeling very "fond" of her tutee and gave him the pseudonym "Nacho" to "provide some humor" for her journal. She was oblivious to the condescending and stereotypical nature of that nickname.

As I read through the journals and papers and reflect on my notes from class discussion, I am struck by how seldom most students mentioned broader issues of inequity. It appeared to be difficult for them to apply their classroom learnings about issues of power and privilege to the concrete experience they were having at their site. I wondered if this project reinforced certain stereotypes some students had when they started. For instance, there was a tendency on the part of some students to "blame the victim" (Ryan 1976). As Joseph said, "I think that many of these kids come from bad

*homes: economically and/or family problems." A frequently heard comment was some-
thing along the lines of "how can migrant parents do this to their kids?" David focused
on this a number of times.*

> *One problem I have for these students is their future. What are they really learning
> from their parents who move constantly? Are they learning to strive for better situa-
> tions? Or are they learning that their future will be in the fields? I know that we need
> people in the fields, but I don't see that as a positive goal.*

*Because the college students did not see migrant parents in the schools, they often
assumed this meant the parents did not care about their children's education. After
decrying the lack of educational commitment from Latino parents, Lisa wrote, "I think
that it is important to first improve the living situation with these migrant families and
then the importance of education will come along with the process." She and other students did not understand the economic pressures or cultural constraints on migrant
parents that may have limited their involvement in the school.*

*While evidence exists, especially in writings later in the semester, that these preser-
vice students did grow in their awareness of the complexity of issues involved in education for Latinos, I became anxious about what had really happened here. I wondered if I
created a situation in which white students act out of an unconsciously paternalistic
mentality rather than being enabled to see the bigger systemic issues behind the project.*

Beth's Perspective: What I Learned   *As I understood the project as Carolyn presented it in the spring of 1996, when I took the class, the fact that it was a service-learning
project seemed to be less important than that it had to do with multicultural issues. As a
result, as I did the project, I focused on the issue of race rather than on the concept of service. This focus had implications for the feelings I had as the project progressed.*

*My classmates and I were scattered all over our area of Minnesota in different
schools or drop-in centers. I was accompanied by a classmate, Mark, to a neighboring
town's high school. Our assignment? Tutoring in an ESL classroom. We had twenty
minutes each way in the car to talk about our feelings surrounding several class topics.*

*Just being in an ESL classroom was a first for both of us. The members of that par-
ticular class were all Latino. Most of them, if not all, were migrant children whose families had made the decision to stay here in Minnesota. The first day, I wondered what
sort of things I would be doing and what sort of things I would be exploring within
myself and within that particular classroom. How could I best treat these students with
respect? Could I empower them and teach them? Would I be sensitive to the students'
needs? How would this work in terms of the class requirement?*

*My first journal entry read, "... I learned that their peers [white students but also
white teachers and staff] cannot necessarily tell them apart." Re-reading this, I remember one Latino boy's description of being called by the wrong name. His tone was quiet
and accepting. To me, the Latino students looked nothing alike, not even the two sisters
in the class. Yet this young boy had accepted the school community's inability to discern among the Latino students. I too have been confused with other blonde, white
women, but in this student's case, it seemed more blatantly racial. I noted to myself
how important it is to remember each student's name to let them know that I could, in
fact, tell them apart. The drawback was that I could not be sure whom I would see from
week to week due to the school scheduling.*

Mr. Kalla, the ESL teacher, was himself a minority in that small community. Three years prior to our introduction, he had moved to Minnesota from an island in the South Pacific. His own experience of being a minority in the community may have been somewhat similar to the students'. I wondered if he had been hired because he was a person of color or because the school (or Mr. Kalla) felt he could relate to the students as another person of color.

That first day, Mr. Kalla made a comment that also struck a chord in me. I overheard him refer to the Latino students in his classroom as "his." This too is a common phenomenon among teachers, but once again, to me it seemed racial. When new Latino students came into this particular school, the administration would notify the instructor that he "had another one." I had a sense that this classroom was very separate from the mainstream classes in the building. I was inclined to believe that the administration and other teachers preferred Mr. Kalla to take responsibility for these students rather than themselves doing so. Mr. Kalla's comments seemed to be connected with his own sense of personal responsibility and the school's lack of attention toward the program.

I believe that in order to take students out of mainstream classrooms, teachers of special needs classes should be going through extensive processes to prove the students' need to be excused. In addition to this, there should be a direct correlation to the students' needs and the special need services that are provided to them. Although it was an ESL classroom, I realized in my third visit that several of the students were there for reasons other than their language skills. Was this typical? Out of about nine students in Mr. Kalla's classroom, at least two identified their first or only language as English. I asked the teacher why there were students in his ESL classroom who, in fact, knew no language other than English. As my journal notes, he told me the school "considers it a time for them to identify with other students [of color]." Apparently, the school's sentiment was that the students needed camaraderie and behavior management training. Minority groups may need to identify with one another to empower one another and share strength, but should it be done during class for a large chunk of the school day? I questioned then and still do whether this action is reasonable. Taking students out of class only serves to further disadvantage them. At the same time, I believe ESL programs, when correctly implemented, have helped students. After I had made several tutoring visits, one of the younger male students shared some personal feelings with me. While he did at one time know Spanish, he said, he no longer could remember it very well. He explained that his parents were displeased with him if he did not use English. "He said he felt stupid when he spoke Spanish with his brothers." In addition to this, when he spoke Spanish at school, he felt that the teachers would punish him since they could not understand what he was saying.

The final day we were there, Mark and I led the class rather than working one-on-one with students. I considered that day my biggest, most realistic opportunity to take action. Naturally, the classroom atmosphere was slightly different with different teachers in control. I converted a vocabulary lesson into a game involving two teams so the students were able to work together in groups. Their honesty and encouragement with one another inspired me. Mr. Kalla also was pleased.

Looking back now, I remember feeling guilty about being in the classroom. We were helping with the one-on-one tutoring, but I also felt that in some way we were being deceitful since the students themselves did not know all our reasons for being there. We were observers, as well as participants, and we were "observing" them in the *context of their status as a color different than our own. I did not know whether it was fair to look at them, talk to them, and teach them, while trying to decipher each of their "stories" about being Latino. Still, individuals in the classroom made my experience what it was. I was enlightened and challenged by what I saw and heard but discouraged for the students involved in that particular program because I saw no significant progress in their acquisition of language or discipline skills during the time I was there.*

The Politics of Service Learning: In Service to Whom?

The politics of the "Social Foundations" service-learning project can be analyzed in a systematic way by focusing on the relationship among interests, conflict, and power (Morgan 1986). In this project, the interests of the predominantly white college students were being met. They were acquiring valuable personal and professional experience in working with students from diverse backgrounds. The interests of the ESL teachers also were being met, since they acquired additional aid in the classroom. The interests of the ESL students—at least some of their interests—were being met as well, since they were getting valuable one-on-one tutoring, which had the potential to increase their agility with the language.

Carolyn: And my interests as instructor were being met on several levels. Engaging in service to the community contributes to my qualifications for tenure at my college. In addition, I provided an opportunity for preservice students to learn what I think they should know, and I placed myself in a position in which local ESL teachers were indebted to me for providing them with free assistants.

It is the parents of the Latino students whose interests are missing. Rather, it is more correct to say that we do not know whether or not their interests were met, since they were an invisible component in this project. Within the schools their children attend, within the social structure of our community, and now within this project, they have little or no power to see that their interests are served. Indeed, the analysis in this chapter—while useful in exploring the limits of a well-intentioned idea—has perpetuated the problem that is at the heart of our critique of our work. No Latino voices are heard in this writing. No "data" were gathered from either Latino parents or their children, and no follow-up was done to rectify this oversight. Our perspectives as teacher and student are valuable, yet the lack of community voice here reinforces the breakdown of this particular school-community relationship. Why are those voices not represented?

Carolyn: I organized this project through a process of networking with community members and teachers who worked with the Latino population. A few of my contacts were Latino, such as the Latina who is the home-school liaison for one school district. The majority, however, were not people of color. One bilingual white woman, for instance, is deeply involved in health education with migrant workers. Of the three ESL educators in the region my project served, none is Latino, and only one spoke Spanish.

No one suggested that I should be speaking with migrant parents or offered to introduce me to key leaders within the migrant community. Likewise, I did not seek this opportunity, internally rationalizing that decision by pointing to the time restraints inherent in academic teaching. I consider myself an antiracist educator who is aware of the ways in which targeted groups are omitted from the decision-making process in systems that affect them. Why did I so easily avoid the crucial step of out-reach to Latino parents and leaders?

The answer, I believe, lies in my own class and race bias, which makes it easy for me—the white professor at the college on the hill—to make decisions about what I think is "good for" a group of people in my community. Looking deeply at what has happened with this project, I have to admit how deep my fears are of truly engaging with migrant families. I am afraid because I do not speak the language and am embarrassed that I don't. I am yet one more monolinguist who won't take the time to learn Spanish. I find that I am reluctant to attempt to communicate with Latino parents who are not fluent in English when I can't speak to them except through an interpreter, even though in months of travel outside the United States, I managed to communicate well enough. Further, as Sleeter (1996) observes, college-educated white faculty members are powerholders in a system in which we have vested interests. Our own self-interest may lead us—consciously or not—to undermine attempts to create multicultural change. Hence, as a privileged, white fac-ulty member, I was able to use my power to avoid potential conflict with members of a racial group different than my own, while still managing to get my interests met.

Unfortunately, too often service-learning practices such as ours fail to embrace a deeper systemic understanding of multicultural issues. Many writ-ers in the field of service learning, for instance, use terms such as *students* or *communities* with the implication that they mean all students when in fact they are referring to white students and middle-class communities. To a critical multicultural educator involved in service learning, these distinctions should be imperative for identifying discrepancies in power interests that arise during the service experience. As Levinson (1990) notes, not addressing these discrep-ancies or conflicts in a service-learning experience denies students the oppor-tunity to look beneath the plight of the "less fortunate" to the "synergistic relationship between social, political, and economic institutions" (74) and may therefore perpetuate stereotypes that students already have. By just attending to whites' interests and sidestepping potentially conflictual situations, white power is reaffirmed and reinforced.

Beth: In class, although I was able to "step back" and assess the broader issues of inequity, I unconsciously placed myself—the white preservice teacher—in the center of the experience. This experience gave preservice teachers a framework to discuss comments and concerns with ESL teachers, co-tutors, and ESL students. We had paid to be trained, right? And in fact, my interests were met as well. The experience served as a catalyst to heighten my motivation to eliminate injustice being done through systematic racism.

Although I was positively affected by the experience, I should not have considered myself the center. Through conversations with Carolyn and fellow students, I realize that the strength of service learning lies in the cooperation and partnership of the com-munity and the students. During the experience, I had considered the feelings and needs of the students I was teaching but not those of their parents or anyone else in the Latino community. In addition, I never actually asked the students what they wanted to learn from me. The students were unaware of our reasons for being there. I now real-ize that my experiential learning may have been at some cost to the community of color.

Without the theoretical underpinnings provided by critical and social recon-structionist multicultural pedagogies, service learning can too easily reinforce oppressive outcomes. It can perpetuate racist, sexist, or classist assumptions about others and reinforce a colonialist mentality of superiority. Nadinne Cruz (1990) places service learning within the historical context of dominance of one group over others. The inevitability of our history, in which groups embedded in conflicting interests have not been equal in power and resources, reinforces racism or oppressive beliefs, even when these are unintentional. Echoing Ivan Illich, Cruz (1990) notes:

> I want us to talk about why, in the context of conflicting interests and the historical dominance of one racial or gender group over another, it is possible that "service" in and of itself, can have racist or sexist outcomes despite good intentions. . . . I think that, in the context of a history of dominance of one group over others, there is an incipient racism in the practice of service that cannot be avoided even if the conceptualization of it includes values and ideals we can respect and the virtues of people who practice it are above question. (322–323)

Carolyn: The issue of classism is pervasive in our experience as well. I do literally teach in a college on a hill and one that does not have a particularly good reputation for attracting or retaining either students or faculty of color. I was fearful that by reaching out to migrant families (most of whom have not yet "made it" into the middle class or to our hill), I would be perceived as condescending. Worse, I may even be condescending in yet another version of academics telling people how they should live their lives without attending to their interests fully. Indeed, my students came away from this project having learned that Latinos *means poor, migrant, and uneducated. I did not help them see the range of socioeconomic class status among Latinos in our area or in the United States.*

My own middle-class upbringing, along with my white racial identity, has given me the habit of power, if you will. I am accustomed to maintaining influence in the spheres in which I move. In this project in particular, I controlled the decision making by using my power to unilaterally decide on the interests and objectives to be addressed and the evaluative criteria to be employed (Morgan 1986). I was able to define the reality of this project and in so doing maintained white power and institutional influence by avoiding potentially unpleasant conflicts of interests.

Students engaged in service, particularly white students, often do not understand the social dynamics of poverty and racism and may accept such circumstances as a given. Service without knowledge, without an understanding of the "embedded inequalities" of our society, means, for example, that students are unable to make connections between the plight of the poor and social policies. For instance, in the "Social Foundations" course, more of the students should have been able to connect the fact that even Latino students whose first language was English were in an ESL classroom to the absence of Latino parents in the educational process. As Ritchie (1995) notes, "[People of color's] ideas and voices risk becoming blurred and buried by constant attempts at understanding people of color from a point of view which reifies a Eurocentric system and academic process of domination under the guise of expanding the current knowledge base. . . . What needs to happen is that our voices not be usurped or interpreted by our 'benefactors'" (310). Going through the motions, just doing service without reflection and without knowledge of political structures reifies dominant-group interests at the expense of those different from ourselves. Service without engagement prepares students to make things "less bad," and it fails to help them make the connections among interests, power, and productive conflict that will lead to change (Morgan 1986).

Beth: My frustration with "action" in the context of this particular service-learning project remains. The political nature of the college-high school relationship did not allow me or any of the other preservice teachers to take dramatic action that would have changed the system. Yet I was learning in our college classroom that action should be taken. I was extremely frustrated that students who spoke English well were in the ESL classroom, apparently so they could "bond" with other Latinos. Not only did this limit their educational potential (since they were capable of much more demanding work), it also reinforced a view of diversity with which I am uncomfortable. The assumption the school made that all members of a "minority" group should be grouped together is disturbing to me. But I did not feel comfortable expressing my concerns about this to anyone in the school, much less trying to actually change what the school did. In dealing with the "experiential learning process" and in situations such as this one, what is considered appropriate and realistic? In addition to being exposed to the issues surrounding diversity, preservice teachers should be able to learn and experience more effective measures of action.

CONCLUSION

At their best, service-learning programs emphasize reciprocity between the "server" and the person or group "being served." This reciprocity emphasizes an exchange of giving and receiving between both parties and avoids connotations of charity. It is not easy to develop and sustain such collaborations. In writing about their own experience with a school-community collaboration, Trubowitz and Longo (1997) emphasize that "the pursuit of mutually beneficial self-interest forms the most enduring basis for a collaborative venture" (44). All members of the collaborative partnership must benefit for the collaboration to prosper, and all must participate in the process of defining what constitutes a benefit.

In a good service-learning program, those being served exercise power through control of the service provided (Kendall 1990). Without this, service learning may tend toward paternalism, particularly for white students engaging in service experiences in communities of color. The U.S. history of white domination of people of color makes such service experiences particularly challenging. Kendall (1990) believes that the word *service* connotes inequity rather than mutuality and cautions against service being used as a "self-righteous, vaguely disguised ticket to salvation for upper- and middle-class people who feel guilty about their access to resources" (24).

As we began to collaborate on the writing of this chapter, we were of differing minds about the value of continuing this project. Initially, Carolyn focused only on the short-term dilemmas and decided to scrap it altogether. Beth, on the other hand, focused on the growth opportunity for students and the long-term benefits to maintaining a college-community collaboration. As we struggled through our own collaborative process, we helped each other forge a new understanding of what aspects of the service-learning project challenged each of us the most.

Carolyn: I feel I haven't lived up to my own rhetoric as a multicultural educator. This experience is a good reminder to me that patient and persistent efforts are needed to change both oneself and larger systemic structures. I do have grave misgivings about whether a white college community is capable of entering into true collaboration with a community of color. The benefits of this project were too inequitably distributed, but I remain committed to engaging white students in experiences that expand their understanding of issues of diversity. I also am committed to forging stronger and more equitable college-community connections, especially with communities of color. I am still convinced that critical multicultural education and service learning have much to offer each other (O'Grady forthcoming). I think there is the kernel of a good idea here, and I'll keep chewing on it.

Beth: I was initially very resistant when Carolyn talked about giving up the project. The service-learning project frustrated me, and I became infuriated by the blatant institutional racism I saw around me, but the objective was to force us, through experience, to reflect on our own power and privilege. I feel I had a useful learning experience. I continue to be frustrated with how I could have taken more action to change the political systems at the school and how I could have taken more action to empower those students. However, I realize that white preservice teachers are not entitled to experiential learning at the cost of the community of color.

As Tellez and colleagues (1995) note, adding more readings on cultural diversity will not increase students' cultural awareness or sensitivity. For that, they need community-based experiences with a variety of racial and cultural groups. We believe that reciprocity between the school and the community is the goal in the best service-learning programs. We also believe that students must have the opportunity to understand the larger context of issues of social justice that can be learned through multicultural education and critical pedagogy. Without this context, service programs may foster an attitude of paternalism on the part of the server and a perpetuation of the power differentials inherent in an inequitable society. As Cruz (1990) observes, "I think it is possible to empower learners (through service learning) and not promote the common good (by reinforcing a sense of inferiority among those 'served' or a false sense of power among those who 'serve'). It is possible to use experience as an integral part of education and simply duplicate the realities we wish to change" (323).

Trubowitz and Longo (1997) remind us that for those involved in forging school-community collaborations, it is crucial to "maintain a balanced perspective regarding what can be done, how soon it can be accomplished, and what results can realistically be expected" (164). We acknowledge the flaws in our own project and Carolyn's complicity in perpetuating these. But we also recognize that this project, like our attitudes to it—like antiracism work itself—is a work in progress.

STUDY QUESTIONS

1. What has been your experience with volunteering or performing service to others? In what way(s) do you feel the service you were doing empowered those you were serving? In what way(s) did it disempower them? What did you learn as a result of the experience?

2. Review some of the literature on service learning recommended in the references? How might you redesign a class to include a service-learning component?

3. Explore the value of incorporating a service-learning pedagogy into several kinds of college courses, such as history, English, biology, physics, and so on. How would this help you learn the content? What kinds of things might you imagine doing as a service project in each kind of course? (It might be helpful to think in terms of what skills and knowledge from each content are used in the world outside of the classroom.)

4. As an undergraduate, how similar is your background to that of Beth? How different? What advice would you offer Beth regarding her concerns about being able to take real action in this project?

5. Do you agree with Beth that it is important to be able to take action to create change in an institution such as a school? What are some ways in which you might take action to change what you consider unjust conditions at your own school or job?

6. Your school has just hired a "service-learning coordinator." You are on the hiring committee and have input into the job qualifications and job description. What should these be?

7. Explore the issue of whether it is realistic for a predominantly white college to engage in collaboration with a community of color. What are the rewards (if any) for each group in doing this? What are the costs (if any) for each group?

8. Carolyn had concerns that this experience may have reinforced the stereotypes some of her students had about Latinos. What advice would you give her to help avoid this possibility in the future?

9. This chapter uses the framework of interests, conflict, and power described by Morgan (1986) in his work on organizations as political systems. Examine the context in which you work, or are a student. What are the issues that arise which create conflict? Whose interests are or are not met in these situations or within the institution? Who has power in that context, and how is that power manifested? (For instance, you may wish to think in terms of who controls resources, who controls information, who controls decision-making processes, etc.)

KEY CONCEPTS

Service learning

Multicultural education

Critical pedagogy

Systemic racism

Paternalism

REFERENCES

Anderson, J. B., and K. Guest. 1994. Service learning in teacher education at Seattle University. In *Building community: Service learning in the academic disciplines,* ed. R. J. Kraft and M. Swadener, 139–150. Denver: Colorado Campus Compact.

Aparicio, F. R., and C. Jose-Kampfner. 1995. Language, culture, and violence in the education crisis of U.S. Latinos/as: Two courses for intervention. *Michigan Journal of Community Service Learning* 2 (fall): 95–105.

Cruz, N. 1990. A challenge to the notion of service. In *Combining service and learning: A resource book for community and public service,* vol. 1, ed. J. C. Kendall et al., 321–323. Raleigh, N.C.: National Society for Internships and Experiential Education.

Hardiman, R., and B. W. Jackson. 1992. Racial identity development: Understanding racial dynamics in college classrooms and on campus. In *Promoting diversity in college classrooms: Innovative resources for the curriculum, faculty, and institutions,* ed. M. Adams, 21–37. San Francisco: Jossey-Bass.

Illich, I. 1990. To hell with good intentions. In *Combining service and learning: A resource book for community and public service,* vol. 1, ed. J. C. Kendall et al., 314–320. Raleigh, N.C.: National Society for Internships and Experiential Education.

Keith, N. Z. 1997. Doing service projects in urban settings. In *Service learning: Applications from the research,* ed. A. S. Waterman, 127–149. Mahwah, N.J.: Lawrence Erlbaum.

Kendall, J. C. 1990. Combining service and learning: An introduction. In *Combining service and learning: A resource book for community and public service,* vol. 1, ed. J. C. Kendall et al., 1–33. Raleigh, N.C.: National Society for Internships and Experiential Education.

Kitano, M. K. 1997. What a course will look like after multicultural change. In *Multicultural course transformation in higher education: A broader truth,* ed. A. I. More and M. K. Kitano, 18–34. Needham Heights, Mass.: Allyn & Bacon.

Levinson, L. M. 1990. Choose engagement over exposure. In *Combining service and learning: A resource book for community and public service,* vol. 1, ed. J. C. Kendall et al., 68–75. Raleigh, N.C.: National Society for Internships and Experiential Education.

McIntosh, P. 1990. White privilege: Unpacking the invisible knapsack. *Independent School* (winter): 31–36.

Morgan, G. 1986. *Images of organizations.* Beverly Hills, Calif.: Sage.

O'Grady, C. R. (forthcoming). *Integrating service learning and multicultural education in colleges and universities.* Mahwah, N.J.: Lawrence Erlbaum.

Ritchie, M. 1995. Whose voice is it anyway? Vocalizing multicultural analysis. In *Multicultural education, critical pedagogy, and the politics of difference,* ed. C. E. Sleeter and P. L. McLaren, 310–316. Albany, N.Y.: State University of New York Press.

Ryan, W. 1976. *Blaming the victim.* New York: Vintage Books.

Sleeter, C. E., and C. A. Grant. 1987. An analysis of multicultural education in the United States. *Harvard Education Review* 57(4): 421–444.

Sleeter, C. E., and P. L. McLaren. 1995. *Multicultural education, critical pedagogy, and the politics of difference.* Albany, N.Y.: State University of New York Press.

Sleeter, C. E. 1996. *Multicultural education as social activism.* Albany, N.Y.: State University of New York Press.

Tellez, K., P. S. Hlebowitsh, M. Cohen, and P. Norwood. 1995. Social service field experiences and teacher education. In *Developing multicultural teacher education curricula,* ed. J. M. Larkin and C. E. Sleeter, 65–78. Albany, N.Y.: State University of New York Press.

Trubowitz, S., and P. Longo. 1997. *How it works: Inside a school-college collaboration.* New York: Columbia University Teachers College Press.

Multiculturalism

Beyond a Zero-Sum Game

Carlos J. Ovando and Peter McLaren

*Multiculturalism in education—so strongly denounced by so many powerful voices
in American life, by historians, publicists, labor leaders, intellectuals, the occasion for
so many major battles in American education during the nineties, and so much
at odds with the course of American culture, society, and education at least up
until the 1960s—has, in a word, won.*
Nathan Glazer, We Are All Multiculturalists Now, 4

Why does our society continue to play a zero-sum game—to declare winners
and losers—with respect to issues of language, race, class, gender, religion, culture, ethnicity, and other differences? Why does Glazer say that multiculturalism has won the battle while at the same time he obliquely laments its victory?
What is it that lies concealed in the hearts of people that keeps society from
passionately embracing human dignity and justice for all its citizens?

As suggested in this anthology, the notion that there always are winners and
losers in U.S. society—the zero-sum game—is deeply anchored in the multicultural and multilingual character of the nation. Comprising many races, nationalities, religions, ethnicities, linguistic backgrounds, geographical regions, ideologies,
and political traditions, the United States has struggled since its violent birth with
issues of diversity, unity, and expansionism. Thus, it is not surprising that multiculturalism came into national prominence late in the twentieth century after a
lengthy and acrimonious war of words between liberals and conservatives over
issues of national and cultural identity and assimilation. Each side in this tug of
war has laid "claim to the mantle of pluralism, though always a pluralism fortified
with some other principle (like a core American 'creed')." (Gordon and Newfield
1996, 83). In more detail, here is what the battle is about:

> Some stress multiplicity and some stress unity. The former is wary that plural-
> ist unity is a nice word for the assimilation of all U.S. groups to Euro-American
> or even Anglo-Saxon norms. The latter insist that pluralist unity can dissolve
> our national institutions into partisan tools of interest-group bickering and
> even civil war. The former group worries about cultural autonomy; the latter is

225

preoccupied with cultural commonality. The former denounces the cultural dominance of the majority, while the latter rejects the cultural separatism of the minority. (Gordon and Newfield 1996, 83)

Acutely aware of the political, epistomological, and ethical import of these ideological issues, the authors of this anthology have articulated in various ways the possibility of creating a win-win scenario for the nation if we hold fast to the principles of critical self-reflection, civil discourse, and democratic pluralism. To create a peaceful and just society, however, some authors have also argued for the centrality of cultural, linguistic, and economic parity. This means that to create a united country out of many diverse peoples, we have to keep working toward the realization of an economic and political infrastructure that is grounded in socially just principles that honor the human family with all its imperfections and potential. And we must do so with an awareness of the fact that we are no longer isolated as a nation but part of the larger global family. As such, we must become aware of how economic and social policies initiated within our shores affect the well-being of our family members throughout the world. As noted in the various chapters, the public schools have several critical roles to play in this mission: integrating examples of the many important contributions of all the people of the United States; developing students' ability to think critically about how knowledge in the social, behavioral, and natural sciences is constructed and influenced by the scientists' own racial, cultural, and social class backgrounds; developing pedagogical practices that affirm the lived experiences of all children and thus create culturally compatible classroom practices; creating empowering sociocultural and linguistic environments where students' lived experiences serve as a springboard for further growth; and affirming the importance of reflection and action (praxis) in all human endeavors within and across cultures (Banks 1995, 4–5).

The editors of this anthology wish that they could celebrate Glazer's premature conclusion that multiculturalism has won (see Clemetson 1998, 38–39). Although we have made progress, as indicated in the various chapters herein, much work still needs to be done to redress the deep structural social and economic inequalities that are pervasive in our globally interconnected society, linking these disparities to issues of social, racial, and schooling injustices. We do, however, hope that the discussions in this anthology have provided the readers with an abundance of ideas about the politics of multiculturalism and bilingual schooling. We hope that the book will inspire the development of policies and school practices that will be more in tune with the multicultural and multilingual realities and dreams of our children—where the future of multiculturalism and a more just and equitable social order rests. Our final wish is that students and teachers will develop a dialogical habit of the mind and heart that will prompt them to step out of their familiar class, cultural, racial, religious, and linguistic frameworks and enter into the experience of others. For, in the words of Carlos Fuentes (1992), "People and their cultures perish in isolation, but they are born or reborn in contact with other men and women, with men and women of another culture, another creed, another race. If we do not recognize our humanity in others, we shall not recognize it in ourselves" (353).

REFERENCES

Banks, J. A. 1995. Multicultural education: Historical development, dimensions, and practice. In *Handbook of research on multicultural education,* ed. J. A. Banks and C. A. M. Banks, 3–24. New York: Macmillan.

Clemetson, L. 1998. Caught in the cross-fire. *Newsweek,* 14 December, 38–39.

Fuentes, C. 1992. *The buried mirror.* Boston: Houghton Mifflin.

Glazer, N. 1997. *We are all multiculturalists now.* Cambridge: Harvard University Press.

Gordon, A., and C. Newfield. 1996. Multiculturalism's unfinished business. In *Mapping multiculturalism,* ed. A. Gordon and C. Newfield, 76–115. Minneapolis: University of Minnesota Press.

Glossary

Critical pedagogy An ambitious and wide-ranging ideological project usually situated within educational contexts and linked to the work of Brazilian educator Paulo Freire. Critical pedagogy represents a montage of ideas and methods emphasizing a strategy of questioning how knowledge is individually constructed and of interrogating the institutions that legitimize one form or domain of knowledge over another. Critical pedagogy offers individuals a lens through which to examine how, as ordinary people, they construct knowledge. As a formal and informal instructional orientation, critical pedagogy informs learning opportunities that guide individuals to an understanding of the sophisticated processes whereby their interactions with institutions and other people advance the co-constructing and safeguarding of specific and regulated forms of knowledge. Critical pedagogy challenges the system of accepted information and common-sense truths that serves to maintain asymmetrical social relations.

Global capitalism For economic growth to be maintained, a global economy has been formed to compensate for the downward profits trend faced by domestic economies that are becoming increasingly exposed to more intense foreign competition. This system of global capitalism is also propelled by an increased level of economic competition between companies, nations, and geopolitical regions throughout the world, de-emphasizing the former preeminence of the nation states. Globalization is marked by the incipience of alternative economic configurations such as "fast capitalism" and the decline of nations to individually guarantee and maintain their economic affluence.

Neoliberalism Refers generally to a trend among contemporary liberals to reconceptualize their ideology and political behavior away from that associated with classical political liberalism first marshaled in during the Roosevelt administration. A key feature of classical liberalism was the notion of "big government" and its role in ameliorating social injustices and inequalities. Neoliberals are a new breed of political actors committed to reconstructing the image and ideology of liberalism to include many of the tenets introduced during the rise of modern conservatism led by Ronald Reagan. Neoliberals purport to be compassionate, fiscally sensible, and morally responsible citizens. In their project to redefine contemporary liberalism, significant social problems such as discrimination, incessant poverty among specific groups, and the positive investment of some members of society to maintain the current social and political climate are topographically addressed. Neoliberals' assessments of the prevailing social conditions are usually rhetorical, and their solutions decidedly provisional and situational, rather than structural. Moreover,

229

neoliberalism has been seen as advancing specific conservative efforts to link schooling to market and materialist relations. The potential contribution of neoliberalism to a project guided by critical multiculturalism is limited.

Hegemony   A theoretical concept largely popularized by the work of Italian social critic Antonio Gramsci. The term describes the condition whereby dominance is accomplished as a matter of consent and shared social institutions and practices among the oppressed, rather than exclusively through the exercise of forcible coercion. Hegemony refers to the sophisticated processes and social practices by which individuals become complicit in their subordination. Hegemony is further accomplished by forming social consensus and social control and then developing institutions that legitimize and preserve this established social arrangement. In this way, an established view of the world becomes transparently embedded in the social, economic, cultural, and linguistic practices of a community, and any questioning of these existent relations then appears to be counterintuitive.

Heterophobic   A new concept among critical discourses, conceptually similar to xenophobia, it describes a panicked or exaggerated reaction to the probability that prevailing social, cultural, and racial relations may be subject to immediate or eventual transformation.

Human capital   With the rise of economic explanation to describe human endeavors, human capital theory purports the belief that humans possess productive capabilities similar to those of inanimate instruments and technologies. By altering or improving the capabilities of individuals, as you would improve either a manual tool or a computer software program, for example, you increase the individual's human capital. Increased human capital is primarily acquired through advanced training such as that received through formal schooling. Human capital is viewed as a composite of acquired skills, abilities, and information.

Nativist   One who practices nativism, a systemic social, political, and legal campaign usually directed at an immigrant population and predicated on the notion that the newcomers are in some way inferior and pose a threat to the extant social and economic relations. Nativism has been offered as the motive behind such actions as the Mexican Miners' Tax of 1850 and Greaser Act (1850), and, more recently, the internment of Japanese Americans during World War II. The Greaser Act is separate from the Foreign Miners' Tax (aka Mexican Miners' Tax), but both were passed in 1850 in California (during the Gold Rush).

Praxis   An action generally understood as the deliberate intersection of theory and practice. That is, the point at which a theoretical tradition, position, or impulse gives rise to and thoroughly informs the concrete actions executed by an individual social agent or group. Praxis is the moment and consequence of informed action.

Index

al Guard to keep nine black students
n, an all-white public school. Phil tried
to settle the matter without military
sent in federal troops to assure the safe
ks, ending the immediate crisis. Phil
roops signaled the failure of the civil
rned what he considered the end of a

in extreme pain. He was unable to stop
distraught about his inability to cope.
ough that particularly difficult period,
rough a series of mood swings. Doctors
d Kay spent as much time as possible
ffectively trying to talk him out of his
The Post, but it was obvious that he had
and startling behavior was his frequent

t that Phil suffered from overwhelming
himself, and indecision about even the
e was completely dependent on Kay and
listen to him at all times. Sometimes he
etimes read, and occasionally he played
e office at all. The couple rarely enter-
ecause Kay was afraid that Phil would
ut word that Phil needed a long rest on
ll the hard work he had put in during the
id quite well with Phil working from over

t had profits of over two million dollars
ion's ninth largest newspaper, ranking
nue in the country. Circulation was over
r 400,000 for dailies. The prices had risen

also began drinking more. As Agnes had done, Phil became more prone to depression, more abusive verbally, and less stable. Sometimes, Phil apologized to Kay after he had lost control due to alcohol. At these times, he said he would not drink to excess any more. When he was sober, Kay tried unsuccessfully to talk with him about his irrational and unpredictable behavior.

When they were getting along well, Phil and Kay talked a lot about the paper. In this way, Kay kept up with many of the new people, ideas, and changes in *The Post*. During these periods, he was exuberant and optimistic. At home he hunted, fished, and hiked with the children. He entertained them with stories and jokes. In public, he was the life of any party, and dynamic in the office. At other times, he was uncommunicative, uninterested, and vague. At home he was more and more critical of Kay—her clothes, the way she kept house, anything and everything.

In several ways, 1953 and 1954 were good years for *The Post*. Phil bought the remaining stock of WTOP. Now he had complete control of CBS radio and television outlets in Washington. Daily and Sunday circulation of passed two hundred thousand.

Phil took on new causes. He proposed an election financing bill to reduce the importance of contributions by special interest groups. His solution was to encourage private citizens to donate more to offset the special interests. Texas Senator Lyndon Johnson worked closely with Phil on this bill. The plan, called the Graham plan, resulted in the draft of a bill in the Senate signed by all but one senator. However, it failed to pass in the House. Phil and Senator Johnson remained good friends. The Grahams spent a weekend at the Johnson Texas ranch. There Kay felt uncomfortable because she believed that Johnson was using Phil for his prestige and power.

In January 1954, Eugene met with a representative of Colonel McCormick. The *Times-Herald* was up for sale due to McCormick's poor health and the fact that the paper was failing with falling circulation and annual losses of about half a million dollars a year. The two men agreed on a selling price of $8.5 million. On March 17, 1954, the deal was finalized. The paper became, temporarily *The Washington Post and Times-Herald*. When Eugene bought the paper, he said, "This makes *The Post* safe for Donny." The boy was then nine years old.

The two papers had served different audiences. The *Times Herald* had lots of features, columnists, sports, crime, and comics. *The Post* served more serious readers with more news-in-depth and more editorials. Phil's immediate job was to see that each audience was satisfied and that current and potential advertisers saw the value in the merger. Eugene printed a declaration of his policy including: "Editorially we shall continue our devotion to the cause of constitutional government, to the protection of civil liberties of every citizen, to home rule in Washington . . . and to international cooperation." Four months after the sale, the circulation for both daily and Sunday editions was just under four hundred thousand.

When Phil was optimistic and relaxed, Kay was also happy. The Virginia farm became a favorite retreat. They built a tennis court and two ponds. One pond was large enough for boating, and the family enjoyed a variety of boats from canoes and sailboats to a strong power boat for water skiing. They had many family meals together as well as lots of guests. Phil had fun with his children, organizing frog-catching expeditions, doing acrobatics, and making up games and riddles.

But this happiness did not last. In Phil's depressed periods, he felt increasingly uncomfortable about Eugene's financial help. He asserted that he could have made it on his own if he had not accepted Eugene's money. He warned Eugene not to interfere with the paper.

Kay also faced increasing problems that she acknowledged only vaguely. She was unhappy. She gained weight and paid little attention to how she dressed. Her mother seemed to her a competitor, not a

Orval Faubus used the Nat
out of Little Rock Central H
to encourage those involv
intervention. But Eisenhow
passage of the black stud
believed this sending in th
rights movement, and he n
dream.

One night, Kay found Pl
sobbing and was complete
A psychiatrist helped him
but soon again he was going
ordered complete rest. He
at Glen Welby with Kay i
illness. Then Phil returned
not recovered. Part of his n
use of gutter language.

Less obvious was the f
self-doubt, a desire to isola
smallest aspects of his life.
insisted that she be there t
visited his psychiatrist, so
golf. He scarcely went to
tained or went out, partly
drink too much. They sen
doctor's orders. Thanks to
last eleven years, the paper
the telephone.

From 1955-57, *The P*
a year. It became the na
seventh in advertising rev
460,000 on Sundays and o

President Eisenhower used federal troops to help racially integrate Little Rock Central High School.

from fifteen to twenty cents for the Sunday edition and from five cents to twenty cents for the daily. *The Post and Times-Herald* increased its lead in circulation over the *Star*. It also increased international coverage with its first foreign office, a bureau in London.

Gradually, Phil seemed to improve, and he felt able to leave the house occasionally. One of his first initiatives was to work with Senator Johnson to push the D.C. home-rule bill. He also spoke at meetings of stockholders. Partly to get out of the house, Kay became more involved in charities. She worked for children's schools, education boards, and for the Department of Public Welfare in its focus on children.

One morning in 1958, Kay found herself almost unable to move. Right away she knew that her emotional problems had taken control of her body. She confided in Phil. He and Dr. Leslie Farber, his psychiatrist, convinced her that Dr. Farber could help Kay at the same time that he helped Phil. This was an unusual decision; husbands and wives seldom have the same psychiatrist. Nevertheless, Kay went along with the idea.

Around the same time, Eugene was diagnosed with both heart disease and cancer. Agnes wanted to continue her activities as speaker and supporter of causes, but she did not want Eugene left without a family member close by. So she asked Kay to look after him while she was out of town. She told her that she and Phil were the only people who could help her father. She added that Phil could be of the most help since Eugene would listen to him better than to anyone else.

Kay was already overwhelmed with her own personal problems, Phil's mood swings, and the care of four children and a large house. She felt that she could not possibly accept another burden, but she felt compelled to care for her father.

In July 1959, eighty-three-year-old Eugene died. In her mourning, Kay felt that the only man who believed in her was gone.

Phil made speeches in late 1959 and early 1960 that showed him as a rejuvenated man. He spoke of a new personal goal, that of examining his own life. When he talked about the paper, he made the frequently quoted comment that a newspaper was a first rough draft of history and the job of documenting this first draft often seemed an impossible task.

In December 1959, Phil outlined strategy to insure Senator Lyndon Johnson's nomination for president in the next year. However, before the nominating convention in July 1960, it became clear that Senator John F. Kennedy would beat Johnson. Phil helped to persuade Kennedy to accept Johnson as a vice-presidential running mate, and he persuaded Johnson to accept the number two spot on the ticket. Kennedy won a close election against Richard Nixon in the November election.

Despite the fact that Phil became heavily involved in work and politics again, Kay felt unsure about his health. She was particularly worried when Phil considered buying the newsweekly magazine *Newsweek* in February 1961. The magazine was over-shadowed by *Time*, its nearest competitor. Kay feared that the pressure of this new responsibility would hurl Phil back into a depression. He countered with the idea that this new venture would do just the opposite for him. He said that this was his first opportunity to work on his own without Eugene's financial and moral support. He needed this opportunity to erase his self-doubt. With some uncertainty, Kay agreed with him.

Kay and Phil planned to go to New York to make the final arrangements to buy *Newsweek*. Just before she left, Kay received a call from her doctor saying that tests showed that she might have tuberculosis. Kay insisted on going to New York anyway, promising the doctor and herself that she would attend to the medical problem as soon as she got home.

With much satisfaction, Phil closed the deal. The Washington Post Company bought 120,000 of *Newsweek's* 180,000 shares, forty-five percent of KOGO-TV, and two radio stations.

When Kay returned to Washington, she was hospitalized with tuberculosis. When she was discharged from the hospital, she was ordered to stay in bed for at least six weeks and to take it easy after that. She accepted the enforced rest and even said that she enjoyed the attention. But this time was difficult for Phil. He assumed some of the tasks that Kay had always taken care of—shopping for the children, taking them places, and talking and listening to them. The unfamiliar responsibilities placed stress on him. Besides, he was used to having Kay at his beck and call.

As fall approached, Kay recovered from tuberculosis, and she was free to spend time with Phil. She was also free to accept invitations from the Kennedys to spend time with them at Cape Cod. "I was very flattered to be included . . . I always felt like a country girl from New York." Phil became more and more dependent on Kay simply to be with him so that he would not be alone.

Chapter Six

"I'm here if you need me"

Then Phil made the most of a period of good health and spirits. He worked to build up *Newsweek* and to create an effective coordination between the magazine and the newspaper. He worked almost feverishly—hiring, firing, promoting, purchasing, organizing. A British journalist described him: ". . . with this wild and restless brilliance he must play Pied Piper to every man and woman that comes into his ken." Phil spent time with the Kennedys. He became so important to the president that when he called the Oval Office, he could usually get put through to the president. He became part of an inner circle at the home of Robert Kennedy, brother of the president.

In October, a *Post* reporter learned that a crisis would arise soon in Cuba. The Soviet Union was erecting missiles in Cuba, missiles that posed a potential threat to the United States. This information, published in *The Post* on a Sunday, enraged Kennedy who thought that he had insured complete secrecy on the situation. He asked Phil not to print any more about the potential conflict. The president did not want to give the Soviets advance information on a possible military response from the United States. Phil agreed. In Monday's edition, a short item declared that any further developments would be kept secret as ordered by the government.

Phil spent more time away from home, both on evenings and over weekends. Kay did not understand the reasons for many of his absences. She spent a lot of time preparing for Lally's coming-out party. Her mother complimented her on the way she arranged the celebration: "Darling, you are very good with lists."

About this time, Phil bought a large plane, the Gulfstream 1. Kay thought the purchase was both unnecessary and extravagant. But instead of questioning Phil, she asked herself what right she had to question or make a judgement. Her answer was that she had no right.

Her long-felt insecurity increased as she grew older. She said about men: "They liked bright men, and they liked girls, but they didn't really know how to relate to middle-aged women . . . we somehow knew we had no place in their spectrum."

She was so afraid of saying the wrong thing, or of being boring that she clammed up when they were out socially. The only time she felt secure socially was when she was with Phil and he was doing most of the talking. Kay's dress and appearance often mirrored her attitude. One acquaintance described her as "dowdy, dumpy almost, in a shapeless dress and a nervous manner, smothered by her husband." Once when Phil was invited to address a large meeting, Kay was invited also. Phil told his assistant to tell the organization that Kay would be delighted to attend. Then, he added ". . . tell Kay how delighted she is."

Kay watched helplessly as Phil showed increasing signs of depression in between his periods of high activity. Both facts and rumors flew about Phil's personal problems. The word got around that he abused both alcohol and prescription drugs. His co-workers knew that in the office he sometimes cried, drank, threw water glasses, made incessant telephone calls, and did a lot of office business lying on the couch. Some office workers kept in touch with Kay, keeping her informed about Phil's behavior.

President Kennedy's aides asked Kay to tell Phil to stop calling the president at all hours of the night. She was unable to stop him. Finally, Kennedy instructed the White House switchboard not to put

President Kennedy had to ask the White House switchboard to not put through
Phil Graham's late night telephone calls.

...nore calls from Phil after nine o'clock in the evening. ...y could not restrain Phil. Once in the president's office, ...d the red emergency phone and yelled into it "Scramble ...Immediately, Kennedy grabbed the receiver and rescind-...er.

...summer of 1962, Kay rented a home on Cape Cod, hoping ...er husband away from busy Washington. The plan would ...en more successful if they had not chosen a home near the ...dy's vacation home. Phil often visited with them despite Kay's ...stions that serious conversations with the president and his ...s would be tiring for him.

On Christmas Eve afternoon, Kay picked up a ringing phone. She ...ard a conversation between Phil and his secretary, Robin Webb, ...at suggested that they were having an affair. As soon as Phil hung ...p, Kay questioned him. He admitted that he loved Robin, but said that he would stop the affair. His family was more important to him than Robin, he said. Then he told her about some of his other affairs. "I felt completely defeated," she wrote later. "It had never occurred to me that we didn't have a great marriage."

Kay told the children. They had not known about Phil's affairs or his heavy drinking. Don scolded Kay for not telling him sooner about the drinking. All Kay could think was that uppermost in her mind was protecting her children.

Phil left the house in anger on the morning of January 12, 1963. Kay sent him a telegram at his office: "I'm here if you need me and I love you." Phil responded with a message that Kay could not understand. It said in part, "And while you need help you will be getting it from me—now and always in this new but loving way. And you shall help me." He seldom came home.

For two weeks, Kay kept the news of Phil's leaving in the family. When she finally confided in a friend, the friend responded immediately that Kay would be better off without him.

Another friend gave her opinion of the marriage: "He [Phil] was charming to the children and nasty to you."

Kay learned, as did many of their friends, that Phil had bought a large house in Washington for Robin, and that they spent a lot of time together there. Sometimes, friends would mention seeing Phil and they would say that he looked well. Kay knew that Phil's apparent good health was only temporary. A depression would surely follow, and then what? If Phil could get help for his problems, would he want to return to her and to the children? Or would he prefer to forget his twenty-two years of marriage and find a new life with Robin? Distraught about the future of their marriage, Kay found a new psychiatrist and consulted with him regularly.

Socially, Phil frequently introduced Robin as the next Mrs. Graham. He and Robin invited his and Kay's friends to dinner parties. Some friends refused the invitations out of loyalty to Kay. At one large dinner party, Phil introduced Lally to Robin. Lally instantly disliked Robin. Kay heard from mutual friends that Phil had a stock answer when someone expressed sympathy about his recent illness. He said things like, "I am not, nor have I been, seriously ill."

In January, Phil lost control of himself at a meeting of publishers in Phoenix, Arizona. Kay was not there, but she heard all about it later. In crude language, Phil criticized well-known people and also the press. Someone finally managed to get him off the speaker's platform and called President Kennedy, who agreed to send a government plane and doctor to take him back to Washington. With the help of tranquilizers, they managed to get him onto the plane. Back in Washington, he was committed to Chestnut Lodge, a mental health hospital in Maryland.

Kay put up a brave front while Phil was in the hospital. She gave parties, and she went out socially. A friend noted that she was consistently loyal to Phil and never complained about him or about the strains of their relationship. Kay visited Phil frequently. Sometimes they had talks about their futures, talks which Phil described as especially good.

In March, Phil left the hospital to spend two weeks in Puerto Rico with Robin. He made it clear that he wanted a divorce. He changed his will so that his children would receive one-third of his estate and Robin would receive two-thirds. He hired a lawyer to handle the divorce. He frequently insulted his employees. Phil talked to the children privately many times. Sometimes he picked up Bill and Steve at school. Kay was frightened by the fact that Phil was unpredictable, and she didn't want to make a difficult situation worse for their children.

For a couple of months, Kay heard nothing directly from Phil. From their friends, she learned that Phil and Robin had renovated a farm, making it much like the Glen Welby estate with ponds and fields. Then she heard from a mutual friend that Phil planned to buy Kay's share in *The Post,* using profits the paper had earned under his management. This news stiffened Kay's backbone. She may be losing Phil, but she was determined not to lose *The Post.*

She did not want to discuss the legal ramifications of a divorce until she could be sure that she would retain control both of their children and of *The Post.* She told one friend that she wished to hold onto the paper only until the children were old enough to run it. The friend scolded her, saying that Kay herself could run the business: ". . . you've just been pushed down so far you don't recognize what you can do."

Phil made a date with Kay to talk about the divorce and to pick up some of his personal things. When the day came, Kay simply could not face him. She stayed away from home. When she returned, Phil had taken most of his clothes and other possessions.

In June, Kay received a call from one of their friends. He was relaying a message from Phil who said that he wanted to be rid of Robin and to come back to Kay. She agreed, and on June 19, he was once again in their home overnight. Once there, he begged to stay instead of returning to Chestnut Lodge for regular treatments. Kay knew that he still needed serious help, and regretfully, she told him that he must return to the hospital until he was better. On June 20, Phil was re-admitted to Chestnut Lodge.

Kay visited him daily. She began to hope that he might recover if he stayed at Chestnut Lodge long enough to complete his treatment. Phil constantly pressured Kay to help him leave the hospital. Finally, with the permission of his doctors, Phil was allowed to go to Glen Welby to spend some time. Kay thought that he might be helped by a relaxing stay at his beloved retreat.

At Glen Welby on August 3, Kay and Phil enjoyed a pleasant lunch together. Then they went upstairs for a nap. After a short while, Phil got up, saying that he wanted to be in his separate bedroom. A few minutes later, Kay heard a gunshot. She found him in the bathroom, dead. Forty-eight-year-old Philip Graham had loaded a gun, put the barrel to his temple, and killed himself.

Chapter Seven

"I went to work"

Kay was in shock and consumed with guilt-filled questions. "Why didn't I remove the gun from the house before he came? Why did I bring him home from the hospital? Why did I leave him alone?" The children gathered at the house to share their grief: Lally from a Mediterranean cruise on vacation from Radcliffe College, Donny from his summer job on *The New York Times* on vacation from Harvard, and William and Stephen from summer camps in Vermont and Colorado.

On the day before the funeral, Kay was asked to speak to the directors of The Washington Post Company. Somehow, she found the strength to speak from notes that Lally had helped her with. She said the company would not be sold.

The funeral service and the following days passed in a blur for Kay. Later, she expressed remorse that she had not spent more of that time with her children, sharing their grief. Then she could only try to explain, "sometimes you don't really decide, you just move forward, and that is what I did—moved forward blindly and mindlessly into a new and unknown life."

Kay's lawyer challenged the legality of the last will Phil had drawn up. Phil's lawyer admitted that he knew that Phil was incompetent when he drew up a will leaving two-thirds of his estate to Robin. He said that he had gone along with Phil, hoping to retain his confidence so that he could change the will when Phil recovered. The challenge to the will was successful, and Kay took control of *The Post* with no significant legal problems.

When she was able to think about her future, Kay summarized her options. "I had three choices. I could sell it (*The Post*). I could find somebody else to run it. Or I could go to work. And that was no choice at all. I went to work."

Until this time, Kay had been a follower, first of her father and then of her husband. Now she was on her own, a frightening thought. She had been raised to take her place in society, not in the business world. She was keenly aware of how little she knew about all aspects of the newspaper—business, editorial, journalistic, technical, managerial, accounting. Later, she admitted that it was impossible to describe how ignorant she felt.

Her constant insecurity made her particularly sensitive to real and imagined criticism and thus more difficult to work with. "I still tended only to see what was wrong and to ignore what was right." Increasing this insecurity was the memory of Phil in his better days, supremely confident and capable—and much stronger than she imagined that she could ever be. Another problem was that her style of management and people-to-people relations was entirely different from Phil's. After his easy-going, nature, she could be considered cool and aloof. Advice from well-meaning associates and friends was formidable, much of it revolving around the fact that she should sell The Washington Post Company.

She set up a heavy schedule for herself: played tennis at 7:00 a.m., showered and changed clothes at the office, and went around the building with a notebook in which to make observations and to write questions. She toured the plant, inspecting and learning about the mechanics of typesetting, printing, and distributing the paper. She took courses and read textbooks and manuals, filling her mind with a new vocabulary—hot and cold type, agate lines, independent distribution, color presses. Each day, she and the management people discussed answers to her questions. Every day she spent an hour reading the paper and scanning the competition. When she read something in *The Post* that she wanted to know more about it, she called in the reporter and asked him/her to explain it. Every week she went to New York to learn more about the operation of *Newsweek*. She attended weekly meetings at which the cover story was decided and discussed. She rarely spoke at these meetings. When asked her opinion, she usually said, "Well, I'm depending on you guys to make it a better magazine."

Despite this intense involvement, she believed that she was simply a bridge between the generations, and that one or more of her children would take over *The Post*. "It never occurred to me that I could manage anything," Kay said about her role. "I assumed everything would go on much as before, with the men already running things continuing to do what they were doing." Many of her peers thought the same thing. She faced many handicaps: inexperience, status as a woman, guilt about Phil's death, and lack of confidence. Someone said about her, "she was so shy she could almost not look at you."

When asked to give a speech, she usually accepted, although she dreaded the occasion. She admitted later: "Speeches and interviews were the hardest thing for me to learn; I wasn't very articulate." An editor pointed out that she too often apologized for herself as she spoke. Other editors helped get her message across. She took voice lessons from a drama coach. A friend said that she went over the same speech forty times before giving it at a company meeting. For added confidence, she had her hair done by Kenneth, one of the best known stylists in the East, and changed her wardrobe to better portray assertiveness and self-confidence. Those who encouraged her to assume responsibility saw her strengths. She had business intuition which she learned from her father, ambition from her mother, strong intellect, and extraordinary courage and determination.

After the suicide of her husband, Kay worked hard to learn all aspects of the newspaper publishing business.

When asked how she did so much in such a short time, she explained, "What I essentially did was to put one foot in front of the other, shut my eyes, and step off the edge. The surprise was that I landed on my feet." She credited three sources of help: Phil's friends, good luck, and her father's advice to "Know everything there is to know, work harder than anybody else, and be absolutely honest."

Agnes helped her daughter. She encouraged Kay and praised her. She helped her to overcome her feeling of blame for Phil's suicide. She was a particularly attentive grandmother to Kay's children.

In September 1963, Kay was elected president of The Washington Post Company. At that time, she announced, "The newspaper shall not be the ally of any special interest, but shall be fair and free and wholesome." She was fortunate that the top executives of the company had been doing a lot of the work as Phil's mental condition had worsened. Now Fritz Beebe, the chairman of the board, called on these executives to help Kay. He also helped her with many decisions, and he did not pressure her to do more than she felt able to do. Beebe's reputation as a sound and shrewd businessman helped to ease the minds of Wall Street, the banks, and others who might have anticipated chaos on Phil's death.

But sometimes she felt a need for more respect. Although she might not show it, she did become angry when she felt belittled by co-workers. One example was an editor who frequently injected into his oral reports the comment that he would explain a point to Kay later when he had more time. When this happened, Kay sometimes went beyond the newspaper and magazine offices for help. One special friend was Defense Secretary Robert McNamara who helped her in business matters and also helped her find confidence in herself.

Lally grew closer to Kay. The two women attended the 1964 Republican National Convention together where they watched Senator Barry Goldwater win the nomination for president.

A few months later, Kay and Lally went to the Democratic

Robert McNamara, who served as Secretary of Defense during the Vietnam War, was Kay's friend and advisor in her first years as publisher of the *Washington Post*.

National Convention. As she was in the airport heading home after the meeting, Lyndon Johnson invited her to come to his ranch for the weekend. Startled, she did not know how to refuse, so she allowed the Secret Service to pick up her luggage, and she sent Lally home. That weekend, she enjoyed being an honored guest. It was obvious that Johnson wanted to get on the good side of *The Washington Post.* Kay admired Johnson and told him that she supported him personally. Still, she told him that the paper would not break its long-held tradition, broken only for Eisenhower, of making no endorsement in the presidential race. In her thank-you letter to the president, Kay wrote: "I feel exactly as though I were the heroine of one's childhood fairy tales . . . carried in three swift jet hours into Never Never Land."

Later, during the campaign, Kay traveled with reporters on a press plane with Johnson. When Johnson asked her to sit by him, she refused, preferring to identify herself with the reporters. She also traveled on a press plane covering Republican candidate Barry Goldwater.

Friends noticed that Kay was increasingly self-confident. She stopped comparing her work to Phil's. She was learning that there was only one way for her to do her job—and that way was to be herself. She signed her name Kay Graham, no longer Mrs. Philip L. Graham. Gradually, she returned to a social life. Although this was painful without Phil, it was even more painful for her to be alone with her thoughts.

She could not control her health the way she controlled her actions. She had another bout with tuberculosis. Stories circulated that she sometimes fell sound asleep at public and private dinner parties. Kay described her nights, telling how she re-played her mistakes in her mind, reliving the embarrassment and shame over and over. She admitted, "I made mistakes and suffered great distress from them, partly because I believed that if you just worked diligently enough you wouldn't make mistakes. I truly believed that other people in my position didn't make mistakes." She found it hard to forgive others' mistakes too. Occasionally, she publicly scolded a reporter for a story. Harsh as her criticism was, she seemed to forget the situation after the scolding. There was no retaliation against the reporter.

Kay had been in charge only a year when the unions threatened to strike in 1964. Kay had once been a proud member of the Newspaper Guild. She felt forced to accept a contract granting her reporters $200 a week, making them the highest-paid in the country. She was not happy about the settlement, and believed that the federal mediators had forced her to accept this contract.

President Johnson won re-election. *The Post* supported the administration's policy on Vietnam, praising American involvement there. In August, Johnson ordered air strikes against Vietnam in retaliation for what he considered unprovoked attacks on U.S. ships by the North Vietnamese.

When Kay went on a trip around the world, she received special attention from American officials in Vietnam in return for the friendliness she had shown to officials in Washington. She talked with the commander-in-chief of the American military forces in southeast Asia, and she toured several villages secured by American forces. This trip made Kay even more positive about the involvement there. She said that as long as American soldiers were already there, they had to stay to protect what they had begun there. Back in Washington, she put a little pressure on editors who suggested that withdrawal from Vietnam might be appropriate.

The Vietnam War became a much-talked about topic. Editorials in other papers were increasingly in opposition to American involvement there. *The Post* still endorsed President Johnson's policies in Vietnam. Some of these papers accused them of playing up to the administration. Meanwhile, Agnes also gained the favor of President Johnson. She worked to pass a bill for federal aid to education, policies to help find and feed hungry children, and establishment of the Health, Education, and Welfare Department. These were all of programs the president wanted to be pushed through the Congress.

In July 1965, Kay asked Ben Bradlee, then Washington bureau chief at *Newsweek* if he would like to move to *The Post*. Ben he said he would love to. He became deputy managing editor for foreign and national news with the understanding that in six months he would become managing editor. He said of his challenge: "I want to have some impact on this town and this country. I want to know they are reading us."

Truman Capote, author of the bestselling true crime book *In Cold Blood*, became Kay's close friend. He wanted to give a party for her, he said, a really nice party to cheer her up. At first she resisted, saying that she didn't need to be cheered up. Capote insisted. He planned an elegant affair at which guests were to wear only black and white clothes, and each guest was to wear a mask. This party, known widely as the Black and White Ball, brought Kay back to society in a significant way. Kay said later that Capote was just looking for an excuse for a party and that he chose her because "I didn't conflict with all the glamorous women he knew."

Newsweek published stories about one of the hottest issues of the day. The racial tensions that increased as African-Americans, Hispanics, Native Americans, and other minority groups pressed for equality in economic, educational, and social opportunities. The magazine took on this topic when other media outlets tried to ignore the burning issue. Still, *Newsweek* was not as profitable as many had expected, possibly because of poor management. Kay decided she needed to improve her management skills. She visited large corporations like Texas Instruments and Xerox. She went to week-long courses to learn more about production, and to learn about computers.

In 1966, The Washington Post Company bought a forty-five percent interest in the *New York Herald Tribune's* Paris edition. A year later, *The New York Times* dropped its own European edition and

Kay's friend Truman Capote organized the Black and White Ball to cheer her up.

joined *The Post* as co-owners of the *International Herald Tribune*. They also opened news bureaus in Tokyo and in the United Nations headquarters.

In 1966, Kay's son Donny graduated from Harvard. Kay had hoped that he would want to pursue a career in journalism, maybe eventually taking over at *The Post*. But Don said he wasn't ready. He said a person couldn't be a good newspaperman if he did had done nothing but work for newspapers all his life. Soon he joined the military and spent a year in Vietnam as a private.

In contrast to Don's enlistment, Bill chose to demonstrate against the war. Like many of his generation, he felt that America had no business sending troops to Vietnam. He was arrested in California for demonstrating in front of a draft center. Kay got a lawyer to keep him out of jail.

Bill's deep feeling against American policy in Vietnam influenced Kay. She began to wonder if the United States should be involved in the war. However, she was not ready to denounce her government. She explained to readers that she thought the United States should continue its commitment, if for no other reason, in order to protect the half million American troops already over there. *The Post* remained firm on this position even in May 1967 when most other main-line publications called for a bombing halt.

In the summer of 1968, Don returned home from Vietnam. Kay asked him to join the newspaper. Instead, he joined the Washington D.C. police force. He told Kay that he wanted to get to know the community before he became a publisher.

Chapter Eight

"Let's Go! Let's Publish!"

In the 1968 presidential campaign, Kay personally endorsed Richard Nixon for president in his race against Democratic Senator Hubert Humphrey. Soon after Nixon was sworn-in as president in January 1969, he ordered increased bombing by the United States in North Vietnam. This bombing increased protests against the war in the United States. Nixon criticized the press for reporting so many stories of anti-war demonstrations. He said that the press did not reflect the views of the majority of the American public. He singled out *The Washington Post* in his criticism.

Bradlee continued to make changes in the paper. One change was in the women's section which he titled "Style." This column focused on people who were "in"—rich, glamorous, and sophisticated. When Kay did not agree with his ideas, she criticized him. Sometimes Bradlee gave the criticism right back to her. Once he said bluntly, "Get your finger out of my eye." After she cooled down, she admitted to herself that she had pushed too hard, that she had a tendency to complain and to push instead of considering a problem rationally.

Kay knew she had a "lifelong tendency to fasten on what is wrong . . . of being overly self-critical much of the time . . . I was seen as always finding fault or second-guessing. I'm sure it made me difficult to get along with." Her insecurity kept getting in the way of her doing the job that she wanted to do. She said that she had picked up the assumption of others of her age that women were intellectually inferior to men. This automatically made them unable to govern, lead, or manage anything outside their homes.

It was confusing to be a woman in a world of men. Days went by when the only women she saw were secretaries or clerks. This was not at all unusual in the 1960s. At times, the problem was openly embarrassing, as when she was in the audience, and a speaker would address himself to "Gentlemen and Mrs. Graham." Other times a speaker would say, "Lady and gentlemen."

In the five years from 1963 to 1969, *The Washington Post* doubled its pretax corporate profit. This was partly the result of Kay's rigorous demand that all employees, especially higher management, do exactly what she said to do. She was quick to censure and then to fire if she suspected disloyalty or inefficiency. She was also adamant that unions would not force her to make salary or conditions adjustments. Some of the profit came from increased advertising revenues. Some came from the number of readers who switched to the paper because of the improvements Ben Bradlee made in the paper. The quality of the reporting was higher. In 1969, The Washington Post Company bought its third television station, this one in Miami. It was named WPLG in honor of Phil Graham.

Editorials and articles in *The Post* continued to infuriate President Nixon. He dropped all contact with the newspaper. Vice-President Spiro Agnew also attacked *The Post* frequently. He said that *Newsweek* was fit only to line birdcages with.

In March 1970, forty-six women who worked for *Newsweek* filed a sex discrimination suit with the Equal Employment Opportunity Commission. At that time, there was only one woman writer at the newsweekly, and she seldom received the big stories. Kay answered that the company did not deliberately discriminate against women. She admitted that there might be grounds for misunderstanding. After several months, they signed a memorandum of understanding.

In her private life, Kay fought against the kind of discrimination that she was charged with at the paper. At a dinner party she refused to go to one room to talk with the women while the men went to another room. She told her host that she was not interested in the conversation the women would have, so she was going home because she had important work to do there. The host gave in, allowing the sexes to stay together for after-dinner conversation.

Kay talked with Gloria Steinem, a leader in the women's' movement. After much conversation, Kay said she began to understand the premise of the movement. She was put to the test. In 1972, more employees sued, citing discrimination against women. Fifty-nine women signed a letter alleging sexual discrimination. The women pointed out that *The Washington Post's* hiring record on male and female writers proved their point. Kay asked the head of personnel to hire more women, and she did so.

William Raspberry, a highly regarded columnist criticized *The Post*. He said, "What is there in the paper for the big, black middle-class out there . . . What is there in the paper for the white plumber? Practically nothing. These people don't make the happenings so they are ignored and we get a false image of our community." Kay spoke to the head of personnel and told her to hire more black reporters, as well as of women.

Don Graham left the police department and became a metro reporter. Later, he moved into different jobs in a number of different departments, including accounting clerk, assistant home-delivery manager, sales representative, and assistant production manager in a California *Newsweek* bureau.

In June 1971 *The New York Times* scooped *The Post* when it published the so-called Pentagon Papers. This was a secret report on the history of U.S. government policy in the Vietnam conflict. The study was authorized by the Department of Defense. The main author of the report, Daniel Ellsberg, had begun working on the history with the belief that the report would help Americans sympathize with the American presence in southeast Asia. But, while writing the report, Ellsberg had changed his opinion, and the papers reflected this change. The publication of the papers created a firestorm of controversy. A federal court issued a restraining order, forbidding further publication.

Bradlee wanted to publish the same information. Although *The Times* did not publish the name of the author of the papers, *Post* national editor Ben Bagdikian guessed who it was, and he contacted the writer. Ellsberg agreed to give the papers to *The Post* if they would promise to publish them. The promise was made. Bagdikian took 4,400 pages of the papers and went straight to Bradlee's house, where reporters met him. They spent hours sorting out the information and making decisions about what to write. At the back of everyone's mind were two questions. If publishing the Pentagon papers was illegal for *The Times*, what would the courts say when *The Post* published them? If they had the papers and didn't publish them, were they true to the ideals of journalism that promoted the citizens' right to know?

Kay was hosting a party at her home when she received a phone call. It was her lawyer. He quickly summarized the reasoning for both printing and for holding back but, he said, the decision was hers alone. She asked him what he would do. He said he would not publish the papers because publication would mean a direct challenge to the government. Then Bradlee and other editors got on telephone extensions and gave their views. Most of them said to publish.

Finally, she said, "Let's go. Let's publish."

As soon as *The Post* published excerpts of the papers, the assistant attorney general called and told them not to publish any more. Bradlee answered, "I'm sure you will understand that I must respectfully decline." The government filed suit against *The Post*. In court, the judge ruled in favor of newspaper. He said that he saw no indication that publication of the papers would injure the nation.

Kay and Ben Bradlee leave the courthouse after the court ruled the *Washington Post* had the right to publish the Pentagon Papers.

A court of appeals reversed this decision. When the case went to the U.S. Supreme Court Chief Justice Warren Berger announced that the Court had decided in favor of the publication of the material.

Kay continued to keep friends among government officials all the way up to the president. She believed that part of her job was to cultivate friendships, to introduce officials to her reporters, and to keep lines of communication open.

In June 1972, five men were arrested in a break-in at the headquarters of the Democratic National Committee. *Washington Post* reporters Bob Woodward and Carl Bernstein investigated and discovered a connection between the White House and the burglars.

In October, shortly before the November election, Woodward and Bernstein reported that the break-in was part of a much larger plan of political spying for the president's re-election efforts. Further, the reporters' stories accused other top Nixon officials of campaign tactics that became known as "dirty tricks."

Nixon's campaign chairman responded to the articles by saying: "The hallmark of *The Post's* campaign is hypocrisy—and its celebrated 'double standard' is today visible for all to see."

For about seven months, Kay did not talk to Woodward and Bernstein about their story for fear of compromising their responsibility to tell the truth. Finally, in January 1973, she asked Woodward if the reporters could authenticate their stories. Woodward assured her that he had a secret source who was completely reliable. He would not divulge this source, referring to it only as "Deep Throat."

Although Nixon won every state except Massachusetts in the 1972 election, Bernstein and Woodward continued their investigative reporting. In April 1973, *The Washington Post* was awarded the Pulitzer Prize for its reporting of the Watergate affair. Both the paper and Kay gained prestige as symbols of journalistic independence and integrity. She modestly insisted, "What I did primarily was stand behind the editors and reporters, in whom I believed."

President Nixon leaving Washington after resigning in August 1974. *Post* reporters Bob Woodward and Carl Bernstein helped uncover the Watergate affair.

Kay named herself chief executive officer and chairman of the board of directors in May 1973. The Washington Post Company's net income for 1973 was over $13 million. But newspaper profits had leveled off. Kay attributed this falling-off to the rising cost of wages.

In a Senate committee investigation in July, a White House aide revealed that there was a taped record of Nixon's conversations in the Oval Office. These tapes revealed that the president had ordered the cover-up of the break-in of the Democratic Headquarters in the Watergate office building. On August 8, 1974, Nixon announced his resignation on national television. Vice-President Gerald Ford became president.

After Watergate, Kay found herself the center of admirers for preserving the integrity of freedom of the press. When someone admired her for her courage to publish, she denied that her act was one of courage. She said that courage applied only when a person has a choice of actions; and that she had seen only one action as responsible. She went on: "Ultimately, Watergate showed what could be done by reporters arduously and painstakingly pursuing investigative work, by editors remaining skeptical and demanding and as dispassionate as possible under the circumstances, and by editorial writers helping to keep the questions foremost in the minds of our readers."

In May 1974, actor Robert Redford visited Kay to ask for her cooperation in making a movie about the Watergate affair, a movie to be called *All the President's Men*. This movie would be based on a book recently released by Carl Bernstein and Bob Woodward. Kay was happy to cooperate at first. Then she learned that the movie would be shot in *The Post* city room. She objected, saying it would disturb the work in an unacceptable way. A compromise was reached when the producers agreed to duplicate the newsroom in a California studio. To create a perfect duplicate of the room, the producers even sent tons of paper and trash from the newsroom to California. Kay was portrayed in one scene. She was relieved, but in another way disappointed, when the producers scrapped that scene.

In the midst of all this publicity, *The Washington Post* continued to flourish. April 1974 marked a highpoint in sales of papers. The paper had a fine reputation for editorial writing. Jill Nelson, a writer for for four years, said that most journalists believed that being hired by *The Post* was the pinnacle of a career.

That same year, Kay was elected the first woman director of the Associated Press. She was also the first woman director of the American Newspaper Publishers Association. *Ms.* magazine said that she had "outgrown her tolerance for silliness, thrown off a life-long cloak of diffidence, and come to accept the heady fact that, within reason, she gets to do whatever she wants." Kay spoke about the burden of being female in a man's world. She explained: "If I do something unexpected, male executives tend to react more than normally by asking 'who has gotten to her.'" Several articles referred to her as the most powerful woman in the world. She replied that the term made her think of a female weight-lifter.

Kay earned a reputation for being quick to fire employees. One of her co-workers said, "She is obsessed with the notion that she dare not fail the tradition behind her. She's always seeking new ideas to improve what she has." Another said, "She loves being the queen bee. And she loves to sting." Kay answered, "They keep yelling at me for firing people. That's not right. They should yell at me for hiring the wrong people in the first place."

Her personal life consisted of many formal dinners and entertainments. In her mid-fifties, Kay was an attractive single woman. Her opinion about another marriage was clear: "I lead such an odd life, always off somewhere, that I'm no bargain. I can't imagine anyone wanting to marry me."

Chapter Nine

"Pay whatever price is necessary"

Kay was still angry about the settlement of the 1964 strike when her reporters had become the highest paid in the country. Now they threatened to strike again. She said that she was willing to offer a fair contract. But she would not be intimidated by threats of a strike. If necessary, she would withstand a strike.

The workers struck. Management told workers to accept the offered contract or to stay out of work. When workers stayed out, forty management employees put out the paper that normally required 400 reporters, copy editors, and photographers. In September 1975, The Washington Post Company hired a public relations firm to take photos, write copy, and get the management side of the story in the public eye. That strike ended, but other problems awaited.

Contracts with nine craft unions came up for renewal. On the morning of October 1, 1975, striking pressmen set fire to the presses, damaged other equipment, and beat one of the foremen. By the time Kay could get to the building, police, fire, and television cameras were there with hundreds of pickets around the building. Inside, electrical wiring was ripped out, machine parts removed, oil drained from the presses, and newsprint rolls were slashed. When questioned, the union leaders said that they had attacked in retaliation to *The Post* management, which was trying to eliminate important clauses in the contracts.

The Post did not publish that day, but management made plans to resume publishing as soon as possible. Six suburban presses agreed to print different parts of the paper. Management arranged for a helicopter to land on the roof of the office building, pick up the necessary film, and deliver it as required. *The Post* missed only one day of publication. A little thin at first, the paper gradually increased editorial copy and advertisements. On Thanksgiving Day, the paper ran 184 pages, all of them trucked up from Florida. Management discovered that it could put out a paper with only six pressmen. No matter what the outcome of the strike, they would not hire back all the thirteen pressmen who had been working there until the protest began.

Demonstrators marched to Kay's house carrying candles flickering in brown bags as a memorial to the pressman. Wives of pressmen stood outside Kay's home pleading for their husbands' jobs. Strikers burned her in effigy. On the outside Kay was consistently calm, so calm that some in the office called her the Iron Lady. She spent many Saturday nights taking classified ads or in the mail room packaging papers for mail subscribers. She explained, "You can't afford to lose control of your organization. Clearly, we had to pay whatever price was necessary to regain control." She said that she owed some of her calmness to Donny, who had just been promoted to assistant general manager. His main duty was to see that the paper was published despite the strike, and he was successful.

When Kay received the Profiles in Courage Award for the coverage of Watergate, a guild officer wrote "Enjoy your dinner, Ms. Graham, while two thousand of your employees are on strike or honoring picket lines. They, too, have the courage to fight for what they believe in."

In October, November, and December, *The Post* made money because it paid much less in salaries. In Washington alone, the number of employees fell from 3,000 to 2,400. This immediate saving, plus the realization that they had been hiring more workers than they needed, gave *The Post* a financial boost.

In December, Kay announced that she would advertise for and hire replacement workers. "My conclusion is that I cannot in good conscience permit a situation to continue in which men and women in our trade unions, many of whom have worked here for many years, are faced with a bleak future because they must honor the picket lines of a group of men who are the highest-paid craft union workers in the building." Demonstrators reacted to her statements by increasing their protests.

On February 15, the mailers voted, 129-58, to accept the new contract. By March 1, the strike was essentially over. When the guild contract expired in April 1976, the company granted only a cost-of-living raise to new employees. The union was broken. Kay said that she had learned at least two lessons. One is that management must always accept the responsibility to manage. Another was that she needed to establish better communications within the company.

Circulation averaged 550,000 for dailies and 766,000 for Sunday editions. The company ranked 452nd on *Fortune* magazine's list of the 500 largest American companies. Kay set a totally new goal for herself. She wanted to expand The Washington Post Company in an orderly and planned way. She looked into available properties. The company traded station WTOP for a station in Detroit, Michigan. It bought a monthly sports news magazine called *Inside Sports*.

The next year, Kay became a member of a World Bank team that was studying how to help developing countries economically, a responsibility once taken on by her father. She was voted the "top leader and shaper of national life" among women by *U.S. News & World Report*.

In 1978, *Washington Post* editorials supported city councilman Marion Barry for mayor of Washington. When Barry won the election many citizens credited the editorials for his victory.

The Washington Star published a five-day profile of Kay, which included comments from both those who loved her and those who hated her. She was called both "Katharine the Great" and Katharine the Terrible." Many readers, including those who knew her best, agreed that the profile was accurate.

In 1979, Deborah Davis published *Katharine the Great*, a partial biography of Kay, which included material about Bradlee and Phil Graham and alleged ties with the Central Intelligence Agency. Bradlee denied any connection to the CIA and found thirty-four other errors. William Jovanovich, head of Harcourt Brace Jovanovich, the publisher of the book, investigated Bradlee's charges. When he found they were true, he withdrew the publisher's name from the book, ordered it recalled from stores and shredded. He further ordered his employees to make sure that all copies of the book were destroyed. Kay applauded Jovanovich's actions. She said that Davis was ". . . just nuts. I never saw her, never went near her, never had anything to do with her." The book was out long enough to receive one review, a review that said it was "rubbish."

In January 1979, Kay announced that Don would take over as publisher of *The Washington Post*. She still kept her office and was chairman of the board and chief executive officer. She also would continue to oversee the business and editorial sides of *The Post, Newsweek*, and the television stations. When the public announcement was made, Don said, "My mother has given me everything but an easy act to follow." Kay admitted that she had withdrawal pangs, but still held a demanding job with The Washington Post Company. She was responsible for a half-billion-dollar company with five thousand employees and two thousand shareholders.

Kay continued to do some interviewing—Russian leader Mikhail Gorbachev was one of her subjects—and continued attending White House dinners and inviting prominent people to her home.

In 1980, Kay became the chairman of the all-male American

Newspaper Publishers Association. She was busy with other challenges as well. She made an extensive study of The Washington Post Company and its affiliates. She devised a policy for future growth, new ideas and new diversification. The introduction of electronic technology in all aspects of the business demanded careful study. And always there were personnel problems. Some of the staff believed that Kay was too quick to criticize and too quick to fire; others believed that she exerted authority only when it was absolutely necessary.

Kay traveled widely in the Middle East with two reporters. They interviewed Prince Bandar in Saudi Arabia and other Arab leaders. In Egypt, they interviewed President Anwar Sadat, and sent back articles for both *The Post* and *Newsweek*. They also talked with the shah of Iran and leaders in Israel.

In the fall of 1980, *Washington Post* reporter Janet Cooke wrote a shocking story of eight-year-old Jimmy who was a heroin addict. According to the story, Jimmy was injected with drugs by his mother's boyfriend. The story won a Pulitzer Prize. Washington Mayor Barry ordered police to find the boy. When he could not be found, Barry denounced the story as a fake. *The Post* investigated both the story and Cooke's credentials. They discovered that she had lied about her education and training in her job application. Cooke confessed that Jimmy was not a single person, but a composite of many children like him. She was fired, and the Pulitzer Prize was taken from her. *The Post* apologized to its readers.

In August 1981, the *Washington Star* ceased publication. *The Post* ran an editorial, trying to assure readers that they had not wanted the *Star* to fail and that they would not change the style of their paper to attract former *Star* readers. They would retain the integrity of *The Post* and would welcome former *Star* readers who wanted to become subscribers. When no one put in a bid for the *Star*, *The Post* bought the building and presses and hired some of the writers.

The Washington Post Company diversified into the cellular phone business. It built some of the first cellular systems in the country. It also launched a weekly edition with a selected reprinting of articles on politics and government. This *National Weekly* enjoyed a mail subscription circulation of 70,000 by 1989.

In 1983, Kay celebrated the fiftieth birthday of *Newsweek* with a lavish black-tie party. More quietly, she celebrated the new financial statistics on The Washington Post Company: the net income had jumped to $68 million.

In 1984, The Washington Post Company bought a test-preparing and tutorial agency, the Stanley H. Kaplan Company. The next year it bought twenty percent of a large media corporation that owned the *Minneapolis Star Tribune* and several other properties.

Lally wrote for *The New York Times Magazine, Esquire,* and *New York,* and was known as an excellent journalist. Kay and Donny hired her to work for *The Post.* There were no complaints about her writing, but there were some about her attitude. Some of her co-workers called her arrogant and said that she demanded special attention. William kept a low profile as a lawyer and investment partner. Stephen was a theatrical producer and part-time owner of the magazine *Spy.*

Kay was voted the most influential woman in America by a group of editors and publishers. She was the only woman CEO of a Fortune 500 company. She claimed that she still shook whenever she had to give a speech. Television cameras bothered her even more than live audiences. To appear at her best, she demanded intensive briefings before each social or business meeting. In a moment of self-reflection, she focused on what she considered her strength. "I'm very concentrated on good management. It's my consuming ambition."

In 1986, management decided to adapt the Sunday magazine section of the paper to reflect the black majority in the Washington community. The first issue highlighted a black rap star and his involvement in drugs. The advertisements pictured only white people. Other issues also highlighted blacks in trouble with the law and also contained advertisements written for whites.

African-American citizens of Washington united against this magazine that they considered insulting and offensive. Individually, they bought copies of the magazine, and as a group they threw them onto the steps of *The Post* building, chanting "Take it back! Take it back!" In all, they dumped about 250,000 copies of the weekly magazine. As a concession to the demonstrators, Don and a black radio talk show hostess agreed to discuss the problem on two hour-long shows. Most African-Americans considered this concession so minor as to be another insult. Over a period of about three months, the number of protestors decreased, until it finally stopped altogether.

In June 1987, Kay celebrated her seventieth birthday and announced that she had no intention of retiring. For the most part, Donny ran *The Post*, but she was still active in *Newsweek*. Her children gave her a birthday party and invited six hundred guests. Among those who attended were President Reagan, Secretary of State George Shultz, senators, ambassadors, and heads of major U.S. companies. She continued to assert that her relationships with government figures helped both the paper and the magazine because they kept communication lines open. She said, "I believe democracy flourishes when the government can take legitimate steps to keep its secrets and when the press can decide whether to print what it knows."

She was sometimes asked about the possibility of marriage again. She answered, "Men who appeal to me are strong, bright, tough, and involved, but that kind of man would probably not accept my own active and absorbing life. It was clear to me that I was married to my job, and that I loved it." Her children were healthy, happy, and successful. Lally had published two books and was writing for several newspapers. Don was, of course, well established in The Washington Post Company. Bill, after being a lawyer and then teaching law, worked in investments. Steve produced plays and founded a theater workshop before he became a book publisher.

Chapter Ten

"I'm looking forward to the future"

In 1991, Katharine Graham resigned her position as CEO of The Washington Post Company. She retained the title of chairman of the board until September 1993, when she gave that up, too. At that time, she became chairman of the executive committee of the company.

In an article in the *Washingtonian* magazine in 1995, her colleagues said of Kay: "The record shows that over the past 20 years she has made virtually all of the key decisions right." They also said that under Kay's leadership, "The Washington Post Company became one of the nation's most successful communications empires."

She passed the title of CEO on to Donny, who remianed publisher of the newspaper. He assumed control of the television stations, cable outlets, *Newsweek*, and other properties. By 1997, The Washington Post Company owned cable systems serving 580,000 subscribers.

Kay now had more time to work with charities. She helped start an early-childhood education project in a poor section of Washington, D.C. to help parents care for their infants and young children.

For several years, Alfred A. Knopf publishers had been asking Kay to write her memoirs. Finally, she signed a contract with them. She hired three people to help—a speechwriter, a research specialist, and a young man to gather and collate material. As though she were writing about someone else, she set up interviews with people who knew her well. With help, she completed two hundred and fifty

Kay won the Pulitzer Prize in 1997 for her memoir, *Personal History*.

interviews. Kay expressed satisfaction with both her life and her book: "It's dangerous when you are older to start living in the past. Now that it's out of my system, I intend to live in the present, looking forward to the future." Living in the present included accepting a Pulitzer Prize in the biography category for her book, *Personal History*.

Kay Graham has made news in many different aspects of her life. She overcame an inferiority complex to become a featured speaker and a welcome dinner guest of some of the most important people in the country. She worked through the agony of the suicide of her husband. She met the challenge of doing a man's job in a man's world. She retained a strong sense of family and the values passed down to her. She is a role model for women who have the courage to follow her lead into the worlds of journalism, management, and publication.

Timeline

1917—born in New York City.
1938—works for *San Francisco News*.
1939—accepts job at *The Washington Post*.
1940—marries Philip Graham.
1942—birth of daughter Elizabeth "Lally."
1945—birth of son Donald "Don."
1948—birth of son William "Bill."
1952—birth of son Stephen.
1963—Philip Graham commits suicide.
1963—elected president of The Washington Post Company.
1973—becomes chairman of the board of The Washington Post Company.
1974—elected first woman director of Associated Press.
1974—leads management to victory over strikers.
1980—becomes chairman of all-male American Newspaper Publishers Association.
1991—steps down from CEO position.
1997—publishes memoirs, *Personal History*.
1998—wins Pulitzer Prize for biography.

Appendix
Newsworthy Events in American Journalsim

NEWSPAPER BANNED FOUR DAYS AFTER PUBLICATION

Boston, 1690—Authorities banned the publication of *Publick Occurrences Both Forreign and Domestick*, the first newspaper published in the colonies, just four days after it came out. The officials cited the report that the English had allied themselves with "miserable savages" as the reason for the ban.

GOVERNMENT AUTHORIZES NEWSPAPER

Boston, 1704—*The Boston News Letter*, published with government approval, will include proclamations, articles about legal matters, and commercial news. The single-sheet paper will cost two cents and, it is expected, enjoy a circulation of 200-300.

PETER ZENGER FOUND INNOCENT

New York, 1734—A jury found Peter Zenger, publisher of the *New York Weekly Journal*, not guilty of charges of unwarranted criticism of the government. Zenger's articles had attacked incompetence, inefficiency, and corruption of public officials. Zenger's lawyer argued successfully that his client had the right and duty to report grievances of citizens and to oppose tyranny.

JOURNALISTS ENGAGE IN POLITICS

Washington,1835—Increasingly, journalists openly support partisan politics. Editor Thomas Hart Benton of the *St. Louis Enquirer* speaks regularly in the Senate in support of President Andrew Jackson. Amos Kendall and Francis Blair, publishers of the *Argus of Western America*, openly advise members of Jackson's cabinet.

NEWSPAPERS FORM ASSOCIATED PRESS

New York, 1848—Six leading New York newspapers have agreed to cooperate in a news-gathering agency to be called the Associated Press (AP).

NUMBER OF U.S. NEWSPAPERS QUADRUPLES

1860—The number of newspapers published in the United States has reached 3,725. This figure includes 387 dailies, 3,173 weeklies, 79 semiweeklies, and 86 triweeklies. In 1790, the total of all U.S. newspapers was 92.

NEWSPAPERS AND MILITARY VIE FOR CONTROL

Washington, 1864—War correspondents are required to submit dispatches to Union Secretary of War Edwin Stanton for approval. Henry Raymond, founder of *The New York Times*, says that military officials prevented him from filing an accurate report of Union losses at Bull Run. Reporter Thomas Knox was jailed on orders from General Sherman, who accused him of helping the enemy.

INVENTION REVOLUTIONIZES PRINTING

New York, 1883—Otto Merganthaler has created a machine which revolutionizes the printing trade. This linotype machine, operated from a keyboard, automatically adjusts each line to the correct length. The type can be used over and over, quickly and continuously. Newspapers are expected to be among the first to take advantage of this innovation.

JOHN PHILIP SOUSA DEDICATES WASHINGTON POST MARCH

Washington, 1889—Conductor and composer John Philip Sousa has dedicated "The Washington Post March" to the newspaper in recognition of its encouragement of young writers. Sousa conducted the Marine Band in a rousing performance of the march as twenty thousand young and hopeful writers listened on the grounds of the Smithsonian Institution. Officials of *The Post* then awarded prizes to winners of the writing contest.

JOURNALIST CLAIMS RESPONSIBILITY FOR WAR

New York, 1896—William Randolph Hearst, publisher of the *New York Morning Journal*, says his newspapers started the Spanish-American war by inciting Americans to support Cuban rebels against Spain. He ordered his photographers to take pictures of Spanish cruelty in Cuba, saying, "You supply the pictures. I'll supply the war."

NEW YORK TIMES LOWERS PRICE

New York, 1898—In a desperate move to save *The New York Times* from financial disaster, publisher Adolph Ochs has lowered the price from three cents to one penny.

WOMAN BECOMES REPORTER

New York, 1908—*The New York Sun* has hired a woman reporter. Agnes Ernst, a graduate of Barnard College, to do "piece work" for the paper. Miss Ernst will earn anywhere from five dollars to forty dollars a week for her work, depending on the number of stories she writes.

GERMAN SPY SUSPECTED IN UP BLUNDER

New York, 1918—Roy Howard, manager of the United Press, suspects that a German spy fed him incorrect information that an armistice had been signed on November 7. Howard cabled this information to newspapers all over the United States, and it was several hours before the hoax was discovered. Howard believes that the spy spread the message to allow the German army a brief respite from its disastrous retreat.

WOMAN NAMED TO HEAD A NEWS BUREAU OVERSEAS

New York, 1925—Dorothy Thompson has been named Berlin bureau chief of the *Philadelphia Public Ledger*. Miss Thompson is the first woman to head a major American news bureau overseas.

NEWSMEN UNIONIZE

New York, 1930—The American Newspaper Guild has won a battle against the Associated Press in the Supreme Court. The Court ruled that reporters have the right to form a union.

NEWSPAPERS BRING WAR HOME

New York, 1945—American newspapers share credit for keeping citizens informed about World War II. Over fifteen hundred radio and press correspondents cover the war in Europe and the Pacific.

NEGRO JOURNALIST RECEIVES ACCREDITATION

Washington, 1947—Alice Dunnigan, free-lance reporter for the *Louisville Defender*, has received accreditation as a White House correspondent. Miss Dunnigan, chief of the Washington Bureau of the Associated Negro Press, is the first Negro woman to receive this press privilege.

WIRE SERVICES MERGE

New York, 1958—The United Press and the International News Service have merged to form the United Press International (UPI). This wire service will compete with the Associated Press.

WASHINGTON POST PUBLISHES PENTAGON PAPERS

Washington, 1971—*The Washington Post* has published excerpts from a top-secret government-sponsored history of the Vietnam conflict. Earlier, a federal court issued a restraining order against *The New York Times* banning further publication of this material called the Pentagon Papers. Sources say that *The Post* defends its decision to publish on the public's right to know.

REPORTERS FORCE PRESIDENT'S RESIGNATION

Washington, 1974—*Washington Post* reporters Carl Bernstein and Bob Woodward are being congratulated for their investigative reporting of the Watergate affair that revealed a government conspiracy leading to President Nixon. High government sources predict that Nixon will resign rather than face certain impeachment.

JOURNALIST STRIPPED OF PULITZER

Washington, 1981—Janet Cooke, reporter for *The Washington Post*, has admitted that her Pulitzer Prize winning story was a hoax. Miss Cooke was given the award for a story about an eight-year-old heroin addict. She revealed to the public and *The Post* that her subject, Jimmy, was fabricated and that she made up the quotes she attributed to him. *The Post* has fired Miss Cooke.

Glossary

article: a factual piece of writing.

beat: area of interest assigned to a reporter.

by-line: name of person/persons who wrote a published article.

caption: written identification of a photo or illustration.

city editor: decides which local stories to investigate and assigns reporters.

city room: office in which reporters, editors, and artists work together.

column: a feature published regularly by a single writer.

copy: any material written for publication.

copy editor: a person who checks punctuation, grammar, spelling and sometimes logic.

deadline: the date/hour at which an assignment is due to an editor.

editorial: an article that states the opinion of the publisher and/or editor.

extra: a special issue of a paper published to celebrate a particular event.

five W's: slang for questions each reporter must answer—Who, What, When, Why, Where.

freelance: a writer who accepts assignments but does not write regularly for any one employer.

mail room: place where papers are counted, stacked and wrapped for delivery.

managing editor: person in charge of overall day-to-day operations.

masthead: information about the publisher, owners, circulation and such topics.

news editor: person who decides where to place news stories in paper.

obituary: notice of the death of a person.

op-ed: a column of signed remarks of readers.

press: a term sometimes used to refer collectively to many newspapers.

press conference: question-and-answer meeting of reporters and the person about whom they are writing.

pressmen: workers who print papers.

Pulitzer Prizes: a series of awards for outstanding achievements in drama, letters, music and journalism.

put to bed: journalists' idiom for sending a newspaper to be printed.

reporter: person who gathers and reports news.

tabloid: newspaper about half the size of a standard newspaper; often focused on sensationalism.

scoop: important story published in one newspaper before other newspapers know about it.

underground newspaper: newspaper with no connection to established journalism sources, usually focusing on a particular life-style or philosophy.

wire service: agency that gathers information for newspapers. Well-known agencies are United Press International (UPI), Associated Press (AP), and Reuters.

Bibliography

Bradlee, Ben. *Conversations with Kennedy*. New York: W.W. Norton & Co., 1975.

Bradlee, Ben. *A Good Life*. New York: Simon & Schuster, 1995.

Davidson, James and Mark Lytle. *The United States: A History of the Republic*. New Jersey: Prentice-Hall, Inc., 1981.

Davis, Deborah. *Katharine the Great*. New York: Harcourt Brace Jovanovich, 1979.

Encyclopedia Americana, vol. 16. Conn: Grolier, 1995.

Felsenthal, Carol. *Power, Privilege, and the Post*. New York: G.P. Putnam's Sons, 1993.

Graham, Katharine. *Personal History*. New York: Alfred A. Knopf, 1997.

Kelly, Tom. *The Imperial Post*. New York: William Morrow and Co., Inc., 1983.

Meyer, Agnes. *Out of These Roots*. New York: Arno Press, 1953.

Nelson, Jill. *Volunteer Slavery*. Chicago: The Noble Press, Inc, 1993.

Pusey, Merlo. *Eugene Meyer*. New York: Alfred A. Knopf, 1974.

Roberts, Chalmers. *In the Shadow of the Power*. Maryland: Seven Locks Press, 1989.

Roberts, Chalmers. *The Washington Post*. Boston: Houghton Mifflin Co., 1977.

Rutland, Robert. *The Newsmongers*. New York: The Dial Press, 1973.

Williams, Carol and Irwin Touster. *The Washington Post*. New Jersey, Prentice-Hall, Inc, 1976.

PERIODICALS

Commentary, August, 1997.

Newsweek, February 3, 1997.

The Progressive, June 1997.

Vanity Fair, July 1996.

Vogue, February, 1997

Washingtonian, November 1995..

VIDEO

A&E Television Networks. *Katharine Graham: Pillar of the Post*. New York, 1997.

Sources

CHAPTER ONE

p.9 "I was the peasant ..." Kelly, Tom. *The Imperial Post.* New York: William Morrow and Co., Inc., 1983, p.129

p.9 "Frightened and tense ... Graham, Katharine. *Personal History*, New York: Alfred A. Knopf, 1997, p. 450.

p.10" I came from ..." Felsenthal, Carol. *Power, Privilege, and the Post.* New York: G.P.Putnam'S Sons, 1993, p.38.

p.10"I thought I was the peasant ..." Kelly, op.cit., 129.

p.10"... beautiful in the classic sense ..." Graham, op.cit., p. 450.

p.10"...a ridiculous sense of achievement ..." op.cit., p.31.

p.12"We ought to have a blackboard ..." Meyer, Agnes. *Out of These Roots*, New York: Arno Press, 1953, p.166.

p.12"My husband would constitute himself ..." Meyer, op.cit., p.122.

p.13"I hated it." *Katharine Graham: Pillar of the Post*, A&E Television Networks, 1997.

p.14"hair-raising" "perilous" Meyer, op.cit., p.123

p.17"Oh, darling ..." Graham, op.cit., p.59.

CHAPTER TWO

p.18"I had a certain lack ..." Felsenthal, op.cit., p.78.

p.18"The Post will have very decided ..." Roberts, Chalmers. *In the Shadow of Power.* Maryland: Seven Locks Press, 1989, p.44.

p.18" ... to print always the good ..." Roberts, op.cit., p.88.

p.19"It will be my aim ..." Roberts, op.cit., p.198.

p.20"Too short under the arms ..." Davis, Deborah. *Katharine the Great.* New York: Harcourt Brace Jovanovich, 1979, p.54.

p.23 "Your mother says ..." Felsenthal, op. cit., p.67.

p.23 "Be a newspaper woman ..." Graham, op.cit., 89.

p.24 "I could picture myself working ..." Kelly, op.cit. p.98.

p.28 "You ought to be in on ..." Graham, op.cit., p.86.

p.28 "...an octopus ...worst of all, deep" Graham, op.cit., p.91.

p.28 "I think I knew ..." Felsenthal, op.cit., p.78.

CHAPTER THREE

p.29 "I thought he was so great." A&E Television Networks, op.cit.

p.30 "...a very objective reporter ..." Felsenthal, op.cit., p.80.

p.30 "Miss Meyer showed ..." Roberts, op.cit., p.367.

p.30 "What I was most interested in ..." Felsenthal, op.cit., p.81.

p.31 "If it doesn't work ..." Roberts, op.cit., p.367.

p.31 "I was really startled .." A & E Television Networks, op.cit.

p.34 "I didn't think I could stand ..." Felsenthal, op.cit., p.101.

p.35 "...a journal of national importance ..." Kelly, op.cit., p.72.

p.35 "...zeal, intrepedity, complete devotion ..." Felsenthal, op.cit., 108.

p.36 "You better watch out ..." Graham, op.cit., p.149.

p.38 "... was honestly convinced ..." Felsenthal, op.cit., p. 111.

CHAPTER FOUR

p.39 "I was put on earth ..." Roberts, op.cit., p. 369.

p.39 "...bright, sharp, and [could] charm ..." Felsenthal, op.cit., p.118.

p.40 "I saw myself ..." A&E Television Networks, op.cit.

p.40 "Yesterday I was saturated ..." Roberts, op.cit., p.331.

p.42 "This is a time ..." Pusey, Merlo. *Eugene Meyer*. New York: Alfred A. Knopf, 1974, p.344.

p.42 "I am withdrawing ..." Roberts, op.cit., p.258.

p.43 "I really felt ,..." Roberts, op.cit., p.369.

p.43 "It [*The Post*] is a vivid demonstration ..." Graham, op.cit., p.177.

p.44 "A man should never feel ..." Felsenthal, op.cit., p.130.

p.44 "Phil thinks I'm an idiot ..." Ibid.

p.45 "...one of the most delicate instruments ..." Roberts, op.cit., p. 271.

p.46 "After a while I got too busy ..." Felsenthal, op.cit., p.135.

p.48 "This is one newspaper's appeal ..." Roberts, op.cit., p. 283.

p.49 "...capital's most independent and vigorous paper" Roberts, op.cit., p. 305.

CHAPTER FIVE

p.50 "...good old Mom" Roberts, op.cit., p.369.

p.50 "He got impatient ..." A&E Television Networks, op.cit.

p.52 "This makes *The Post* safe ..." Felsenthal, op.cit., p.226.

p.52 "Editorially we shall continue ..." Roberts, op..cit., p.316.

p.53 "I was always the butt ..." Roberts, op.cit., p. 369.

p.53 "an energetic charmer" Kelly, op.cit., p.119.

p.53 "I would talk to him ..." A&E Television Networks, op.cit..

p.58 "I was very flattered ..." Graham, op.cit., p. 289.

CHAPTER SIX

p.59 "I'm here if you need me..." Graham, op.cit., p. 308.

p.59 "With this wild and restless brilliance ..." Kelly, op.cit., p.125.

p.60 "Darling, you are very good ..."*Columbia Journalism Review*, May/ June 1997, p.69.

p.60 "They liked bright men ..." Graham, op.cit., p.290.

p.60 "Dowdy, dumpy almost ..." Roberts, op. cit., p.369.

p.60 "...tell Kay how delighted ..." Graham, op.cit., p. 295.

p.62 "Scramble the planes" Felsenthal, op.cit., p. 200.

p.62 "I felt completely defeated ... " A&E Television Networks, op.cit.

p.62 "I'm here if you need me ..." Graham, op.cit., p.308.

p.62 "And while you need help ..." Graham, op.cit., p.309.

p.63 "He [Phil] was charming ..." Graham, op.cit., p.319.

p.63 "I am not, nor have I been..." Graham, op.cit., 321.

p.64 "...you've just been pushed down ..." Graham, op.cit., p.319.

CHAPTER SEVEN

p.66 "I went to work" Roberts, op.cit.,p.369.

p.66 "...sometimes you don't really decide ..." Graham, op.cit., p. 338.

p.67 "I had three choices ... " Roberts, op.cit., p. 369.

p.67 "I still tended ..." Graham, op.cit., p. 414.

p.68 "Well, I'm depending on you ..." Felsenthal, op.cit., p. 230

p.68 "It never occurred to me ..." A&E Television Networks, op.cit.

p.68 "She was so shy ..." Ibid.

p.68 "Speeches and interviews were the hardest ..." Roberts, op.cit., p 371.

p.70 "What I essentially did ..." Graham, op.cit., p. 341.

p.70 "Know everything there is ..." Davis, op.cit., p. 195.

p.70 "The newspaper shall not be the ally ..." Roberts, op.cit., p.370.

p.72"I feel exactly as though ..." Roberts, op.cit., p.372.

p.72"I made mistakes and suffered ..." Graham, op.cit., p.371.

p.74"I want to have some impact ..." Roberts, op.cit., p.379

p.74"I didn't conflict ..." Vanity Fair, July 1996, p.126.

CHAPTER EIGHT

p.77"Let's go! Let's publish!" Graham, op.cit., p.589.

p.77"Get your finger out ..." Graham, op.cit., p. 414.

p.77"...a lifelong tendency to fasten..." Graham, op.cit., 389.

p.79"What is there in the paper ..." Kelly, op.cit., 170.

p.80"Let's go. Let's publish." Graham, op.cit., p.450.

p.80"I'm sure you will understand ..." Roberts, op.cit., p.420.

p.82"The hallmark of the *Post's* campaign ..." Roberts, op.cit., p.436.

p.82"What I did primarily ..." *Commentary*, Aug. 1977, p.51.

p.84"Ultimately Watergate showed Graham ..." Graham, op. cit., p. 506.

p.85"...had outgrown her tolerance ..." Kelly, op.cit., p.244.

p.85"If I do something unexpected ..." Roberts, op.cit., p. 464.

p.85"She is obsessed with the notion ..." Felsenthal, op.cit., p. 332.

p.85"She loves being the queen bee ..." Ibid.

p.85"They keep yelling at me ..." Ibid.

p.85"I lead such an odd life ..." Felsenthal, op.cit., p. 324.

CHAPTER NINE

p.86"Pay whatever price ..." Felsenthal, op.cit., p.348.

p.87"You can't afford to lose ..." Ibid.

p.87"Enjoy your dinner, Ms Graham ..." Graham, op.cit., p. 555.

p.88"My conclusion is that I cannot ..." Graham, op.cit., p. 563.

p.88" ...the top leader and shaper ..." Felsenthal, op.cit., p. 364.

p.89"Katharine the Great and ..." Felsenthal., op.cit., p.365.

p.89"...just nuts. I never saw ..." Felsenthal, op.cit., p.370.

p.89"My mother has given me ..." Kelly, op.cit., p.243.

p.91"I'm very concentrated ..." Forbes, April 9, 1984, p.86.

p.92"Take it back!" Nelson, Jill. *Volunteer Slavery*. Chicago: The Noble Press, Inc., 1993, p.71.

p.92"I believe democracy flourishes ..." *Progressive*, June 1997, p.44.

p.92"Men who appeal to me ..." Graham, op.cit., p 615.

CHAPTER TEN

p.93 "I'm looking forward to the future ..." Graham, op.cit., p. 625.

p.93 "The record shows that ..."*Washingtonian*, Nov., 1995, p.44.

p.94 "It's dangerous when you are older ..." Graham, op.cit., p. 625.

Index